ANTIGUA
BOOKS

JOHNS HOPKINS STUDIES
IN ATLANTIC HISTORY
AND CULTURE

Editorial Board
Rebecca J. Scott, *Chair*
Sidney W. Mintz
Michel-Rolph Trouillot

Coffee, Society, and Power in Latin America

EDITED BY

William Roseberry
Lowell Gudmundson
Mario Samper Kutschbach

The Johns Hopkins University Press

Baltimore and London

This book was prepared under the auspices of the Joint Committee on Latin American Studies of the Social Science Research Council and the American Council of Learned Societies, with funds from the Andrew W. Mellon Foundation.

The Johns Hopkins University Press
2715 North Charles Street
Baltimore, Maryland 21218-4319
The Johns Hopkins Press Ltd., London

Library of Congress Cataloging-in-Publication Data
will be found at the end of this book.
A catalog record for this book is available from the British Library.

ISBN 0-8018-4884-9
ISBN 0-8018-4887-3 (pbk.)

Contents

Illustrations

Tables

Preface

THE IDEA for this book began at a conference on the history of coffee in Costa Rica in comparative perspective, sponsored by the Universidad Nacional of Costa Rica in 1986. Impressed by the work presented at the conference, and by the recent appearance of excellent monographs on coffee production, social relations, and politics in Latin America, a group of participants agreed that the time had come to attempt a more ambitious comparative work. Four of us, Lowell Gudmundson, Marco Palacios, William Roseberry, and Mario Samper Kutschbach, volunteered to serve as coordinators of this effort.

We then approached the Joint Committee on Latin American Studies at the Social Science Research Council, which agreed to support a preliminary effort to organize a conference, and then generously supported the conference itself, with funds provided by the National Endowment for the Humanities. Marco Palacios, then rector of the Universidad Nacional of Colombia in Bogotá, was able to commit the university to providing matching funds and a venue for the conference itself. That conference, which brought together over thirty scholars from Europe, Latin America, and the United States, was held in Bogotá and Sasaima, Colombia, in September 1988, thanks to the organizational, social, and intellectual gifts of Clemente Forero, then dean of the School of Economic Sciences at the Universidad Nacional.

We then began the rather different task of composing a book that would not simply be a volume of proceedings from the conference but would communicate the results and perspectives of this exciting collaborative and comparative work to a wider audience. Three scholars committed themselves to writing essays that were not presented at the conference: William Roseberry wrote a comparative introduction, Michael Jiménez wrote an essay on coffee consumption in the United States in the early twentieth century, and Mauricio Font contributed an essay on class and politics in Brazil. Two scholars who wrote essays for the conference, Laird Bergad and Joseph Love, chose not to contribute to the book.

We thank the participants in the conference and the contributors to this book for their active engagement and stimulating work. Among the scholars invited to comment on essays at the conference, we especially thank Eric Hobsbawm for the generosity with which he shares his intellectual gifts and historical knowledge. His closing summary was a model of comparative exposition; his insistence on a global frame and a serious linkage between consumption and production motivated us to solicit Jiménez's essay for this volume.

We have benefited from the advice and counsel of three coordinators of the Joint Committee on Latin America and the Caribbean. Joan Dassin served during the planning stages of the conference and committed the committee to full support; Silvia Raw served during the conference itself; and Eric Hershberg has moved us gently but persistently toward a book. He and the SSRC have assisted us enormously in arranging for publication, as has Jacqueline Wehmueller, editor at the Johns Hopkins University Press, who has approached the project with interest, support, and patience. Marie Blanchard has edited the manuscript with skill and grace. Rebecca Scott, Sidney Mintz, and Michel-Rolph Trouillot, editors of the Johns Hopkins Studies in Atlantic History and Culture, have encouraged us with this project; more importantly, they have promoted a body of work of consistently high quality. The series was our first choice as an editorial venue for a comparative work of this kind and scope. The Research Foundations at the University of Oklahoma and Mount Holyoke College have provided Lowell Gudmundson with support that has aided our editorial work. We thank all of these individuals and institutions for their encouragement and support.

Coffee, Society, and Power
in Latin America

One

Introduction

WILLIAM ROSEBERRY

HISTORIANS AND social scientists continually struggle to understand and account for the unity and diversity of Latin American social life. On the one hand, the vast territory has been subjected to common historical forces and processes: conquest and colonization; the wars of independence and the nineteenth-century processes of state formation and nation building; the development of export economies as Latin American regions became primary product exporters in an international division of labor; the common mid-twentieth-century struggle of Latin American countries to alter their positions in the world economy by developing import substitution schemes; the nineteenth-century experience of *caudillo* rule; the twentieth-century development of strong military forces and regimes; the emergence of "new," "middle" social groups and classes and the development of "populism"; and so on.

Some of our most influential interpretive models have sought to capture the commonality of these forces and processes. Some, such as reference to a "latifundia-minifundia complex" (an agrarian structure based on the preponderance of huge landholdings) or Latin American dependency, seek to capture a continuity in Latin American experience in space and time; they hope to characterize certain common features in Latin American history from the colonial period to the present. Others, such as models of nineteenth- and twentieth-century liberalism or of "oligarchic pacts," of populism or bureaucratic authoritarianism, or the recently proclaimed "democratic transition," have dealt with more carefully circumscribed periods of time while developing general political and economic models that can be applied to a variety of Latin American states.

On the other hand, common historical forces and processes have always been experienced differently in particular Latin American regions. Though the Spanish colonial bureaucracy sought to impose a uniform body of regulations and institutions on its vast empire, colonial forms and processes were inserted within and shaped by remarkably different social spaces. The *encomienda* was one institution in the Valley of Mexico but something else altogether in, say, the lands that were to become Paraguay or Venezuela.[1] Liberalism took on almost as many faces as there were individual liberals, and populisms under Perón, Vargas, or Cárdenas shared certain features while developing in fundamentally different political regimes. Export economies may have occupied similar positions within an international division of labor, but they differed markedly and importantly in their internal structures and dynamics.[2]

In recent decades, historians and anthropologists, along with other social scientists, have contributed to our knowledge of such local and regional diversity, challenging earlier understandings of colonialism, agrarian structures and processes, economic dynamics, political regimes and ideological formations. The present book is a product of and contribution to this literature. Based on the work of scholars who have studied regional processes of class formation and politics, it presents some of that work, recognizes its challenges to more general social science models and interpretations, and begins to ask new comparative questions.

We do this by analyzing a single commodity, coffee, toward the production and export of which many Latin American regions turned in the second half of the nineteenth century, with surprisingly different dynamics and results. Indeed, of all the agricultural commodity exports developed in Latin America from the sixteenth through the twentieth centuries, coffee was both one of the most widely distributed geographically and least restricted to a single farm size or technological repertoire. For the most part, the individual essays concentrate on particular aspects of distinct regional experiences — differences in agrarian structure, the role and fate of small-scale production, class and ethnic relations, state structures, and the like. We begin, however, with two more general statements of orientation: the present introduction, which explores some of the dimensions of difference in Latin American coffee economies and offers a modest proposal for strategies of comparative analysis, and Michael Jiménez's reflections on transformations in coffee consumption in the early-twentieth-century United States and their implications for and ramifications among Latin American producing regions.

The Coffee Century

Although coffee consumption had been introduced in Europe in the seventeenth century (primarily via the coffeehouse), and the first coffee trees had been introduced in the New World in the eighteenth century,[3] the

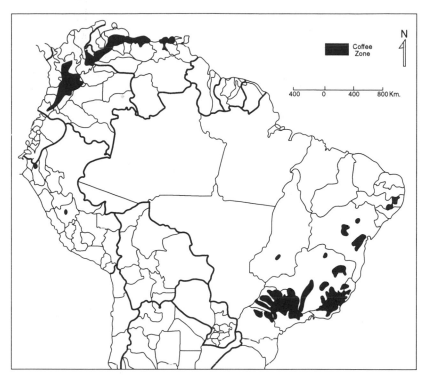

Map 1.1. Coffee Zones of South America, ca. 1930

nineteenth century (that is, roughly, from 1830 to 1930) was *the* coffee
century in Latin America. It was a period that witnessed a dramatic increase in world trade in coffee (from 320 metric tons in 1770, mostly from
Asia; to 90,000 metric tons in 1820, with half coming from Brazil; to
450,000 metric tons in 1870; and to 1,600,000 metric tons in 1920)[4] and
per capita consumption (in the United States, from three pounds in 1830
to ten pounds in 1900 and sixteen pounds in 1960).[5] And it was a period
in which coffee production was associated with a profound transformation of landscape and society in several Latin American regions. In most of
the regions that concern us, the expansion of coffee cultivation coincided
with territorial expansion, the movement of settlers into frontier zones
where tropical forests were destroyed, "new forests"[6] of coffee and shade
planted, towns established, roads and railroads built, regional identities
forged. Whether we think of the westward expansion of coffee estates in
Rio de Janeiro and São Paulo, or the movement of capital and settlers
from the Sabana de Bogotá to the subtropical slopes to the west, or the
Antioqueño colonization, or the occupation of the Central Valley in Costa

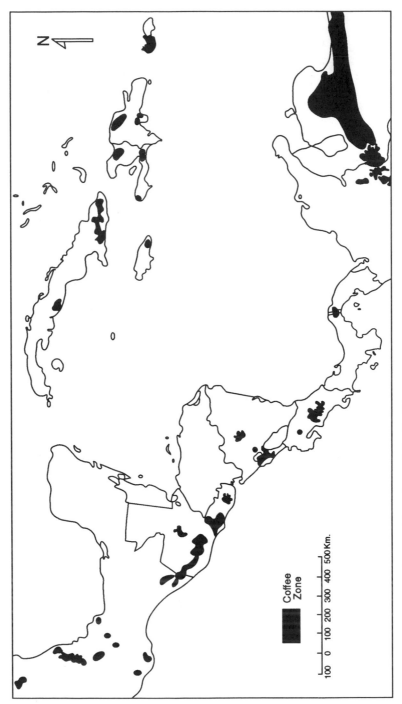

Map 1.2. Coffee Zones of Central America and the Caribbean, ca. 1930

Coffee
Zone

100   0   100   200   300   400   500 Km.

Rica, coffee was associated with important processes of internal migration and settlement as frontiers were transformed into poles of development. Rare was the case such as El Salvador, where the coffee zone corresponded with an area of dense settlement from the colonial or precolonial period.

It is not surprising, then, that we find some of the same processes and themes repeated from coffee-producing region to coffee-producing region — the incorporation of regions within an expanding world market, the establishment of outwardly focused development strategies with the export of a primary product the price of which fluctuates significantly but is beyond the control of local producers and exporters, the building of roads and railroads (generally with foreign capital) to carry the coffee from the newly settled interior to port cities, the ambiguous question of land ownership in frontier zones and conflicts between rural settlers and urban investors, the related legal revolutions in landed property and labor regulations, and the ubiquitous concern for the labor problem — the "*falta de brazos.*"

What is perhaps more surprising is the remarkable variation in social, economic, and political structures and processes among coffee-producing regions, the radically distinct structures of landed property and the different resolutions of the labor problem encountered in Brazil or Costa Rica or Colombia. Compare, for example, the extremes of Brazil and Costa Rica. With the expansion of coffee cultivation in Rio and later São Paulo, the large estate held sway. There a coffee plantation worth the name should have at least one hundred thousand coffee trees and could often contain several hundred thousand, supporting a baronial household in Rio or São Paulo. The plantations were worked first by slaves and then by *colonos*.[7] In the expansion of settlement and coffee cultivation in the Central Mesa of Costa Rica, however, the small producer predominated. Although coffee processors and merchants held large farms that might average sixty thousand trees, the bulk of the land was held by small-scale producers, and a commercially oriented peasantry emerged.[8] Between these two extremes, we find a variety of alternative developments. In Guatemala, for example, the piedmont plantations developed in thinly populated areas and depended upon state-enforced migration of highland Maya populations for extended periods of plantation labor.[9] In Colombia, three distinct regions (the Santanders in the northeast, the central cordillera of Cundinamarca and Tolima, and the west of Antioquia and Caldas) turned to coffee, each at different moments with distinct rhythms and processes and with markedly different social and political structures. Cundinamarca, for example, was characterized by large haciendas (up to and well beyond one hundred thousand trees). The *hacendados* were often Bogotá merchants who depended upon resident administrators and peasant tenants and who exported their coffee directly to the exterior. While Antioquia also developed large farms, small farmers growing their own coffee and selling it to urban merchants for processing and sale constituted an important segment of the population.[10]

Each of these regions turned toward coffee at *roughly* the same time (that is, within a few important decades of each other): Brazil, Costa Rica, and Venezuela had important coffee economies by mid-century; Guatemala, El Salvador, and Colombia turned to coffee several decades later — the 1870s, 1880s, and beyond. Each was producing the same primary product for export to the same European and North American ports (though one might export primarily to London, another to New York, another to Hamburg). The structure of trade (that is, the relationship between local exporters and international firms) was roughly the same (though important differences developed in Brazil as it came to dominate the market). Each of the regions became "dependent" on a single export commodity, suffering the same reverses and enjoying the same booms.

Despite the commonalities in their incorporation within the world market, however, their most basic social relations, including those associated with labor mobilization and "the specific economic form, in which unpaid surplus-labour is pumped out of direct producers,"[11] were fundamentally different. Easy assertions about Latin American dependence or the dominance of the "latifundia-minifundia complex" are out of place, as are more complex arguments that recognize variation but subsume it within a common emergence of two "large nodes of decision-making bodies" with the incorporation of regions within the world economy — one based on the "plantation" solution and the other based on the "merchant" solution (in which merchants dominate and capture the production of small farmers).[12] Such assertions explain away difference rather than confronting it.

We need instead to confront these differences in the coffee-growing regions in Latin America. We need to ask why such fundamental differences in landed property and labor mobilization occurred and what effects these differences might have had for their respective societies. A variety of easy resolutions are closed to us. None of the distinctions in timing or markets noted above could be considered causal or determinative. Nor do we have access to a mechanical opposition between closed and open frontiers or to different land and labor ratios. If our only contrast was one between El Salvador and Costa Rica, such oppositions and ratios might be convincing, but most of the regions were open frontiers, with different results of settlement that are too important to gloss over with grids and causal diagrams. A more considered examination of the societies in which the frontiers were opened and settled, the social, economic, political, and cultural contexts in which coffee became an important export crop, is necessary.

One approach that is especially useful in furthering such a sociological understanding is that sketched by F. H. Cardoso and Enzo Faletto in their call for studies of the "internalization of the external" in Latin America. Surveying the emergence of capitalism in various Latin American countries, they argue:

The very existence of an economic "periphery" cannot be understood without reference to the economic drive of advanced capitalist economies, which were responsible for the formation of a capitalist periphery and for the integration of traditional noncapitalist economies into the world market. Yet, the expansion of capitalism in Bolivia and Venezuela, in Mexico or Peru, in Brazil and Argentina, in spite of having been submitted to the same global dynamic of international capitalism, did not have the same history or consequences. The differences are rooted not only in the diversity of natural resources, nor just in the different periods in which these economies have been incorporated into the international system (although these factors have played some role). Their explanation must also lie in the different moments at which sectors of local classes allied or clashed with foreign interests, organized different forms of state, sustained distinct ideologies, or tried to implement various policies or defined alternative strategies to cope with imperialist challenges in diverse moments of history.[13]

What we need, according to this view, is a "history of . . . diversity," a sense that "the history of capital accumulation is the history of class struggles, of political movements, of the affirmation of ideologies, and of the establishment of forms of domination and reactions against them."[14] With the introduction of coffee in a variety of Latin American contexts, we encounter a range of examples of the internalization of the external. In each case, particular societies or regions were subjected to new economic and political forces emanating from the centers of the world economy — from London, Hamburg, New York. These forces were not uniform. Exporters in particular regions developed ties with importers in particular cities, just as particular importers bought on spot markets or loaned funds to merchant houses in particular regions. In this multiplicity of relations, there was some room for maneuver and strategy, within limits set by the price cycle itself and, from the turn of the century, the growing concentration and centralization of the trade.

The most important site for variation, however, was in the different contexts — the different fields of power — into which coffee traders and capital moved. The essays in this book offer detailed considerations of such contexts or fields of power. Far from being a collection of "case studies," we offer these studies as a theoretical contribution to the comparative analysis of the history of capitalism in Latin America; we offer a history of diversity. In our view, it is important to contrast those situations in which coffee production involved the occupation of a frontier with those in which existing forms of landholding were transformed, just as one must understand the size of that frontier and the demographic trends associated with the occupation of space. But it is equally important to understand the different class and ethnic relations, themselves the complex products of different colonial experiences, that provided the initial social, political, and cultural milieux for the occupation of Brazilian, Costa Rican, and Colombian spaces. It is only in such terms that we can understand the extension of the great estate and slavery in the Brazilian interior, or the movement of highland Indians and mestizos to the subtropical slopes of central Colombia, or the peasant migration in Costa Rica's Central Mesa.

We need, in sum, to examine Latin American coffee economies in the context of preexisting and emergent fields of power—the occupation of space and transformation of landed property within the regions that turned to coffee; the position of these regions within interregional trade networks; the location and development of roads, ports, and processing facilities; the mobilization and reproduction of labor; the organization and capitalization of markets; the class and ethnic structure of regions and states in the late eighteenth and nineteenth centuries; the relative power of regional landholders in relation to other regional elites as well as power holders in other regions and the central state; and so on.

In the discussion that follows, I organize a schematic comparison of various coffee regions in terms of such questions. Connecting them, as an economic and political problem for coffee elites and as an analytical theme for us, is the labor question. Although labor might seem to be a simple "economic" issue, in practice it inflects all dimensions of the social field. Liberal politics revolve around it; merchant-peasant relations are, in an important dimension, labor relations, as are, centrally, gender and household relations, and so on.

Three examples suffice. First, as is clear from several essays in this book, large landholders attempting to attract laborers were not acting in isolation. They might be competing with growers from other regions, with urban entrepreneurs, or, in the case of immigration schemes, with planters or entrepreneurs in other countries. This is not to say that landholders were powerless and a free market prevailed: the monopolization of land in some regions was the most effective means for securing a labor force. It is to say that planters acted within particular contexts, particular sets of constraints, and that the systems they devised to attract workers in the first place, or to assure more careful tending of coffee trees, or to feed the working population, often created further constraints. Structures of decision making and control could become quite diffuse as coffee groves and food plots were let out to tenants.

Second, labor mobilization schemes were never static. It would be insufficient to set up a comparison in simple spatial terms with large estates and the colonato in Brazil, peasants and processors in Costa Rica, *haciendas* in Cundinamarca, and peasants in Antioquia — the large estate regions being characterized by "oligarchic" domination and the peasant regions seen as more "democratic." In each of these regions, labor regimes changed over time. Haciendas in Cundinamarca began to disintegrate in the 1920s and 1930s, for example, partly due to economic problems encountered much earlier and partly due to the increasing organization and militance of their tenants. Careful attention to the fault lines created by *hacendados'* resolution of labor mobilization problems in previous decades is essential for an understanding of their problems in the twenties. In the smallholder regions, in turn, we need to be sensitive to changes over time. In Costa Rica, for example, small farmers faced increasingly difficult pressures from the middle of the nineteenth century to 1930, as open lands closed off or as relations with processors became more exploitative or as household heads found it increasingly difficult to provide an inheritance for all of their children (see Gudmundson, this volume, for an important example of how careful attention to such questions can illuminate fundamental social processes and political relations).[15]

Finally, if we think about labor mobilization in terms of contexts, constraints, and fault lines, and if we consider the way particular resolutions of the labor problem change over time, we open up an important area for investigation. One of the intriguing developments that emerges in the literature on coffee in Latin America is the frequency with which elites experiment with different strategies. The most famous is probably the Vergueiro experiment in Brazil with immigrant sharecroppers in the mid nineteenth century, four decades before the end of slavery.[16] But we also find other experiments in, for example, Cundinamarca in the twenties[17] or Guatemala in the twenties and thirties (see McCreery, this volume). Indeed, as McCreery's essay demonstrates, careful attention to such experiments and debates can illuminate the most profound economic, political, and cultural dilemmas confronting coffee elites. As we examine the kinds of solutions that are attempted and the solutions that are not even considered, we are able to sketch the limits of the possible (which include the limits of the socially constructed mental and cultural horizons of the elites at a particular time) in various coffee-producing regions. An apparently simple "economic" question (how labor was organized), then, need not lead to a labeling exercise. A discourse about labor is seldom "just" about labor. Examining one such discourse, we may begin to explore the sociology of racism in Guatemala or Brazil or Costa Rica; in examining another, we may begin to understand the particular features of liberalism in, say, early-twentieth-century Colombia.

Let us turn, then, to a preliminary sketch of the common forces and structures through which Latin American coffee economies were formed, and of the distinct social fields in which these forces and structures were implanted.

Comparative Dimensions

As Eric Hobsbawm pointed out at the conference that led to this book, coffee is both a product of "free trade" ideology and practice and the first "drug food" not controlled by colonial or imperial trading blocks. For those newly independent countries from southern Mexico to southern Brazil with exploitable subtropical soils, coffee served as a principal point of linkage to an expanding world economy, the means by which they could turn toward an "outwardly focused" model of development. It could be stored for long periods with relatively little spoilage; it had a high value per kilogram, making transport costs relatively low and making inland territories valuable in a way they could not be for crops such as sugar;[18] and it enjoyed a growing and lucrative acceptance in European and U.S. markets. For merchants and trading firms from countries entering the new Latin American markets (first England, later Germany and the United States), coffee became a focus of trade.

For the period that concerns us in this volume, coffee production and marketing followed classic free-trade patterns. Control of production was highly dispersed, both among coffee-producing countries and among producers within countries. While international trade was controlled by merchant houses in London, Hamburg, and New York, there was no significant concentration among the houses until the early twentieth century. As concentration began to occur, it responded at once to changing processing and marketing structures in consuming countries (see Jiménez's discussion in Chapter 2) and to crisis periods in producing countries, during which foreign firms might take more direct and active roles (as happened in Brazil and Colombia in the early twentieth century).

International coffee firms would establish credit and commercial relations with exporters and merchants in particular Latin American countries, loaning funds to exporters with which the exporters would acquire coffee—often by means of further loans to local producers and merchants. Certain general features of these arrangements deserve emphasis. First, despite the close connection between European or North American firms and Brazilian or Costa Rican exporters and producers, local merchants and exporters were not subsidiaries of European or North American firms for most of the period under discussion. Even where the exporters were German or English expatriates, they were expatriates acting as individual entrepreneurs and adventurers, often with a privileged and preferred relationship with a particular London or Hamburg house, but the tie that bound them was one of credit and shared nationality rather than ownership. Second, exporters, acting with their own funds or with borrowed funds from abroad, were the principal sources of credit for local producers and merchants. For most of the period that concerns us, national or international banks were not involved in the coffee trade. Third, with purchasing and credit arrangements linking particular international firms and exporters, producers and merchants alike were subject to price fluctuations. Exporters lacked the means to withhold coffee in periods of low prices. There were no local coffee exchanges, and states were not involved in the coffee trade. It was only with the onset of the first general overproduction crisis in the 1890s that discussions began what finally resulted in Brazil's valorization scheme of 1906. With this scheme, the first chinks in the free-trade armor appeared.

For much of the nineteenth century, rapidly increasing supply met with expanding demand. Price fluctuations were often related to more general economic conditions and cycles in the consuming countries. For example, one of the more serious price declines of the second half of the nineteenth century, that of the 1870s, was precipitated by the European crisis of 1873 but was cushioned by the departure of Java from the supply market.[19] The doubling of prices in the 1880s corresponded with the expansion of production in such countries as Colombia, Guatemala, and El Salvador, and especially with the expansion of coffee into western São Paulo. The increase in land planted in coffee in the 1880s did not affect actual production until the 1890s. This introduces an aspect of coffee production that needs to be highlighted: although the coffee trade fit well within the model and ideology of free trade during the nineteenth century, neither supply nor demand curves respond quickly to price fluctuations. On the demand side, high prices may result in lower consumption, as we know from various consumer revolts in this century. But low prices do not necessarily lead to rapid increases in consumption patterns, as per capita consumption is relatively stable on the short term. Jiménez's essay (Chapter 2) provides a good analysis of the strategies of North American firms in trying to increase per capita consumption in the early decades of this century.

On the supply side, response is necessarily more sluggish. Coffee is a perennial, and planters do not enjoy the first full harvest until some five years after planting. Thus a myriad of planters in several regions may respond to a high price period by planting coffee (let us say, in 1890), only to find a slight reduction in prices at the first full harvest (1895) and a sharply declining price curve in the years thereafter. But the coffee trees will not stop producing simply because the market situation is unfavorable, and the planter will hesitate to rip out a long-term investment.

This is roughly the situation that confronted coffee producers in the late 1890s — increasing production, decreasing prices, increasing "visible supply" (unsold but marketable coffee stocks from previous years), and stable world demand. Thanks in part to São Paulo's valorization scheme starting in 1906, prices had begun to recover by the early teens. With the exception of a price trough during World War I and a sharp decrease in 1920–21, the general trend in prices during the 1910–29 period was upward. With the onset of the Depression, prices dropped sharply and remained quite low during the 1930s. With the closure of the European market in World War II, the United States and fourteen producing countries signed the International Coffee Agreement of 1940, setting export quotas for the various countries. The agreement was the first of a series of international control schemes that stabilized the market and facilitated a dramatic postwar price increase. It also corresponded with (indeed required) the formation of national coffee-marketing boards of the sort established in Brazil much earlier, marking the effective end of the free-trade model of coffee marketing — until the neoliberal reforms of the 1980s and 1990s.

Furthermore, the market was not homogeneous. In general, European consumers have preferred the "quality" milds produced in Costa Rica, Colombia, and Guatemala, and European markets were the principal outlets for the milds. These export markets were cemented with long-term arrangements with particular foreign houses (e.g., England [as entrepot] for Costa Rica, Germany for Guatemala). Indeed, during the free-trade period much of the quality coffee was exported not as Colombian or Costa Rican coffee but, "like French wines,"[20] under the mark of a particular Costa Rican processor (*beneficiador*) or Colombian hacienda. The United States, on the other hand, has served as a market for the harsher, less expensive, coffees, especially from Brazil, but also as a subsidiary market early on for the other countries. As with all generalizations, this one requires some temporal specification. In the first place, no producing country exported solely to a single consuming country. European markets were important for Brazil, and European firms were active in Rio and Santos. Second, during the twentieth century the U.S. market became increasingly important throughout Latin America, accounting for 38.9 percent of the world total during the 1909–13 period and 51.7 percent by

1939. Moreover, the United States became the primary market during the two world wars, with the closure of European markets.[21]

The segmentation of the coffee market is an important feature, however, not simply in terms of a broad distinction between milds and lower-quality coffees but in terms of complex grading hierarchies based on the size, color, and polish of the bean and the number of imperfections. Although soil conditions and cultivation methods affect quality, quality control can also be exercised in the harvesting and processing of beans.

There are two principal methods of processing coffee, within each of which there is significant room for variation. The outer layer of the coffee cherry is a mucilaginous pulp. Once this has been removed, the two beans are still enclosed within a loose parchment and a more tightly fitting membrane, the silver skin. The object of both methods of processing is to remove these three layers so that the beans can be polished, sorted, and, eventually, roasted. The dry method involves drying the cherries, generally in the sun, until the pulp becomes quite hard. The dried pulp, parchment, and silver skin are then removed in a single hulling operation. Under the wet method, the cherries are depulped by machine with a constant flow of water. The parchment- and mucous-covered beans are then placed in fermentation tanks for twelve to eighteen hours, which dissolves the mucous. The first two stages must be accomplished immediately after the cherries have been picked. The parchment-covered beans are then dried; once dried they can be stored or shipped in the parchment or hulled in a manner similar to that used in the dry process.[22]

The hulling itself can be accomplished by a variety of means — from simple pounding with sticks, through horse- or oxen-drawn stone mills, to water-, steam-, or electricity-driven machinery. There are, then, few *technical* requirements that lead to economies of scale. The small, undercapitalized coffee farmer needs little more than a drying floor (of dirt, brick, concrete, or wood) and relatively simple processing equipment — for example, a mortar and pestle. Different processing techniques produce different qualities of coffee, however. Partly because the wet method requires perfectly ripe cherries while the dry method requires overripe cherries (or, in the case of Brazil, a mixture from the stripped coffee tree branches), and partly because the dry method may involve excess fermentation and spoilage during the initial drying, the wet method produces "superior cup quality and certainly a superior roasted appearance."[23] Even here, however, the machinery and equipment (including water supply and tanks) necessary for the initial depulping and fermentation can be quite small-scale, within the reach of a small farmer.

Nonetheless, given differences in quality that result from soil and climatic variation, the more sophisticated the processing machinery (with

more control over, for example, drying), the higher the quality of the
coffee bean. Given a marketing environment permeated by a discourse of
quality and a pricing system based on the grading hierarchies, this provides an important point of control for coffee processors, especially where
the processors are also merchants. In any given region, then, there will be
profound *social* and *economic* pressures favoring particular processing
techniques and relations. To understand some of these pressures, we need
to consider the transformation of spaces in the nineteenth century in terms
of four broad questions: the occupation and structuring of social space,
the mobilization and reproduction of labor, the processing, marketing,
and financing of the product, and the political and ideological formations
through which these transformations were effected.

The New Forests: Land and Labor in the Coffee Republics

The frontier character of many of the coffee regions has often been
stressed in regional studies. If it has impressed historians and social scientists, it has also impressed historical actors, both at the moment of frontier
settlement and in memory. The memory of cutting down the subtropical
forest (*tumbando montes*), or the image of a people forged in settlement
and transformation (for example, "the ethos of the *hacha*"[24] [an ax] in
Antioquia) is strong.

Most of the areas converted to coffee cultivation attracted population
migration and settlement. In Brazil, the early-nineteenth-century expansion into the Paraíba Valley in Rio set the stage for a westward movement
into the western plateau of São Paulo and Minas Gerais that was to continue throughout the nineteenth century and into the twentieth.[25] In Costa
Rica, the sparsely settled Central Mesa was occupied and a commercially
oriented peasantry forged from the early decades after independence.[26]
Two of the regions that were to dominate the Colombian coffee economy
contained vast stretches of subtropical forest before the late-nineteenth-
century move toward coffee: one (the western slopes of the eastern *cordillera* in Cundinamarca and Tolima) depended upon the migration of
highland peasants to new coffee farms; the other (the Antioqueño west)
experienced a prodigious colonization of settlers from around Medellín.[27]
While the first Venezuelan coffee cycle occurred in regions of colonial
settlement, expanding commercial cultivation onto hillsides that had been
devalued by cacao planters, its expansion in the second half of the nineteenth century attracted migrants from the western plains or *llanos* into
the western Andes, transforming a colonial backwater into an export
center.[28] In Puerto Rico, the central highlands had been an "internal frontier" prior to 1850, as the commercial activity and population had been

concentrated in the sugar zones along the coast. Here, too, the expansion of coffee attracted investors and settlers as a backwater became an economic center.[29] Guatemala and El Salvador serve as counterpoints in this story, in that both were densely populated. Even in Guatemala, however, the microregion that was to become the most dynamic production zone — the piedmont areas of Amatitlán, Suchitepéquez, Sololá Quetzaltenango, San Marcos, and the Alta Verapaz — contained much unused land.[30] Only in El Salvador did the coffee zone correspond with a region of relatively dense colonial settlement, and only in El Salvador did the expansion of coffee and the transformation of landed property that accompanied it involve a widespread displacement and expropriation.[31]

The building of the new forests brought with it the foundation of new towns. Palacios comments that "the coffee hacienda was the result of the encounter between urban merchants and agrarian societies,"[32] neither of which was static. From region to region, we find new agrarian societies and new urban centers, new groups of merchants (often recently arrived from Europe), and new roads and (eventually) railroads connecting recently opened interior provinces with coastal ports. Coffee cultivation on a large scale was inconceivable without this developing human and material infrastructure. The settlement itself, however, and the first important moves toward coffee, often preceded it. Settlers on the western plateau of São Paulo, for example, might plant food crops and sugar cane before turning the *terra roxa* to coffee.[33] Or as settlers moved beyond the San José/Heredia nucleus in Costa Rica's Central Mesa, they would devote their newly opened lands to food crops and pasture before coffee became a feasible (profitable) crop.[34] Even when and where settlers turned directly to coffee, however, coffee cultivation was rarely a monoculture. Regardless of the size of the farm, planters also had to plant food crops and pasture for their mules. In Colombia, for example, one can speak of "the activities that have always accompanied coffee cultivation: sugar cane, plantains, manioc, maize, and livestock."[35] With this mixture, it was not at all uncommon for the majority of a coffee farm's holdings to be devoted to food, pasture, and uncultivated forest. This is not to say that a balance between coffee and food production was always maintained; in particular microregions such as the San José/Heredia nucleus in Costa Rica, a virtual monoculture emerged in the nineteenth century,[36] and coffee displaced food crops in the Puerto Rican highlands.[37] Such displacements could not make the food and pasture problem disappear, however, and the manner in which farmers in particular regions resolved the coffee-production/household-and-farm-reproduction dilemma constitutes an important (and as yet insufficiently explored) arena for comparative discussion.

Despite the frontier character of much of the coffee expansion, however,

most of the "wildernesses" into which coffee farmers moved were already
encumbered by people, entailing overlapping and competing claims to land
and conceptions of space, time, and justice — in short, "history" — before
the coffee expansion began, and these encumbrances shaped their respective coffee economies even as the regions were transformed by the move
toward coffee. In Brazil, for example, the western lands were settled by
squatters who displaced indigenous populations. Squatters' rights to their
holdings were not recognized by the Portuguese crown or the Brazilian
empire, however. As the state ceded large land grants to favored subjects,
and as grant holders began to turn their imprecisely marked holdings into
plantations, squatters were displaced farther westward.[38] In central Colombia, some of the lands opened in Cundinamarca and Tolima involved
the dissolution and displacement of preexisting cattle and sugar cane lati-
fundia as Bogotá merchants invested in farms and organized migrant flows
from the highland plateau to the new coffee farms along the slopes.[39] In
Venezuela, settlers from the llanos who moved into the Andes, and merchants from Italy and elsewhere who settled in emerging market towns,
encountered a sedimented colonial economy and society based on highland
wheat and potato production. Many lands that were to become central to
the coffee economy were already claimed by indigenous communities or
the descendants of colonial settlers.[40]

Examples of preexisting claims and populations can easily be expanded. The transformation of frontiers into rural provinces occurred in
radically different contexts, and we learn much about the different coffee
economies that emerged by exploring the variety of social and political
"encumbrances" that pioneers encountered, and the manner in which
different emerging states resolved the conflicts that ensued. While Brazil,
for example, refused to recognize squatters' rights and favored the claims
of large grant holders, Colombia passed land laws that recognized and
protected the claims of settlers on unoccupied national lands (terrenos
baldíos), and Costa Rica adopted homesteading laws that offered clear
title to any settlers that occupied national lands and planted coffee. An
examination of such laws and their uneven enforcement, or of the competing claims that were expressed in the debates surrounding the laws and
their implementation, can serve as a point of entry for an examination of
the different political regimes that developed coffee economies. It can also
serve as a starting point for an examination of different land and labor
regimes in the coffee zones.

Once we have established some basic contrasts concerning the occupation of space and the emergence of distinct landed regimes, we must consider the mobilization and reproduction of labor in the new forests. The
coffee farmer must plant coffee, food crops, and pasture, which will re-

quire an initial capital fund that might be obtained on credit; he must be in a position to maintain the coffee trees during the initial five-year growth period before the first harvest and during annual weedings and prunings; he must harvest the coffee during a relatively short period when his coffee and the coffee of neighboring farms is ripe; he must process the coffee and get it to market. Each of these tasks indicates a potential point of failure. For the small farmer, secure in newly granted or purchased title, access to credit, processing facilities, and markets presents a series of mechanisms (to be examined in the section on commercialization, below) that may compromise that title, mechanisms through which small farmers might lose land to landlords or merchants. For the large farmer, especially in frontier regions but also in a country like Guatemala in which there is a spatial disjunction between the coffee estates and the potential laboring population, finding the labor necessary to plant and maintain coffee, and to harvest and process it, presents a problem and potential fault line. The "falta de brazos" therefore becomes an oft-repeated economic and ideological complaint among coffee elites. Some of the available methods for resolving that problem could result in a diffusion of control over the coffee estate, presenting a potential social basis for the future fragmentation of the farm. Coffee farmers large and small were therefore placed into relationships with markets, merchants, processors, and laborers that could alter the very structure of landholding.

For example, if our understanding of the large estate in Brazil begins with a discussion of the occupation of space and the granting of large tracts of land to favored individuals, our analysis of the dynamics must quickly turn to an examination of the estates' labor forces. In the expansion into the Paraíba Valley as well as the early expansion in São Paulo, planters depended upon slave labor. Paradoxically, however, planters were resorting to slaves during a period in which slavery was increasingly costly and impractical. The coffee boom of the 1850s and 1860s in Rio, for example, occurred after the international slave trade had been banned, and internal slave prices had doubled. Moreover, by the 1870s, legislation had begun to limit slavery. Behind the picture of wealth and aristocratic privilege, then, lay a social reality of waste, decay, and impending crisis.[41]

In the 1870s and 1880s, planters in São Paulo began to actively pursue other forms of labor; as they did so they depended upon the active involvement, finance, and direction of the state of São Paulo. The *colonato* that emerged depended upon the state-subsidized immigration of millions of workers, largely Italian, to serve short-term contracts on coffee estates. Beyond its payment of the immigrants' passage, the state also coordinated planter needs and labor supply. Immigrants would be transferred from Santos to a hostel in São Paulo, where the state would serve as labor contractor. While at the hostel, the immigrant family would sign a contract to work on a particular plantation and would then be given railroad passage from São Paulo to the interior.

The contracts they signed represented a unique form of labor mobilization. First, they received a fixed wage per thousand coffee trees weeded and maintained during the year, regardless of yield. Second, harvest labor was compensated on the basis of yield (so much per fifty liters of cherries). Third, they received a house, and fourth, they received a food plot. Variations might appear in regions where coffee was being planted, allowing *colonos* to plant food crops between rows of recently planted coffee. The system preserved some of the advantages of a sharecropping regime (some of the risk was reduced with the harvest compensation tied to yield; costs were reduced with the provision of a food plot) but eliminated some of sharecropping's disadvantages (the set wage for tending a number of trees allowed more space for planter control of the labor process).

Because of state subsidization of immigration and the elimination of debt as a social and economic relation between planter and colono, there was extraordinary movement of persons in the São Paulo west at the close of each annual cycle. Colonos on one plantation might leave and move farther west, especially to zones of expansion, where contracts were perceived by colonos as being more lucrative. As long as the immigrant stream was maintained, however, the instability in terms of personnel was of little concern for the planter. A dependable, state-subsidized and state-controlled mass of cheap and replaceable labor remained available.[42]

Once implanted, the colonato system dominated coffee production in São Paulo throughout the period that concerns us in this book, lasting until the 1960s. The combination of incentives to individual laborers, cost-reducing features, and a structure of labor discipline proved a powerful source of planter power in the early decades of this century. Stolcke emphasizes, for example, that planters were able to weather increasingly frequent periods of low prices because the provision of food plots allowed planters to reduce wages and compensate for decreased prices.[43] One of the more interesting debates in the recent literature, however, concerns what we might call the fault lines within this labor regime. Holloway and Font, for example, stress social mobility among colonos, arguing that significant numbers were able to establish their own farms in the westward expansion of São Paulo settlement. Others, like Love and Stolcke, discount the importance of such mobility as a threat to the power of the planters. The problem takes on added importance when we move beyond the São Paulo countryside and consider the composition of those social groups who moved toward the industrialization of São Paulo and agitated for a dismantling of the republic in the 1920s.[44]

One of the most remarkable systems of labor "recruitment" e
Guatemala, as described by David McCreery in this volume a
essays.[45] Coffee growers accumulating land in the piedmont faceu
labor shortages and turned their attention to the highlands, home to a
densely settled Mayan population. Unfortunately for the planters, the
villagers showed little desire to journey to the coast and work, preferring
to remain in their villages and farm their own lands. Fortunately for the
planters, the liberals who came to power with planter support in 1871
were anxious to find a solution to the problem. The principal means
devised by the regime of Rufino Barrios was the *mandamiento*, modeled
after the colonial *repartimiento*. Under this system, outlined in the labor
law of 1877, a planter would request a certain number of laborers from a
departmental governor, who in turn would order a particular town to supply the workers, with stipulations on length of service and wage, which
would be paid in advance.

That highland Indians became the primary source of labor on coffee
plantations does not mean that it was obvious to elites in the early 1870s
that they *should become* the primary labor force. "What the Liberals
wanted," McCreery reminds us,

was a "modern" white working class which would accept the wages and conditions which centuries of European rule had forced upon the Indians. By "bleaching
out" the lower classes they sought a radical transformation of the ethnic but not
social structure. "An infusion of fresh and vigorous life" provided by mass white
immigration would "speed the clogged blood" of the nation. An influx of Europeans would increase the "intelligent" work force available, revolutionize agricultural production, and spread civilized morals and values among the lower order.[46]

In the early seventies, the government set up an Immigration Society,
which set up offices in the United States, printed pamphlets for distribution in the United States and Europe encouraging immigration, and, in
1878–79, welcomed a few boatloads of Italian and Tyrolean immigrants.
Immigration could not become a realistic option, however, partly because
of the larger context of European emigration and the emerging importance of the United States, Argentina, and Brazil as ports of entry. With
state subsidization of immigration in Argentina and Brazil, Guatemalan
planters were placed at a decided disadvantage. They could not finance
the passage themselves, encountering the same problems of enforcing debt
obligations faced by São Paulo planters, and the Guatemalan state lacked
the resources of the São Paulo state. Luckily for the planters, "not only
were local Indians accustomed to the low rewards and the harsh realities
of existing conditions, but the government was free, limited only by the

danger of provoking a total revolt, to enact measures which reduced their cost as a production factor, without fear of consular intervention or gunboat diplomacy."[47]

The mandamiento was not the only means by which Indian labor was mobilized, though it provides a necessary context for understanding other forms. One means by which highlanders could evade work for one planter was to demonstrate that they were already indebted to another planter and were working off the previously acquired debt for that planter. Thus the twin systems of forced labor drafts and reinvigorated debt peonage complemented each other, securing a labor force for the plantations. The two systems also worked together to secure the various types of labor needed by coffee farms — the characteristic alteration between a permanent year-round force and the increased demands during the harvest.

Such systems, based on large landholdings and elaborate state-sponsored schemes for securing and moving laborers, can be contrasted with those regions in which smallholders predominated. Costa Rica's Central Mesa, the Antioqueño west in Colombia, parts of the Venezuelan Andes, and the Western Highlands of Puerto Rico serve as examples of regions in which the spread of coffee cultivation facilitated the expansion of groups of small-scale, commercially oriented farmers, and they have attracted increasing interest from historians and anthropologists over the past two decades. We need to avoid the temptation of treating smallholder regimes as the basis for a "rural democracy," in contrast to the "oligarchy" that characterized planter regimes in Brazil, Guatemala, and central Colombia. Smallholders produced and sold their coffee — and secured labor for their coffee plots — within hierarchical social fields that deserve careful analysis. Of special importance is the relationship between small-scale producers and urban merchants who provided credit, purchased and processed coffee, and sold trade goods. In such situations, landholding was not the primary route to power. Both the accumulation of land and access to labor depended on one's position within and access to accumulated commercial wealth.

Even so, it would be inappropriate and simplistic to make rigid distinctions between smallholder and plantation regions. Smallholders in western Venezuela, Antioquia, and Costa Rica existed alongside and in economic and social relation with large landholders. Their conflicting interests and requirements, especially with regard to labor recruitment, deserve careful attention. The large landholder in regions characterized by small-scale production, such as Costa Rica's Central Mesa, was attempting to recruit workers to cultivate or harvest coffee, but the workers they were mobilizing were also farmers trying to cultivate or harvest their own coffee patches. Given the situation of the large estate within a smallholder milieu, estate owners attracted permanent and seasonal laborers with relatively high wages. The Costa Rican *peón*, as Cardoso stresses, "was basically an employee, a wage labourer and not a 'serf.' "[48] Yet landlords were unable to mount any sustained effort to attract additional laborers to Costa Rica. On the one hand, this represents their more modest resources in a world in which other countries — Brazil and Argentina — had begun massive subsidized immigration schemes. On another, it represents the limits of their own mental and cultural horizons. The 1862 colonization law specifically forbade settlement by blacks and Chinese, and Tomás Guardia rejected Chinese workers in 1875, claiming they were "gamblers, thieves, and opium smokers."[49] Moreover, even when contracts were signed for the construction of a railway to the Atlantic coast, the Costa Rican government stipulated that the West Indian laborers brought in to work on the railway were not to enter the Central Mesa.[50]

Like French Wines: Merchants, Processors, and Markets in the Era of Free Trade

As we turn to a discussion of marketing and processing networks and hierarchies, some of the general characteristics of the coffee trade delineated above need to be emphasized:

— the dominance of a free-trade model in international trade;
— the diffuse nature of control exercised through exporters, trading companies, and local merchants;
— the segmented nature of the international coffee market; and
— the importance of a discourse of quality.

Segmentation and diffusion were at once sources of relative autonomy for local producers, providing some room to maneuver *and* sources of power and control for particular merchants. In their control over grading hierarchies, over the market and market prices, over credit, and sometimes over processing, merchants and traders occupied nodal positions within a variety of hierarchical networks. We can learn a good deal about distinct coffee economies by sketching some of these networks and their changes over time.

In Brazil, for example, large planters processed their coffee on their own estates but entered into complex social and financial relations with their buyers (factors or *comissarios*) in Rio or Santos. For much of the nineteenth century, factors served as principal sources of credit for planters, and they were entrusted with handling economic and social affairs for planters as well. Once a relationship between planter and factor had been established, the factor would open a current account, accept the coffee as it arrived, credit the account upon sale to a sacker, and attend to the planter's needs, purchasing goods requested by the planter and arranging for their shipment to the countryside as necessary and even lodging the planter and his family when they traveled to Rio. Factors stored and graded coffee from individual planters and sold it to sackers, who blended various lots of coffee and arranged for the sale of the lots to exporters, who acted as agents for foreign firms. While factors in Rio tended to be Brazilian or Portuguese, a much smaller group of foreigners, especially British and North American, dominated the exporters.[51]

While this three-tiered system characterized the second half of the nineteenth century, the overproduction crisis that became apparent during the 1890s provoked a major transformation in Brazil's marketing system and in the international coffee trade. In response to continued overproduction, the state of São Paulo, in cooperation with foreign firms (Crossman and Sielcken of New York) and banks (Disconto Gesellschaft of Berlin) removed millions of bags of coffee from the market, for sale in later years. This, the first of a series of "valorization" schemes during the early twentieth century, initiated a number of structural changes. First, the schemes increased foreign control over coffee production and trade, in the holding of Brazilian stocks and in the increased dependence of the São Paulo and later the federal state on foreign banks. Second, it facilitated and required greater participation by the state, creating a set of state institutions, regulations, and protections that undercut the free-trade model. The most important of these was the National Coffee Department, which controlled Brazilian trade in the decades following the depression of the 1930s.[52]

Costa Rica presents an interesting contrast, in terms of market niche, processing methods, commercialization networks, and power hierarchies. Costa Rican coffee was able to occupy the quality segment of the European market because, unlike Brazil, Costa Rican coffee was processed by the wet method almost from the beginning. Due to the efforts of early planters who installed patios and machinery, the consolidation of a European market for Costa Rican coffee in the late 1840s coincided with a recognition of its high "quality," in part a function of sophisticated processing machinery. With wet method processing hegemonic in terms of market acceptance, less sophisticated and expensive processing methods were effectively closed off to small farmers, who sold their coffee to processors (beneficiadores) from the 1840s on. Processors would in turn act as exporters and served as principal creditors for small farmers.[53]

Processors' provision of credit, in conjunction with their control of processing in a quality market, gave them effective control over the coffee sector. Despite the establishment of a few banks (with English capital) in the late nineteenth and early twentieth centuries, the banks had no system of agricultural credit until the 1930s and 1940s. The major source of credit was the English and other European importing firms, who would advance funds to processors, who in turn would make advances to small farmers in return for coffee, to be delivered to the processing facility upon harvest, at a price to be determined upon delivery or upon sale in London.[54]

Given the importance of the coffee sector within Costa Rica, the processors were able to establish themselves as an economic and political elite, composed of Costa Rican and, increasingly, foreign (French, German, English, and Spanish) families. While foreigners processed 5 percent of Costa Rican coffee in 1850, they or their descendants processed 20 percent of it by 1900 and 33 percent in 1935. While most processors would also establish coffee farms of up to 60,000 trees, especially in the fertile San José/Heredia sector of the Central Mesa, their power lay in their control over processing and credit.[55]

By the 1920s, the small producer/processor divide had become the object of political dispute and protest, especially from farmers outside the San José/Heredia sector who received lower prices for their coffee. With the crisis of the thirties, protests became quite acute, with the formation by farmers of the Asociación Nacional de Productores de Café in 1932 and the creation by the state of the Instituto de Defensa del Café in 1933, designed to regulate relations between producers and processors with mechanisms for fixing prices and regulating payments. An organ for mediating conflicts between producers and processors, it was also set up to defend the coffee sector in a period of crisis. In this function, and in its mediating role, it remained under the control of processors until after the 1948 revolution. As Samper Kutschbach argues in this volume (Chapter 6), the producer movements of the thirties never reached the pitch that characterized tenant movements in central Colombia at the same time. An understanding of the contrast requires attention to the different production regimes, the mediated character of commercial exploitation between processors and small farmers, and — as Gudmundson shows in chapter 5 of this volume — the differentiation that had occurred in the small farmer sector by the onset of the crisis of the thirties. In any case, the small farmer/processor divide remains quite vivid in political and historiographical imagery.[56]

Merchant dominance over small producers could be found in other regions as well, most notably in Antioquia, Colombia, where merchants in Medellín exercised control over processing and credit for producers in a variety of small towns and producing centers,[57] and in the Venezuelan

Andes. Unlike Antioquia and the Central Mesa of Costa Rica, however, merchants in Venezuela's Maracaibo and Andean commercial centers depended upon their control of credit for their dominant position. Venezuelan coffee did not occupy a "quality" niche in international markets and was processed by the dry method with simple technology available to the small grower.

Where merchants could control processing, credit, and the export trade, they were in a position to exercise effective control over the coffee sector. In Colombia, for example, the most important of them formed a secret combine in 1908 called the Negocio X y Y to fix prices on coffee bought at local plazas, on processing fees, and on transport. Each of the houses had separate relations with small merchants in towns throughout the west, and, as Palacios describes it,

to preserve the secret character of the society, each member had its own agency in the municipalities, so that producers and small intermediaries would believe that there was competition among the various agencies and coffee processors.

Orders were transmitted in code to municipal agents, and the sender would invent ingenious combinations so that not even the agents would suspect the existence of the business. Thus, for example, when a lower price was ordered in a municipality in which there were two or more member agencies, orders would be given over a three-day or one-week period to take away any suspicion of joint action.[58]

By 1913, in a period of rapid expansion in Colombian production and of relatively high prices after the near collapse of the first decade of the century, several Medellín firms, especially some who had been active in Negocio X y Y (Vásquez y Correa, Alejandro López & Cia, Pedro A. López & Cia, etc.), opened offices in New York and began to act as importers of Colombian coffee for the New York market. The firms drew their financing from Antioquian sources, especially the Banco de Sucre.[59] After World War I, prices nearly doubled as European markets reopened and wartime stocks were released, but they began to drop almost as quickly and steeply in early 1920. During the price rise, however, Colombian elites celebrated their good fortune with a wave of consumption and importation.

With the price collapse of 1920, Colombian banks and firms that had financed the wave of imports found themselves overextended and quickly went bankrupt as New York and London banks refused to extend further credit. This created an economic space for more direct foreign control of Colombian trade, especially through the Mercantile Bank of the Americas, formed in New York. Through their association with Alfonso López, son of Pedro López and future president of the republic, they were able to control some 40 percent of Colombian trade by 1919. With the collapse of Colombian houses the following year, the Banco Mercantil bought and restructured several of them.[60]

At the Banquet of Civilization: Ideas, Ideals, Ideologies, and Politics in the Coffee Republics

The coffee transformations of the late nineteenth and early twentieth century provide windows through which we can view the formation of liberalism and the dependent state. At various points in this book we refer to "the state" — in terms of land laws, abolition, immigration subsidies, mandamientos, valorization schemes, coffee marketing boards, and the like. We also refer to certain kinds of ideas — of free trade, of progress, of the necessity of "bleaching" the population or of the imagined dangers of blacks and Chinese, those notorious "gamblers, thieves, and opium smokers." We need to consider each in turn. Although the moment captured by Jiménez in Chapter 10, in which Jesús del Corral called upon fellow coffee planters to "redouble our efforts, gird ourselves for combat, and prepare to attend the magnificent banquet of civilization," was unique, one is tempted to extend the vision and battle cry to other moments and locales. In this phrase are captured the combat and *sense* of combat that accompanied the coffee transformations, the sense of progress and civilization that carried coffee entrepreneurs to the frontiers, and — implicitly — the disdain for and fear of the "barbarians" who were not up to the civilizing task and threatened to undermine the whole project. These ideas and sentiments, and the politics of the civilizing mission, require further consideration.

One way of approaching the state would be to see the coffee republics as exemplars of the liberal, dependent state, forged with the implantation of the outwardly focused development model in the late nineteenth century, undermined by the economic, social, and political forces that had emerged by the collapse of that model in the 1930s. Here we could with reason point to the "oligarchic pacts" that emerged in the late nineteenth century, the way in which state policies and practices responded to or "expressed" the needs of the planters and merchants, and the coffee planters who held positions of state power in the various republics. With state subsidization of a massive immigration scheme in São Paulo, such expression was quite direct. As Holloway notes, "the economic dominance of coffee was unquestionable. Among the property-owning sectors of society the right of the planters to control the political system was unquestioned, and the mass of working people — slaves, freedmen, native Brazilian peas-

ants, and immigrants—had no political voice. The government of São
Paulo was itself the *instrument* of the coffee planters."[61]

The examples can be multiplied, from the implementation of a state-
enforced system of forced labor in Guatemala to the commitment of state
resources to build railroads and open ports in Guatemala and Costa Rica,
to the passage of sweeping land reforms in El Salvador. At this level, the
class nature of the state is none too mysterious: it can be seen, as Marx and
Engels saw it, as "a committee for managing the common affairs of the
whole bourgeoisie." The demise of that state can then be connected with
the demise of the coffee bourgeoisie and of the free-trade period of the
global economy, and the rise, internationally, of imperialist monopolies
making direct investments in Latin American countries, and, nationally, of
a much more ramified state intervening directly within the economy and
of new economic and social groups (industrialists and "middle sectors")
associated with the new economic forces. Unlike the "liberal" state, the
emergent "populist" state, while still "capitalist" and "dependent," would
then have a less obvious, more mediated relationship with bourgeois rule.

Though I wish to suggest that such a vision is inadequate, its inadequacy lies not in its attempt to link class interests with state power. In most
of the cases that concern us here, such linkages were transparent. But both
class and state were in formation: the bourgeoisie was not "whole"; the
state was not a "perfected power." Several dimensions need to be stressed
here. One is the regional character of the coffee transformations and of the
planters and merchants that came to dominate them. A second is the sustained and pervasive struggle, both within and between regions, among
segments of a regional coffee elite, between coffee elites and others, between "peninsulares" and "criollos," and so forth. This might take the
form of regional and extra-regional warfare, most famously in Colombia
but also elsewhere, or it might concern disputes among differently situated
elites over, for example, transformation of credit laws protecting landowners in Brazil, the passage of a homestead act in Colombia, or the
imposition of an export tax to finance market intervention. Pérez-Brígnoli
expresses this well for Central America:

Who took power with the Liberal reforms? At least in the beginning, they were
socially a heterogeneous group: landowners, merchants, middle-class urban dwell-
ers, not to mention the many newcomers and quite a few newly converted conservatives. What the new business establishment had in common was their vision of
the opportunities for investment. . . . With the Liberal reform, the state could free
up resources to develop the agricultural export economy and greatly broaden the
economic basis of the new coffee producers. It might almost be said that the
Liberal state "created" its own ruling class.[62]

That the state should serve their i
by those elites who sought to contrc
their interests and *what* were the r
icies to further those interests mig
reflects, on the one hand, the di
tested for state power. Coffee elit
them did not act in a vacuum bu
included elites wedded to other
local and national markets. Is
slavery in Brazil in the 1880
the same period, or the passa
century Colombia, or the en
of coffee-marketing boards (or the failur
zuela, in the context of the dominance of petroleum ..
resolved unambiguously in favor of "coffee interests." The in..
bankers and merchants on the one hand and of growers on the other
would be quite opposed in, say, a credit reform, even though both interests
might claim to be "liberal."

On the other hand, the uneasy fit between "interests" and "policies" reflects the changing regional, "national," and global worlds in which elites
acted. The planters of Guatemala might have wanted white laborers from
Europe, but they could not compete with Brazilian and Argentine subsidization of immigrant streams. The beneficiadores of Costa Rica, with hacendado pretensions, might have wanted an infusion of laborers, but they
were not willing to contemplate the introduction of nonwhites in the Central Mesa. The planters of Colombia might have wanted railroads to ship
their coffee to distant ports, but the massive program of road and railroad
building drained labor from their farms; and the completed railroads,
under monopoly control, did not lower their freight costs. The planters of
Brazil wanted the state to buy their coffee in a period of market collapse,
but they did not want to pay an export tax to finance the program.

From coffee republic to coffee republic, this *contingent* character of
class and state rule needs to be emphasized. A comparative analysis of
class formation and power that concentrates on the ways in which particular elites confronted and resolved particular problems — the demise of
slavery, the inadequacy of state revenues, the collapse of the market — can
take us beyond programmatic statements about particular kinds of states
and illuminate the dynamics and contradictions of class and state formation in the late nineteenth and early twentieth centuries. Two essays in this
volume offer models of the sort of analysis that carry such discussions
forward. McCreery's examination of debates concerning free labor in
Guatemala in the 1920s and 1930s (Chapter 8) exposes an elite that surely

28

as reached a juncture at which it has no confidence
to do. Old solutions to the labor problem no longer
new solutions that might involve "free" forms of labor
e threatening. That McCreery's analysis includes an exam-
e larger social field in which planters acted — including, most
y, the changing social, economic, and political situations and
s of indigenous villagers — gives his essay special power. Jiménez's
nation of the "limited" or "imperfectly constituted" hegemony of
ral Colombian planters in the early twentieth century (Chapter 10) is
especially fine example of the social and political insights to be gained
when we place our analyses of class and state formation and power in
more problematic, historically contingent terms.

Likewise, we are impressed by the *practical* character of liberal ideas
and ideologies during this period. We may view liberalism as a common
ideology among the coffee elites, even where those elites might call their
ideology "conservative." Palacios, for example, considers two Colombian
exceptions — the dominance of the conservatives under the late-nineteenth-century "*Regeneración*" *during* the first great expansion of Colombian production, and the nominally conservative character of Antioqueño
politics in the nineteenth century. Of the second, he suggests that Antioquia, unlike regions of longer settlement, was not characterized by major
ethnic differences (the "barbarians" in their midst) nor by an entrenched
oligarchy from the colonial period against which an aggressive group of
free-trade merchants would have to mobilize politically and intellectually.
The two — the barbarians and the conservative *godos* ("Goths") — provided twin objects for liberal disdain; in their absence, Antioqueño elites
could forge a primarily regional political identity.[63] Of the first, Palacios
suggests a convergence of liberal and conservative interests before the
emergence of the famous liberal-conservative pact:

Our thesis is this: Manchesterian liberals and Regenerationists supported the agro-
export model with different shadings, and for the same fundamental reasons,
given that the two visions were penetrated by the same hope for economic progress. The fundamental differences between liberals and conservatives were expressed in the political definition of their relations with subaltern and dominated
classes. Liberals were convinced that capitalism would promote individual liberty
and political democracy and that social mobility would be uninterrupted through
the long process of development. Conservatives and regenerationists thought that
"spontaneous" capitalism would corrode the pillars of any type of progress: authority, religious tradition, and the central State. Before achieving all of its attributes, capitalism would require a stable social order; the discipline of all social
classes was a prerequisite for modernity.[64]

While it is important to delineate the intellectual and ideological lineage of liberal doctrines among economic elites and political actors during this period, it is also necessary to analyze the adaptability and malleability of such ideas under changing circumstances. Here again we need to concentrate on the *problems* the liberals confronted. It is interesting to note how easily liberals might call upon the state to resolve their economic problems, despite their free-trade ideology. State subsidization of immigration with the demise of slavery, or state intervention in the market with the collapse of international prices, might provoke debate (and market intervention inspired an especially intense debate), but the resolutions were essentially practical, transforming and undermining the "liberal state." Likewise, if we turn our attention to the issues that actually motivated liberal dreams and actions — the building of a road or railroad, the abolition of a tax, the reform of credit laws — we are able to approach a much more concrete understanding of the variety of liberalism*s* in the nineteenth- and twentieth-century coffee republics.

This is not to say that ideas and ideologies did not matter. Many planters and merchants, and their political supporters, felt themselves to be "at the banquet of civilization." Ideologies of progress and order, of global civilization, and of a combat with the forces of backwardness or an ever-present and threatening barbarism were central to Latin American liberalisms. I simply want to suggest that the ideas were not abstract in their various expressions. Thinkers and speakers had in mind real (and changing) barbarians and combats — among the barbarians, they had in mind the slaves in the *senzala*, the Indians in the hills, the Chinese, the blacks; among the combatants, they had in mind General Fulano, *los godos*, and so on. We need to pay close attention to these specific and changing objects and contents. We need, for example, careful studies of the various "economic societies" and "agricultural societies" that were formed in coffee-growing regions — often while elites were still out of state power but coming to see themselves as having common interests and needs which were articulated in the economic society's pamphlets, journals, and meetings and which might serve as blueprints for eventual state policies.[65] We also need studies of the various socially and politically constituted racisms that colored elite ideologies. They find their clearest and most public expression as elites are attempting to resolve their labor problem, when we see what elites are not willing to consider (free black laborers, for example, or "Chinese") or would prefer not to consider but eventually have to settle for (the "Indians"). Here again we find ideologies taking concrete, specific forms; we also have a collection of texts through which we can examine the socially constructed mental and cultural limits of the possible for specific groups of coffee planters and merchants.

Conclusion

We began with a paradox — the common transformation of Latin America's coffee republics in the late nineteenth century and the radically distinct experiences that transformation engendered. If we now ask *why* these different forms and relations emerged, I would suggest that such understanding can only be sought in the comparative exercise itself. "The determinate 'cause' of such changes," writes Sidney Mintz concerning another problem, "is a context, or a set of situations, created by broad economic forces."[66] In this case, I have tried to sketch radically different social, economic, political, and cultural contexts into which these broad economic forces were inserted, and I now wish to suggest that these different contexts "determined" the different directions the coffee economies took.

Despite appearances, this is not simply an argument that coffee economies were different because they were different. It is, instead, an attempt to work through, by means of comparative historical analysis, one dimension of the "history of diversity" that Cardoso and Faletto regard as necessary for an understanding of the emergence of capitalism in Latin America. We regard this book as a contribution to such a history, one that outlines and explores a variety of Latin American fields of power. Despite the diversity of approaches to individual studies in this volume, two controlling or limiting criteria can be discerned. First, most obviously, we have limited ourselves to a single commodity and an examination of the social fields in which Latin American coffee economies were formed. Second, less obviously, the authors take to their investigations a set of questions that fit quite comfortably within a historical materialist framework: the occupation of space and the transformation of landed property, the mobilization and reproduction of labor, the organization and capitalization of markets, and the political and ideological processes associated with state formation and the emergence of hegemonic blocks. The authors understand and approach particular questions differently, and some emphasize one or another of the questions at the expense of others. We have resisted imposing the questions as a set of structured categories or boxes which each author must fill for his or her particular region. This would too quickly lead to the sort of formalism that undermined and discredited mechanical materialisms in the first place.

Rather than offering summaries of basic structural features, most of the essays explore those features by concentrating on particular problems facing elites or smallholders at particular moments. Michael Jiménez's first contribution (Chapter 2), for example, begins with a crisis in levels of coffee consumption and oversupply in U.S. markets in the early twentieth century. Examining the strategies devised by coffee traders, merchants, and distributors, he reveals structural changes in coffee processing, marketing, and distribution in the United States, and in coffee-producing regions as well. His second essay (Chapter 10) examines the failure of the central Colombian coffee planters to form a hegemonic block that could effectively lead a Colombian "nation" and thus is able to question the existence of an "oligarchic pact." David McCreery (Chapter 8) takes the debate about "free labor" in Guatemala in the 1920s and 1930s as a political and economic problem that provides an important glimpse of the structure and dynamics of the state, and of the labor regime that characterized Guatemalan coffee production. Lowell Gudmundson (Chapter 5) examines inheritance strategies among smallholders and finds a basis for and evidence of internal differentiation among them, with implications for an understanding of the appeal and character of social democracy, as well as its class and gender biases, in mid-twentieth-century Costa Rica. And so on.

Our comparative strategy, then, is one that concentrates on the local and particular, with questions about the appropriation and mobilization of land and labor, the investment of capital and the organization of markets, and the administration and imagination of power. As we ask these questions, we are acutely aware of other questions unasked or inadequately answered, of further work that needs to be done. I close this essay, then, by pointing to some of the more important problems for comparative research.

One of the themes that emerges in this book is the importance of small-scale, familial or household-based production units, even within the largest estates. Large haciendas in central Colombia depended on peasant renters, and huge estates in Brazil depended on household production units with the colonato. The coffee regions of Costa Rica, Antioquia, Venezuela, and Puerto Rico provide important examples of the importance of a quasi-independent peasantry engaged in export production in the nineteenth and early twentieth centuries. The differences among sharecroppers on large estates and independent peasants are important, but given a literature that has stressed the dominance of a "latifundia/minifundia" complex in Latin America, the coffee regions provide an important point of entry for an alternative vision. Beyond alternative visions, however, a number of important issues concerning household production remain to be explored.

One of the most important concerns food production by estate based and independent peasants. One question is the extent to which coffee displaced food production, as it seems to have done in particular regions and microregions (for example, the nucleus of Costa Rica's Central Mesa[67]).

But in most regions, coffee was associated with other crops — maize, sugar cane, bananas, and pasture (each of which could be commercialized) — for the reproduction of the labor force and the provisioning of mules, horses, and other stock. Many rental arrangements or labor agreements (e.g., in Cundinamarca and São Paulo) reserved for the estate owner control over the coffee but granted the tenant control over food, creating conflict over the labor time of tenant family members but also giving the tenant a potential power base.

Once the importance of reproduction is recognized through an emphasis on food production, an analysis of gender relations and decision making within household production units becomes essential. It is woefully underdeveloped in most studies of coffee economies, including those that stress the importance of household production. An important exception is the work of Verena Stolcke, both in her monograph[68] and in her contribution to this volume (Chapter 3). Her analysis of "the exploitation of family morality" opens up an important and neglected social, political, and cultural dimension of the field of power. While Stolcke finds evidence of the manipulation of "family morality" by planters, and its collapse with the demise of the colonato system leading to wage labor, Gudmundson finds that a male-dominant land inheritance pattern emerged as part of a process of smallholder consolidation. The uses of "family morality" and the insights of a gender-specific analysis invite further comparative research.

Attention to household production units and reproduction over time will also facilitate the sort of careful analysis of the internal relations and contradictions of coffee-producing peasantries pioneered by Picó (Chapter 4), Gudmundson (Chapter 5), and Samper.[69] Here, too, we need to see peasant producers confronting real problems — which themselves change over time — of recruiting labor, balancing food and commodity production, arranging for the children's inheritance, surviving a bad harvest or a price collapse. The ways in which these problems are resolved have important consequences for the processes of class formation and, as Gudmundson shows, the emergence of new political movements.

One of the most important results of this book, and an area for further research, is the radical questioning of prevailing analyses of political domination during the period. Whether in analyses of "limited hegemonies" or in studies of the contradictions imposed upon planters by the means in which they solved problems associated with the "falta de brazos," more attention needs to be paid to the fissures within oligarchic groups, and the fault lines in their domination. Jiménez's second essay in this volume (Chapter 10) is a model of the kind of work that is missing in much of the Latin American literature. As McCreery shows (Chapter 8), one of the more strategic ways of getting at such fissures is to examine a period when fundamental social and political relations seem unstable, when elites are discussing and arguing among themselves about the best means to assure their labor supply, or markets, or tax exemptions, or whatever seems to threaten the world they have made.

Finally, we need more studies of commercialization, both within countries and in the international arena. One of the areas that needs work here is the examination of the activities of merchant houses in the importing centers and their linkages with houses in exporting centers—the changing structures of their purchasing and credit operations. Another is the study of coffee consumption and the transformation of trade and consumption in the United States and various European countries. Jiménez's discussion in Chapter 2 is quite suggestive in this regard.[70] It is no criticism of his fine work, or of any of the essays in this book, to suggest that much remains to be done.

Notes

I wish to thank the contributors to this volume for their stimulating essays, without which I could not have attempted this synthesis. More specifically, I have benefited from the criticisms and suggestions of Lowell Gudmundson, Michael Jiménez, David McCreery, Mario Samper Kutschbach, and Verena Stolcke.

1. Charles Gibson, *The Aztecs under Spanish Rule* (Stanford, 1964); Eduardo Arcila Farías, *El régimen de la encomienda en Venezuela*, 2d ed. (Caracas, 1966); Elman Service, "The Encomienda in Paraguay," *Hispanic American Historical Review* 26 (1951): 230–52.

2. See as well Ian Roxborough, "Unity and Diversity in Latin American History," *Journal of Latin American Studies* 16 (1984): 1–26.

3. See Michel-Rolph Trouillot, "Motion in the System: Coffee, Color, and Slavery in Eighteenth-Century Saint Domingue," *Review* 5 (1982): 331–88.

4. J. de Graaf, *The Economics of Coffee* (Wageningen, Netherlands, 1986), 26.

5. U.S. Department of Commerce, *Coffee Consumption in the United States, 1920–1965* (Washington, D.C., 1961), 5.

6. M. Palacios, *El café en Colombia, 1850–1970*, 2d ed. (Mexico City, 1983), 178.

7. Stanley Stein, *Vassouras, a Brazilian Coffee Country, 1850–1900: The Roles of Planter and Slave in a Plantation Society*, 2d ed. (Princeton, 1985); Warren Dean, *Rio Claro: A Brazilian Plantation System, 1820–1920* (Stanford, 1976); Thomas Holloway, *Immigrants on the Land: Coffee and Society in São Paulo, 1886–1934* (Chapel Hill, 1980); Verena Stolcke, *Coffee Planters, Workers, and Wives: Class Conflict and Gender Relations on São Paulo Plantations, 1850–1980* (New York, 1988).

8. Carolyn Hall, *El café y el desarrollo histórico-geográfico de Costa Rica*

(San José, 1976); Lowell Gudmundson, *Costa Rica before Coffee* (Baton Rouge, 1986).

9. David McCreery, "Coffee and Class: The Structure of Development in Liberal Guatemala," *Hispanic American Historical Review* 56 (1976): 438–60; idem, "Debt Servitude in Rural Guatemala, 1876–1936," *Hispanic American Historical Review* 63 (1983): 735–59; idem, "An Odious Feudalism: Mandamiento Labor and Commercial Agriculture in Guatemala," *Latin American Perspectives* 13 (1986): 99–117; Carol A. Smith, "Local History in Global Context: Social and Economic Transitions in Western Guatemala," *Comparative Studies in Society and History* 26 (1984): 193–228; J. C. Cambranes, *Coffee and Peasants: The Origins of the Modern Plantation Economy in Guatemala, 1853–1897* (Stockholm, 1985).

10. Palacios, *El café*; Mariano Arango, *Café e industria: 1850–1930* (Bogotá, 1977); idem, *El café en Colombia, 1930–58* (Bogotá, 1982); Absalón Machado, *El café: de la aparcería al capitalismo* (Bogotá, 1977).

11. Karl Marx, *Capital* (New York, 1967 [1894]), 3: 791.

12. Immanuel Wallerstein, *The Modern World-System III: The Second Era of Great Expansion of the Capitalist World-Economy, 1730s-1840s* (San Diego, 1989), 152–53.

13. Fernando Henrique Cardoso and Enzo Faletto, *Dependency and Development in Latin America* (Berkeley, 1979), xvii.

14. Ibid., xvii, xviii.

15. See as well Mario Samper Kutschbach, "Enfrentamiento y conciliación: comentarios a propósito de las relaciones entre productores y beneficiadores de café," *Revista de Historia*, Special number (1985): 207–12.

16. Dean, *Rio Claro*, 89–123; Holloway, *Immigrants on the Land*, 70–72; Stolcke, *Coffee Planters, Workers, and Wives*, 1–9; Emilia Viotti da Costa, *The Brazilian Empire: Myths and Histories* (Chicago, 1985), 94–124.

17. Machado uses articles written by hacendados in the *Revista Cafetera de Colombia* outlining the benefits of new forms of tenancy which they had recently adopted. Machado uses the articles as evidence of particular forms of sharecropping, but they are also interesting as elite discourses, with the planters simultaneously trying to present themselves to each other in a particular way and trying (*publicly*) to resolve increasingly intractable problems as their tenants left the farms and worked on public works projects (Machado, *El café*, 179–99).

18. See Laird Bergad, *Coffee and the Growth of Agrarian Capitalism in Nineteenth-Century Puerto Rico* (Princeton, 1982), 38.

19. Antonio Delfím Netto, "Foundations for the Analysis of Brazilian Coffee Problems," in C. M. Peláez, ed., *Essays on Coffee and Economic Development* (São Paulo, 1973), 50.

20. Arango, *Café e industria*, 184. The analogy, while suggestive, is inexact. Coffee is subject to a grading system, at first developed by traders in consuming countries and in recent decades developed by marketing boards in producing countries as well. It has never been associated with the sort of politically and commercially charged designation of lands which produce grapes that can be processed into wines with certain appellations, and within appellations, the desig-

nation of grapes and the lands that produce them into grand, premier, and lesser crus; nor can it be. Nonetheless, that a discourse of quality can give to a coffee processor a control analogous to that exercised by, say, a wine *negociant* is, at the least, an interesting possibility.

21. V. D. Wickizer, *The World Coffee Economy with Special Reference to Control Schemes* (Stanford, 1943), 13.

22. Brief descriptions of both processes (and of other technical aspects of coffee production) can be found in de Graef, *The Economics of Coffee*, 42–47, and C. F. Marshall, *The World Coffee Trade: A Guide to the Production, Trading and Consumption of Coffee* (Cambridge, 1983), 32–35.

23. Marshall, *The World Coffee Trade*, 35.

24. Palacios, *El café*, 294.

25. Stein, *Vassouras*; Dean, *Rio Claro*; Holloway, *Immigrants on the Land*; Stolcke, *Coffee Planters, Workers, and Wives*.

26. Hall, *El café*; Gudmundson, *Costa Rica before Coffee*; Mario Samper Kutschbach, *Generations of Settlers* (Boulder, 1991).

27. Palacios, *El café*; Arango, *Café e industria*; idem, *El café*; Machado, *El café*.

28. Domingo Alberto Rangel, *Capital y desarrollo: la Venezuela agraria* (Caracas, 1969); William Roseberry, *Coffee and Capitalism in the Venezuelan Andes* (Austin, 1983).

29. Bergad, *Coffee and the Growth of Agrarian Capitalism*; Fernando Picó, *Libertad y servidumbre en el Puerto Rico de del siglo XIX* (Río Piedras, 1979); idem, *Amargo café* (Río Piedras, 1981).

30. McCreery, "Coffee and Class"; idem, "An odious feudalism"; idem, "Debt Servitude."

31. David Browning, *El Salvador: Landscape and Society* (Oxford, 1971); Ciro F. S. Cardoso, "Historia económica del café en Centroamérica (Siglo XIX): Estudio comparativo," *Estudios Sociales Centroamericanos* 4 (1975): 14–15; see Pérez Brignoli, Chapter 9, this volume; Aldo Antonio Lauria Santiago examines land tenure and local processes of land concentration in the context of the expansion of the coffee economy in El Salvador, arguing that smallholding was more widespread and tenacious than has been asserted ("An Agrarian Republic: Production, Politics, and the Peasantry in El Salvador, 1740–1920" [Ph.D. diss., University of Chicago, 1992]).

32. Palacios, *El café*, 124.

33. Dean, *Rio Claro*, 24–25.

34. Mario Samper Kutschbach, "La especialización mercantil campesina en el noroeste del valle central: 1850–1900. Elementos microanalíticos para un modelo," *Revista de Historia*, special number (1985): 49–98.

35. Palacios, *El café*, 70.

36. Hall, *El café*, 80–81.

37. Bergad, *Coffee and the Growth of Agrarian Capitalism*, 94–95.

38. An excellent general treatment of land policy is in da Costa, *The Brazilian Empire*, 78–93. For treatments of the conflicts between squatters and grant holders in Rio and São Paulo, see Stein, *Vassouras*, 10–17; Dean, *Rio Claro*, 11–20; Holloway, *Immigrants on the Land*, 112–14.

39. Palacios, *El café*.

40. Roseberry, *Coffee and Capitalism*.

41. Stein, *Vassouras*, 65–67.

42. This summary has depended on descriptions in Stolcke, *Coffee Planters, Workers, and Wives*; Holloway, *Immigrants on the Land*, and Dean, *Rio Claro*.

43. Stolcke, *Coffee Planters, Workers, and Wives*, 28–34.

44. Mauricio Font, "Coffee Planters, Politics, and Development in Brazil," *Latin American Research Review* 22 (1987): 69–90; idem, "Perspectives on Social Change and Development in São Paulo: A Reply," *Latin American Research Review* 24 (1989): 143–57; Joseph Love, "Of Planters, Politics, and Development," *Latin American Research Review* 24 (1989): 127–35; Verena Stolcke, "Coffee Planters, Politics, and Development in Brazil: A Comment on Mauricio Font's Analysis," *Latin American Research Review* 24 (1989): 136–42.

45. McCreery, "An Odious Feudalism"; idem, "Debt Servitude."

46. McCreery, "Coffee and Class," 452–53.

47. Ibid., 452–56.

48. Ciro F. S. Cardoso, "The Formation of the Coffee Estate in Nineteenth-Century Costa Rica," in Kenneth Duncan and Ian Rutledge, eds., *Land and Labour in Latin America* (Cambridge, 1977), 194.

49. Hall, *El café*, 57.

50. Ibid., 57. This makes all the more interesting a consideration of the famous mural depicting Costa Rican economy and society in San José's National Theater. The romanticized picture of coffee and banana workers shows them all to be white, an obvious misrepresentation of the banana zone, an accurate representation of an elite's self-image.

51. J. E. Sweigart, *Coffee Factorage and the Emergence of a Brazilian Capital Market, 1850–1888* (New York, 1987), 27–31.

52. Thomas Holloway, *The Brazilian Coffee Valorization of 1906* (Madison, 1975); Delfím Netto, "Foundations for the Analysis," 54; and C. M. Peláez, "An Economic Analysis of the Brazilian Coffee Support Program: Theory, Policy, and Measurement," in C. M. Peláez, ed., *Essays on Coffee and Economic Development* (Rio, 1973).

53. Hall, *El café*, 49–52.

54. Ibid., 45–47.

55. Ibid., 51–53. For an important study of a processing firm, see Gertrud Peters Solorzano, "La formación territorial de las grandes fincas de café en la meseta central: estudio de la firma Tournon (1877–1955)," *Revista de Historia* 9–10 (1980): 81–167.

56. Hall, *El café*, 47–49; Victor Hugo Acuña Ortega, "Clases sociales y conflicto social en la economía cafetalera costarricense: productores contra beneficiadores: 1932–1936," *Revista de historia*, Special number (1985): 181–212.

57. Elsewhere in Colombia, urban coffee merchants held a different position in the processing and commercialization hierarchy. Cundinamarca, for instance, was characterized by the dominance of the large coffee *hacienda*. During the period of hacendado ascendance, the hacendado (who was often a Bogotá merchant) controlled processing and exported his coffee directly to the exterior, contracting

debts with European and North American importing firms. Though the hacendado was simultaneously a merchant in this case, it would be inappropriate to equate this situation with that of Antioquia or Costa Rica. It was the hacendado's ability to control land, processing, and trade that allowed him to become an exporter and avoid the situation that plagued small producers elsewhere.

58. Palacios, *El café*, 287; for the entire discussion of Negocio X y Y, see pp. 286–92.

59. Ibid., 291–92.

60. Arango, *Café e industria*, 199–214.

61. Holloway, *Immigrants on the Land*, 39.

62. Hector Pérez Brignoli, *A Brief History of Central America* (Berkeley, 1989), 94.

63. Palacios, *El café*, 33–35.

64. Ibid., 29.

65. Gudmundson points out that petty bourgeois reformist tracts appear repeatedly in the *Revista del Instituto de Defensa del Cafe* in the 1930s in Costa Rica. The journal was the organ of the Instituto de Defensa del Café, set up in 1932 to coordinate elite concerns, demonstrating how disputed even the most hegemonic institutions can be (see Chapter 5).

66. Sidney Mintz, *Sweetness and Power: The Place of Sugar in Modern History* (New York, 1985), 181.

67. Hall, *El café*, 80–81. For the displacement of food production in Puerto Rico's highlands, see Bergad, *Coffee and the Growth of Agrarian Capitalism*, 94–95 et passim.

68. Stolcke, *Coffee Planters, Workers, and Wives*.

69. Mario Samper Kutschbach, "Uso de la tierra y unidades productivas al finalizar el siglo XIX: Noroeste del valle central de Costa Rica," *Revista de Historia* 14 (1986): 133–78.

70. See as well William Roseberry, "Yuppie Coffees: The Beverage of Postmodernism" (paper presented at the session on "Histories of Commodification: Essays in Honor of Sidney Mintz," at the 1992 meeting of the American Anthropological Association, San Francisco).

Two

"From Plantation to Cup": Coffee and Capitalism in the United States, 1830–1930

MICHAEL F. JIMÉNEZ

> Coffee is universally considered a nerve food, a "factor" of the economical forces.... There is nothing like a good cup of coffee to wipe out the languishing nutrition of city dwellers, to reanimate their moral sense so prone to decay, and to sustain the vigor and flexibility of the body and the spirit, to even up the waste of strength and to stop the desegregating movement of human energy.
>
> E. Monin (1927)

IN JANUARY of 1927, Gus Comstock, a barbershop porter in the small Minnesota town of Fergus Falls, drank eighty cups of coffee in seven hours and fifteen minutes. The *New York Times* reported that near the end, amid a cheering crowd, Comstock's "gulps were labored, but a physician examining him found him in pretty good shape."[1] A nationwide marathon coffee-drinking spree had been set off two years earlier by news from the Department of Commerce that imports into the United States amounted to five hundred cups annually per resident.[2] While amused by this "newest form of athletic exercise" on the North American scene, the coffee industry nonetheless expressed dismay at the possible negative impact of "such things uncommon" on its efforts to promote the healthfulness of the beverage.[3]

The coffee-drinking contests of the mid-1920s occurred amid an intense, multifaceted campaign to expand consumption by a lobby composed of retailers, wholesalers, roasters, and importers working with the technical and financial assistance of foreign merchants and governments, most notably from Brazil. This interest used novel marketing methods in these years to complete the beverage's century-long transformation from a luxury item into a commonplace in the North American diet. At the same time, having acquired organizational coherence and political influence after the turn of the century, coffee importers, processors, and merchandisers joined other North American elites to promote greater openness toward foreign trade. This essay examines the history of this commodity in the economic, social, and political history of the United States during the century before the Great Depression. It focuses particularly on the structural, institutional, and cultural changes in that period which made coffee the paramount beverage of that emergent consumer society.

Coffee and the Market Revolution

A century earlier coffee drinking had been largely an elite and often more private affair than the raucous event at Fergus Falls. With cocoa, sugar, and tea, it was one of a bundle of tropical commodities consumed by the upper strata in the North Atlantic basin for several centuries.[4] In 1830 the United States imported some 38 million pounds of coffee, and annual per capita consumption was only three pounds annually.[5] High import costs from the still largely inaccessible producing areas in Asia and Latin America confined its usage mostly to the eastern seaboard, where it had become the centerpiece of a distinctive coffeehouse culture among the new nation's republican patriciate. In the fragmented regional economies of the United States, coffee found limited purchase among often isolated and relatively impoverished outlying populations with their own various regional brews made from chicory and nuts.[6] Such constraints on demand precluded any major innovations in grinding and roasting. On the other hand, service technologies available to elite consumers grew ever more sophisticated, with elaborate, French-influenced design of percolators, drip services, and porcelain and metal pots.

After 1830, however, coffee consumption expanded dramatically, accompanied by major changes in the processing and marketing of the bean in the United States. Imports grew sixfold over the next four decades, from 38,363,000 to 231,174,000 pounds; annual per capita usage doubled in the same period, reaching a new high of six pounds after the Civil War.[7] Coffee consumers became both more geographically and socially diverse. The increased use of the beverage accompanied the demographic growth, the spread of commercial agriculture, and the rise of manufacturing in a belt stretching from New England to the Midwest.[8] It became more commonplace not only in that thickly populated zone, but also at the outer edges of the frontier beyond the Mississippi River.[9] Coffee was now more

generally consumed by middle-class townsfolk, farmers, and workers in
the middle decades of the nineteenth century despite the slow growth in
discretionary income among the lower classes.[10] The social upheaval and
physical mobility of the Civil War years likely contributed to the regular
use of a beverage which became, in Richard Hooker's words, "an occasional drink and one to accompany meals."[11]

Crucial improvements in processing and merchandising of the bean
during this period increased coffee's presence in ever-widening markets.
At mid-century, several manufacturers in the Connecticut Valley improved coffee-processing machinery; among them, Jabez Burns, son of a
Chartist immigrant, patented a discharging roaster which applied heat
more evenly to the beans and allowed for their automatic removal without
shutting down operation. Other innovations followed, including coolers,
mixers, and granulators. Within the decade after the Civil War, grocers
and household consumers could acquire a cheaper, higher-quality product
from commercial roasters. At the same time, major marketing changes led
to the introduction of paper packaging and company trademarks. The latter included Lewis Osborn's Java sold in New York, the Ariosa brand sold
by Pittsburgh's John Arbuckle, and the Buckeye from Columbus, Ohio.[12]
Moreover, several firms specializing in imports and wholesale distribution
acquired national reach; amongst these were the St. Louis grocers Stein-
winder and Stoffregen, whose move to New York in the early 1870s
opened up a new era of marketing.[13] At the retail level, small grocers faced
stiff competition by large chain stores, most notably The Great Atlantic
and Pacific Tea Company (A&P) founded in 1859 and expanding within a
decade to over one hundred outlets between Virginia and Minnesota.[14]

During the four decades after the Civil War, coffee acquired a secure
niche in the consumer habits of a continentally expansive and industrial-
izing United States. Between 1870 and 1900, imports increased from
231,174,000 to 748,801,000 pounds and annual per capita consumption
grew from almost six to over thirteen pounds just after the turn of the
century.[15] In the industrial East and Midwest, the expanded working class
grew accustomed to its use in their homes and eateries surrounding the
mills and factories. Among the burgeoning white-collar class, coffee became the ideal "nerve food" to counter what George M. Beard called the
"pressures of the machinery of civilized life."[16] Finally, in the expanding
western frontier the bean became, in the words of one contemporary
observer, "an unfailing and apparently indispensable beverage, served at
every meal . . . Even under the boiling midday sun, the wagoner will rarely
fail to replenish a second time, his huge tin cup."[17]

The restructuring of industrial capitalism in this period spurred coffee
consumption.[18] A new phase of manufacturing with novel energy and

production technologies led to an increasing homogenization of the working class as factory hands were deskilled and levelled.[19] The resulting cultural unity and coherence of a large portion of the United States population served as the core of a national market enlarged and consolidated by two additional factors: first, a rise in discretionary incomes as a result of dramatic increases in agricultural productivity in the trans-Mississippi granary from the 1870s which reduced foodstuff prices, and, second, the greater, more efficient carrying capacity of the national and world-wide transportation system which substantially diminished transfer costs within the United States and globally, thereby affecting the demand for products such as coffee from abroad.[20]

The accelerated pace of industrial innovation in the United States had a major impact on bean processing as economies of scale and technological improvements reduced costs significantly. Roasters successfully utilized German gas technology to standardize roasting and Naperian urns provided mass service to restaurants and hotel patrons cheaply and more efficiently. At the same time, the development of household grinders, improved coffee pots, and filters stimulated greater household usage. Finally, the once largely elite service technologies became more widely used by the growing middle classes.[21]

Paradoxically, however, bean selection and processing did not improve despite a marketing revolution at the retail level in which coffee became a major item for chain grocers and numerous specialty distributors replaced the brown paper bag with colorful vinyl packets and strawboard containers.[22] Deception and adulteration were commonplace, with chicory, cereals, acorns, and even sawdust passed off as coffee.[23] The fragmentation of the import and roaster sections of the coffee industry partly accounts for the absence of any major drive toward product control and standardization in this period. A commission-house structure and a mentality characteristic of the Front Street district in New York City persisted.[24] At the same time, most major industrial centers had their own roasters provisioning local markets. The result was a regionally differentiated industry as well, with an older northeast coffee community, several major midwestern groups, a rising Pacific coast interest in San Francisco, and another rapidly growing element in New Orleans close to Latin American producers. Unlike sugar, the other major tropical commodity consumed in the United States, coffee did not experience a dramatic consolidation in both processing and marketing.[25]

The world coffee economy also precluded any drive toward major investments or concentration in the processing and marketing of the bean. Little incentive to monopolize trade existed for a product grown in so many different parts of the world. Despite the enormous weight of Bra-

zilian producers, the continuing importance of East Indian coffees and the
growing presence of mild varieties from Colombia and Central America
made for a highly fragmented global trading structure. In addition, the
endemic instability of world commerce in tropical commodities became
particularly marked for coffee in these years.[26] Unpredictable harvests
characterized a tropical commodity from so many diverse sources and
with so many variously sized producers, circumstances which also limited
standardization.[27] Consequently speculation was commonplace, with repeated episodes of market manipulation such as the 1880–81 Trinity
Syndicate episode which led to losses of upwards of $5 million.[28] The New
York Coffee Exchange, founded in 1884, did establish a futures market
and import regulations, but these changes could only dampen the vol-
atility of the trade and not rescue it from persistent structural problems.[29]
In short, by century's end, what Francis Thurber in 1881 referred to as the
journey "from plantation to cup" remained in thrall both to the vagaries
of the North Atlantic economies and the unpredictability of production
and commerce in the tropics.[30]

The Challenges of Corporate Capitalism

By the early twentieth century, coffee had become practically a staple
among U.S. consumers. Over the following three decades, it would be
fully enthroned as that society's paramount beverage, commonly used in
households, available in ever more numerous public spaces, and offered to
consumers in many novel forms (e.g., soluble, iced, and decaffeinated).
Between 1900 and the mid-1920s, imports almost doubled, from 748,801
to 1,468,888 pounds, but per capita consumption grew at a slower pace
and oscillated between ten and twelve and a half pounds.[31] A Boston study
of working-class consumer habits revealed that typical menus "gave coffee
everyday and tea about five times a week, with the result that over a seven-
week period, three pounds of coffee were consumed and only one third a
pound of tea."[32]

Major changes in the structure of the United States economy encouraged greater consumption during the first third of the century. The homogenization of work begun in the late nineteenth century now accelerated
through novel systems of labor specialization and hierarchy. Simultaneously, industrial reorganization and new management techniques split
workers into numerous categories of skills and responsibilities and led to a
much expanded white-collar work force.[33] This crucial redesign of North
American capitalism helped crystallize national markets for durable and
perishable goods above necessaries, a process which simultaneously pro-

moted a homogeneity of demand even as it conduced specialty markets. Moreover, the merchandising systems which had evolved after the Civil War became increasingly complex and sophisticated, as did the advertising industry to which the coffee interests now irrevocably hitched their fate.[34]

Coffee benefited from these changes. A more coherent national market drove out most competing beverages, such as chicory, from the popular diet. In addition, the dramatic transformation of urban life led one-fifth of the population to consume food and beverages away from the home by the early 1920s.[35] The growth of suburbs and the increased separation of workplace and residences for blue- and white-collar workers alike accelerated the establishment of restaurants and eateries in business districts and factory zones.[36] Finally, the prohibition of alcohol after the First World War gave a fillip to coffee consumption; the conversion of a Buffalo, New York, brewery into a coffee roaster and distributor signaled the coffee interest's efforts to take advantage of this potentially radical change in popular drinking habits.[37]

Despite the positive impact of these major economic and social changes on consumption, the coffee interest faced numerous obstacles after 1900. Stagnation in the growth of per capita consumption was marked in the first decades of the century, the thirteen-pound level in 1902 not reached again until forty years later. For various reasons the market appears to have been saturated well before the First World War. Slower population growth after the turn of the century contributed as well to a greater inelasticity of demand for many consumer products beyond necessaries. Other structural problems in the United States economy imposed restraints on greater coffee consumption. Between the 1890s and the 1920s, recurrent crises in world grain markets led to steadily rising prices for wheat and other staples, thereby threatening to marginalize coffee and other products purchased with discretionary income. Simultaneously, the dynamic interplay between agriculture and industry which had driven the North American economy during the last decades of the nineteenth century began to fray as real wage growth declined and the gap between the rich and the poor widened after the mid-1890s. In effect, the managerial reorganization and technological innovation set in place between the 1870s and the 1890s did not lead to any major increases in purchasing power among the bulk of United States consumers after the turn of the century. These circumstances braked the previous long-term, if uneven, growth in demand for tropical commodities by North Atlantic consumers, thereby presenting a substantial challenge to the coffee interest in the United States, the world's largest consumer of this beverage.[38]

Continuing instability in the international coffee trade also destabilized the product's position in North American markets. Dramatic price varia-

tions continued to plague the industry in the three decades after 1900.
Prices remained low immediately after the turn of the century; they rose to
1896 levels of 14.2 cents a pound only by 1912 and remained relatively
high for the next several years. The cost of the bean doubled at the end of
the First World War, from 12.1 to 24.8 cents a pound between 1918 and
1920. This upswing was followed by an equally dramatic fall in prices in
the early 1920s, but then a recovery to 24.5 cents a pound by 1926. Prices
continued to be erratic through the end of the decade, finally slipping to
13.2 cents a pound in the year after the October 1929 financial crash.[39]

Periodic price rises led to several episodes of public outrage in the
United States and political debates over the so-called coffee question.
Early on, the alleged monopolization of the coffee trade, abroad and in the
United States, came in for harsh criticism. Populist Nebraska congress-
man George Norris denounced importers, roasters, and foreign interests
on the floor of the House of Representatives in April 1911 as a conspiracy
to gouge consumers. He suggested the federal government file suits against
coffee importers for violation of the Sherman Anti-Trust and Wilson Tariff
Acts in order to assure the application, in his words, of the "doctrine of the
Golden Rule to all people on the earth."[40] This campaign shifted its focus
from the coffee trust in the United States to harsh rebukes of Brazil's
several attempts to prevent further price declines by a withdrawal of coffee stocks from the market orchestrated by the government of São Paulo
and funded by an international consortium of financiers.

The repeated episodes of valorization in the three decades before 1930
aroused considerable ire in the United States against Brazil.[41] In 1908,
Harry Jones, of the National Grocer Company, condemned the first valorization as a "scheme (that) does not appeal to us in any way. We believe
that if the natural law of supply and demand should rule, the market
would be better today."[42] During the second valorization in 1913 Julius
Klein at the Commerce Department labeled it "an attempt on the part of
the government [of Brazil] to control the value of coffee arbitrarily."[43]
Over a decade later, in the midst of widespread criticism of commodity
controls by tin, oil, and rubber producers throughout the globe, one observer remarked on the "nationwide clamor . . . because of Brazil's attack on our breakfast cup via high prices."[44] Commerce Secretary Herbert Hoover threatened financial boycott and a trade war against the
Brazilians.[45]

Facing a weakened market position and criticism by populists and
xenophobes, the dealers in this commodity were also caught in the under-
tow of fierce debates concerning its moral and physical salubrity. Before
World War I, some medical experts posited a negative link between alcohol and coffee, noting that "fried foods and strong coffee form the bulk of

the American workingman's diet . . . [and] this causes indigestion and of itself fosters a thirst for stimulants which the saloon readily provides."[46] A 1917 report on women workers by the Massachusetts Department of Health concluded that "the large use of tea and coffee may have promoted undue irritability among women."[47] During Prohibition coffee was seen in some quarters as a danger to good health and sobriety. In 1926, coffee retailers were warned about "the Moral League for the restriction of other people's pleasures . . . this earnest group [which] glorifies in the fact that they use neither tea, coffee, nor tobacco and have been inducing Sunday school pupils to sign pledges of abstinence from these immoral practices. . . . The coffee trade that this 'League' has killed in any fair-sized town would give some roaster a very comfortable living."[48]

Remaking the Coffee Interest

The coffee interest responded to flattened demand, consumer skepticism, and political problems in various ways: first, by seeking lower costs of importing, processing, and distribution; second, through a major advertising campaign designed to secure an unassailable market niche for coffee; and third, in the promotion of an ideal of economic cosmopolitanism among business elites, government authorities, and the public at large so as to cushion the trade against xenophobic and anti-internationalist sentiment.

Cost reduction after the turn of the century was a major goal. It certainly involved encouragement of increased production and quality controls among growers and processors in the Tropics. Large United States importers devoted special attention to Brazil, exerting pressure there for bean standardization.[49] But they also encouraged diversity of sourcing in order to overcome Brazil's preponderant position in the market, 62.4 percent of the market share in 1924.[50] In the 1920s, United States firms took over export activities from most national commission houses in Colombia, supported in these ventures by commercial banks located in New York City.[51] Similarly, Central America saw the vigorous expansion of North American coffee interests in the 1920s, with W. R. Grace taking over the profitable Guatemalan trade from the Germans.[52] As a result, non-Brazilian producers in Latin America acquired stronger positions in the North American market, with Colombia's share growing from 4.3 to 9.1 percent between 1909 and 1923 and El Salvador and Guatemala each having a 3 percent share by the mid-1920s.[53]

Having sought to assure a steady flow of inexpensive, high-quality beans from abroad, the domestic coffee interest also faced head on several internal obstacles to their penetration of national markets. Coffee lobbyists supported infrastructural improvements at major ports of entry, including New York, New Orleans, and especially San Francisco as the latter became a major entrepot for Central American and Colombian imports after the First World War.[54] In addition, processing innovations involved the further application of gas and electric technologies to the roasting, granulating, and milling of the bean. Also, new products such as decaffeinated and soluble (instant) coffees were introduced to the public after a decade of laboratory research. Service technologies underwent major improvements as well, primarily through filtration and percolation devices.[55] With the invention of the automatic urn in 1906, the beverage was available to ever larger numbers of people in eateries and workplaces; the electric coffee pot became commonplace in the growing number of middle-class households. Finally, the problems of uneven quality were effectively resolved. Coffee, ever more colorfully packaged and brand-specific, arrived fresh to consumers with the introduction of the vacuum-packed can by San Francisco's Hills Brothers Company; other improvements in cardboard and metal containers reduced waste and allowed for longer periods of storage.[56] Quality controls in the Tropics had their analogue in the development of cup evaluation procedures after the turn of the century. With standardized grading at ports of entry, Coffee Exchange officials categorized beans by size and roasting potential.[57] This, in turn, encouraged the introduction and spread of increasingly popular blends.[58]

These changes in processing, distribution, and consumption technologies occurred within the context of major shifts in the structure of the coffee industry.[59] After the First World War, import firms specializing in coffee faced serious challenges from several quarters. Many were taken over by a handful of roasters, banks, and larger, more aggressive firms such as W. R. Grace with multiple interests in the Caribbean and South America. For example, in 1919 the Mercantile Bank of the Americas acquired Hard and Rand, one of nation's principal importers. The following year, the same bank bailed out several prominent Colombian commercial houses and assumed control of the prominent New York firm Levy and Sons.[60]

Within the United States, specialty wholesalers and chain stores took up the challenge of a still highly fragmented and decentralized coffee trade.[61] Tennessee's Cheek-Neal Company, producer of the Maxwell House brand named after a Nashville plantation, successfully broke into New York and Los Angeles markets in the 1920s after having gained widespread acceptance throughout the South.[62] The A&P intruded most successfully into the domain of the traditional coffee merchants in this period. Its subsidiary, the American Coffee Corporation, founded in 1919, replaced domestic and foreign exporters in many parts of Latin America, purchasing coffee directly from cultivators, processing the bean in its own plants, and offering the final product to the public in A&P stores as the famed Eight O'Clock brand.[63] Such economies of scale, financial flexibility, and brand identification earned firms such as A&P, in the words of one admiring observer, "the right to stand as one of the progressive and economic industries of this great progressive country."[64] Small, independent grocers selling coffee in small lots and with little frill could hardly compete, issuing laments such as that of the 1920 California Grocer's Association Report: "Why make the consumer pay for a worthless can? Why cease to be a merchant in the best sense of the term? Why a cog in another fellow's wheel, grinding out a profit for the proprietor of a well-advertised brand?"[65]

Despite the example of the A&P roasters, firm concentration was less pronounced in processing than distribution, with 93 percent of the nation's roasting done by 42 percent of the firms in the early 1920s.[66] Some within the industry emphasized the need to rationalize markets and reduce wasteful competition among the multitude of small roasters. At the 1924 annual convention of coffee roasters, their president, Carl Brand, argued on behalf of mergers as a solution to the fragmented processing sector.[67] But such jawboning had little immediate effect on the structure of the industry, which remained quite decentralized well into the 1930s as firms with less than twenty workers still did 90 percent of processing.[68]

Brand's appeal for greater efficiency and firm consolidation nonetheless reflected the growing coherence of the coffee lobby in the years before the Great Depression. Early in the century there had been separate regional associations of roasters and "green-coffeemen" trading in unprocessed beans. Midwestern roasters became the backbone of a national coffee lobby, beginning in 1911 when a St. Louis group formed the National Coffee Roasters Traffic and Pure Drug Association (eventually known as the National Coffee Roasters' Association). Over the following two decades, as the NCRA's membership grew rapidly, it promoted product research and development, sought to protect the industry against levies and other forms of government intervention, and supported advertising campaigns.[69] For many years, roasters remained at odds with importers and jobbers, especially the powerful New York Green Coffee Association with its array of Puerto Ricans, Cubans, Jews, and other immigrants. The former group, largely from the North American industrial heartland, held the latter in contempt. Scarcely veiling their xenophobia, they barred the green coffeemen from the NCRA's 1913 national convention because "the gentlemen from New York are speculators who are making your business and my business unprofitable."[70]

The outbreak of the First World War swept away many differences, however, leading to a close collaboration between the two groups and the formation of the Joint Coffee Publicity Committee with the financial support of the Brazilian government. This first national business lobby assisted by a foreign government underwrote an extensive advertising campaign and research during the following half decade.[71] Although the Brazilians withdrew from the enterprise in the mid-1920s, the intense cooperation between roasters and greenmen in that period spurred the establishment of the National Coffee Association in 1928.[72]

The formation of the Joint Coffee Publicity Committee under Carl Brand's aegis signaled another major aspect in the evolution of the coffee interest, namely its increasingly internationalist business orientation. Brand, a Cleveland roaster and dealer who became president of the NCRA in the early 1920s, expanded his investment portfolio to include real estate, automotive manufacturing, and even Mexican mines. His ascension in 1930 to the vice-presidency of Standard Brands, the newly formed national foodstuff firm, climaxed a career symbolic of the growing rapprochement between various regional and sectoral elites.[73] In effect, men like Brand from the coffee industry helped midwife what Thomas Ferguson has referred to as a "multinational bloc" made up of "capital-intensive industries, investment banks, and internally oriented commercial banks."[74]

From Substance to Circumstance

"The public has been made coffee conscious as never before," declared Felix Coste, the energetic manager of the Joint Coffee Publicity Committee in 1924.[75] From the late 1890s, as limits of market expansion became evident, the industry attempted to expand consumption through greater efficiencies in processing, packaging, and transport, as well as greater cooperation with the United States government and, in the case of the Joint Committee, the Brazilian authorities. Equally important, however, was the multifaceted campaign to extend coffee usage beyond the calculus of the pocketbook into the realm of psychological and cultural marketplaces hopefully less vulnerable to price fluctuations.

The lobby took advantage of widened media opportunities after the turn of the century on billboards, the radio, daily newspapers, magazines, and the cinema.[76] In this way, a more coherent interest worked to transcend the fragmented, often parochial market horizons of the late-nineteenth-century importers, jobbers, wholesalers, roasters, and grocers engaged in the coffee trade. The alliance of Front Street and Madison Avenue forged by the larger firms and the more unified and powerful national lobby sought to invest coffee with a symbolic value which resonated to the prevailing social norms in the United States and drew on that society's major sources of cultural legitimation after the turn of the century.

The coffee industry targeted the mushrooming numbers of hotels, restaurants, cafeterias, and other public eateries after the turn of the century.[77] One contemporary observer noted that many of these institutions "catered to this highly developed taste for coffee to such an extent that [their] popularity rests on their ability to hit the taste of the consumers in this one particular."[78] The search for new public settings was relentless. In one case, waitresses served moviegoers cups of coffee during intermission.[79] Afternoon visits to local eateries were identified as moments of respite and recuperation. A 1921 Joint Coffee Publicity Committee ad urged consumers: "Along about four o'clock drop in at a convenient restaurant or soda fountain and get a good, hot cup of coffee. It will lift you up over the zero-hour of mid-afternoon."[80] An effort to assure coffee's niche as an all-season beverage led to campaigns on behalf of iced coffee.[81]

The theme of the beverage's regenerative powers became even more salient in a full-scale program during the second decade of the century to establish the "coffee break" in workplaces throughout the United States. In 1912 A. L. Burns declared before the NCRA national convention that "coffee increases the capacity for both muscular and mental work."[82] The lobby soon financed research on the relationship between coffee and labor productivity which concluded that the natural rhythms of mid-morning and mid-afternoon lassitude could be countered by consumption of the beverage at those times of the day.[83] By the early 1920s, these studies had been disseminated to a wide variety of workplaces, which were also given information and assistance in setting up coffee stations and cafeterias.[84] In turn, demand for large-scale delivery technologies increased as did greater usage of the beverage between meals, at or near work.[85] Coffee thus effectively became a handmaiden in the making of the new industrial order which emerged in this period.[86]

The lobby worked with equal determination to more completely integrate this product into the private realm of the household. Industry leader E. Aborn proposed in 1913 a national program to educate housewives on the subject of coffee.[87] By the early 1920s, intensive efforts were under way to inculcate good coffee habits among women "for even such a staple . . . requires some system of consumer instruction."[88] The Joint Coffee Publicity Committee established a Home Economics Service as part of its coffee promotion program in those years.[89] One spring newspaper campaign related "what June brides should know about coffee."[90] Written almost in the form of a factory manual, advertisement copy detailed methods to ensure a well-brewed cup. This included promotion of electrical processing devices flooding homes throughout the United States as part of the industrialization of household management in those years.[91] Such advertising techniques guaranteed homemakers that these products would free them from drudgery, attention to detail, and expenditure of energy.[92] Hoping to seal a mystical bargain of sorts with housewives, Faust Instant Coffee was promoted in the mid-1920s as "involving no trouble, no cooking, no waste."[93]

This stratagem cut deeper still as part of the repatriation of women to the home following the upheavals of the First World War and the triumph of the suffragist movement in the United States.[94] Beyond informing them on the cheapness of the product and the means of efficient preparation, advertisers directly associated women's self-esteem to their ability to make a good cup of coffee. Consumption of this product in the home had a mark of civility and grace in patriarchal families conforming to a post-Victorian domesticity. A 1927 MJB ad showing a group of well-dressed men in a study or smoking room proclaimed that "men demand full-bodied flavor in their coffee." The picture and copy signaled the subordination of the absent women and their careful offering of coffee as an expression of their attentiveness to the "demands" of their men.[95] The coffee interest was disarmingly frank in this matter. MJB's chairman, in an essay entitled "Healing the Injured Pride of Masculinity," revealed his company's determination "to make a direct appeal to men." In doing so they were also appealing to women, "because every wife wishes to please her husband and buy the coffee he likes." Otherwise, he warned, men might become "coffee cranks."[96] Another advertising campaign in the same period highlighted the anxieties of the housewife in this regard: "Mrs. Roberts was dead tired" and "Mrs. Fredericks was worried" were countermanded by "Mrs. Bradley surprised her husband" with a good cup of coffee and "they lived happily ever after."[97]

Other symbols of legitimation became the provenance of the coffee lobby. The medical profession, then acquiring new cultural authority, played a crucial role in turning back the widespread criticisms of coffee as unhealthful, and caffeine as particularly threatening.[98] In 1923 the industry cited British medical studies that this was indeed "the beverage of the intellect," which, moreover, could find "friendly association with the cigarette."[99] Advertising in medical journals became a key tactic to resist negative opinions about coffee, "for what 200,000 physicians read counts for more, in its immediate and widespread influence than, as a rule, what ten times as many lay people read, because it is the physician who molds the habits of his patients and holds it within his power to suggest or promote habits of diet or even thought."[100] To dispel any doubts, the Joint Coffee Publicity Committee established a research fund in 1921 and contracted

Samuel C. Prescott, former United States Army Surgeon General and Professor of Industrial Microbiology at the Massachusetts Institute of Technology to undertake a major study. His 1923 report proclaimed that "coffee is a beverage which properly prepared and rightly used, gives comfort and inspiration, augments mental and physical activities, and may be regarded as a servant rather than a destroyer of civilization."[101]

The nation's public schools also drew the attention of a lobby hopeful "that when boys and girls of the classroom grow up, they will know what coffee really is and will, therefore, not only be users of the beverage, but will see that their children get no silly notions in their heads regarding the universal drink." Representatives from the Joint Coffee Publicity Committee and secondary school administrators cooperated in order to assure the "triumph of the truth about coffee and its value as an aliment." Exhibits and pamphlets urged students to "Get a Reputation for your coffee" and enjoined them to become acquainted with the "Six Rules for Making Better Coffee." Likely directed at adolescent girls, this campaign extended the reach of highly gendered coffee advertising already evident in the broader media.[102] At the same time, however, it served efforts in the 1920s to socialize youth into the rationality of the new industrial order, within and outside the home.

Another campaign revealed more clearly the dovetailing of business interests around increased coffee consumption in this period. Acknowledging the rapid spread of electrical coffee pots and similar devices, some local utilities informed their customers on ways to improve home preparation of the beverage. Coffee spokesmen reveled in such support for their product, for "coming from so dignified and highly respected a corporation as the local electric light utility, these representations bear surprising weight. . . . In light of all this, it is readily apparent that the public utilities are performing a splendid and estimable service to the coffee trade."[103]

The promoters of coffee did not, of course, independently make it the paramount beverage of United States capitalism after the turn of the century. Their product had particular properties well suited to the imperatives of modern industrial life. Its qualities as a stimulant could be easily harnessed to the logic of the modern capitalist order: an instrument to sharpen the rational and energetic completion of everyday tasks and the handmaiden for leisure and sociability in the home, public arenas, and the workplace. In anticipation of the workday and at work, coffee, together with other products such as sugar, cocoa, and tea, provided the bursts of energy to sustain productivity and also allowed the recouping of that energy in various public and private contexts, each with its own elaborate rhetoric and rites. Given the context of a powerful alcohol prohibition movement in this period, coffee found a particular niche as "a passage to work," in Joseph Gusfield's words.[104] But more than an instrument to raise productivity, the particular way in which coffee helped construct the nature and purposes of leisure time reflected the emergence of a consumer society in the United States, which "meant a culture of work and spend . . . [where] time was converted into money on and off the job."[105] Completing in this period what Roland Barthes has referred to as the transition from "substance" into "circumstance," coffee became in both material and symbolic terms one of the seemingly indissoluble links holding together modern capitalist society in the United States.[106]

The Rise of Economic Cosmopolitanism

The coffee lobby early recognized the urgent need to educate the public that the use of their product "set in motion some of the tremendous currents of the world that flow through the year and pour a ceaseless stream of green and yellow and brown berries . . . into a marketplace which is never quite satisfied."[107] After 1900, the coffee interest became embroiled in a major debate in the United States regarding the links to the rest of the world as erratic prices, speculation, and the several episodes of market intervention by the Brazilians provoked xenophobic and anti-internationalist responses. Its principal leaders acknowledged that while the trade depended on its capacity to ensure a cheap, consistent product, it should also promote a greater awareness regarding the benefits of North American participation in the global economy.[108] Thus "coffee-consciousness" possessed a meaning far wider than merely assuring its customary and natural use by reducing the price and connecting it to the particular contours of public and private life in this emergent consumer society. In effect, the coffee lobby found it necessary to push the horizons of the market far beyond what few ordinary citizens of the United States had likely heretofore imagined.

The coffee trade appears, in retrospect, to have been a singularly appropriate vehicle by which to promote economic cosmopolitanism in the United States. Widely traveled businessmen in the Tropics had been reporting for several decades on their experiences in isolated plantation districts and processing centers at railheads and port cities and on their encounters with workers, foremen, local traders, and the most powerful and wealthy citizens of coffee-producing societies, particularly in the Americas. "A born trader, a fighter, commercial wizard, an experienced merchant in politics, weather, and geography," in the words of one observer, the green-coffeeman scrutinized the globe for those places where a profit might be turned.[109] Before the turn of the century, a vast array of guides to coffee-producing areas had provided encyclopedic information to importers, jobbers, and investors.[110] These would be followed by extensive reportage on the Tropics in the trade media and the popular press, including *World's Work*, the *Magazine of Business*, *National Geographic*, and *Scientific American*. This new geography of profit presented customarily precise, informative, and often vivid accounts of climate, terrain, cultivation and processing, marketing arrangements, and transportation systems in coffee growing. While differing from the period's highly exotic travel literature, these writings portrayed trade with the Tropics and investment in those latitudes as a civilizing crusade.[111]

The capitalist realism of the green coffeemen's reportage took on greater significance as the U.S. coffee industry confronted widespread public uneasiness about foreign manipulation of the trade, before and after the First World War. In October 1902, during a major price downswing, at a meeting of the New York Coffee Exchange of coffee merchants, United States officials and representatives from producing nations cautioned that the crisis threatened "the internal peace of impoverished nations. . . . For it is unfortunately true that misery breaks asunder the ties of order." The conference recommended lowering tariffs on tropical imports into the United States, official propaganda campaigns to increase consumption, and, most importantly, support for valorization because, in their words, the "restriction of supply . . . is a sacrifice that may become necessary in order to avoid having to make larger ones."[112] In 1912 a delegation of coffee roasters visited Brazil and reported favorably on the valorization program, insistent that "conditions at the time of very low prices were so near universal bankruptcy as to fully justify the government in the various steps it took for the protection of its principal industry."[113] A year later, in the midst of a public reaction to higher coffee prices following the implementation of the first Brazilian valorization program, Herman Siecklen, one of its principal New York financiers, testified in defense of the program before a hostile congressional committee. Having raised $75 million to finance valorization, he firmly rejected the commonplace view that producing countries "should sell products at the lowest price and we at the highest."[114]

Such unorthodox notions would gain greater currency in the 1920s as greenmen and roasters closed ranks and the coffee lobby acquired greater unity and organizational clout. A principal exponent of the new economic cosmopolitanism was E. A. Kahl, longtime manager of W. R. Grace operations in San Francisco and vice-president of the multinational firm in 1924. This German immigrant with extensive experience in Central America and Colombia argued repeatedly in his reports on behalf of a more pragmatic vision of international trade.[115] In his view, the interests of the United States would hardly be served if coffee producers were reduced to "starvation prices . . . as only a prosperous Latin America can take our exports." Insisting on the growing economic interdependence of the United States and Latin America, Kahl declared that "much of what we pay them for coffee is not leaving our country, but remains here in the shape of increased exports."[116]

Some observers worried about rising prices, either as a result of valorization or the demands of Latin American coffee workers for higher wages. Such increases, in the view of the editors of a major trade publication in late 1925, imperiled the trade, "for the goose that lays the golden egg is not immortal."[117] Yet Kahl warned against what he called "price antagonism" in the United States against Latin America's coffee growers, pointedly comparing the latter with the desperate situation of North American farmers at the time. Upon close scrutiny of the "showing of coffee-producing countries for the last twenty years," he insisted, "one cannot possibly consider that the periods of so-called high prices interspersed with starvation prices have been very sufficient to make coffee producing a very attractive venture from the standpoint of investment and average profit."[118]

Kahl prescribed market regulation as an antidote to the trade's endemic instability. Echoing the views of Siecklen and others before the First World War, the W. R. Grace executive vigorously defended Brazilian valorization. "Let us realize," he wrote in January 1926, "that coffee is still ridiculously cheap in cost per cup. . . . The Regulation of receipts applied in Brazil to the proper distribution of their crops can no longer be viewed as a weapon by the producing countries to dictate prices, as performance has already shown that, at best, regulation means little more than stabilization which should be welcomed rather than decried."[119] Later that year the editors of *Spice Mill* impressed on their readers in the coffee community that they need not apologize for supporting valorization because the "American consumer has never suffered from the coffee price . . . paying for roasted coffee less comparatively, than for other articles of household use or human need, foreign or domestic grown or manufactured, if we take pre-war costs as a basis."[120] In effect, this notion of international corporatism suggested a means by which cooperation between the state and private enterprise might reduce the arbitrariness and destructiveness of the market and benefit consumers and business alike.

Such reassessment of the free-market ideal by industry leaders such as Kahl found echo among government figures in the United States, especially after the First World War.[121] In 1923 William O. Schurz, the commercial attaché in Rio de Janeiro, wrote a sympathetic report to his superiors on the Brazilian valorization program. The Ohio-born Schurz, with an advanced degree in history from the University of California at Berkeley and experience as a foreign trade adviser to President Woodrow Wilson, suggested that the United States needed to replace the historic oscillation of its Latin American policy between indifference and intervention with a more coherent, mutually beneficial program of commercial and financial cooperation. Schurz and others in the government privy to Kahl's reports served as interlocutors between the coffee lobby, Brazilian officials, and the United States government.[122] These internationalist bureaucrats and their corporate allies made some progress by decade's end; Hoover, in retreat from his long-standing antagonism toward the Brazilians, acknowledged the dangers of this "uneconomic warfare in industry which, like any other warfare, is wasteful."[123]

While the globalist dimension of what Emily Rosenberg has called the "promotional state" was contested in this period, the coffee lobby, together with other groups, helped lay the foundations for a new vision of the international order. The free-trade ideal, of course, remained strong, with the director of the Bureau of Foreign and Domestic Commerce, Julius Klein, in 1928 warning supporters of "raw material controls" that "international business relations are governed by economic laws whose working cannot be long postponed, evaded, or thwarted."[124] Soon thereafter the coffee trade would be dragged down into the Great Depression, crushing both the consumers and producers of what had come to be known as the "brown gold."[125] Nonetheless, the growing internationalist sensibility stirred by the coffee lobby and other segments of the business community oriented toward foreign trade in the 1920s would inform the Good Neighbor Policy during the following decade.[126] And ultimately the notion of an interconnected global economy requiring the substantial coordination foreseen by Kahl, Schurz, and others would emerge in a more comprehensive manner in the 1940s and 1950s as the United States acquired global hegemony.[127]

Conclusion

Fernand Braudel has cautioned against regarding "the appearance of a great number of foodstuffs [in the early modern period] as mere anecdotal history."[128] The same could be said about coffee and other tropical commodities such as sugar, tea, cocoa, and bananas which acquired critical niches in modern consumer societies during the last century and a half. In this regard, the history of coffee provides important insights into the dramatic transformation in market relations in the United States and its relationship to the global economy during the century before the Great Depression.

The multiple and novel uses of this beverage indicate the depth and completeness of the profound social and cultural changes that accompanied the making of a new order based on relentless technological innovation, high labor productivity, and a widened capacity to consume goods and services by a substantial segment of the population. Initially an exotic item reserved mostly for wealthier consumers, it became unequivocally the premier beverage of a mass consumer society through the parallel evolution of greater control over the work force and ever more sophisticated marketing. Coffee stood, Januslike, at the intersection of cultural processes which simultaneously separated and conjoined work and leisure at a crucial moment in the emergence of a modern consumer society in the United States.

At the same time, coffee's journey from plantation to cup involved the dramatic expansion of the horizons of North American consumers into the global arena. In this process, it was one of several vehicles through which the ideal of economic cosmopolitanism was forged in the United States, effectively the notion that the contours of citizenship in a liberal society were shaped as much by the will and capacity to buy and sell in a market with an increasingly global ambit as by the prerequisites and responsibilities of republican political ideas and practice. In effect, coffee provides a prism through which to examine the links between the remaking of taste, identities, and discourses of work, leisure, and sociability in the North American marketplace and their relation to the world in the past one hundred years.

Finally, the history of coffee helps illuminate the patterns of elite restructuring in a crucial period of capitalist transformation in the United States and elsewhere in the North Atlantic in the century before the Great Depression. While export elites in Latin America and elsewhere in the Tropics ascended toward the apex of their wealth and power during these years, the United States witnessed the emergence of a new ruling class configuration composed of internationally minded merchants, financiers, and industrialists. These elements of the multinational bloc in the United States elaborated a multifaceted program to overcome a series of economic, institutional, and cultural barriers to foreign trade and investment abroad. Those involved in the commerce and processing of coffee and other tropical commodities played key early roles in the formation of this new elite alignment. In the end, their efforts to promote the outward thrust toward the global economy hastened the further maturation of the world capitalist system whose legacy, for good and for ill, is ours.

Notes

I wish to thank Professors Michael Bernstein, of the University of California at San Diego, and William Roseberry, of the New School for Social Research, for their close reading of this essay. Officials at the National Coffee Association in New York City and the staffs of Baker Library at the Harvard Business School and the New York Public Library extended every courtesy. Daniel Cunningham assisted in the original research and students of an undergraduate research seminar at Princeton University on the Social History of Tropical Commodities also provided valuable commentary.

1. *New York Times* (January 12, 1927).

2. *Spice Mill* (March 1925): 533.

3. *Spice Mill* (December 1926): 2478.

4. On the place of these commodities in the North Atlantic during the early modern period, see Fernand Braudel, *Capitalism and Material Life, 1450–1800* (London, 1973), 152–58; Reay Tanahill, *Food in History* (New York, 1973), part 5; and Barbara Norman, *Tales of the Table: A History of Western Cuisine* (Englewood Cliffs, N.J., 1972), chap. 5. On coffee in particular, see William H. Ukers, *All about Coffee*, 2d ed. (New York, 1935), and Heinrich Jacob, *Coffee: Epic of a Commodity* (New York, 1935).

5. Ukers, *All about Coffee*, 521, 529; U.S. Department of Commerce, *Coffee Consumption in the United States, 1920–1965* (Washington, D.C., 1961), 11–12.

6. On the economic and social contours of production and consumption in the United States during this period, see Charles Sellars, *The Market Revolution: Jacksonian America, 1815–1846* (Oxford, 1991), chap. 1.

7. Ukers, *All about Coffee*, 521, 529; U.S. Department of Commerce, *Coffee Consumption in the United States, 1920–1965*, 11–12.

8. For a discussion, from differing perspectives of these economic changes, see David Gordon, Richard Edwards, and Michael Reich, *Segmented Labor, Divided Workers: The Historical Transformation of Labor in the United States* (New York, 1982), 54–78; W. W. Rostow, *The World Economy: History and Prospect* (Austin, 1978); and Alfred Chandler, *The Visible Hand: The Managerial Revolution in American Business* (New York, 1977), chaps. 3–4.

9. Cleveland Amory et al., *The American Heritage Cookbook and Illustrated History of American Eating and Drinking* (New York, 1964), 52.

10. Jeffrey G. Williamson and Peter H. Lindert, *American Inequality: A Macroeconomic History* (Indianapolis, 1981), 130.

11. *Food and Drink in America: A History* (Indianapolis, 1981), 130.

12. Ukers, *All about Coffee*, 435–54, 541–43, and 595–98.

13. *Spice Mill* (January 1926): 107–8.

14. On the history of A&P, see Richard Tedlow, *New and Improved: The Story of Mass Marketing in America* (New York, 1990), chap. 4.

15. Ukers, *All about Coffee*, 521, 529; U.S. Department of Commerce, *Coffee Consumption in the United States, 1920–1965*, 11–12.

16. Cited in Alan Trachtenberg, *The Incorporation of America: Culture and Society in the Gilded Age* (New York, 1982), 47.

17. Josiah Gregg, cited in Hooker, *Food and Drink in America*, 185. See also Marjorie Kriedberg, *Food on the Frontier: Minnesota Farm Cooking from 1850 to 1900* (St. Paul, Minn., 1975).

18. On this process, see David Landes, *Prometheus Unbound: Technological*

Changes and Industrial Development in Western Europe from 1750 to the Present (Cambridge, 1969); W. Arthur Lewis, *Growth and Fluctuations, 1870–1913* (London, 1978), chaps. 2–3; Michel Aglietta, *A Theory of Capitalist Regulation: The U.S. Experience* (London, 1979), 65–79; and E. J. Hobsbawm, "The Crisis of Capitalism in Historical Perspective," *Socialist Revolution* 6 (October–December 1976): 77–96.

19. Gordon, Edwards, and Reich, *Segmented Labor, Divided Workers*, 112–27.

20. Williamson and Lindert, *American Inequality*, 46–51, and Paul A. David and Peter Solar, "A Bicentenary Contribution to the History of the Cost of Living in America," in Paul Uselding, ed., *Research on Economic History*, vol. 2 (Greenwich, Conn., 1977).

21. Dorothy Rainwater, "Victorian Dining Silver," in Kathryn Grover, ed., *Dining in America, 1850–1900* (Rochester, 1987), 173–204.

22. Ukers, *All about Coffee*, 256–58.

23. Government reports on coffee adulteration are discussed in Oscar E. Anderson, *The Health of a Nation: Harvey W. Wiley and the Fight for Pure Food* (Chicago, 1958), and James Harvey Young, *Pure Food: Securing the Federal Food and Drug Acts of 1906* (Princeton, 1989).

24. For a vivid portrait of the New York trade in the last decades of the nineteenth century, see Abram Wakeman, *Reminiscences of Lower Wall Street* (New York, 1914).

25. The contrast with sugar is evident in Chandler, *The Visible Hand*, 328–29, and Alfred S. Eicher, *The Emergence of Oligopoly: Sugar Refining as a Case Study* (Baltimore, 1969).

26. For contrasting perspectives on the changes in the world economy and the role of tropical commodity production and trade in this period, see W. Arthur Lewis, *Aspects of Tropical Trade, 1883–1965* (Upsalla, Sweden, 1969), and Eric R. Wolf, *Europe and the People without History* (Berkeley, 1982), chap. 11.

27. Antonio Delfím Netto surveys the cycles of production in the world's principal source of coffee in this period, in "Foundations for an Analysis of the Brazilian Coffee Problems," in *Essays on Coffee and Economic Development* (Rio de Janeiro, 1973). For the Colombian case, see Marco Palacios, *Coffee in Colombia, 1850–1870* (Cambridge, 1980).

28. For a narrative of the unstable trade in coffee, see C. K. Trafton, "Coffee Trade: Booms and Panics," *Tea and Coffee Trade Journal* (November 1920): 536–67.

29. The origins and operation of the Coffee Exchange are examined in F. W. Rowe, *Primary Commodities in International Trade* (Cambridge, 1965), and Julius B. Baer and George Woodruff, *Commodity Exchanges and Futures Trading: Principles and Operating Methods* (New York, 1949).

30. *From Plantation to Cup* (New York, 1881).

31. Ukers, *All about Coffee*, 521, 529; U.S. Department of Commerce, *Coffee Consumption in the United States, 1920–1965*, 11–12.

32. Frances Stern and Gertrude Spitz, *Food for the Worker* (Boston, 1917), 117.

33. Gordon et al., *Segmented Labor, Divided Workers*, 127–76; Jurgen Kocka, *White-Collar Workers in America, 1890–1940: A Social Political History in International Perspective* (Beverly Hills, 1980).

34. On advertising, see Daniel Boorstin, *The Americans: The Democratic Experience* (New York, 1973), part 2; Stuart Ewen, *Captains of Consciousness* (New York, 1976); and T. J. Jackson Lears, "From Salvation to Self-Realization: Advertising and the Therapeutic Roots of the Consumer Culture, 1880–1930," in Richard Wightman Fox and T. J. Jackson Lears, eds., *The Culture of Consumption: Critical Essays in American History, 1880–1980* (New York, 1983), 1–38.

35. *Spice Mill* (May 1921): 751.

36. For an entertaining survey of the restaurant business in a large metropolitan center in these years, see Michael and Ariane Batterberry, *On the Town in New York from 1776 to the Present* (New York, 1973), 110–95.

37. *Literary Digest* (July 10, 1920): 126; *Printer's Ink* (July 6, 1933): 10–11.

38. Williamson and Lindert, *American Inequality*, 75–82; Gordon et al., *Segmented Labor, Divided Workers*, 127–62; Lewis, *Growth and Fluctuations*, chap. 4.

39. The material on coffee prices in this period is drawn from Steven Topik, *The Political Economy of the Brazilian State, 1889–1930* (Austin, 1987), 82; and Ukers, *All about Coffee*, 521, 529. For an overview of the declining position of tropical commodities on international markets, see Charles P. Kindleberger, *The World in Depression, 1929–1939* (Berkeley, 1973), chap. 4.

40. Richard Lowitt, *George W. Norris: The Making of a Progressive, 1861–1912* (Syracuse, 1963), 215.

41. For a history of valorization, see Thomas Holloway, *The Brazilian Coffee Valorization of 1906: Regional Politics and Economic Dependence* (Madison, 1975); Delfím Netto, "Foundations for Analysis of the Brazilian Coffee Problem," 76–105; V. D. Wickizier, *The World Coffee Economy, with special reference to control schemes* (Stanford, 1943); Stephen D. Krasner, "The Politics of Primary Commodities: A Study of Coffee, 1900–1970" (Ph.D. diss., Harvard University, 1971), 1101–65; Topik, *The Political Economy of the Brazilian State*, 59–92.

42. *Spice Mill* (August 1908): 585.

43. U.S. House of Representatives, *Crude Rubber, Coffee, etc. Hearings before the Committee on Interstate and Foreign Commerce, House of Representatives*, 69th Cong., 1st sess., on H. Res. 59, January 6–22, 1926, 290.

44. R. D. Fleming, "Brazil's Corner in Coffee," *Industrial Digest* (January 1926): 18.

45. Joseph Brandes, *Herbert Hoover and Economic Diplomacy: Department of Commerce Policy, 1921–1928* (Pittsburgh, 1962), 130–38.

46. Cited in Harvey A. Levenstein, *Revolution at the Table: The Transformation of the American Diet* (Oxford, 1988), 100.

47. Lucile Evans, *The Food of Working Women of Boston* (Boston, 1917), 174–75.

48. *Spice Mill* (June 1926): 1026.

49. Antonio Delfím Netto, *O problema do café no Brasil* (São Paulo, 1959), chap. 3.

50. Mary L. Bynum, *International Trade in Coffee* (Washington, D.C., 1926), 3.

51. Fabio Zambrano, "El comercio de café en Colombia," *Cuadernos colombianos* 3:11 (1977): 391–436.

52. *Tea and Coffee Trade Journal* (September 1921): 350; and *Spice Mill* (August 1926): 1414–17. For a detailed account of efforts by United States interests to improve coffee cultivation and processing in Central America, see Mauricio T. Domínguez, "The Development of the Technological and Scientific Coffee Industry in Guatemala, 1830–1930" (Ph.D. diss., Tulane University, 1970).

53. Bynum, *International Trade in Coffee*, 3.

54. *Spice Mill* (March 1923): 438–48; *Spice Mill* (August 1926): 1414–20; and *Spice Mill* (September 1926): 1608–11.

55. L. G. Zinmiester, "Increased Efficiency in the Roasting Industry," *Spice Mill* (December 1914): 1266–68; *Spice Mill* (September 1924): 1266–68; and Ukers, *All about Coffee*, 604–22.

56. Richard Bach et al., "Color and Style in Containers," *Tea and Coffee Trade Journal* (July 1926): 24–28, 82–92. On the history of the vacuum can, see T. Carroll Wilson, *A Background Story of Hills Brothers, Inc.* (San Francisco, 1966).

57. *Spice Mill* (April 1921): 590–92, and V. D. Wickizier, *Coffee, Tea, and Cocoa: An Economic and Political Analysis* (Stanford, 1951), 35–62.

58. The expansion of blended coffees can be seen in comparisons between Joseph M. Walsh's review of the trade in *Spice Mill* (September 1908): 550–51, and a report in *Spice Mill* (January 1925): 590–92.

59. An outline of the mechanics of the coffee trade in these years is in William H. Ukers, *Coffee Merchandising* (New York, 1930), and in J. W. F. Rowe, *Primary Commodities in International Trade* (Cambridge, 1965).

60. *Tea and Coffee Trade Journal* (June 1919): 540–41, and *Tea and Coffee Trade Journal* (October 1920): 458–66.

61. *Spice Mill* (January 1926): 56.

62. *Printer's Ink* (September 22, 1927): 165–74; *Printer's Ink* (October 11, 1928): 131–32. In 1928, Postum Cereal, which would be renamed General Foods Corporation, purchased the Cheek-Neal Company for $16 million. Krasner, "The Politics of Primary Commodities," 313.

63. Ukers, *All about Coffee*, 736.

64. *Spice Mill* (October 1926): 1912, and Tedlow, *New and Improved*, chap. 4.

65. *Tea and Coffee Trade Journal* (July 1920): 48.

66. *Spice Mill* (October 1924): 2154.

67. *Spice Mill* (October 1924): 2204.

68. U.S. Office of National Recovery Administration, "The Coffee Industry," Statistical Materials Series No. 265. (February 1936): 15–16.

69. On the NCRA, see a review of its first decade in *Spice Mill* (November 1922): 1900–08, and the official history of the lobby by the National Coffee Association, *Half Century of Service* (New York, 1961).

70. *Spice Mill* (October 1924): 2180–81.

71. On this unique cooperation of a foreign government and United States

business interests, see "Promotion Work That Backs up the National Advertising," *Printer's Ink* (January 1921); "Coffee Advertising Campaign Apportioned on a New Basis," *Printer's Ink* (April 7, 1921): 19–20; "Coffee Trade Committee Reports," *Printer's Ink* (March 23, 1922): 153–54; and "Growers Invest $1,028,025.17 in Advertising," *Printer's Ink* (October 30, 1924): 147–48.

72. *Spice Mill* (February 1925): 220–21, and the National Coffee Association, *A Half Century of Service*.

73. "Starting at $8 — The Story of Carl Brand," *Spice Mill* (July 1924), 1308–12, and *The National Encyclopedia of American Biography*, vol. 31 (New York, 1944), 475–76.

74. "Industrial Conflict and the Coming of the New Deal: The Triumph of Multinational Liberalism in America," in Steven Fraser and Gary Gerstle, eds., *The Rise and Fall of the New Deal Order, 1930–1980* (Princeton, 1989), 7.

75. *Printer's Ink* (June 9, 1924): 158–68.

76. Trends in coffee marketing in the first half of the twentieth century are detailed in James P. Quinn, *Scientific Marketing of Coffee* (New York, 1960). Roland Marchand, *Advertising the American Dream: Making Way for Modernity, 1920–1940* (Berkeley, 1985), presents a broader context.

77. Levenstein, *Revolution at the Table*, chap. 15.

78. Forrest Crissey, *The Story of Foods* (Chicago, 1917), 366.

79. Felix Koch, "Coffee at the Movies: A Middle-western Innovation," *Spice Mill* (March 1925): 640–43.

80. *Spice Mill* (October 1921): 690. See also, "Important Place of Hot Coffee in Soda Fountain Service," *Spice Mill* (January 1921): 108; "Linking up Coffee with Delicatessens and Restaurants," *Spice Mill* (April 1922): 554–55; and, "Is the Coffee Shop an Important Outlet?" *Spice Mill* (April 1926): 640–43.

81. On iced coffee, see *Spice Mill* (July 1914): 733, and *Printer's Ink* (July 28, 1927): 170–72.

82. *Spice Mill* (November 1912): 1901.

83. In its pamphlet, *Coffee as an Aid to Factory Efficiency* (New York, 1920), the Joint Coffee Publicity Committee presented this information to factory and white-collar office managers.

84. "Spread of the Coffee Station Idea," *Spice Mill* (June 1921): 950–54. See the guide to the establishment of cafeterias and restaurants published by the National Industrial Conference Board, *Industrial Lunch Rooms* (New York, 1928), and Evans, *The Food of Working Women*, 161–67.

85. *Printer's Ink* (June 19, 1924): 164.

86. On this broad shift in labor management strategies, see Samuel Haber, *Efficiency and Uplift: Scientific Management in the Progressive Era, 1890–1920* (Chicago, 1964); Harry Braverman, *Labor and Monopoly Capital — The Degradation of Work in the Twentieth Century* (New York, 1974); and Richard Edwards, *Contested Terrain: The Transformation of the Workplace in the Twentieth Century* (New York, 1979).

87. *Spice Mill* (November 1922): 1901.

88. *Spice Mill* (September 1922): 1605. See also the report by the director of the Home Economics Service of the Joint Coffee Trade Publicity Committee,

Helene Louise Johnson, "The Prescott Report in Home Economics," *Spice Mill* (October 1924): 2250–52.

89. The director of the service, Helen Louise Johnson, presented a paper at the 14th Annual NCRA Convention in October 1924 showing how the Prescott Report data had been integrated into direct appeals to housekeepers. *Spice Mill* (October 1924): 2250–52.

90. *Spice Mill* (April 1921): 608.

91. The six rules for making good coffee were: (1) keep the coffee airtight; (2) measure carefully; (3) use grounds only once; (4) use boiling water; (5) serve at once; and (6) scour the coffee pot. *Printer's Ink* (April 7, 1921): 19. For a contemporary discussion of the application of the new management styles to the home, see Mary Pattison, *Principles of Domestic Engineering* (New York, 1915).

92. Ruth Schwartz Cowan, *More Work for Mother: The Ironies of Household Technology from the Open Hearth to the Microwave* (New York, 1983).

93. *Good Housekeeping* (March 1921): 98.

94. On the reintegration of the middle-class housewife into the home during the 1920s, see Ruth Schwartz Cowan, "Two Washes in the Morning and a Bridge Party at Night: The American Housewife between the Wars," *Feminist Studies* 3 (1976): 147–72, and Dolores Hayden, *The Grand Domestic Revolution* (Cambridge, 1981), chaps. 1, 12, and 13.

95. *Spice Mill* (March 1921): 532. Women's particular responsibility for such rituals is carefully explicated in Emily Post, *Etiquette* (New York, 1922), 223–24.

96. *Printer's Ink* (November 3, 1927): 10–11.

97. *Spice Mill* (September 1922): 1605.

98. On the growing influence of physicians in this period, see E. Richard Brown, *Rockefeller Medicine Men: Medicine and Capitalism in America* (Berkeley, 1979), and Paul Starr, *The Social Transformation of American Medicine* (New York, 1982).

99. *Spice Mill* (May 1923): 839.

100. *Spice Mill* (January 1923): 36.

101. *Spice Mill* (May 1921): 766; *Spice Mill* (November 1923): 2177. The final results of the study are in Samuel C. Prescott, *Report of an Investigation of Coffee* (New York, 1923).

102. "Enlightening the Young on Coffee," *Spice Mill* (May 1923): 934.

103. "How the Public Utility Promotes Coffee Consumption," *Spice Mill* (January 1926): 27.

104. "Passage to Play: Rituals of Drinking Time in American Society," in Mary Douglas, ed., *Constructive Drinking: Perspectives on Drink from Anthropology* (Cambridge, 1987), 83.

105. Gary Cross, *Time and Money: The Making of a Consumer Culture* (London, 1993), 5.

106. "Towards a Psychosociology of Contemporary Food Consumption," in Robert Forester and Orest Ranum, eds., *Food and Drink in History* (Baltimore, 1979), 172. A provocative comparison with sugar in an earlier period is Sidney W. Mintz, *Sweetness and Power: The Place of Sugar in Modern History* (New York, 1985).

107. *Tea and Coffee Trade Journal* (October 1921): 473.

108. Materials on the United States' involvement in the world economy are in Myra Wilkins, *The Maturing of Multinational Enterprise: American Business abroad from 1914 to 1970* (Cambridge, 1974), 3–163, and Emily S. Rosenberg, *Spreading the American Dream: American Economic and Cultural Expansion, 1890–1914* (New York, 1982).

109. *Business Week* (February 5, 1930): 44.

110. In addition to many British and other European manuals on coffee, the principal North American volumes published during the last quarter of the nineteenth century are Robert H. Hewitt, *Coffee: Its History, Cultivation, and Uses* (New York, 1872); Chase and Sanborn, *Coffee* (Boston, 1880); Francis Beatty Thurber, *Coffee: From Plantation to Cup* (New York, 1881); B. B. Keable, *Coffee: From Grove to Consumer* (New York, 1881); and Joseph W. Walsh, *Coffee: Its History, Classification, and Description* (Philadelphia, 1894).

111. See, for example, Samuel Crowther, *The Romance and Rise of the Tropics* (Garden City, 1929).

112. U.S. Department of State, *Production and Consumption of Coffee, etc.: Message from the President of the United States, transmitting a Report from the Secretary of State relative to the Proceedings of the International Congress for the Study of the Production and Consumption of Coffee*, 57th Cong., 2d sess. Senate. Document No. 35, 57.

113. Cited in Krasner, "The Politics of Primary Commodities," 125.

114. U.S. House of Representatives. Subcommittee of the Committee on Banking and Currency, *Investigation of Financial and Monetary Conditions in the United States* (Washington, 1913), 55.

115. *Spice Mill* (February 1927): 315.

116. *Spice Mill* (December 1925): 2580.

117. *Spice Mill* (December 1925): 2851.

118. *Spice Mill* (January 1926): 56.

119. *Spice Mill* (January 1926): 56.

120. *Spice Mill* (April 1926): 603.

121. Robert Neal Siedel, "Progressive Pan Americanism: Development and United States Policy toward South America, 1906–1931" (Ph.D. diss., Cornell University, 1973), argues that Kahl's memorandums received wide circulation at the Department of Commerce and may well have contributed to the more favorable United States policy toward coffee-producing countries toward the end of the decade (p. 47). On the interaction between the business community and the state over foreign trade and investment, see Richard H. Werking, "Bureaucrats, Businessmen, and Foreign Trade: The Origins of the United States Chamber of Commerce," *Business History Review* 52 (1978): 321–41.

122. Schurz, who wrote *Valorization of Brazilian Coffee* (Washington, D.C., 1923), and on whom biographical data can be found in *Who's Who in America*, vol. 4 (Chicago, 1968), advised the Cuban government on economic policy in the late 1920s, served as director of Johnson and Johnson's Latin American division and as a consultant for the Walter J. Thompson advertising agency for Latin America in the 1930s, and returned to the State Department during the 1940s as

Acting Chief of the American Republics Division. After the war, he was professor and dean of the faculty of the American Institute of Foreign Trade in Phoenix, Arizona, a training school for United States international corporate managers.

123. Siedel, "Progressive Pan Americanism," 487.

124. *Frontiers of Trade* (New York, 1928), 115.

125. For a description of the downward spiral in tropical commodities and other staples in the late 1920s, see Kindleberger, *The World in Depression, 1929–1939*, chap. 4. See also Instituto Internacional de Agricultura/Food and Agriculture Organization, Studies of the Principal Agricultural Products of the World No. 9., *The World's Coffee* (Rome, 1947), 3–30.

126. Irwin F. Gellman, *Good Neighbor Diplomacy: United States Policies in Latin America, 1933–1945* (Baltimore, 1979), chap. 4.

127. For a broad overview of the role of the United States in the reconstitution of the global economy after the Second World War, see Fred L. Block, *The Origins of International Economic Disorder* (Berkeley, 1977), and Thomas J. McCormick, *America's Half-Century* (Baltimore, 1989), chaps. 1–2. More specifically with regard to commodity policy, see Christopher P. Brown, *The Political and Social Economy of Commodity Control* (London, 1980).

128. *Afterthoughts on Material Civilization and Capitalism* (Baltimore, 1977), 11.

Three

The Labors of Coffee
in Latin America: The Hidden Charm
of Family Labor and Self-Provisioning

VERENA STOLCKE

B Y THE MIDDLE of the nineteenth century Latin America was becoming the main coffee producer for the world market. Thereafter,
stimulated by rising European demand and by foreign and national capital
investment, coffee production in Brazil, Colombia, Venezuela, the Central
American countries, and the Caribbean expanded rapidly. The history of
these Latin American coffee economies has received growing attention
from scholars since the 1980s.[1] Their case studies have gone a long way
toward illuminating the class relations and conflicts that shaped the formation of the national coffee economies. What they reveal, however, is
neither a common story nor the whole story. The picture that emerges is a
mosaic of productive arrangements with very diverse fortunes. And most
of these studies focus solely on the systems of labor exploitation that
developed in coffee cultivation, paying little attention to the important
ways in which the family, as a set of social and economic relationships,
contributed to the success of the coffee economies.

The significant contrasts in the way coffee was introduced and expanded in Latin America as one of the major cash crops for export and the
circumstances under which it was grown provide an excellent opportunity
for beginning a comparison that will help us not only to better understand
the reasons *why* coffee production structures varied so markedly but also
to advance our comprehension of Latin American agrarian history in general. An overall comparison of Latin American coffee economies would,
however, be an unwieldy task. My aim in this essay is a more modest one. I
want, instead, to analyze one hitherto largely neglected dimension of labor systems in coffee cultivation. My primary intention is to compare the

role the family, as an ideal and as an actual set of relationships of social reproduction, played in shaping strategies of accumulation adopted by coffee capital and the way this influenced the fortunes of the respective coffee economies on the world market. There is by now a vast literature on the family, often informed by a feminist concern with women's experiences of oppression and the sociocultural meanings of different family forms as well as intrafamiliar relationships and their economic implications. The unit of analysis in these studies is the family, within which economic decisions are made, set against the background of prevailing intra- and extrafamiliar structures of domination.[2]

By contrast, mainstream historical-economic studies of agricultural development rarely take into account the multiple ways in which prevailing family morality, understood as a set of cultural values which establish the reciprocal rights and obligations that obtain between family members and their expected contributions to its survival, intersects with economic-political processes and how the latter, in turn, shape family structures and gender hierarchies. This theoretical "disencounter" between family studies and the history of Latin American coffee economies is neither random nor inconsequential. Studies of Latin American coffee economies usually take the individual, "formally free" worker as their unit of analysis or as their point of reference for interpreting prevailing systems of labor exploitation and the changes they undergo. Even those studies that have stressed the importance of family composition and the allocation of the labor of women and children under particular productive arrangements have generally not gone far enough in assessing the consequences for the viability of the coffee economies of this dynamic link between productive and reproductive systems and their implications, especially for women.[3]

I want to challenge this "family-blind" and above all "gender-blind" methodological individualism for entailing a triple omission. First, workers, just as are landowners, are always endowed with a family morality and are embedded in kinship relationships. As a consequence, family ideals, goals, and practices play as fundamental a role in shaping strategies of labor exploitation as do workers' labor market commitment and economic-political behavior. Second, by focusing analysis on production, to the exclusion of the sphere of reproduction, a hidden source of surplus extraction is often overlooked, namely the many ways in which family values and labor, especially that of women and children, can contribute to accumulation. And, third, because the gendered nature of laborers has implications for designing systems of labor exploitation, the consequences of forms of labor use, in particular for the experience of women, are generally neglected. My general aim, then, is to draw attention to the relevance of the family and gender relations in their cultural-moral as well as socioeconomic dimensions for an analysis of economic process and change. As one São Paulo coffee estate owner made a special point of remarking in the late 1930s,

The choice of rural workers and of other help is the responsibility of the administration. A well colonized *fazenda*, with well organized families, strong people, well disposed to work, acquainted with the job, functions by itself. . . The workers must have their family on the *fazenda*. The single worker is restless, a nomad, he does not grow roots, lacks motivation. Rural life more than that in town imposes the organization in families.[4]

Related to researchers' "family blindness," there is often yet another recurrent omission. Many authors have regarded coffee as a monoculture whose expansion tended to displace subsistence agriculture, overlooking the fact that coffee has often been grown together with food crops. I will attempt to show, instead, that attention to forms of exploitation of family labor reveals yet another facet of coffee production in many Latin American contexts, namely the frequent combination of coffee as a cash crop with food production for self-provisioning by family labor.

Coffee is a very peculiar crop. It has long been the second commodity after oil in terms of pecuniary value in world trade, but it lacks any nutritional value or any utility as a source of energy. Rather than in response to local needs, coffee growing in Latin American began wholly in response to foreign demand for a beverage that was endowed with social meanings and believed to contain a stimulating quality. Hence, from the start coffee production meant the incorporation of producing countries into the international market. Within this shared market, a cursory overview of diverse local coffee economies reveals great structural variety in the organization of production.

In view of these varied and "peculiar" productive arrangements, it is perhaps not surprising that the interpretation of Latin American agricultural development should have been highly polemical. Research has often been informed by what I would call a "labeling" or "nominalist" approach, intent on establishing the "semifeudal," "noncapitalist," "precapitalist," or, inversely, "capitalist" character of prevailing land tenure arrangements and forms of labor exploitation. The decisive criterion in this conceptual controversy was either the existence or absence of a free labor market of wage workers, or the circulation of commodities produced for the market. But this diversity cannot be ordered along a simple historical continuum of progressively more "capitalist" forms of production. There is, for example, the São Paulo plantation system, which was in fact worked by a particular type of sharecropper hired in family units. This *colonato* system lasted until the 1960s. From a conventional historical-materialist perspective, the replacement in the Turrialba region of Costa Rica of wage workers (*peones*) by a very similar colonato system, around 1915, appears as even more anachronistic.[5] Colombia provides yet another example, where early in this century small family farms progressively took the place of large *haciendas* as the main coffee-producing sector. Hence, rather than establishing a teleological taxonomy, we need to uncover the specific economic and political circumstances and cultural logic that together accounted for these diverse productive systems as well as their transformations.

Little attention has hitherto been devoted to the political dynamics under which concrete labor systems operated in Latin America, in particular to the ways in which workers resisted their exploitation and the consequences of different forms of resistance in transforming systems of labor use. I argue that we need to study the historical contexts of the particular forms of labor exploitation under which coffee is grown, focusing especially on the class contradictions and struggles which have shaped and transformed these systems. Any type of labor exploitation is embedded in a power relationship which entails a form of domination. In turn, coercion always means that a potential exists for resistance to exploitation by the workers. Rather than focusing primarily on the so-called factors of production — that is, land, labor, and capital, as they interacted in the expansion of coffee — I want to rescue the political dimension of social relations of production, its subjects: coffee planters and workers, women and men. Through their actions and reactions, inspired by specific class interests and mediated by a family morality, they shaped the history of coffee production.

Wherever available information allows I will therefore explore the *politics* of labor exploitation, that is, the contradictions and conflicts generated by particular forms of labor use as a fundamental factor of economic change. These three phenomena are related. The hidden role played by the family and gender in shaping strategies of surplus extraction, as well as self-provisioning by family labor, constitute a neglected dimension not only of the economics but also of the politics of exploitation. Different systems of exploitation of family morality — under family labor systems, by contrast with individual wage labor, for example — influence forms of resistance to exploitation in different ways.

As I have shown elsewhere, coffee workers in São Paulo in the 1970s perceived their work situation to be the result of the power relations in which they were embedded and offered resistance in multiple, subtle ways.[6] Dona Maria, a day laborer on a large coffee plantation in São Paulo, for instance, explained why she had to work for a wage to make a living, rather than having a piece of land of her own: "This business of rich and poor began a long time ago when the land was not sold. The shrewd ones fenced in the land and the others were left with their mouths open and worked for the others. In those days the most cunning appropriated everything. The others were fools. Now this is no longer possible; when you are poor it is difficult to become rich. Working, one does not become rich." As another woman worker elaborated, it seemed to her that, without the poor, agriculture would not exist:

Because, you see, someone who is rich, not even if he knew how to, not even jokingly, would take a hoe and work. But you see that the bread of everyday comes from the dust of the earth, doesn't it? It comes from the hands of the poor... Thus, the rich want money and we, the poor, want food. Now, if everybody was rich nobody would want to work... Those who are rich, even those who are somewhat better off, don't want to have anything to do with work; they will prefer to pay somebody else, the poor, to making an effort themselves, because they think that working is a sacrifice. Now, people like us who are poor, who need to work, we face it. We have already been born for this struggle.

Sr. Dito, yet another day laborer, who died recently, summed up the logic of capital:

What gives the landlord his profit is labor. Not the land. Without labor it does not give anything. That's logical. It is the profit of capital. But if you do not apply labor it does not give anything. You have to be a fool not to perceive that. If you leave the capital in a corner you should see what comes of it. If you do not weed the land, you should see what happens, nothing! To me all that is produced is produced by the laborers. The landowners think that we are all suckers.

These workers visualize society as divided between those who work because they are dispossessed and those who don't need to work because they own the land and reap their profit from those who, having been expropriated, need to work to make a living. The "rich," using the power they possess, have expropriated the "poor" because they were powerless. These day laborers worked in gangs controlled by an overseer who organized the work process and saw to it that they worked "properly." The very existence of the overseer is only one indication that labor discipline was always open to challenge.

Specific forms of labor exploitation depend, then, on the power of those who own the land and on the capacity for resistance of the landless under concrete historical circumstances. Relations of production and politics are, therefore, intertwined and must be analyzed jointly in order to fully comprehend forms of labor exploitation and why they change.

Forms of Labor Appropriation in
Latin American Coffee Economies

For a comparison of structures and fortunes of Latin American coffee economies, the São Paulo case can serve as example and background for an inquiry into the ways in which the politics of exploitation and the exploitation of family morality has shaped labor appropriation. Coffee was introduced to Brazil in the late eighteenth century, first appearing in the Paraíba Valley north of the then imperial capital of Rio de Janeiro, thereafter moving gradually into northern São Paulo and southern Minas Gerais in the second half of the nineteenth century. As late as the 1870s the Paraíba Valley still accounted for 60 percent of the total production, Minas Gerais for 25 percent, and São Paulo for only 10 percent. By the end of the century, however, the province of São Paulo had become the country's principal coffee producer, a position it was to maintain until the 1950s.[7] In every case coffee was grown without shade on large estates. In the Paraíba Valley coffee was cultivated exclusively by slaves. In São Paulo and Minas slaves predominated on the coffee plantations until the 1870s, but experiments with free immigrant labor, in particular in São Paulo, had begun already in the early 1850s. In Minas, by contrast, more abundant native-born labor was to take the place of the slaves after abolition in 1888.

As coffee expanded in late-nineteenth-century São Paulo and Minas Gerais, large estates predominated, worked by a growing labor force of either immigrant or native-born labor. One significant characteristic in both cases was that labor was generally hired in family units, in São Paulo under the colonato system and in Minas as sharecroppers. That is, in the center-south of Brazil coffee production destined for the international market gave rise to a plantation economy run with labor hired in family units under very different wage-incentive systems.

The first free laborers introduced to São Paulo coffee plantations in the 1840s were mostly Swiss and German immigrant families. Their arrival coincided with the passage of a land law which consolidated private property rights in land. This law was intended to *prevent* the native-born laborers and immigrants from becoming independent farmers by simply settling on public lands. The vast expanses of unoccupied territory were already posing a serious obstacle to hiring the scattered native-born population of free workers.[8] By 1855 about 3,500 immigrant laborers were employed on thirty Brazilian-owned plantations in the province of São Paulo, often working side by side with slaves.

From the start São Paulo coffee planters insisted on hiring immigrant labor in family units, initially as sharecroppers, rather than as individual wage labor. One reason for their preference for family labor was, presumably, their experience with slaves, among whom women and children had proved to be a valuable labor reserve, in particular for the coffee harvest when labor demand rose markedly.[9] As I will argue later, these coffee planters fully appreciated the comparative profitability, under certain circumstances, of labor hired in family units. However, without abandoning the family labor system, planters soon replaced sharecropping with a labor-leasing contract, that is, a straight piece-work system under which laborers were paid by the quantity of coffee tended and harvested. In the 1870s, finally, labor leasing gave way to the typical colonato system which was to prevail on São Paulo coffee plantations well into the 1960s. At the same time, by contrast, in the Zona da Mata of Minas Gerais coffee was mostly grown on estates which followed the production patterns of the Paraíba Valley, that is, by an abundant and free, native-born labor hired as sharecropper families.[10]

The history of the Colombian coffee economy, arguably the most complex in Latin America, contrasts notably with that of the center-south of Brazil.[11] Until the 1940s, coffee was the leading sector of the country's economy in terms of area planted and employment. Haciendas predominated in the late nineteenth century, but by the 1920s an ever increasing volume of coffee was being produced by small family farms, which gave a powerful boost to the whole economy, while a liberal coffee bourgeoisie developed as merchant exporters.

Coffee was first introduced in Colombia in Santander. Large coffee estates worked by sharecroppers continued to dominate in this region until the mid twentieth century, side by side with a growing sector of small family farms, with production stagnating after 1913. Between 1880 and 1895 Bogotá and Medellín merchants opened new coffee haciendas in Cundinamarca, becoming both *hacendados* and exporters. A decade later coffee spread into Tolima and southwestern Antioquia. In the latter region, in particular, while haciendas occupied the fertile lowlands, small family farmers colonized the slopes, planting coffee combined with subsistence crops. Cundinamarca haciendas turned out to be more vulnerable economically for at least two reasons. Production was highly specialized in coffee. This diminished their ability to withstand periods of depression in the world coffee market. Moreover, although the *arrendamiento* labor system entitled the renter families to grow food alongside coffee, it also gave them a measure of autonomy which seems to have generated intense conflicts over land. Tenants preferred to work on their own plots rather than in tending coffee for the hacienda, and their efforts to secure better and/or larger plots of land favored labor mobility. Estate owners' attempts to reduce production costs in response to economic difficulties in the early

1930s led to severe land conflicts. As a result of tenants' struggle for land, some of the Cundinamarca haciendas were taken over by *arrendatarios*. In Antioquia, by contrast, hacendados adopted a form of labor use midway between sharecropping and renting, the *agregado*, a family labor system which entitled the workers to housing and a self-provisioning plot on the estate. As Palacios indicates, Antioquia estate owners endeavored, however, to separate the agregados' dwelling from their subsistence plots, precisely to curtail potential aspirations to independence in a family-based economy.[12] In contrast to Cundinamarca, in Antioquia the growing number of smallholders were the result of informal land occupations rather than organized tenants' movements.

Although the exact fate of haciendas during the first coffee depression at the end of the century remains unclear, by the 1920s the predominance of small family farms in coffee growing is well established. Moreover, after the stagnation in production around the turn of the century, from 1910 onward Colombian coffee production grew steadily, unscathed by the 1929 recession until the 1960s. The country became the second coffee producer for the world market after Brazil, while marketing was progressively taken over by North American capital.

The production structure and fortunes of the coffee economies of Venezuela and Puerto Rico contain both parallels and significant differences. In both countries, coffee became the main export crop in the second half of the nineteenth century, earlier than in Colombia and at a time when Brazil was emerging as the leading Latin American producer.[13] Coffee was introduced in the Venezuelan Andes when national merchant capital, financing commodity-producing farmers, consolidated landed property and gave rise to a peasantry. The expansion of coffee accelerated the demarcation of a previously ill-defined, if European, landed property, and of indigenous reserves which were legally divided into smaller units. Public land was occupied by squatters who established family farms. From this process came a merchant class tied to Maracaibo and a coffee-producing peasantry. As Roseberry has shown, these small-scale farmers, while independent of landlords, depended on the merchants for credit and for the marketing of their produce. Estate owners, who had also moved into coffee, hired resident workers and renters entitled to self-provisioning plots, and acted as creditors to peasant proprietors in an attempt to secure scarce labor. The Venezuelan coffee economy stagnated during the overproduction crisis at the end of the century but did not collapse. After the 1929 depression the area planted in coffee increased, and exports rose again as merchants pressed for debt repayment in coffee at current, depressed prices, even though productivity declined.[14] It is significant that the Andean region, where farm size was smaller than the national average, proved to be more resilient than other coffee regions in the country in the face of the successive market crises. Early in the century petroleum replaced coffee in Venezuelan foreign trade without destroying the coffee sector. Diversification of the economy reached the Andean region only in the 1950s and 1960s. At the same time, the coffee peasantry proved little receptive to government programs of coffee renovation, and instead some family members sought wage work outside the farm, further eroding smallholders' viability.

By contrast with the Venezuelan Andes and Colombia, coffee expansion in the Cordillera Central of Puerto Rico, while it was still a Spanish colony, entailed the progressive concentration of land ownership to the detriment of small farms in a process that was dominated by and consolidated the hold of immigrant merchants.[15] Land concentration was particularly intense where merchants also became coffee hacendados (as in the Yauco region), instead of repatriating capital as the Mallorcan and Catalan merchants operating in the Lares district did. Former agregado and renter families living and toiling on large and medium estates, usually with self-provisioning rights, were partly replaced by *jornaleros*, that is, seasonal day laborers who migrated from the coast to the coffee regions attracted by high wages at the time of the coffee boom, while expropriation advanced and the agricultural frontier closed over the mid nineteenth century. Whereas in the 1850s about half of the population had access to land, by the 1870s this proportion had declined to 17 percent. Thus, although smallholders predominated numerically, most coffee was produced on large estates. The Ley General de Jornaleros, passed by the colonial government in 1849 to create a supply of free labor for coastal sugar plantations (by forcing all males who could not demonstrate they owned land to seek employment on legally titled farms), increased the demand for land on the one hand, and on the other speeded the proliferation of minifundia and of outright expropriation. One result was that coffee in Puerto Rico became a monoculture in the true sense of the word, displacing subsistence crops in particular, although the production structure of smallholders is not clear. A sudden end befell a very prosperous coffee economy when it collapsed during the first coffee crisis in the late 1890s. Bergad underlines as a primary factor in this collapse the danger inherent in the exclusive dependence of a landed elite, stimulated by a colonial merchant class in pursuit of quick profit, on a single cash crop for the world market.[16]

In the Central American republics of Costa Rica, Guatemala, and El Salvador, finally, coffee was introduced and became the main foreign exchange earner in the second half of the nineteenth century.[17] Land tenure structures and systems of labor exploitation developed in quite different ways, however. In Costa Rica, the country with the lowest population density of the three, coffee was first introduced on the fertile Meseta Central, near San José, where land concentration occurred slowly up to at least 1935. Ciro Cardoso attributes the prolonged predominance of small coffee farms to the scarcity of labor and shortage of capital. Competition for labor by the United Fruit Company at the end of the century is thought to have further aggravated labor scarcity, although the rate of natural population growth appears to have been high throughout the period, to the point of intensifying the subsistence crisis. All official immigration projects, designed to create a peasantry of European origin, failed for reasons which are not quite clear, but a constant if minuscule stream of immigrants entered the country attracted by the economic prospects coffee offered. Indeed, this alleged labor scarcity seems rather paradoxical considering natural population growth coupled with the constant arrival of immigrants and a subsistence crisis. As in the Venezuelan Andes, the coffee peasantry enjoyed autonomy as growers but depended on large merchants for the processing and marketing of their crop. When, by the end of the century, public lands were no longer available on the Meseta Central, smallholders increased coffee cultivation, apparently to the exclusion of food crops, which were moved to marginal lands. Simultaneously, coffee expanded into the Reventazón valley around Turrialba, stimulating a process of severe land concentration. On the largest hacienda in the Turrialba region, however, a colono system similar to that which prevailed on São Paulo plantations partly replaced waged day labor in 1915, allegedly as a way to deal with marked seasonal fluctuations in labor demand.[18] Hence, in Costa Rica two distinct production structures developed, a freeholding peasantry on the Meseta Central and large estates in the Reventazón valley and Turrialba that were worked predominantly by wage labor.

In Guatemala and El Salvador, by contrast with Costa Rica, the state played a decisive role in creating the conditions for the development of a coffee economy based on large estates.[19] Under the liberal reforms in Guatemala in the 1870s extensive church lands were confiscated and sold or distributed. In addition, a form of land rent in perpetuity was abolished, with renters being forced to purchase the land. And public lands were sold or allocated, under the condition that the recipient grow coffee or other commercial crops. One consequence of these reforms was the creation of a land market. Another was the expropriation of the mostly indigenous peasantry who lacked the resources to buy the communal land they had cultivated, even though indigenous communal lands were not formally abolished. At the same time, the archaic financial system was overhauled to make capital and credit available for commercial agriculture. As regards labor supply, early on attempts had been made to attract the abundant highland population by offering payment in advance for work on the coffee estates located in the western coastal regions of the country where population was scarce, but with little success. Also, in order to ensure and control labor supply a Reglamento de Jornaleros was passed in the 1870s which thereafter permitted forcible recruitment of labor from the indigenous communities, which were subjected, as were resident wage workers, to rigid discipline. By the 1880s about one-fourth of the economically active population was made up of landless laborers and another one-fourth of indigenous smallholders who worked part of the year on coffee estates. Traces of forced labor recruitment persisted well into the 1940s, indicative of the reluctance of Indians to work on the estates even though a minimum wage had been introduced at the beginning of the twentieth century.[20]

In El Salvador the liberal reforms of the 1880s aimed instead at the abolition of traditional indigenous communal land rights, in particular in the volcanic central plain of the country, the most densely populated region of the country and also the best suited for coffee growing. Coffee production had already expanded substantially in the 1860s, threatening indigenous land rights. The liberal reforms endowed this ongoing process of expropriation with a cloak of legality. The consequence was the consolidation of a coffee oligarchy, one landlord owning several medium sized estates at a time, while mestizos (*ladinos*) tended to become medium and small farmers on lands unsuited for coffee. Initially, coffee planters attempted to attract labor by granting subsistence plots. According to Cardoso, the expansion of coffee made this method of labor recruitment nonviable, although for reasons that remain unclear. In the 1880s a new form of labor procurement gained force which consisted in settling workers in villages established in the vicinity of estates — veritable company towns — without rights to self-provisioning. Laborers' subsistence was provided by the estate owners for whom they worked. This was an alternative to forced recruitment under the aegis of the state as imposed, for example, in Guatemala. The state intervened, instead, to enforce compliance with work agreements and to repress attempts at resistance to labor discipline, as well as rebellions such as the peasant revolt of 1889 in the west of the country.

In El Salvador the massive and radical expropriation of the indigenous population and their displacement created a dispossessed population available for seasonal work on the coffee estates. During the dead season they survived on marginal lands which, as Cardoso suggests, made methods of forced labor like those used in Guatemala redundant.[21]

The Discreet Charm of the Family for
the Politics of Labor Exploitation

Brass offers an example of extreme formalist conceptualization of labor systems in Latin American coffee economies. He defines free labor as that which is independent from access to land and free from the control of a particular employer. He argues that "the increased demand for labor-power arising from the expansion of an export-oriented yet labor-intensive capitalist agriculture in a location where labor is scarce is met not by free wage labor but rather by recourse to unfree labor." That is, scarce labor in a context of abundant land apt for cultivation leads to "unfree labor." Debt peonage was the most common method of restricting labor mobility in Latin America, another way to delay wage payment. Brass cites as one example the indebtedness of immigrant sharecroppers working on coffee plantations in the Río Claro region of São Paulo in the 1850s, which he mistakes for indentured immigrant workers.[22] While agreeing that "the supply and demand for labor depends upon a variety of interconnected factors including population size, land demand and availability, wage rates, and changes in international market conditions," Bergad emphasized, in replying to Brass, the changing interaction of these factors over time.[23]

The bone of contention here is the definition of labor scarcity. It is, therefore, all the more remarkable that neither author pays any attention whatsoever to the fact that workers are always part of a family, a "hidden dimension" of labor availability which qualifies the supply of labor power in a very important way. The decision of the largest coffee planter in Aquiares, in the Turrialba district of Costa Rica, in 1915 to adopt a colono system — very similar to and possibly following the São Paulo experience — is a particularly intriguing example of the exploitation of family morality under an incentive wage system, for it was introduced to partly replace wage labor itself. Norris related the option for colonos to marked seasonal fluctuations in labor demand but concluded that "the colono system serves to guarantee permanent, dependable labor at a minimal cost to the owner."[24] The colonos were recruited for the care and harvest of coffee and were paid a fixed price per *fanega* of coffee produced. In addition to housing, they were given a self-provisioning plot but did not receive compensation for the work of the members of their family in the *colonia* (the plot). The workers hired had formerly been peones (wage laborers) and, by contrast with the mobility of São Paulo colonos, stayed on the hacienda for decades. They enjoyed high social prestige and were also considered advantageous for the estate. This form of labor use persisted until the 1950s, alongside resident day laborers and administrative staff, when it was abolished by a new owner committed to gang wage labor.[25]

São Paulo planters' early experiments with free labor, when it became clear that slavery was doomed, provide perhaps the clearest example of how their acknowledgment of the virtues of family labor systems shaped their strategies of labor exploitation and of how subtle forms of labor resistance forced readjustments in production organization. The colonato system, the end product of these experiments, came to predominate on São Paulo coffee plantations precisely in the 1880s when a free labor market was constituted, which goes directly against the grain of orthodoxy regarding the "capitalization" of agriculture. São Paulo coffee planters initially hired immigrant families as sharecroppers. The colonato, a mixed-task and piece-rate system, replaced sharecropping in the 1870s and predominated on São Paulo coffee plantations until the 1960s, as I have shown elsewhere.[26]

Interpretations of sharecropping have differed substantially.[27] Liberal scholars have regarded sharecropping as less efficient than wage labor. Receiving only part of the product, sharecroppers would allegedly stop work sooner than wage laborers. More recently, the use of sharecropping has been attributed to its greater efficiency in risk aversion and dispersion.[28] In Brazil in the case of Minas Gerais it has been interpreted as a way of binding labor to the estate, that is, as a kind of debt bondage.[29] All these interpretations obscure, however, two fundamental traits of sharecropping built into this system of family labor exploitation, namely, the distinctive *incentive/motive*. Sharecropping in a situation of expensive and/or scarce labor is more efficient than wage labor, provided the employer has the political clout to enforce a profitable distribution of the product. It is a form of labor use similar to a carefully negotiated piecework system, a way of securing extra effort from labor, of making laborers work harder and better for only a small increase in total pay over that of wage laborers. Pay, in the form of a portion of the product, constitutes an incentive for the laborers to intensify their effort, since it is on the amount produced that their income will depend. They will cultivate with greater care, again because part of the output will accrue to them. The extent to which management supervises production seems to vary, but control of work discipline is exercised by the laborers themselves.[30]

When coffee was introduced in São Paulo it was a frontier region. Although there may have been no shortage of *potential* workers, available free labor was scarce.[31] The planters' decision to recruit immigrants meant that labor costs in São Paulo were initially high. Employers had to advance the transport and installation costs of the immigrants. Coffee is a very labor intensive crop. Due to the incentive element of sharecropping, it could be expected that sharecroppers would tend more coffee trees per worker than would wage laborers. Consequently, fewer workers would be required, and initial investment would be lower. Now, sharecroppers were usually hired in family units. Planters had always opposed recruiting single men since, they argued, immigrant families were less prone to abandon the plantation. This may have been so, but surely equally important was the fact that the immigrants' families constituted a cheap labor reserve. A sharecropper usually accepts a division of the harvest that does not fully cover the hypothetical market price of family labor, which would otherwise remain under- or unemployed. The planter obtained this additional labor at a cost well below that which he would have had to pay had he hired them on the market as wage labor.[32] Since labor needs during the harvest were greater than during cultivation, the workers' wives and children could cover this additional demand well. Finally, the laborers were allotted a food plot on which they were expected to grow only what they needed for their subsistence. Self-provisioning was usually the women's and children's task during the coffee cultivation season, which required less labor than the harvest. Men generally did the weeding. Family labor was thus used to the fullest extent. Self-provisioning by family members, and in particular by wives, without compensation, contributed to reducing the cost of labor reproduction and generated a labor rent. To interpret self-provisioning by the workers, therefore, as a right to the usufruct of land, as some authors have done,[33] conceals this indirect form of labor power appropriation, especially of family members and among them particularly of women. Not only did women produce most of the food for the family, thereby reducing their reproduction cost as workers, but in addition the labor power that went into this self-provisioning was not compensated.

Nonetheless, sharecropping as the predominant form of free labor use was short-lived on São Paulo coffee plantations. Early in this century, after the first overproduction crisis, some planters proposed that sharecropping be reintroduced in São Paulo. But, revealingly, laborers were unwilling in the context of falling coffee prices to accept sharecropping instead of the by then predominant colonato system which granted them a basic fixed income.

In Minas Gerais, by contrast, sharecropping persisted in a situation of available native-born labor.[34] It was presumably accepted by the workers, despite the greater labor intensity it entailed in comparison with wage work, because of the incentive element coupled with self-provisioning under circumstances where there were no better alternatives available. They lacked the bargaining power to demand more favorable work conditions. At the 1878 Agricultural Congress, Minas Gerais planters opposed large-scale immigration as a solution for the labor problem. They wanted to see antivagrancy legislation passed, as well as the creation of an immigrant peasantry as a labor reserve. São Paulo coffee growers, however, used their growing political leverage to successfully demand subsidized mass immigration instead.[35]

The crucial point of contention between labor and capital in sharecropping is the setting of the "share" level, which depends on the bargaining power of both parties. Interests are opposed. When profits are low landowners prefer sharecropping to labor earning a fixed wage, whereas the workers prefer the latter, and vice-versa. The early failure of sharecropping in São Paulo in the late 1850s has generally been attributed to a much publicized revolt by Swiss immigrant laborers triggered by frauds committed by planters, as well as to an alleged decline in interest in free labor among planters. However, these abuses only added to the growing discontent of immigrants with their living and working conditions. Immigrant labor required an initial investment by the planters, which they attempted to retrieve by retaining half of the workers' share in the coffee produced. Consequently, the immigrants started out already burdened with a debt which weighed heavily on their future income, their returns from coffee cultivation being markedly lower than the stipulated 50 percent.

Sharecropping on São Paulo plantations cannot, therefore, be interpreted as a form of debt peonage resulting from the indebtedness of the immigrant families, comparable, for example, to the advances offered Indian labor in Guatemala to retain them on the estates.[36] The debt arose from the planters' attempt to recover the investment made in hiring the laborers. This debt, moreover, undermined the very logic of sharecropping, namely the incentive element. The productivity of labor in coffee turned out to be extremely low. The workers, in a kind of spontaneous, family-centered form of resistance, diverted much of their labor power to self-provisioning, a reaction comparable to that of the Cundinamarca arrendatarios.[37] The planters lacked any means of imposing labor discipline short of firing the workers, which would have only further deprived them of their investment. Nonetheless, rather than abandoning free labor and reverting to slavery, the more farsighted planters adjusted the labor system to solve the problem of supply and to achieve higher productivity through more effective labor discipline, at the same time pressuring the state for support.

By 1886 the provincial government of São Paulo began subsidizing mass immigration, flooding the labor market with cheap and disciplined labor, evidence of the political power the planter class had by then acquired. In the next three decades almost one million predominantly Italian immigrants entered São Paulo, mainly in agriculture. After a further readjustment of the labor use system, which led to the colonato, labor productivity in coffee rose from about 700 coffee trees cultivated per worker per year in the late 1850s, to between 2,500 and 3,000 trees.

Under the colonato system that replaced sharecropping, coffee weeding was paid at a fixed annual rate per thousand trees tended, a sort of fixed minimum wage intended to induce immigrant families to cultivate a larger number of trees. A piece rate was paid for the harvest, which permitted labor costs to be adapted to annual fluctuations in yields. Food plots were now allocated in proportion to the number of trees tended. Planters also emphasized their preference for hiring especially large families, a way to reduce unit labor costs. The more workers per consumers there were in a family, the lower the cost of reproduction of each individual worker and, consequently, the lower the piece or task rate could be. A Prussian agronomist duly acknowledged this feat of the São Paulo coffee planters:

> One fact in relation to this labor system [the colonato] . . . is of outstanding importance: it educates workers for intensive work. . . I have mentioned this point here as evidence for my assertion that the labor system predominating now on the plantations of São Paulo deserves to be regarded as an almost ideal one. Let us honor the untiring ambition and intelligence of São Paulo planters who by introducing this labor system . . . have made an outstanding contribution to solving the social question.[38]

The Cost Flexibility of Combined Coffee and Food Crop Cultivation

The profitability of combined food and cash crop family labor systems, as compared with individual wage labor, should be clear by now. The failure of sharecropping in São Paulo had to do with the class conflicts it generated rather than with purely economic reasons. The symbiosis of coffee with food crops had, however, a further advantage beyond generally reducing labor costs, namely its cost flexibility.

At the turn of the century about 80 percent of the agricultural labor force of the state of São Paulo was engaged in coffee cultivation under the colonato system. Coffee production increased fivefold between 1890 and 1907. Labor productivity had risen markedly in response to the wage incentive of the colonato system, which was no longer eroded by an initial debt. But organized, collective political action now replaced the earlier resistance to exploitation by individual families. The following three decades saw not only two overproduction crises but also a succession of colono strikes. Nonetheless, coffee continued to expand steadily in São

Paulo until World War II, and with it the production of food crops by the colonos.

The belief that coffee monoculture for export expands to the detriment of domestic market crops often rests, in effect, on a misconception that obscures the multiple advantages of self-provisioning by family labor. Under the São Paulo colonato system and wherever coffee was grown by family labor units in combination with food crops, as in Colombia and Venezuela by peasantries, by smallholders in the Meseta Central of Costa Rica, under the Turrialba colono system, and by the early forms of service tenancy (agregados) or renters in Puerto Rico, a symbiotic relationship obtained between coffee and food crops which provided planters or merchants a measure of flexibility in the face of price slumps on the world market that they would not have enjoyed with wage labor.

São Paulo coffee planters, in effect, were able to weather quite successfully overproduction crises and the fall in coffee prices by about 50 percent at the beginning of the century and again in 1929, not only on account of state price support but significantly by reducing task wages and increasing self-provisioning instead. The colonato as a family labor system, combining a cash crop with self-provisioning by the workers, operated as a kind of cushion that helped absorb part of the impact of adverse market conditions. Although embedded in a plantation system, the colonato was not dissimilar in this sense from coffee peasantries dependent on a merchant class elsewhere. These peasantries also continued producing coffee when prices were low, at the cost of increasing family self-exploitation and by cultivating food crops on the side. The only difference was that in São Paulo the beneficiaries were both the plantation owners and the merchant houses, whereas, for example, in Colombia and also in the Venezuelan Andes it was the coffee merchants alone who profited from the coffee peasants' self-exploitation.[39] Other combined cash and food crop family labor systems, such as the early agregados and the arrendamiento, surely entailed similar advantages. Coffee interests were well aware of this. Mariano Ospina Pérez, the president of the National Federation of Coffee Growers, for example, explained Colombia's competitive superiority on the world market in the following terms in 1934: "Colombia, because of the enormous parcelization of its coffee properties and the multiplicity of crops grown within each coffee farm, is in a very favorable position to endure a price war. Even supposing that a great part of the coffee harvest were lost or that the price of coffee were to fall considerably, the people of the coffee zone could count on a considerable part of the products they need for their subsistence."[40]

The difference between shaded and nonshaded coffee is also relevant in this respect. Shaded coffee in Colombia, for instance, presumably did not allow for growing food crops between the rows as in São Paulo, where it further increased planters' room for manuever vis-à-vis coffee price fluctuations. Workers preferred intercropping of food to cultivating a separate plot because it meant saving labor on their part. In effect, in times of low prices São Paulo planters allowed food growing even in the rows of mature coffee trees, which was known to diminish yields, as a compensation for wage cuts.

The cost flexibility inherent in growing coffee in combination with food crops was thus an additional bonus of family labor systems hidden to those analysts who fail to pay attention to the family. Individual wage work would have meant that the cash crop competed with food crops for a single worker's labor power. There are, of course, instances where the family members of wage workers grew food on marginal land outside the coffee estates, but this made it much more difficult for planters to preempt potential labor conflicts by compensating a wage cut with more extensive self-provisioning.

Still, this does not mean that the combined cash and food crop systems of labor appropriation — by large coffee growers or by a merchant class — and the cost flexibility they permitted were devoid of tensions between estate owners and laborers, as well as among planters themselves. The strikes by São Paulo colonos were usually over harvest piece-rates, or the reduction of self-provisioning at times when coffee prices rose, and they were organized by families. On the other hand, self-provisioning, which ensured their basic livelihood, enhanced the colono families' staying power during these strikes. Planters were well aware of this. One way of defeating the workers, beyond repression by police forces, was to deny them the purchase of those subsistence items for which the colonos depended on the *fazenda*, such as sugar, salt, dried meat, and other staples.[41] The conflicts over land between estate owners and arrendatarios in Cundinamarca, Antioquia estate owners' attempts to grant self-provisioning plots to the agregados at a distance from their dwellings to curtail their autonomy as a family economy,[42] early São Paulo sharecroppers' tendency to divert labor power to self-provisioning to the detriment of coffee cultivation, and the colonos' haggling over the size of food plots and their proverbial nomadism in search of more favorable self-provisioning conditions elsewhere, are all further evidence of the contradiction between laborers' and estate owners' interests in self-provisioning. The laborers sought a measure of independence, even at the cost of self-exploitation, while estate owners sought to ensure a greater rate of profit than they would have achieved with wage labor.

More attractive conditions for food growing in new coffee regions in São Paulo also intensified competition for labor between estates, and hence labor instability. That the Aquiares colonos in Costa Rica, by contrast, should have been more dependable and stable would seem to have been due not only to their own preference for this labor system, as compared with wage labor, but also to the lack of similar work opportunities on other estates, which, incidentally, raises the question of why this colono system had not, to my knowledge, been adopted elsewhere but was regarded rather with distrust. Aquiares colonos, at any rate, stressed the greater degree of independence and prestige they enjoyed. By contrast, they were more skeptical about their monetary advantages.[43]

The labor arrangements of the coffee economies in Puerto Rico, Guatemala, and El Salvador contrasted notably with the cases discussed above.[44] In all three countries the state (in Puerto Rico the colonial administration, but in Guatemala and El Salvador a liberal state) played a crucial role in creating the conditions for the development of large coffee estates. In São Paulo state intervention took the form of subsidized labor immigration and price support at times of market crises, incidentally benefiting all other world coffee producers. In Puerto Rico and Guatemala, the state enacted antivagrancy laws, subjecting the country's indigenous population to a system of forced labor which facilitated labor supply in the second half of the century. In El Salvador, finally, the state abolished indigenous communal lands outright, in order to eliminate this impediment to coffee's expansion and the recruitment of indigenous labor.

The structure of Puerto Rican coffee production comes closest, in a way, to what has been considered the classical model of a capitalist plantation economy.[45] Large and medium coffee estates accounted for the bulk of coffee produced and retained a core of agregados entitled to self-provisioning, but these were complemented by migrant seasonal wage laborers (that is, the proverbial "free laborers"), in particular during the harvest season. It was on these large estates that coffee seems to have become a monoculture in the true sense of the word. Coffee expanded at the expense of subsistence agriculture. With the onset of the first overproduction crises in the 1890s the coffee economy collapsed, thus revealing the economic fragility of monoculture and providing further evidence of the comparative advantages for coffee capital of the combined cash and food crop family labor systems.

Bergad has argued that, "as coffee expanded, population increased, land became concentrated in fewer hands, the frontier was closed, and a large rural work force emerged subject to the domination of landed society."[46] This interpretation is just one more example of the widely held notion that landed interests prefer straight wage labor when labor market conditions permit.

If coffee plantation systems worked by "free labor" were an exception rather than the rule, this suggests that we may need to invert the questions commonly posed. Instead of searching for the proverbial "free laborer," we may need to pay more attention to the comparative economic advantages of family labor systems involving self-provisioning in order to understand why, for example, they disappeared in nineteenth-century Puerto Rico and about a century later in São Paulo, Colombia, and Venezuela.

In Guatemala and El Salvador coffee interests had to overcome very special obstacles. Both countries had large indigenous populations which lived embedded in traditional communities. Traditional rights and cultural values limited coffee growers' access to labor and/or land. The solutions found were distinct in each case, depending on whether indigenous communities constrained only labor supply, as in Guatemala, or also competed with coffee interests for land, as in El Salvador.

In Guatemala some coffee growers initially settled poor peasants on their properties, paying them a wage in addition to granting them a plot to grow food, understood as partial compensation for their services. Even so, Indians generally refused to work away from their communities for meager pay and preferred to look after their own crops.[47] When, by the end of the 1860s, coffee growing and coffee producers were well established in the country, it became more urgent to ensure the labor supply. The solution found was the legalization of forced indigenous labor, which permitted the enlistment of Indians for work on coffee estates for specified periods of time. In addition, debts resulting from arbitrary fines and exorbitant food prices were used to tie them to the estates. Whereas in São Paulo, for example, wage cuts in the face of falling coffee prices had to be compensated by more extensive self-provisioning, in Guatemala hyperexploitation only intensified during the first coffee crisis. Workers' nominal wages were not only reduced but paid in devalued paper money,[48] evidence of the extraordinary power wielded by Guatemalan coffee growers backed by the state.

In El Salvador, indigenous communities occupied the central volcanic highlands most suited for coffee cultivation. In the 1880s the state eliminated this double obstacle to coffee's expansion by abolishing the Indian communities, "liberating" not only thousands of Indians for work on coffee estates but also their ancestral lands. After unsuccessful attempts to attract colonos by offering them food plots, workers were settled in villages established in the vicinity of coffee plantations. They were forbidden to grow their own food, which they had to obtain from the estates. Laws were also passed forbidding Indians to occupy untitled land and imposing severe labor discipline. Instead of instituting forced labor, as in Guatemala, the state in El Salvador, supported by the military, repressed any form of peasant rebellion.[49]

In Guatemala and El Salvador the particularly draconian forms of labor recruitment and exploitation did, in effect, generate widespread social tension, at times resulting in open peasant revolts, which were put down by the military.[50] The structure of class domination which allowed for intensified labor exploitation during coffee price slumps ensured continued coffee production and export despite its having become a monoculture in these countries.[51] Coffee prospered but food production declined dramatically, and the living conditions of the landless worsened. In Guatemala, according to Cambranes, "the scarcity of food, growing every day, was intimately related to the rural expropriation of the communities, because earlier peasants had enough fields to rotate them according to the needs of the soils which were submitted to the temporal cultivation of maize, kidney-beans and other food stuffs. The lack of food in the country . . . became a national and permanent problem since the appropriation of the best cultivation lands by the *impresarios*."[52] The expropriated Indians were forced to work permanently for the plantations, no longer able to attend to the maize fields. The government encouraged the rental of land to poor peasants "in exchange for part of the harvest or work services" to improve food production, and the number of such tenants increased considerably in the 1870s. Cambranes does not make it clear, however, how coffee and the growing of food were combined.[53]

Western family structure and morality played a significant role in allowing coffee interests to design their strategies of exploitation by adopting combined coffee and food-crop family labor systems of demonstrable profitability in the cases discussed initially. In Guatemala and El Salvador, by contrast, traditional indigenous community structure and cultural values constituted a serious impediment for coffee's expansion. This was so not only because Indians enjoyed access to land of their own. I would suggest that, in addition, that because traditional indigenous social and kinship structures could not be put to the service of labor appropriation by coffee interests, they protected the Indians against exploitation by strangers. As a consequence, indigenous communities needed first to be dissolved and their cultural values destroyed to ensure the labor supply for coffee production. A measure of the tenacity with which Indians defended traditional rights and cultural values is the very brutality with which they were enlisted for work on coffee estates.[54]

Why Did Family Labor Systems Change After All?

If, as I have attempted to demonstrate, combined coffee and food-crop family labor systems were comparatively more efficient and profitable for

employers than wage labor was, even if they entailed specific contradictions, abandoning these forms of labor appropriation appears, at first
sight, paradoxical.

Many histories written of Latin American coffee economies end either
with the first (1890s) or the second coffee crisis.[55] Other authors have
taken their studies up to the 1970s or even the 1980s.[56] As I have indicated
above, combined cash and food-crop systems allowed coffee growers to
withstand price slumps quite successfully. Market and price fluctuations,
by contrast, had much more direct repercussions for the survival of coffee
monocultures. Coffee cycles in particular countries, therefore, also depended to some extent on the systems of labor exploitation adopted.

The colonato system predominated on São Paulo coffee plantations
well into the 1960s, when seasonal wage labor gradually began to replace
the colonos, owing to political circumstances.[57] Also in the 1960s, and as
an indirect consequence of the 1957–62 overproduction crisis which gave
rise to new state intervention in the coffee economy, the coffee peasantries
of Colombia and the Venezuelan Cordillera Central experienced significant change. The state began to intervene more systematically in the coffee
economies of these countries, through credit policies and by furthering
technical innovations very much inspired by the modernization philoso-
phy of the times propagated by international development agencies.[58] In
the context of more intensive competition for world market shares and the
diversification of the respective economies, state policies aimed at improving competitiveness by raising the productivity of land while reducing production. But, whereas in Brazil state intervention in the form of exchange
policy and attempts at raising land productivity through technical innovations did not affect production relations, in Venezuela official coffee policy
seems to have resulted in a transformation of the traditional coffee peasantry. Large family farms remained stable, but through fragmentation the
number of small farms rose at the expense of middle-sized farms. Increasingly, some members of these small family farms, among whom technical
innovations found little acceptance, pursued wage work off the farm,
which affected farming strategies and viability in turn.[59] In Colombia by
1970 government programs to raise productivity of land with the aid of
more intensive cultivation techniques in regions especially appropriate for
coffee growing, to restrict overall coffee production, and to further agricultural diversification appear to have had a similar effect. They led to an
increase in small, low-output farms in marginal areas; family members of
other small producers became seasonal wage laborers, another group of
coffee smallholders was transformed into commercial family farms; and in
the more dynamic regions coffee production became more concentrated.[60]
It remained, nonetheless, uncertain at the time whether the marked de-

cline in the traditional coffee peasantry meant its total eclipse. Palacios attributed the earlier success of Colombia's peasant-based coffee economy to the country's "liberal model of development" and its protagonists, the coffee bourgeoisie. He does not seem to realize that it was the peasant producers who made this possible.[61]

State coffee policy in the 1950s and early 1960s not only differed between São Paulo and Colombia or Venezuela. Its impact was also distinct. By contrast with the prewar period, when state coffee price support prevailed, during the 1950s foreign exchange policy (what was disparagingly called "exchange confiscation" of coffee earnings) in support of import substitution industrialization assumed a central role in Brazil. Nonetheless, as I have shown elsewhere, São Paulo coffee planters were able to protect their interests quite effectively against excessive encroachments by the state.[62] Attempts at improving coffee quality to make it more competitive were timid for the time and had no effect on the production structure of coffee. The forces of change came somewhat later, from class conflict. The situation in Colombia and Venezuela seems to have been the reverse. It was precisely state policy, designed to raise coffee productivity if not production, which had a lasting effect — the disintegration of the traditional coffee peasantry. This was so because the coffee peasantry lacked the power and the means to resist. Instead, a "modern" production structure progressively took its place. Thus the distinct structures of domination in the respective coffee economies, coupled with the organization of coffee production itself, determined the impact state coffee policy would have. In Colombia and Venezuela the traditional coffee peasantries were unable to withstand state intervention favoring powerful merchant interests. In contrast, São Paulo coffee planters held onto the colonato system until challenges to their unlimited traditional power by the landless defeated its original purpose.

In São Paulo casual or day wage labor replaced the colonos in the 1960s in response to the enactment, in 1963, of labor legislation which granted rural workers the benefits industrial labor already enjoyed, foremost among them job security and indemnity for dismissal. The Rural Labor Statute of 1963 was, however, the outcome of progressive political polarization over the agrarian question in the late 1950s and early 1960s. Until then landowners, through their representatives in Congress, had succeeded in vetoing any attempt to extend protective legislation to rural workers. When the clamor for land reform gained momentum, however, the Labor Statute seemed the lesser of two evils and a palliative to contain growing rural unrest. When the military government which took power in the 1964 coup did not abolish the statute as landowners demanded, planters used a legal loophole and replaced resident colonos, as far as coffee cultivation allowed, with *volantes* (casual or day labor) who were not entitled to job security and indemnification or severance pay. It was these measures which landowners objected to most, for they curtailed the absolute freedom to hire and fire at will that they had long enjoyed.[63]

These transformation in production systems, in turn, undermined the coffee workers' family structure and their ability to grow food. In Boconó in Venezuela, and in the Colombian case as well, wage work by family members outside the farm introduced conflicting individual interests, not unlike what happened with São Paulo seasonal workers.[64] And technical change was introduced in coffee cultivation in São Paulo only in the 1970s, when planters became disenchanted with the low productivity of casual wage labor. Until then, labor demand for coffee cultivation remained high. Therefore, a significant number of colonos became resident wage workers, but they were now denied self-provisioning rights because food crops could not be discounted from the legal minimum wage. Moreover, planters attempted to deny them their "rights" whenever they could. Their families were transformed into a pool of resident day laborers deprived of any legal protection. As regards intrafamiliar relationships, under the colonato extrafamilial economic imperatives put a premium on a corporate labor organization, which was reinforced by a family morality that encouraged cooperation among family members and sustained the husband/father's authority within it. Individualized wage work posed new contradictions. It assumed the pooling of resources within the family by paying an individual wage well below the cost of reproduction of the family's members as individuals. On the other hand, individual interests pull the family apart. The consequences have been multiple, namely growing intrafamiliar tensions, women's proverbial double burden, and men's demoralization at the loss of part of the authority they had hitherto enjoyed. Women gained little from these changes but increasingly became the target of much of men's frustration.

Unfortunately but revealingly, none of the studies I have used for this comparison offer any insights into laborers' family organization, the authority structures obtaining within the household unit, the sexual division of labor, or gender relations. Women, and for that matter their children, are nowhere to be seen.

Conclusion

It is this general invisibility of the family and gender relations and the neglect of self-provisioning in the history of Latin American coffee economies that no doubt have constituted one of the main obstacles for properly understanding coffee planters' and/or merchants' longstanding success in weathering often very adverse market conditions precisely by holding on to the family. In these times of economic recession and insistent calls for the regeneration of the family to assume the functions of the faltering welfare state, it might be expected that future histories and future historians of Latin American agricultural change will also be more sensitive to the virtues of the institution of the family and the particular costs it entails, especially for women.

Notes

1. Marco Palacios, *Coffee in Colombia, 1850–1970: An Economic, Social, and Political History* (Cambridge, 1980); Laird W. Bergad, *Coffee and the Growth of Agrarian Capitalism in Nineteenth-Century Puerto Rico* (Princeton, 1983); William Roseberry, *Coffee and Capitalism in the Venezuelan Andes* (Austin, 1983); Ciro F. Santana Cardoso, "Historia económica del café en Centroamérica (Siglo XIX): estudio comparativo," *Estudios Sociales Centroamericanos* 4 (1975): 9–55; J. Castellanos Cambranes, *Coffee and Peasants: The Origins of the Modern Plantation Economy in Guatemala, 1853–1897* (Guatemala, 1985); José de Souza Martins, *O cativeiro da terra* (São Paulo, 1979); A. L. Duarte Lanna, *A transformacão do Trabalho: a passagem para o trabalho livre na Zona da Mata Mineira, 1870–1920* (Campinas, 1988); Verena Stolcke, *Coffee Planters, Workers, and Wives: Class Conflict and Gender Relations on São Paulo Plantations, 1850–1980* (London, 1988); F. Pérez de la Riva, *El café: historia de su cultivo y explotación en Cuba* (Havana, 1944).

2. A few relevant studies are Louise Tilly and Joan W. Scott, *Women, Work, and the Family* (New York, 1978); Carmen Diana Deere and Alain de Janvry, "Demographic and Social Differentiation among Northern Peruvian Peasants," *Journal of Peasant Studies* 8 (1981); Kate Young, "Formas de apropiación y la división sexual del trabajo: Un estudio de caso de Oaxaca, México," in Magdalena León, ed., *Debate sobre la mujer en América Latina y el Caribe*, vol. 2, (Bogotá, 1982); Veronica Bennholdt-Thomsen, *Bauern in Mexico: Zwischen Subsistenz- und Warenproduktion* (Frankfurt, 1982); also Roseberry, *Coffee and Capitalism*.

3. See, for instance, Thomas H. Holloway, *Immigrants on the Land: Coffee and Society in São Paulo, 1886–1934* (Chapel Hill, 1980).

4. Stolcke, *Coffee Planters, Workers, and Wives*, 347.

5. T. L. Norris, "A *Colono* System and Its Relation to Seasonal Labor Problems on a Costa Rican *Hacienda*," *Rural Sociology* 18 (1953); T. L. Norris and P. C. Morrison, "Some Aspects of Life on a Large Costa Rican Coffee *Finca*," *Papers of the Michigan Academy of Science, Arts, and Letters* 38 (1953). The Cuban coffee colonato, by contrast, should not be confused with the colonato system developed by large São Paulo coffee growers. In Cuba coffee was introduced in the eighteenth century, expanded early in the following century, and began to decline thereafter.

Coffee was usually grown on a small scale, largely for domestic consumption, sugar cane and tobacco being the main export crops. As Pérez de la Riva suggests, the colonato was introduced in Cuba at a time of agricultural decadence on account of declining prices and scarcity of labor after abolition. Under these circumstances, sugar cane and coffee planters divided their properties, engaging colonos to cultivate plots of land, the produce of which they handed over to the landowner, who paid them either a preestablished percentage of the returns or a share of the processed product. In the case of coffee, by contrast with sugar cane, hiring the so-called colonato led to neglect of coffee groves and aggravated the decline in production. It is not clear, however, why the coffee colonos did not respond to the incentive motive. In the early twentieth century a variety of colonato arrangements prevailed in coffee, ranging from sharecropping to tenancy agreements. In the older coffee regions colonos were on occasion entitled to self-provisioning. On the whole, the condition of colonos was precarious and the coffee produced was of low quality. Because the Cuban colonato covered a variety of sharecropping arrangements adopted at a time of low profits, the outcome was quite different from that of the São Paulo colonato, which was designed to overcome underproduction and neglect of coffee trees and turned out to be an extraordinarily efficient form of labor exploitation once a free labor market had been created. Pérez de la Riva, El café, 60ff, 85ff, 219ff.

6. See Stolcke, Coffee Planters, Workers, and Wives, chaps. 4 and 5.

7. Boris Fausto, "Expansão do café e política cafeeira," in O Brasil Republicano, vol. 3, pt. 1, Estructura de poder e economia, 1889–1930 (São Paulo, 1975), 196–97.

8. Emilia Viotti da Costa, "Política de terras no Brasil e nos Estados Unidos," in Da Monarquia a República: momentos decisivos (São Paulo, 1977). Liberals opposed to the landowning interests opposed this law, arguing for the donation of land to immigrants as an incentive to attract foreign settlers to "civilize" the country. José de Souza Martins, A imigracão e a crise do Brasil agrario (São Paulo, 1973), 51–54.

9. The conventional image of slave owners as preferring male slaves is being revised by recent studies which suggest the extensive use of slave women for the cultivation of crops such as sugar cane in Bahia or coffee in the Paraíba Valley. Thus it may be that the imbalance in the sex ratio of slaves was due not to the nature of demand but to that of supply. Stuart Schwartz, Sugar Plantations in the Formation of Brazilian Society: Bahia, 1550–1835 (Cambridge, 1985), 357. J. B. Moore, Parliamentary Papers, House of Commons and House of Lords, Select Committee on the Slave Trade, 1847–48, 22:322, 436.

10. Duarte Lanna, A transformação do trabalho.

11. The following discussion is based on Palacios, El café.

12. Ibid., 82.

13. Roseberry, Coffee and Capitalism; Bergad, Coffee and the Growth of Agrarian Capitalism.

14. Different criteria can, however, be used to assess the efficiency of a productive sector, its resilience to external constraints, its productivity and/or the returns to the productive effort made. Roseberry chose productivity. If he had focused on

the range of crops and the use of family labor he would have been able to shed more light on why, despite declining prices and productivity, the peasantry did not collapse.

15. Bergad, *Coffee and the Growth of Agrarian Capitalism.*

16. Ibid., 204ff.

17. Santana Cardoso, "Historia económica del café"; Castellanos Cambranes, *Coffee and Peasants.*

18. Norris, "A *Colono* System."

19. Santana Cardoso, "Historia económica del café."

20. Ibid., 28.

21. Ibid., 30.

22. Tom Brass, "Free and Unfree Rural Labor in Puerto Rico during the Nineteenth Century," *Journal of Latin American Studies* 18 (1986). The interpretation of productive relations in coffee in nineteenth-century Puerto Rico, and the existence or absence of a free labor market, led to an exchange between Bergad and Brass. See Bergad, "Coffee and Rural Proletarianization in Puerto Rico, 1840–1898," *Journal of Latin American Studies* (hereafter *JLAS*) 15 (1983): 83–116; Brass, "Coffee and Rural Proletarianization: A Comment on Bergad," *JLAS* 16 (1984): 143–52; Bergad, "On Comparative History: A Reply to Tom Brass," *JLAS* 16 (1984): 153–56; and Brass, "Free and Unfree Labor."

23. Brass, "Free and Unfree Rural Labor," 153.

24. Norris, "A *Colono* System," 378.

25. Ibid.

26. Stolcke, *Coffee Planters, Workers, and Wives*, chap. 1.

27. *Journal of Peasant Studies*, Special Issue on *Sharecroppers and Sharecropping*, 10 (1983).

28. Alfred Marshall, *Principles of Economics* (London, various editions); S. N. S. Cheung, *The Theory of Share Tenancy* (Chicago, 1969); Thomas H. Holloway, "The Coffee Colono in São Paulo, Brazil: Migration and Mobility, 1880–1930," in Kenneth Duncan and Ian Rutledge, eds., *Land and Labour in Latin America* (Cambridge, 1977).

29. Duarte Lanna, *A transformação do trabalho*, whose interpretation of sharecropping on Minas coffee estates not only fails to acknowledge the extensive literature on sharecropping but, in addition, contradicts itself by trying to demonstrate, on the one hand, that national labor was abundant in contrast to São Paulo but, on the other, that sharecropping was a means to recruit labor.

30. Stolcke, *Coffee Planters, Workers, and Wives*, chap. 1.

31. Bergad, "On Comparative History," 153.

32. Stolcke, *Coffee Planters, Workers, and Wives*, chap. 1.

33. See, for example, Bergad, *Coffee and the Growth of Agrarian Capitalism.*

34. Duarte Lanna, *A transformação do trabalho.*

35. Stolcke, *Coffee Planters, Workers, and Wives*, 13–14.

36. Santana Cardoso, "Historia económica del café."

37. Palacios, *El café*, 82.

38. K. Kaerger, *Brasilianische Wirtschaftsbilder, Erlebnisse und Forschungen* (Berlin, 1892), 335.

39. Palacios, *El café*, who similarly shows that the plot was a source of tension between arrendatarios and hacendados because laborers preferred to work on their own plot rather than for the hacienda. Efforts to secure a better and/or larger plot generated considerable mobility of labor. In the case of São Paulo, labor mobility was also high due to differences in self-provisioning rights and quality of soil between the older and newer coffee regions.

40. Quoted in Charles Bergquist, "Colombia" (unpublished paper, 1982).

41. Stolcke, *Coffee Planters, Workers, and Wives*, 34–36.

42. Palacios, *El café*, 82.

43. Norris, "A *Colono* System," 377; Antonio Manuel Arce, "Rational Introduction of Technology on a Costa Rican Coffee Hacienda: Sociological Implications" (Ph. diss., Michigan State University, 1959).

44. Bergad, *Coffee and the Growth of Agrarian Capitalism*; Santana Cardoso, "Historia económica del café."

45. Bergad, *Coffee and the Growth of Agrarian Capitalism*.

46. Ibid., 222. Bergad's suggestion that São Paulo colonos enjoyed significant opportunities for social mobility (based on Holloway, *Immigrants on the Land*) is debatable, as I have argued; see Stolcke, *Coffee Planters, Workers, and Wives*, 36–43. In a recent article, Font suggests not only that São Paulo colonos were able to accumulate but that this led to the fragmentation of the coffee sector and the loss of hegemony by the traditional large coffee planters as early as the 1920s due to the emergence of a coffee peasantry of immigrant origin and its growing share in production. Mauricio A. Font, "Coffee Planters, Politics, and Development in Brazil," *Latin American Research Review* 22 (1987). Yet the size of this peasantry and its coffee production is still open to dispute. For a commentary and debate on Font's article, see Joseph Love, "Of Planters, Politics, and Development"; Stolcke, "Coffee Planters, Politics, and Development in Brazil"; and Font, "Perspectives on Social Change and Development in São Paulo: A reply," *Latin American Research Review* 24 (1989).

47. Castellanos Cambranes, *Coffee and Peasants*, 101 and 106.

48. Ibid., 321.

49. Santana Cardoso, "Historia económica del café," 29–30.

50. Castellanos Cambranes, *Coffee and Peasants*, 317–18.

51. Santana Cardoso, "Historia económica del café," graph no. 3.

52. Castellanos Cambranes, *Coffee and Peasants*, 311.

53. Ibid., 314.

54. See also M. Schmolz-Haberlein, "Sklaverei im 'wahren Frieden' — Zur verstarkten Rekrutierung der indigenen Arbeitskraft im Guatemala der 1930er Jahre. Ursachen und Auswirkungen am Beispiel der Region Alta Verapaz" (Master's thesis, Universitat Augsburg, 1993).

55. Santana Cardoso, "Historia económica del café"; Castallanos Cambranes, *Coffee and Peasants*; Bergad, *Coffee and the Growth of Agrarian Capitalism*; Holloway, *Immigrants on the Land*.

56. Roseberry, *Coffee and Capitalism*; Palacios, *El café*; Stolcke, *Coffee Planters, Workers, and Wives*.

57. Stolcke, *Coffee Planters, Workers, and Wives*, chap. 3.

58. Palacios, *El café*, chap. 11; Roseberry, *Coffee and Capitalism*, chap. 6.

59. Roseberry, *Coffee and Capitalism*, 171ff.

60. Palacios, *El café*, 241–47.

61. Ibid., 256.

62. Stolcke, *Coffee Planters, Workers, and Wives*, 77ff.

63. Ibid., chap. 3.

64. Roseberry, *Coffee and Capitalism*, 180. Palacios does not discuss the effects of wage work on the peasant family or on gender relations. For more details on family change and gender hierarchy, see Stolcke, *Coffee Planters, Workers, and Wives*, chaps. 4 and 5.

Four

Coffee and the Rise of Commercial Agriculture in Puerto Rico's Highlands: The Occupation and Loss of Land in Guaonico and Roncador (Utuado), 1833–1900

FERNANDO PICÓ

FROM THE SIXTEENTH to the eighteenth centuries, there were repeated attempts to spur the development of an export-oriented agriculture in Puerto Rico. Nonetheless, the export economy did not take hold, in a continuous and developed fashion, before the second half of the eighteenth century. In the commercial agriculture of that period, coffee cultivation came to hold a position second only to sugar cane.

The Arabian coffee shrub (*arábigo*) was introduced in Puerto Rico in 1736, and Governor Miguel de Muesas offered fiscal incentives for its cultivation in 1768.[1] However, from the decade of the 1770s to the early 1820s, coffee was planted in unpropitious soils in the warmer areas along the coast, where it competed directly with sugar cane, which was better suited for the coastal climate and soils. After 1837, coffee declined in importance while sugar cane cornered the available financing, workers, and political favors. Only after 1855 did coffee grow in importance again, but now in the central mountainous area, whose clay soils and fresher climate favored the Arabian variety of coffee.

Some peculiarities of coffee cultivation in Puerto Rico are explained by the long-lasting preference for the Arabian variety. The higher and cooler terrain yielded the best harvests. Coffee was cultivated under the shade of tall, leafy trees. The absence of chemical fertilizers led to dependence on the layers of vegetal compost in the coffee groves. As a rule, the Arabian coffee shrub took five years of growth before producing its first harvest, which meant that the coffee grower needed access to sufficient credit to develop his land during that period of time and turned to fast-growing staples and cattle raising to complement his coffee plantings.

Moreover, coffee required access to sources of water and water tanks for the washing and dehusking of the grain. In the mid nineteenth century, the dehusking machines were relatively cheap, frequently hand made by the coffee growers themselves. Coffee was dried on canvas or on pavements called *gláciles*. Later in the century, the more prosperous farmers availed themselves of heavy drawers which slid on rails, and which could easily be pulled back to shelter when the frequent and sudden mountain rain squalls descended. After drying, coffee was winnowed in hollowed-out mango trunks called *pilones*.

For most of its history as one of the principal Puerto Rican export crops, coffee was cultivated on small units called *estancias* in nineteenth-century records, but in popular parlance *fincas*, translated here as *farms*. But in each coffee municipality and in certain *barrios* (political subdivisions of the municipality), larger units became important, and these, by analogy with the sugar-producing ones, were called *haciendas*. By the end of the nineteenth century, the volume of hacienda coffee production ranged between 30 and 40 percent of the total crop of each principal coffee-growing municipality.[2] Actually, haciendas had an even greater role in the coffee economy, because many of the small coffee farmers delivered their unprocessed coffee to them in payment of debts and crop advances. With sufficient human and material resources for the washing, husking, and winnowing, better access to financing, and contacts with exporters on the coast, the haciendas concentrated in their hands the processing of the coffee for sale.

The Land

After the sixteenth-century conquest the process of settlement of the central mountain range of Puerto Rico was exceedingly slow. The demographic collapse of the sixteenth and seventeenth centuries and the distribution of land in large units (*hatos*), passed undivided from one generation to another, hindered the development of formal settlements in the interior of the island. From 1734, when residents of Arecibo bought the Otoao hato and began to settle it, the rate of settlement in the interior accelerated. But it was not until the 1820s that many Puerto Ricans, displaced by the development of sugar cane on the coastal plains, set out for the mountains. The appropriation of mountain lands took several forms. In some cases, the old hatos subsisted well into the nineteenth century, and in others their division resulted in the creation of the nuclei of future haciendas. In the majority of known cases, however, the hatos were subdivided among multiple heirs, who often enough sold their portions to immigrants from the coast or from outside Puerto Rico.

With the division of hatos, as well as municipal commons and formerly untitled crown lands, some settlers succeeded in obtaining title to their lands. In the first half of the nineteenth century, these family-owned lands were dedicated both to cattle raising and subsistence crops, but they also occasionally entered the market with tobacco, coffee, or other crops. These lands were frequently impoverished by rapid deforestation and imprudent agricultural practices, or they were subdivided among numerous heirs. Thus many of the original *estancias* or farms gave rise to widespread *minifundia* in the mountain area.

Spontaneous settlements in crown lands were the object of titling efforts in the 1820s and 1830s. The titling authorities required proof of the poverty and need of the claimants. In a shift in policy in the second half of the nineteenth century, however, the government favored with titles those who could offer some guarantee that the land would be cultivated. Thus many families lost possession of the land because they could not afford the expense of securing title, or they could not offer sufficient guarantees for cultivation of the land they occupied. By the 1880s, most crown lands had been distributed. The government tried to review the grants, to obtain the return of those lands which had not been improved. But by the end of Spanish rule in Puerto Rico (1898), few of the unimproved lands had been returned, and the new government did not pursue their devolution.

In the highlands, farms changed hands rapidly as coffee cultivation intensified. With the breakup of properties among multiple heirs and the sale of plots came the proliferation of minifundia. Land also became concentrated in the hands of hacienda owners who combined adjoining farms. Debts to ecclesiastical institutions or to the public treasury also brought about dispossession and land sales. But it was especially the debts to merchants and *hacendados* that led to forced sales of land by heirs.

Thus the explanation for the frequent collapse of small and middle-sized farms often rests on an examination of the prevailing credit system. Since merchants extended goods and cash on credit to enable the coffee farmers to develop the land during the several years preceding the first harvest, coffee growers delivered their harvests to their creditors in payment of their debts. Thus merchants reaped a double profit: on their sales to growers and the accumulated interest on the farmers' accounts as well as on the price at which they received the farmers' coffee, which they then resold at a profit to the exporters on the coast. This double burden on their income exposed the coffee growers to situations of high risk, so that a bad harvest, an erratic pattern of consumption, or a family crisis, such as the death of the head of the household with the attendant medical, burial, and legal costs, could force a coffee farm into foreclosure proceedings or at least force the sale of a substantial portion of the land to pay off debts to merchants.[3]

These economic explanations (the expanding haciendas' need for land and labor and the merchants' system of financing) should be complemented with the study of other economic and noneconomic factors. In this essay, I will attempt to present a comprehensive explanation for changes in land tenure in one area of the largest nineteenth-century coffee-growing municipality, Utuado. I have examined all of the landholding families of the barrios of Guaonico and Roncador and traced their origins and fortunes throughout the nineteenth century. I am attempting to come to some conclusions, applicable to the whole group of non-hacienda coffee farmers, which may be useful in developing a hypothesis as to the causes of such changes elsewhere in the coffee regions of Puerto Rico.

The Loss of Land in Guaonico-Roncador, 1833–1900

Río Guaonico and Quebrada Roncador merge before the enlarged Río Guaonico flows into the Río Grande on its way to the city of Utuado. The two bodies of water gave their name to the mountainous barrios of Guaonico and Roncador. It was along their banks in the late eighteenth century that the first Puerto Rican families who settled the area planted their subsistence crops and raised modest herds of cattle. In the late 1820s and early 1830s, the two barrios were often merged in the fiscal lists as Guaonico-Roncador. By 1833 there were twenty-two heads of family paying duties for their land in the area.[4] Subsequent development resulted in a more dense settlement of Roncador, where land was particularly apt for coffee cultivation. In 1867 Guaonico had twenty-seven farms and Roncador forty-seven; by 1900, however, there were only eighteen and twenty-two farm units, respectively.[5] Thus the concentration of agricultural lands in fewer hands was more pronounced in Roncador than in Guaonico.

If one closely examines the list of landholders for both barrios prepared in 1900, one can identify five successive stages of land occupation and cultivation in nineteenth-century Guaonico and Roncador. The names of the landholders of 1900 have a story to tell; they are like an archaeologist's strata, revealing the successive changes in the composition of the barrio's landowners. The thirty-four different surnames of the 1900 list, belonging to forty landowners, evoke the five stages in the agricultural evolution of the barrios: (1) the subsistence agriculture and cattle raising of the first wave of Puerto Rican settlers, who arrived in the second half of the eighteenth and early decades of the nineteenth centuries; (2) the modest coffee farms of mid-nineteenth-century Utuadeños, who came from other parts of the municipality upon obtaining land grants or buying land from previous owners; (3) the more ambitious coffee farms of Puerto Ricans who came from other parts of the island in the 1860s and 1870s and bought land in the barrios; (4) the coffee farms of Spanish immigrants, some of whom lived in the city of Utuado and had concurrent business activities there; and (5) the extensive landholdings of commercial houses, which invested in land during the end-of-century coffee boom or held foreclosed farms and were waiting for a favorable opportunity to sell them at a profit.

Let us examine the fortunes of each of the landholding groups, using the 1833 land tax list, the oldest complete *padrón de terrenos* extant, as a starting point. The twenty-two landholders of Guaonico-Roncador paying land duties in 1833 declared twelve surnames among them. Family reconstructions done with the help of the household-by-household census of 1828[6] as well as parish records allow us to establish the fact that all of the tax-paying families of 1833, and even those who are known to have been residing in the area and obtained title to their land in subsequent decades, were born in Puerto Rico and were related to each other either by descent or by marriage. Family relationships cut across official racial classifications and at that time bore no rigid relation to the size of land holdings. But there was a developing pattern of endogamous marriages, which the high number of young people of marriageable age and the small number of families in the area made inevitable.

The biggest problem besetting the estancia owners of Guaonico in the 1820s was that of communications. To shorten their traveling distance to town, inhabitants of Guaonico had taken to cutting across the lands of Cristóbal de Montalvo, a large landowner in the neighboring barrio of Salto Arriba. This practice resulted in litigation, which served to clear rights of way in the area.[7]

Montalvo had not objected to the earlier traffic, and one can guess the reason: of the few early-nineteenth-century families living in Guaonico most of the heads of household were either his first or second cousins, or were related by marriage. But by the 1820s the situation had begun to change, precipitating the need to clarify rights of way. Montalvo was selling his lands in Salto Arriba, and settlers from other parts of the municipality were obtaining land grants in Guaonico and hauling logs to town.

The first coffee boom, which was modest locally,[8] had encouraged some Utuadeños to seek land in the mountains, away from the old trails and river beds, and to obtain title to it. Grants made in the area accelerated the clearing of the land and reduced the possibilities for squatters of obtaining title.[9] Thus by the mid-1840s land in Guaonico and Roncador had begun to be commercialized. One large family of squatters, headed by Feliciano Maldonado, was dispossessed as a result of a suit which established that it had no title to its holdings.[10] By mid-century, twenty-two sons of the landowners of 1833 in Guaonico and Roncador had to register as day laborers because they did not own land.[11] In some cases, they evaded subsequent application of Governor Pezuela's edict on day laborers by returning to live on their families' lands. But for others, there was no return: the land had already been sold or subdivided among numerous heirs.

Dispossession for these sons of the 1833 landowners meant the loss of access to public lands, which but a generation earlier had seemed unlimited. The younger generation in Guaonico and Roncador lacked the means, both economic and political, to begin the process of soliciting, measuring, and obtaining title to a land grant. Persons from other parts of the municipality or from elsewhere, interested in coffee cultivation and with readier access to town officials and cash to pay for the paperwork, had obtained title to the available land. The old landowners, who had been paying tax for relatively modest amounts of land, had to bequeath small holdings to their heirs.

By 1851, Guaonico had 36.5 *cuerdas* under coffee cultivation and Roncador 30; in both cases the number of cuerdas dedicated to plantains and rice was greater.[12] But the following decades saw the number of cuerdas titled and the number of landowners in the area rise (see Table 4.1).

The increase in the number of tax-paying cuerdas registered between 1833 and 1867 reflects the distribution of crown lands among applicants in the middle decades of the century. Very little is added to the total

TABLE 4.1

Landownership in Guaonico and Roncador, 1833, 1867, 1900

Year	Total cuerdas[a] paying land tax	Number of landowners	Number of different surnames among owners
1833	2370	22	12
1867	4719	73	38
1900	4778	40	34

Source: Land tax lists.

[a]One cuerda = .97 acre.

between 1867 and 1900, but the number of landowners shrinks dramatically. As for the surnames of landowners, they more than triple in number between 1833 and 1867 with the inflow of recipients of land grants, but between 1867 and 1900 they decline at a much more modest rate than the number of landowners. The proportion of surnames to landowners is much closer to 1:1 in 1900 than in 1833, reflecting the dissolution of the family ties that once encompassed the barrios.

The families of earlier settlers had by no means been entirely displaced by 1867. Ten of the twelve surnames of the 1833 list still appeared in 1867. But in the next three decades, when coffee planting intensified and became the area's main crop and the value of land grew apace, surnames of the earlier settlers disappeared from the ranks of landowners.

Thus only two landowners among the forty in the 1900 tax list are patrilineally descended from those listed in 1833: Segundo Arza and Manuel Maldonado. When one examines the holdings of the Maldonado and Arza family groups in the different fiscal lists, the change in the composition of the landholders in Guaonico and Roncador is even more evident. Six Maldonados held 975 cuerdas in 1833, and ten Maldonados 434 cuerdas in 1867; by 1900 the only one appearing, Manuel, had 39 cuerdas. On the other hand, two Arza households, one of which had thirteen children and the other eighteen, had between the two of them 150 cuerdas in 1833. In 1867 only one Arza, Segundo, appeared as a landholder, and he had 250 cuerdas. He was the same one who reappeared in 1900 with 95 cuerdas.

It is evident that the descendants of the first group of settlers did not profit from the coffee boom period, but rather lost their estancias in Guaonico and Roncador. Was the second wave of landowners more successful? Among the seventy-three landowners in the 1867 tax list there are thirty-eight different surnames that had not appeared in the 1833 *padrón*. One can readily identify among them thirty-three members of twenty-one *criollo* (Puerto Rican–born) families who had been living in other parts of Utuado before coming to own land in Guaonico and Roncador. Some had obtained their land through crown grants, others had purchased it, and still others, like Juan del Carmen Avilés,[13] had married into landholding families. In 1867 the Utuadeño newcomers to the two barrios held the majority of the tax-paying land, but only a portion of their holdings was cultivated.[14] In the transactions recorded in the notarial records, one can note that their principal agricultural activity was coffee cultivation, and that they relied heavily on financing provided by the town merchants to develop their land and sustain themselves during the years before their coffee shrubs came into production.

Although only two patrilineal descendants of the ten landholding families of 1833 who reappear in the 1867 padrón survived as landowners until 1900, fifteen of the forty landowners in the 1900 padrón belong to Utuadeño families who had settled in Guaonico and Roncador since the 1830s. More important, these fifteen owners, with thirteen surnames among them, account for 1,789 cuerdas, or 36.45 percent of the land in the 1900 list. Thus one can conclude that the second wave of settlers of Guaonico and Roncador, constituted by Utuadeños from other areas of the municipality, was more successful in holding on to their land throughout the coffee boom period than the first occupants of the land. Twelve out of the twenty-one new Utuadeño surnames of 1867 are still represented in the 1900 list. With the three other Utuadeño families that had obtained land in the barrios after 1867, they account for a substantial portion of the land.

Let us now look at a third group of landowners who appear in the 1900 list. They are members of criollo families who came to Guaonico and Roncador from other parts of Puerto Rico in the second half of the nineteenth century. By the 1894 *catastro* one can see that coffee is their principal agricultural activity.[15] In 1900, fifteen landowners from Mayaguez, San Germán, Adjuntas, and other municipalities account for 1,034 cuerdas (21.06 percent of the land): Genaro Nazario, Francisco Beauchamp (from Mayaguez), the Jiménez brothers (from Mayaguez), José Concepción Rosado, Miguel Pérez Gómez, Juan Toro (from San Germán), and Manuel Sepúlveda (from Adjuntas) account collectively for 834 cuerdas (17.45 percent of the total). Particularly successful among them, in terms of land held, were the sons of Manuel Antonio Jiménez, a Mayaguczano who combined coffee cultivation with loans to his neighbors and built up a large farm, which by 1900 was subdivided among his heirs. Juan Toro had 168 cuerdas, but the rest held portions of less than 100 cuerdas.

Was this criollo group in the process of displacing the Utuadeños at the time of the coffee boom? Aside from the Jiménez family there is little evidence of sustained aggrandizement at the expense of neighbors. Moreover, these criollos, most of them born in the coffee-rich western part of the island, were slow to enter into relationships with neighboring Utuadeño farmers. The godparents chosen in the 1890s by the Jiménez, Beauchamp, Toro, and Sepúlveda families for their children did not come from neighboring Utuadeño families, but from their own kin in Mayaguez, Las Marías, and clsewhere. Coffee cultivation had rooted them in Guaonico and Roncador, but it would take them some time to create permanent links with the barrios.

A fourth group of landowners in the 1900 padrón consisted of immigrants from Spain. There were five of them, owning 889 cuerdas (18.11 percent of the land): Jaime Aimery, Mariano Artau, Pedro Ripoll, Jaime

Sureda, and Guillermo Bernard. To trace their itinerary is to retell the experience of countless other immigrants to the highlands in the last third of the nineteenth century:[16] the impoverished and demographically over-burdened native municipalities in the Balearic Islands, Catalonia, Canary Islands, Cantabria and Asturias; the trip to the New World financed, per-haps, by some distant relative and paid for with years of quasi-indentured labor as foreman, store attendant, assistant, factor, or legal representa-tive;[17] the marriage to some modest local heiress; the tenacity in planting coffee, supervising hired hands, overseeing the harvest; the loans to neigh-bors, thrift in consumption, and patient garnering of neighboring plots; the two-story house, built to accommodate the harvest; the patience, the suffering, the plodding progress; the exceptional successes, the neighbors' envy, the reluctance to speak out about local issues; the anticlericalism, nurtured at home, reflecting the homeland's tensions; the nephew coming from Spain; the temptation to liquidate holdings and return home; the si-lent decision to stay where one had put down roots. The stories vary, the pedigrees may be more exalted or humble, the years spent behind the counter of a small store may have been many more than those dedicated to agriculture, but the dynamics of the process were common. Among the Spaniards listed in the 1900 padrón, a Balearic named Sureda who was a factor for an Arecibo commercial house in the 1880s struck out on his own, succeeded, and served a term as justice of the peace.[18] The land in Roncador represented an investment, but his main interest remained commerce. Artau was a Catalán businessman. Ripoll, from Mallorca, became a coffee farmer, and his descendants still occupy land in the sec-tion of Guaonico bordering on Adjuntas.[19] Of Aimery and Bernard little is known at present.

Still another portion of the land was owned in 1900 by commercial houses: Casanovas y Delgado had 158 cuerdas in Guaonico, and M. Rozas y Cia. had 379. Santoni Hermanos had 525 in Roncador. A total of 1062 cuerdas, or 21.63 percent of the land in the barrios, belonged to these firms. These holdings corresponded to the peak years of the coffee boom, when some commercial houses had decided to invest their profits in land.[20] Usually this land was leased out for short periods to farmers, who had little inducement to make permanent improvements, since in two or three years the lease would expire and chances were that the rent would increase. In subsequent years the commercial houses, pinched by their overcommitments, liquidated their holdings and returned to their tradi-tional economic activities. Perhaps if the boom had continued longer, a greater share of the land might have come into the commercial houses' possession, thus helping transform the organization of coffee production. As it was, the traditional pattern of divesting themselves of the land they acquired by foreclosure proceedings or other methods was reestablished.

The five groups of turn-of-the-century landholders in Guaonico and Roncador described in the foregoing pages thus represent five stages in the appropriation and use of land in the two barrios. The coming of each new group diminished the chances of the foregoing one to obtain additional land and even to retain the family patrimony. In the case of the first settlers, they had titled enough land for their immediate needs and assumed a permanent availability of land for their descendants. The granting of crown lands to Utuadeños from other barrios, however, drastically reduced the possibilities of the earlier settlers' children becoming squatters or obtaining title to land. Thus Pezuela's edict on day laborers caught twenty-two of them without any land, and they had to register and carry a passbook.

In turn, coffee cultivation by the second Utuadeño wave encouraged criollos from other parts of the island to buy land in the territory that was opening up for coffee cultivation. The development of better communications with the coast, access to financing, and availability of labor stimulated the investment in land for coffee farming. And as the price of land rose, and the competition for financing and labor became keener, the second wave of settlers could have been elbowed aside by the newcomers from the rest of the island. But the resilience of these second-wave settlers was great, and many of them were able to pass on their land to their children.

The third wave of settlers, those coming from other parts of the island, had immigrants from Spain following on their heels. Although the criollos were familiar with the techniques of coffee cultivation, the Spaniards had better financial backing, since they often had ties to their countrymen's commercial houses. Besides, as with the cases of Sureda and Artau cited above, they often combined farming with storekeeping or with officeholding. But in Guaonico and Roncador these individuals did not constitute as much of a threat to the landholding pattern of the district as did the commercial houses themselves.

Had the commercial houses come to dominate landholding in the coffee region, the structure of coffee cultivation could have been rationalized along market-oriented lines. But the invasion of 1898, the devastation wrought by the 1899 hurricane, the tumble in world coffee prices, and the new opportunities for sugar in the newly guaranteed American market diverted the merchants' interest away from coffee. Thus most coffee cultivation stayed in the hands of farmers and hacendados who lived on their fincas and hedged their investment in coffee with the cultivation of tobacco, bananas, oranges, and vegetables.

Throughout the second half of the nineteenth century, landholders in Guaonico and Roncador with less than one hundred cuerdas constituted a stable sector but with a changing membership (see Table 4.2). Of the

TABLE 4.2
Structure of Land Tenure in Guaonico and Roncador, 1833–1900

Year	Less than 100 cuerdas		100–199 cuerdas		200–399 cuerdas		More than 400 cuerdas		Total area
	Area	Percentage	Area	Percentage	Area	Percentage	Area	Percentage	
1833	640	27	670	28.3	600	25.3	460	19.4	2,370
1837	441	17.7	700	28.1	600	24.1	750	30.1	2,491
1842	380	15.2	700	27.9	600	23.9	825	32.9	2,505
1848	378	18.5	814	39.9	850	32	—	—	2,042
1850	378	12.7	814	27.4	950	32	825	27.8	2,967
1855	986	21.2	910	19.6	1,150	24.8	1,600	34.4	4,646
1858	1,570	33.2	812	17.2	250	5.3	2,100	44.4	4,732
1866	1,409	29	1,246	25.7	1,600	32.9	600	12.4	4,855
1900	1,261	25.7	620	12.6	1,970	40.1	1,057	21.5	4,908

Sources: Padrones de terrenos in FMU and in Obras Públicas, Propiedad Pública.

landholders with less than one hundred cuerdas, those who experienced the greatest loss of land were the families who had first settled and opened up Guaonico and Roncador. Of these families the records tell us that they shared some characteristics: they titled relatively modest portions of land; they had many children in each household, because they tended to marry early, a practice which the availability of nontitled land encouraged. They were illiterate, as can be seen by the fact that they did not know how to sign (early in the 1870s there was still only one head of household who could write in Roncador). They planted only modest plots of coffee, as can be seen by the agricultural census of 1851. But their land was valuable, not only because it was suitable for coffee planting, but also because, since it was the land first occupied, it was near the Utuado-Adjuntas road and the principal bodies of water. Thus access to transportation and to abundant water supplies enhanced the desirability of the land.

These families of older settlers could not adapt well to the changing economy. They had limited previous experience with coffee cultivation, and they marketed their coffee with the aim of obtaining a modest cash income; coffee was not their principal source of subsistence. They could not keep written accounts, and they became consumers in the commercial establishments of Utuado, purchasing imported goods on credit against the next harvest, but these goods became more expensive with the accumulated interest of their debts. Multiple heirs to shrinking estancias, they wound up selling their plots of land to their creditors or to eager newcomers who paid what then must have seemed good prices (because they were so much higher than their families had paid) for their land.

The families that lost their land in Guaonico and Roncador during the coffee boom decades therefore tended to be the ones that had resided longer in the barrios, had hitherto cultivated only modest plots of coffee, had many children, were headed by illiterates, and had good access to the Utuado-Adjuntas road and to the principal bodies of water. They were dispossessed because the cumulative weight of their disadvantages did not prepare them to adjust to the challenge of an era when there was no longer an open frontier of untitled land to which they or their children could have recourse when their titled land became mortgaged or fragmented into small, individual plots belonging to the many heirs of a deceased couple.

Land Fragmentation in Guaonico and Roncador

Of the landholders of Guaonico and Roncador, this original group was the most vulnerable to losing their land. But why did they actually lose it, at a time when coffee prices were starting to increase and opportunities for credit and marketing had notably improved? From the reconstruction of the family histories of the 1833 land taxpayers, one can gather a fivefold explanation: (1) low productivity of the group's estancias, (2) credit structures, (3) the developing land market, (4) traditional attitudes to land exploitation, and (5) multiple divisions of patrimonial land. Let us consider each of these in turn.

As one can see by the agricultural census of 1851 and by the percentage of land under cultivation in the land tax lists of 1866–67 and 1867–68, most of the land on the traditional estancias was not under cultivation. Members of the household constituted the labor usually employed by the estancias. But family labor, in the precoffee boom period, was not oriented to market production.[21] The family unit was individualistic, varied in numbers and composition from year to year, and often shifted from productive to monetarily nonproductive activities. It seldom engaged in long-range planning. The family labor unit could not easily adapt to an intensive coffee-growing economy. Productivity remained low while consumption of goods in merchants' stores rose, collection of taxes became more persistent, and personal credit was strained.

Credit structures were flexible enough to allow an *estanciero* to plant coffee and wait for the five years before the plot was ready for harvesting. But the flexibility in extending credit from one year to the next presupposed that the creditor would be receiving the coffee crop in payment of the debts and of the accrued interest (usually from 1 to 1.5 percent, computed monthly). The double profit extracted from the estancieros (from imported goods sold on credit, and from buying the harvest at a price fixed by the local merchants) handicapped their earning potential and left them exposed to the hazards of natural disasters.

Increasing coffee prices stimulated the market for land that was appropriate for planting the beans, and especially for land where a portion had already been planted and was about to enter into production. Thus merchants, officeholders, and other persons with some cash to invest stimulated land speculation and put pressure on estancieros to pay off their debts with their land. The unprecedented land prices may have tempted even solvent farmers to sell a portion of their patrimony for what must have looked like good prices.

Traditional attitudes to land exploitation among the families with the earliest documented presence in Guaonico and Roncador not only resulted in the low productivity recorded in the *Censo Agrícola* and the padrones but also precluded property investments and soil conservation practices. Accustomed to a shifting pattern of land use, relocating their *bohíos* as each slash and burn operation opened up a new portion of the mountains, the Utuadeños, even when they titled the land they happened to occupy, did not reflect in their transactions that proprietary attitude of the well-to-do criollo families with a strong sense of lineage attached to land transmission from one generation to the next. Land was gambled off at cockfights, exchanged, parceled off to illegitimate children, sold off in plots to the stranger who came begging for a piece in which to build a bohío, or to the town merchant who wanted to set up a rural outlet. Later, when there was no more untitled land to be had and land had become a commodity, litigations and blood feuds over boundaries developed. But the families of Guaonico and Roncador that entered the coffee boom period with traditional attitudes to the land had little commercial conception of its value and were thus particularly vulnerable to offers to buy it.

The price of land in the two barrios, which had averaged a peso per cuerda in the infrequent sales recorded for the first half of the century, started to increase in the 1860s and rose sharply in the 1870s (see Table 4.3).

In any case, after two generations, the division of land by inheritance

TABLE 4.3
Land Purchases and Prices in Guaonico and Roncador, 1863–1877

	Roncador			Guaonico		
Year	Total sold (cuerdas)	Price (pesos)	Average price	Total sold (cuerdas)	Price (pesos)	Average price
1863	1272	4350	3.41	686	1993	2.9
1868	720	5213	7.24	350	3600	10.28
1873	416	5151	12.38	326	3475	10.65
1877	102	2871	28.14	580	11750	20.25

Source: Protocolos notariales for indicated years.

TABLE 4.4
Landholders, Number of Cuerdas, and Number of Known
Children, Guaonico and Roncador, 1833

Head of household	Cuerdas	Number of known children
Gregorio Arza	50	14
Justo Arza	100	15
Marcelo Arroyo	200	16
Juan Baez	100	10
Juan Colón	100	8
Antonio de Jesús	60	1
Manuel González	30	5
Antonio Maldonado	460	9
Feliciano Maldonado	200	14
Isidoro Maldonado	100	8
María Nieves, widow of Juan Maldonado	170	14
Juan Portalatín Maldonado	40	9
Rafael Maldonado	75	6
Sebastián Maldonado	100	5
Pablo Martín	60	6
Antonio Montalvo	25	8
Felipe Montalvo	60	5
Juan de Montalvo	40	12
Manuel Montalvo Arza	100	10
Manuel Montalvo Martín	70	4
José Raimundo Ramos	30	5
José Rodríguez	200	12
(Totals)	2370	196

Sources: Padrón of 1833 and municipal census of 1828 and ca. 1835 in
FMU, and Utuado's parish registers.

among members of this group quickly reduced titled land and crown grants to minifundia. A list of the 1833 landholders in Guaonico and Roncador, with the number of cuerdas for which each of them paid the land tax and the number of children known to have been born in each household, illustrates the potential division in each generation (see Table 4.4)). Of the 196 children represented in the table, 27 (13.8 percent) are known to have died before the age of sixteen, 97 (48.9 percent) are known to have married in church, one to have had a child out of wedlock, and 20 (10.1 percent) to have died single without issue. Of the remaining 53, several appear as adults in day laborer lists, but their marital status is unknown. The rest are still untraced.

Counting only the known children of the 1833 land-tax payers of Guaonico and Roncador who married or died as single adults, and divid-

ing the 2,370 cuerdas among these 118, the average portion that would
have fallen to them in inheritance was 20 cuerdas. Admittedly, many of
them married members of the same group, thus potentially doubling the
average portion per second-generation household. But not all the 1833
landowners had managed to retain their land by the time of their deaths;
one has to remember that twenty-two of their sons had to register as day
laborers in 1849–50 because they were landless.

Occasionally an effort was made by one of the heirs to reassemble the
patrimony, but it was an uphill, and ultimately futile, effort. Of the sixteen
recorded children of Marcelo Arroyo, ten are known to have survived him
and inherited his land. In his will of May 1854, Arroyo declares that he
owes 180 pesos to the commercial society Casalduc and Nicolau, 37 pesos
to three other persons, and to Don José Salas, whatever his account books
might show.[22] If Arroyo's 250 cuerdas (he had added 50 to the 200 for
which he paid tax in 1833) are valued at 500 pesos, their market value the
year of his death, his known debts, not counting those to Salas, amount to
43 percent of the value of his land.

One of Marcelo Arroyo's sons, Santiago, bought portions of the land
from his siblings. By 1863 he had 50 cuerdas, and by 1868, 125. Like his
father Marcelo, Santiago Arroyo received goods on credit from the successive commercial houses of which Felipe Casalduc was the major partner.
Like his father, Santiago was unable to pay off the debt, which amounted
to 464 pesos, 80 cents, owed to Casalduc, Sandoval and Co. in 1868. His
land had a market value of 1,250 pesos that year; if Santiago Arroyo had
no other debts, he owed 37 percent of the value of his land. But 1868 was a
difficult year for creditors, who felt the pinch of the economic crisis and of
the government's drive to raise and collect taxes. Thus Santiago Arroyo
was forced to mortgage his land. In the 1870s his position did not improve, and with the permission of his creditors (Iglesias, Casalduc, y Her-
mano had succeeded Casalduc, Sandoval), he sold portions of his land to
relatives and neighbors to pay his debts.[23] By the 1890s no Arroyo appeared in the Guaonico land-tax lists.

To sum up, the loss of land in Guaonico and Roncador during the last
third of the nineteenth century was most acute among the families who
had first settled the area. A fivefold explanation of why these families were
particularly vulnerable to forfeiting their patrimony takes into account
the low productivity of their estancias, credit structures, the developing
land market, traditional attitudes to land exploitation, and land divisions
among multiple heirs. Yet the alienation and loss of land by this group led
not to the formation of haciendas but to the aggregation of estancias into
medium-sized coffee farms such as the ones that appear in the Catastro of
the 1890s and the Utuado land tax roster of 1900. Commercial houses are

intermediaries in the process; by pressing for payment of their debts, they induced the landowners to mortgage and to sell, but if they took possession of the land the commercial houses usually sold it quickly.

Much more work needs to be done, of course, before one can identify a clear pattern for the coffee-growing central mountain region. But in Guaonico and Roncador one can see that economic change did affect the tenure of the old subsistence estancias, and that efforts to turn them into coffee farms by the illiterate and inexperienced descendants of the earliest settlers by and large failed. It would be interesting to follow the fortunes of the landholders of 1900 and their descendants up to the collapse of coffee production in the early 1960s. Coffee is still grown in Utuado, but the more productive farms are shifting to nets (*mallas*) for harvesting and are depending on intensive fertilizer use, rather than shade, for the protection and development of the shrubs. The new coffee agronomy will probably result in still another change in the composition of the region's landholders.

Notes

1. Altagracia Ortíz, *Eighteenth-Century Reforms in the Caribbean: Miguel de Muesas, Governor of Puerto Rico, 1769–76* (East Brunswick, N.J., 1983), 183.

2. See Laird W. Bergad, *Coffee and the Growth of Agrarian Capitalism in Nineteenth-Century Puerto Rico* (Princeton, 1983), 178, 187.

3. See Laird Bergad, "Towards Puerto Rico's Grito de Lares: Coffee, Social Stratification, and Class Conflicts, 1828–1868," *Hispanic American Historical Review* 60 (1980): 617–42; Carlos Buitrago, *Los orígenes históricos de la sociedad precapitalista en Puerto Rico* (Río Piedras, 1976); Vivian Carro, "La formación de la gran propiedad cafetalera: La hacienda Pietri, 1858–1898," *Anales de investigación histórica* 2 (1975).

4. Archivo General de Puerto Rico (henceforth AGPR), Fondo Municipal de Utuado (FMU), "Partido de Utuado 1833 Padrón nominal de propietarios de terrenos," 11 r.

5. Ibid.: "Pueblo de Utuado Padrón General de Fincas Rurales Año de 1867 a 68," 10 v and 11 v; AGPR, Obras Públicas, Propiedad Pública, Utuado, "Ciudad de Utuado Relación de los terratenientes que existen en este término municipal según el padrón de contribuciones del año de 1900 a 01," 5 r and 13 r.

6. AGPR, FMU, box 3, Untitled expediente with 1828 census, 42 r-43 v and 44 r-45 v.

7. AGPR, Obras Públicas, Caminos Vecinales, Utuado, box 1460, "Espediente instruido por el Ayuntamiento sobre las quejas de los vecinos de la Chorrera y Guaunico de esta jurisdiccion; por haber cerrado los caminos que tenían por sus estancias D. Juan Basquez y D. Cristoval Montalvo" (1823).

8. Coffee production in Utuado rose from 700 hundredweights in 1818 to

6,104 in 1832; figures for the late 1830s have not been obtained. AGPR, Fondo de los Gobernadores Españoles de Puerto Rico (FGEPR), Censo y Riqueza, box 12, "Estadáistica de riqueza, Utuado, 7 de diciembre 1818"; Pedro Tomás de Cordoba, *Memorias geográficas, históricas, económicas y estadísticas de la Isla de Puerto Rico*, 2d ed., vol. 2 (San Juan, 1968), 134.

9. The expedientes of individual grants are found in AGPR, Obras Públicas, Propiedad Pública, Utuado. One can also check the acts of the Junta Superior de Terrenos Baldíos in the same series.

10. Feliciano Maldonado appeared in the 1833 land-tax list with 1 *caballería* (200 cuerdas). There are references to the suit in AGPR, Protocolos Notariales, Utuado, Otros Funcionarios, 1850, 277r-279 v and in F. Picó, ed., *Registro general de jornaleros de Utuado, 1849–50* (Río Piedras, 1977), nos. 266–67 and 447.

11. Ibid., nos. 7, 204, 221, 225, 240, 266, 267 (and 800), 319 (and 769), 325, 430, 441, 447, 481, 568, 578, 579, 684, 731, 738, 810, and fragments of the Registro de Jornaleros of 1855–57 in FMU, nos. 197 and 206. Moreover, in 1850 one of the 1833 landowners, don Antonio Montalvo, had lost his land (25 cuerdas), and registered as a day laborer (*Registro*, no. 378).

12. FMU, "Riqueza Agrícola: summaries for Guanico and Roncador."

13. Fernando Picó, *Amargo café* (Río Piedras, 1981), 109–12.

14. FMU, "Pueblo de Utuado. Padrón general de fincas rurales Año de 1866 a 67," 6 r and 18 r; "Pueblo de Utuado Padrón general de fincas rurales Año de 1867 a 68," 10 r and 11 v. In 1867 in Guanico there were 204 cuerdas cultivated (7.92%) and 2,369 cuerdas not cultivated (92%). In Roncador there were 238 cultivated (11%) and 1,908 not cultivated (88.9%).

15. AGPR, Catastro de Fincas Rústicas, Utuado.

16. Esperanza Mayol, *Islas* (San Juan, 1974); Buitrago, *Los orígenes históricos*; Francisco Ramos, *Viejo rincón utuadeño* (Utuado, 1946); Estela Cifre de Loubriel, *La formación del pueblo puertorriqueño: La contribución de los catalanes, baleáricos, y valencianos* (San Juan, 1975); Astrid Cubano Iguina, "Economía y sociedad en Arecibo en el siglo XIX: los grandes productores y la inmigración de comerciantes," in Francisco Scarano, ed., *Inmigración y clases sociales en Puerto Rico del siglo XIX* (Rio Piedras, 1981); Fernando Picó, *Al filo del poder* (Río Piedras, 1993), 73–90.

17. In 1865 the Catalán Miguel Artau and his son Baldomero (brother of Mariano, the landholder of 1900) and Antonio Cabañas agree, through arbitration, to settle their differences on mutual claims arising from the five years that Baldomero Artau served as clerk in Cabañas's store in Utuado. Cabañas had paid Artau's passage from Barcelona and medical expenses incurred while Artau was in his service as well as ordinary expenses for room and board. He claimed that Artau still owed him money. Artau claimed that Cabañas owed him back pay. A third party resolved the controversy in Artau's favor, but for a more modest sum, 80 pesos, than the one originally claimed (230 pesos) (AGPR, Protocolos Notariales, Utuado, Osvaldo Alfonzo 1865, 145 v-147 v).

18. Interview with his niece, Doña Ana Sureda Boysen, in her house in Arecibo, July 22, 1977.

19. Parroquia de San Miguel de Utuado, book 36 of Bautismos, part 240, and

interview with Francisco Maldonado Alvarez, then secretary of the parish archives, January 11, 1982.

20. Of the three, only Santoni Hermanos, an agricultural society, had land in 1890 (575 cuerdas) (AGPR, FMU, "Año de 1890 a 91 . . . Riqueza Agrícola," Roncador.

21. Eric R. Wolf, "Types of Latin American Peasantry: A Preliminary Discussion," *American Anthropologist* 57 (1955): 452–71; Picó, *Amargo café*, chap. 4.

22. AGPR, Protocolos Notariales, Utuado, Federico Porrata, 1854, 65 v-67 r.

23. Ibid., Prot. Not. Osvaldo Alfonzo 1867, 93 v-94 r, 95 r-v; Osvaldo Alfonzo 1868, 189 v-191 r; Osvaldo Alfonzo 1870, 152 r-153 r 153 r-154 v; Otros Funcionarios 1872, 31 r-32 v.

Five

Peasant, Farmer, Proletarian: Class Formation in a Smallholder Coffee Economy, 1850–1950

LOWELL GUDMUNDSON

A LTHOUGH REFERRED to as the noble grain throughout Latin America, coffee was produced at a wide variety of social levels, from the peasantry to the plutocracy. Unlike sugar, its sister tropical export crop, coffee did not always require large production units or farm sizes, or heavy capital investment in mechanization. While large coffee plantations emerged in several regions, such as Brazil, Guatemala, and El Salvador, no general farm size owing to inherent economies of scale characterized the activity in Latin America. Indeed, of all of the major agricultural export activities developed in the region after the middle of the nineteenth century, coffee was perhaps the most reconcilable, in certain contexts, with small-scale land ownership and cultivation.

References to smallholding in coffee cultivation appeared quite frequently in early-twentieth-century works praising the alleged positive, democratic consequences of smallholding, particularly in Colombia, Puerto Rico, and Costa Rica. The study of smallholders themselves has been advanced recently by works on Puerto Rico by Picó and Bergad, on Venezuela by Roseberry, and on Italians in Brazil by Holloway.[1] Beyond these and a relatively few other works little is known regarding the origins and evolution of smallholder society in coffee economies.[2] Indeed, most references to smallholders, even in the cases of greatest presumed importance (Colombia, Puerto Rico, and Costa Rica), have been based on inferences drawn from anonymous statistics on land tenure and its evolution over time rather than on detailed study of the smallholders themselves. Even the extraordinarily detailed descriptions offered by Picó for Puerto Rico are limited to four family histories with no attempt to generalize based on a statistical profile of such experiences.[3]

Colombia and Costa Rica are perhaps the two societies most highly identified in the popular imagination with smallholding in coffee culture. Surprisingly, neither has taken the lead in the historical study of smallholders themselves. Major works in both nations, by Hall, Cardoso, Pérez, Stone, and Peters for Costa Rica, and by Palacios, Machado, and Bergquist for Colombia, have all offered insights into the evolution and function of smallholder society, but in nearly every case based on inferences drawn from either *hacienda* or census records in aggregate form.[4] Smallholders themselves, the heroes of earlier nationalist historiography, remain shadowy figures still in this more systematic and less partisan modern scholarship.

Within Costa Rican historiography in particular, smallholders have figured both as a sort of endangered species to be saved by reformist politics in the mid-twentieth-century literature, and later as fundamental building blocks of abstract models of social and economic evolution.[5] The existence and numerical importance of smallholders in Costa Rica have been shown conclusively with studies of both hacienda records and the 1935 coffee producer census.[6] Beyond this, however, little light has been shed on the origins, evolution, and significance of smallholding.[7] Who were the smallholders? Where did they come from socially and how did they acquire their land? What were their chances for success and how was it achieved, or failure suffered, with the expansion and increasing specialization of coffee cultivation? If indeed such a thing as a petty or "peasant bourgeoisie," to use Franz Schryer's suggestive if contradictory term, developed in coffee cultivation, then who were these people and what were their relations with merchants, large landowners and processors, and those poorer than themselves? What explains their success and the failure of their less fortunate brethren, and how large a group did they constitute over time? While answers to questions such as these for coffee culture throughout Latin America lie well beyond the scope of this essay, the study of class formation in the one case most highly identified with and characterized by smallholding, Costa Rica between 1850 and 1950, can contribute to this end.

Costa Rican coffee-based society witnessed a "peasant to farmer" transition in agriculture, by which a subsistence-oriented peasantry was transformed into propertied and propertyless, employer and laborer classes. This was a lengthy and highly ambiguous process to be sure, but one in which a wealthy smallholder group, or rural petty bourgeoisie of sorts, was consolidated by the early twentieth century. This process involved both political mobilization and social change, particularly the growing restriction of partible inheritance to favor sons over daughters. Of all the social classes present in the countryside the well-to-do producer (non-processor) group is the primary focus of this study.

The formation of a rural petty bourgeoisie and its evolution in one coffee-based economy has a paradigmatic importance well beyond the case at hand. In an era in which revolutionary and reformist agitation in Latin America most often based itself in the ranks of salaried workers in the export sector, with purportedly leftist, laborite ideology, coffee-producing smallholders and their leaders in Costa Rica elaborated an anti-labor, anti-Marxist doctrine of social change and national liberation.[8] They sought both to defeat labor-based political movements and to pre-empt their program for societal transformation, employing a "construc-tive," "interventionist" liberalism and state support for a coffee producers' cooperative movement.[9] The importance of such antileft, petty-bourgeois reformism in the cold war era can hardly be overestimated.[10] Understand-ing the dynamics of class formation, particularly among the propertied, in the society most highly identified with successful petty-bourgeois reform-ism may offer comparative insights for societies elsewhere in Latin Amer-ica in this period and beyond.

The Setting

The area chosen for study lies in the heart of the classic smallholder coffee zone of the Costa Rican Central Valley in the area from Santo Domingo upward to San Isidro in Heredia province (Map 5.1).[11] Within this area settled during the early to mid eighteenth century, Santo Domingo's popu-lation increased from roughly 1,500 to 2,000 in the mid nineteenth cen-tury, to just over 6,000 in Santo Domingo and 2,700 in newly separate San Isidro in 1927. This entire region north of San José was one of the earliest converts to coffee cultivation, in the period 1850–70, and eventually be-came the most monocultural coffee zone by the 1930s, owing to its un-rivaled ecological conditions and the volcanic-ash fertility of its soils.[12] According to the 1935 coffee census, Santo Domingo had the fifth highest (of forty-four districts nationwide) average coffee yield at 9.9 *fanegas* per *manzana* (San Isidro was twenty-second with 6.6), and the highest ratio of coffee farm residents to total population at 58 percent (San Isidro reported 51 percent).[13] Average sizes of farms in Heredia province, at 2.0 manzanas (1 manzana equals .7 hectares), were slightly smaller than the average for other coffee-producing areas in 1935, and more provincial residents held property (16 percent) than the national average (12 percent) in 1927.[14]

However, similar processes of growing land scarcity and value, im-poverishment of many people, and commercial concentration were at work throughout Costa Rica in this period. In Santo Domingo, as we will see in greater detail below, the number of reported property owners was

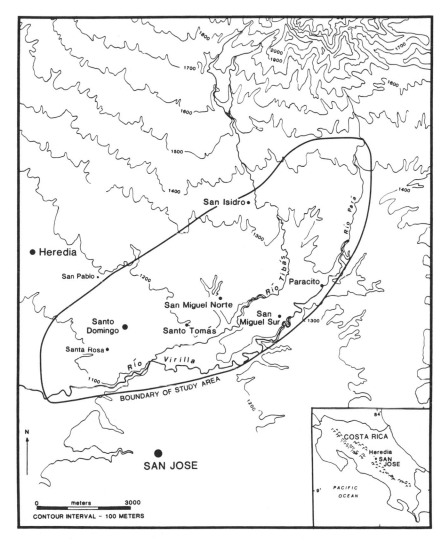

Map 5.1. Santo Domingo de Heredia and Its District, 1850–1950

roughly halved between 1935 and 1955, continuing a longstanding trend in that direction.[15] Equally ominous was the extreme reduction in the number of processing plants or *beneficios*, from fifty-three in 1887 (all in Santo Domingo and its dependent hamlets) to only six in 1935 (five in Santo Domingo and one in San Isidro).[16] While a district of only thirty-two square kilometers such as Santo Domingo could hardly be expected to continue to support over fifty beneficios as technical modernization of these plants progressed, the survival of only five, belonging primarily to major capitalists resident in Heredia (Julio Sánchez Lepiz) and San José (Tournón and Company), led to rising protests on the part of coffee producers. Indeed, San Isidro de Heredia was one of the earliest sources of support for coffee producers' cooperatives after the 1930s.

Further consequences of this growing inequality and land scarcity in Santo Domingo were the growth of a landless laboring population (discussed in detail below) and rapid out-migration. Early migratory movements, during the 1860s and 1870s, were to higher elevations on the contiguous "frontier" in the direction of San Isidro, primarily by the ambitious children of the already propertied of Santo Domingo, often with highly successful results. Thereafter, migratory flows became notably more economically precarious, with those involved seeking out ever more illusory opportunities, particularly in western colonization zones of Alajuela province after the 1880s and 1890s. According to the 1950 population census, Santo Domingo (26 percent) and San Isidro (40 percent) had some of the highest net emigration indices of the entire nation. Fully 39 percent of those born in Santo Domingo resided elsewhere, and 44 percent of those born in San Isidro resided elsewhere in 1950.[17]

Coffee and the Origins of Smallholding

Prior to the development of coffee culture Santo Domingo was a thinly settled area of cattle raising and shifting cultivation of corn and beans with little privatization of land ownership. The original settlers had received small grants of land which they paid for as part of the neighborhoods led by petty crown officials whose family names were often retained in place names such as (Paso de la) Quintana, Rincón (de los) Álvarez, Ruíz, Torres, Chaves, Rojas, "el común" de los Zamora, or simply "la Bermúdez."[18] The original grants to such individuals, grouped together "in common" to petition for land, were quite small, nearly always less than fifty and usually less than twenty manzanas. As the number of residents grew, dependent hamlets such as Santa Rosa, Santo Tomás, and San Miguel grew up in order for residents to be closer to their fields and herds.

Land tenure, even for the precoffee wealthy, was not fundamentally a system of private, exclusively held property, however. The typical cultivator made use of either common lands or unclaimed forest for shifting yearly crops of corn and beans. The wealthy of the era usually owned cattle herds in addition to a "home place" in the countryside.[19] Although some of these leading settlers might have made their home along the trail to their particular area or *rincón*, the great majority not only lived in either

Santo Domingo or one of its suburban hamlets, but they grew crops in several distant points in the surrounding countryside and pastured cattle on land claimed as far away as western Alajuela province. Crops within vaguely claimed lands were valued separately (in probate inventories) from the land itself and up to a dozen or more such disparate land/crop claims might be listed throughout the district and beyond. In several cases a land claim (of slight monetary value to be sure) was made to a general *derecho*, or right, in either *la montaña* or an area held by a particular clan (Zamora, Rodríguez, etc.) without the claimant's either surveying or ever having cultivated the land. Clearly, even for the relatively wealthy, highly abundant land was primarily of value for impermanent use rights to annual food cropping, while private property referred to house lots, "home places" in the countryside (which were as often sheds and cattle pens as "houses"), and livestock.[20]

In a land-rich, labor-starved society such as this even the wealthy saw no need for, nor practical possibility of, denying ready access to annual planting lands. Coffee would soon change all this by permanently investing land with past labor in a perennial crop, by increasing land values, and by concentrating family land claims within a short distance of the "home place," driving out cattle and pasture first and then excess people themselves. Those who remained increasingly moved outward to the hamlets and roadside farms which grew up along with commercial agriculture and fully privatized land holding.

The legal framework that accompanied this transition to generalized private ownership of land was highly favorable to the pretensions of local residents with some capital or influence. While many of the village poor would lose access to annual cropping lands in the surrounding countryside, those who could assert claims based on settlement, customary usage for cultivation, purchase, or homesteading were usually successful in obtaining title to the land eventually. The opening of the Public Property Registry in 1864 was an important stimulus to registration of deeds, but far more important in practice were public lands policies which granted homesteading rights and confirmed ownership in older settlements based solely on peaceful occupation for ten years or more.[21] Many probate inventories of the 1860–80 period include parallel legal processes for inscription of land title based simply on peaceful occupation of the deceased, with positive results in virtually every case. Overall, a single property owner of land suitable for cultivation (as distinct from mountainous pasture or forest at higher elevations) throughout Santo Domingo and San Isidro rarely held more than several dozen manzanas over the nineteenth century.

If the several paragraphs above describe "how" smallholding was consolidated and transformed in Santo Domingo by coffee culture, then "who" were those who were most likely to secure a place as a smallholder? Rural households in Santo Domingo entered into this process with markedly different resource bases and most were very, very poor. Thus from the very start petty bourgeois prosperity was not the likely outcome for the majority, but neither was it unheard of nor limited to the already wealthy. On the basis of a comparison of the 1846 census with probate inventories one can positively identify some 60 individual heads of household (53) or spouses (7), out of a total of some 471 households listed (only heads of household and their spouses' names are given). However, to say that only 53 of 471 households held substantial real property would be very misleading given the fragmentary nature of surviving probate records. In fact, being able to identify so many on the basis of so few probate records from the pre-1880 period suggests that a very considerable minority held private property sufficient to pay for probate proceedings.

Not everyone, of course, shared equally in this new-found village prosperity. Santo Domingo and San Isidro were home to several dozen interrelated clans over the period 1850–1950. At any one point in time only thirty surnames accounted for 50 to 75 percent of all inhabitants. Given such repetition in surnames and intense intermarriage, it is hard to establish who "winners" and "losers" were simply on the basis of clan membership or surname. Within the most and the least successful clans there were those whose experience diverged radically from the group norm. Nevertheless, certain clans were inordinately prominent and influential. The Zamoras, for example, were distant descendants of the first crown official in the district in the late seventeenth century and their original home base was still referred to as the "Hacienda Zamora" in San Miguel Sur in the 1927 census. A leader of the clan, Santiago Zamora, was listed as a "*beneficiador*" in the list of five local residents in 1878. Other families who were "winners" in the process, the Arce, Rodríguez, Madrigal, and Barquero clans, and especially the Villalobos family in San Isidro, appear in Table 5.1. Certain other families were dramatically underrepresented, such as the Calvo, Hernández, and Ulate surnames, as well as the Torres and Córdova clans.

In such a clan-based village society undergoing commercial agricultural development and land privatization, wealth maintenance and enhancement depended upon land colonization efforts, inheritance patterns, and marriage strategies. For successful clans partible inheritance would be respected, but its leveling effects counteracted. This could be achieved by a combination of circumspection in the choice of (preferably landed) marriage partners to recombine fragmented holdings, by conveying house lots and "home places" to dependent daughters or daughter/son-in-law unions

TABLE 5.1
Paternal Surnames in Census and Probate Records, Santo
Domingo, 1840–1955

Paternal surname		Percentage of those appearing		
	1846 census	1927 census	Probate deceased 1840–1940	1955 census proprietors
Zamora	4.1	5.3	3.5	7.6
Arce	3.6	6.3	8.0	3.9
Rodríguez	3.2	4.6	7.6	6.0
Madrigal	0.3	0.8	2.4	2.5
León	1.5	1.0	3.2	1.8
Barquero	1.4	2.7	3.7	4.5
Villalobos	4.9	7.5	9.9	9.4
Calvo	0.4	1.4	0.5	0.2
Hernández	0.5	1.9	0.3	0.7
Ulate	1.1	1.3	0.8	0.2

Source: ANCR, Congreso, No. 5,424 (1846); Estadística y Censos, Censo de Población, 1927, nos. 201–5; Sección "Mortuales de Heredia (630 cases from Santo Domingo and San Isidro, 1840–1940); uncataloged microfilm from the archives of the Dirección General de Estadística y Censos, rolls 83 and 85 (1955). All documents held by the ANCR.

(attracting similarly motivated suitors from other landed clans), and by stimulating sons to build their own houses upon marrying, in town, on outlying "parcels" of the home place, or in public lands farther up the mountainside toward San Isidro. Only much later, during the twentieth century, would siblings in once wealthy clans have to content themselves with minuscule house lots "all in a row." Only then would daughters begin to pay the price for the demise of partible inheritance of ever more scarce land.

Class Formation in Smallholding Society

Within the central coffee districts of Costa Rica smallholding was the overwhelmingly predominant form of land ownership between the mid nineteenth and early twentieth centuries. However, the farm-owning percentage of the population declined rapidly during the twentieth century as more and more residents either moved away or were reduced to houses with garden plots and wage laboring. Overall impoverishment of the less and less landed majority seems an inescapable conclusion of virtually all contemporary documentation. Intensely seasonal demand for labor (November to January) during the coffee harvest meant that, paradoxically,

coffee could simultaneously be described as a "family" and, more fan-
cifully, a "socialist" enterprise owing to its combined autarchic and (wage)
distributive aspects.[22] Only coffee's wealthiest producers employed significant wage labor year round. Family farm coffee producers of a middling
sort lived a reality in which they could plausibly see themselves as virtually
self-sufficient at least ten months of the year, and then only relying on
wage-earning "help" (often attracted through kin ties as well) for the
harvest.[23] Such was the local, crop and historically determined face of
agrarian capitalism in Costa Rican coffee culture.

Over time, however, social classes slowly became more sharply defined
and clearly antagonistic. Initially the basic division and antagonism had
been between processors and producers of whatever size, with wage labor
a distinctly secondary phenomenon. Nevertheless, by the twentieth century there emerged ever more clearly three social classes, in theory separ-
able, with two basic contradictions. The classes might be described as
processor/estate owners, nonprocessor producers, and land-poor produc-
ers/wage laborers, while the basic contradictions were between processors and producers, on the one hand and all land owners and wage laborers, on the other. Nevertheless, class boundaries were always highly
fluid and contradictions nearly always purposefully confused or muted.

Before returning to a discussion of the evidence for impoverishment
and class polarization by the early to mid twentieth century, it may be
useful to briefly describe representative experiences within this three-part
class structure. In order to do so, and to suggest the diversity of experience
within such a process of social differentiation, we will employ four categories: (1) the processor oligopoly; (2) wealthy but nonprocessor producers;
(3) smallholders in various stages of decline; and (4) semiproletarian and
fully proletarian households. However, one must keep in mind the fact
that real individuals could and did inhabit the borders between such abstract social classes. Moreover, the general tendency (not the universal
experience, however) was for downward mobility for those who remained
in Santo Domingo during the first half of the twentieth century.

The Processor "Trust"

Coffee processing[24] ranged from exceedingly primitive and dispersed, in
economies such as those of Puerto Rico and the Venezuelan Andes, to
highly complex and concentrated, in Costa Rica and El Salvador. Tem-
porally, variation was also very great. Santo Domingo went from having
fifty-three beneficios in 1887 to only six larger-scale plants in 1935. Local
residents such as Santiago Zamora and Rafael González had been pro-

cessors in 1887, whereas during the twentieth century three outside firms came to predominate in the local processing industry: Julio Sánchez Lepiz of Heredia, Tournón and Company of San José, and Emilio Challe Loubet, a merchant resident in San José.[25]

Julio Sánchez was reputedly the single wealthiest individual — and probably the largest coffee producer — in Costa Rica at his death in 1934. His vast estate was conservatively estimated at some two million pesos, or roughly half a million dollars. He had functioned as a bank of sorts for producers whose crop he processed and he regularly lent money for yearly operating expenses to poorer growers. While hardly a self-made man, Sánchez was much admired for his entrepreneurial drive in many different agroindustrial concerns. His father had made a fortune during the late nineteenth century as a coffee grower and transporter with his own oxen and cart fleet.[26] With a "common touch" in both his family tree and daily work habits, Sánchez was one of the least frequently criticized members of the processor "plutocracy" denounced by reformist leaders.

Tournón and Company was a major producer, processor, and lender in Santo Domingo after the late 1870s. However, despite their best efforts at land acquisition through purchase and foreclosure, the company was only able to accumulate a wide variety of tiny plots throughout the district, and it remained dependent upon private growers, many of whom it financed against land mortgages, for two-thirds of the crop that it would process as late as the 1930s. By the 1950s Tournón had begun to develop a strategy of urbanizing its close-in coffee lands in response to lucrative possibilities for commercial, industrial, and housing uses. Tournón, the corporate "outsider," was the far more frequent object of reformist attacks than Sánchez, but even its variety of holdings and profit sources allowed it to escape being made a scapegoat.

Processor/producer conflicts were virtually a constant feature of Costa Rican political life after the 1890s. The first major legislative initiative was forthcoming in 1932, purportedly regulating crop liquidation and finance terms between the parties.[27] Far more important was official support for the creation of state bank financing of coffee growers and the creation of a producers' cooperative sector of beneficios, circumventing in both areas the much resented processors' control.[28] These latter changes, consequences of the successful political revolt of 1948, forced the processors to grow increasing amounts of their own beans in order to utilize their existing plant capacity, as they would lose nearly two-thirds of "third party" crop to cooperative plants by 1980. A major reason for the rapid expansion of coffee planting in areas peripheral to the Central Valley since 1950 has been precisely this new impetus for processor diversification.

Well-to-Do Coffee Growers

A substantial number of residents of Santo Domingo, San Isidro, and their outlying hamlets owned very valuable estates without engaging in coffee processing. A few such families had once been processors and continued to lend money at interest or engage in retail trade. Likewise, a few families were able to maintain some of their descendants at this wealthy farmer level, while most could be expected to lose ground through partible inheritance and subdivision.

Fortunes of the well-to-do peasant-cum-farmer ranged from as little as ten thousand pesos just after the mid nineteenth century, to an occasional one- or two-hundred-thousand-peso fortune by the 1920s and 1930s. Land ownership and use changed even more dramatically than values. Initially, the wealthy owned considerable amounts of land (from perhaps twenty-five to over one hundred manzanas) at distant points throughout the district, most with little development or declared monetary value. By the early twentieth century wealthy households usually held smaller amounts of more spatially concentrated land (twenty to fifty manzanas perhaps), but nearly all of it fully developed with coffee or other intensive uses. Thus, not only were estate values higher as time went on, but at least the first generation (after 1850) or two of the wealthy could partially subdivide the land area among their children without giving them less monetarily than they themselves had "started with."

The well-to-do struggled to maintain their social position. While they were generally unable to continue their role in coffee processing, they did not meekly slide into dependency and impoverishment. As we will see below, their sons married later (and more carefully, one might presume), they migrated, and they eventually restricted partible inheritance to avoid further erosion of their position. They could and did suffer bitter conflict with processors over indebtedness and occasionally were the victims of foreclosure proceedings.[29] However, major nonprocessor coffee producers retained substantial land and cash resources quite independent of any other social class. Their obvious dependence in crop processing and marketing was not matched by a direct financial dependence on the major processors. Indeed, one of the most striking features of both probate and agricultural census records is the relative infrequency of the use of credit by wealthier producers.[30]

Probate records for wealthy growers disclose a pattern of rapid specialization in coffee; their land values were soon five to ten times that of undeveloped or annual cropping land. Nevertheless, wealthy landowners often produced commercial quantities of corn and held substantial, if declining, amounts of pasture land, especially in the more recently settled and mountainous San Isidro. Equally striking in these records is the near total lack of luxury consumer goods. Perhaps only the appearance of an occasional sewing machine after the 1890s betrays a greater degree of consumption and comfort, however utilitarian such a "luxury."

The productive arrangements of wealthy households are poorly revealed in the probate records. Only when estates were disputed or administered for a time by an executor of the estate do we gain a glimpse of day-to-day operations. In one such case Gregorio de Jesús Azofeifa Chacón died unexpectedly in 1923 at age thirty-three.[31] He held rights in some twenty-one properties with a total value of 79,000 pesos, but worth a net of only 43,000 pesos. His 1923–24 coffee harvest brought in the sum of 17,769 pesos. Coffee picking was done in both December and January, but we only have the temporary labor bill for two and a half weeks of January when some twenty-five members (male and female, young and old) of six families were able to earn 580 pesos. During nonharvest periods through October of 1924 the daily labor bill (*jornales*) oscillated between roughly thirty and one hundred pesos per week. In addition, there were ten permanent male employees whose earnings were not listed.

Even in this very wealthy household, day-to-day operations could be directed and supervised by the owner, with larger, temporary harvest labor recruited as kin groups composed primarily of women and children. Labor, for owners such as these, was neither menacing nor part of their self-definition as economic actors. Although they were in need of seasonal "help," *agricultores* usually conceived of labor/capital relations in exceedingly paternalistic and voluntaristic terms. Such could be the case because so few year-round workers were needed and only a handful of owners required massive labor contingents for harvest. In 1955 only forty-three of six hundred land owners employed more than twenty workers (their own family plus salaried workers) in the peak of harvest, and only five employed fifty or more.

Perhaps one particularly detailed example of wealthy households and their fate will provide an idea of the resources controlled by nonprocessor coffee producers in Santo Domingo. From the earliest times the Zamora surname was one of substance in Santo Domingo. As colonists (place names such as Quintana and "El Común de los Zamora" bear witness to this), as crown officials, and as early coffee growers and even processors, the Zamoras controlled a great deal of the district at one time or another. When in 1920 the children of Bernardino Zamora and Rudecinda Chacón (Lizano) — Florinda, Nereo, José Procopio, Graciliano, Aurelia, and Teodorico — gathered to dispose of their parents' estate, they faced the prospect of dividing just over fifty hectares in nineteen properties of all kinds, conservatively estimated to be worth 84,591 pesos, or theoretically

14,099 each.[32] Each heir received properties and cash, forming a virtual line of households in central Santo Domingo. José Procopio Zamora Chacón, for example, lived in a house in 1927 surrounded by "Zamoras," two or three in a row on each side. Of the six heirs, Florinda moved just north to Barva, and José Procopio, Graciliano, and Teodorico were listed as heads of household, all owners of farms, employers, and registered voters, in the 1927 census. While some of the "Zamora" listings in the 1955 agricultural census are virtually illegible (and thus useless for our reconstructive purposes), one can locate several of the members of José Procopio's household. His widow, Orfilia Chacón Vargas, held 25 manzanas of land, 14.5 in coffee. She harvested 150 fanegas and employed some eleven workers at harvest time. Their children fared just as well. Rogelio Zamora Chacón held 33 manzanas, 18 in coffee, harvesting 170 fanegas with eleven workers; Nereo (named for his uncle no doubt) held 43 manzanas, 30 in coffee, harvesting 370 fanegas with thirty-nine workers; Lile was now married to a Fonseca but held on her own account 50 manzanas, 27 in coffee, harvesting 125 fanegas with twenty-six workers, while Eida (married to a Rodríguez) held 28 manzanas, 23 in coffee, harvesting 150 fanegas with thirty-seven workers.

Not everyone could be found amid such prosperity, however. Of the Zamora Chacóns described above only Zoveidee, eight years old in 1927, could not be found among the landed in 1955. Likewise, none of Teodorico's six children (Zamora Zamoras) nor Graciliano's son (Rodrigo Zamora Chacón) could be positively identified in the 1955 listing. Given the problems of legibility in the 1955 microfilm, it would be too much to say that José Procopio's line had inherited most or all of the parents' fifty-hectare estate in 1920, but his heirs seem to have fared exceptionally well. In any event, "smallholders" such as these were anything but small in the local context. Well-to-do, nonprocessor coffee producers were the on-the-ground antithesis of poverty and wage laboring, however effectively their direct ownership, operation, and residence in Santo Domingo may have allowed them to identify, as family farmers, with producer interests and against outside processor interests.

Smallholders in Demise

Those less fortunate than the Zamoras described above regularly faced difficult choices with each generation's transmission of landed property. For those whose land base proved insufficient and who refused the alternative of ending partibility and favoring one or few heirs over others, there were basically two related options: financing out-migration of heirs in the hope of avoiding conflict over the "home place" when the time came, or equitable distribution of the farm into large or small house lots, each with road frontage if possible. Out-migration and what might be termed "lotification" were the typical responses of smallholder society as it came under the pressure of increasing land scarcity. The first of these options was intended to avoid entirely the issue of land scarcity and pro-letarianization, while the second was a graceful acceptance of them, con-ferring small income sources, housing sites, and semiproletarian status equally on the once self-sufficient. While many such heirs hoped to rebuild the family farm through guile, industry, and well-chosen marriage, the likelihood of their success was far less than for those whose wealth main-tenance strategy was based on out-migration.

Lotification was a rather straightforward affair. Coffee groves and yields were so finely calculable and highly monetarized that intransigent heirs could and did demand an exact accounting and nearly microscopic "material division" of land. In one such case a marginal smallholding family gave rise to six households with tiny lots. The six heirs of Félix Valerio Ramírez and Simona Zamora Ocampo met to divide their estate in 1900.[33] In total they held only eighty-seven areas in corn and pasture, sixty-nine areas in coffee, and a seventeen-area house and lot in Santa Rosa. Its gross value was only 1,268 pesos, leaving a net value of 858, or 143 pesos each. In order to finalize the division, the eighty-seven-area parcel was sold to provide cash for costs, each male heir received a lot of seventeen areas of coffee, and the daughters took their part in the house and lot. The youngest of the sons, Pedro, was listed in the 1927 census as a fifty-four-year-old "laborer" living as a "guest" along with his nine-year-old daughter, Alicia Valerio Alvarado, in the house headed by the laborer Juan Salas Valerio, a relative no doubt. Pedro owned no property, was illiterate, a *peón labrador en cafetal*, but was registered to vote. This may have been a case of extreme downward mobility, but the reality of the experience was no less onerous for the individual involved.

Out-migration involved both winners and losers. In the mid nineteenth century, movement to San Isidro often proved successful for those in-volved, but the area was quickly settled and those seeking land were forced to look elsewhere. A favorite target area for land-hungry *domin-gueños* after the 1880s was Naranjo in western Alajuela, two or three days' travel on foot or horseback. Two examples of smallholder immi-grants to Naranjo will illustrate the extremes of success and failure within this option. When Jacoba Zamora Vargas died in Santa Rosa in 1887, her widower, José Rodríguez Álvarez, was forced to sell the family's house lot and coffee grove of barely seventeen areas for 644 pesos in order to cancel a debt of 450 pesos. Their eldest daughter, Ignacia, had been given an "advance" on her inheritance of 12 pesos to help her emigrate to Naranjo.

At 12 pesos she likely received more material aid than her six younger siblings, who remained at home and suffered through the experience of dispossession.[34]

At the other extreme were the Rodríguez Madrigals. When their mother, Lorenza Madrigal Arce, died in 1883 at forty-five years of age, their father divided an estate worth 1,787 pesos and made up of some five manzanas and a house lot in Santo Domingo, and nearly thirty manzanas and a house in Naranjo. The widower had purchased much of this land and three of his elder sons (aged sixteen to twenty-two) already lived in Naranjo, while the eldest son, all the daughters, and the minor sons inherited pieces of the home place.[35] Whether as successful as Juan, José, and Secundino Rodríguez Madrigal, or as desperately impoverished as Ignacia Rodríguez Zamora, domingueño emigrants in Naranjo all represented an attempt at solving the equation which led inexorably to the demise of many of the smallholders in Santo Domingo's coffee economy.

Poor Relatives and Other "Help"

Studying the propertyless on the basis of proprietary documentation would seem a contradiction in terms. Certainly, the perpetually dispossessed and the transient will be forever outside the purvey of probate and agricultural census records. However, many very poor households appear in the 1927 census records and a few of these can be linked with earlier probate records to provide a glimpse of the lives of the materially most disadvantaged.

Those most likely to fall out of smallholder society into the ranks of the laboring poor and servant populations were those whose father or mother died very young and indebted, or those whose home and yard needed to be sold to cancel debts and pay probate inventory and burial expenses. However, the fate of those who suffered through such a traumatic experience varied enormously. The following examples provide some idea of the lives of those near the bottom of society.

Belisario León Ocampo appeared as a head of household renting his dwelling in Santo Domingo in 1927. He was a forty-two-year-old employer/owner of a butcher shop in the city and he supervised, as a widower alone, the upbringing of his five minor children. Although a renter without real property, he was literate. He had received a primary school education (all of his children had also attended school), and he was both an employer and a registered voter. Noteworthy indeed was such modest prosperity, coming as it did from an heir whose family's modest house had been sold to pay debts upon the death of his widowed mother in 1903.[36]

None of his four siblings could be located in either probate or census records.

Nearer the other extreme was the experience of one Gabriel Arce. The widower of twenty-six-year-old Ana Arce Chacón in 1906, he and his five minor children were forced to sell their only two pieces of property, worth a mere 450 pesos, to meet burial expenses and debts.[37] At that time they claimed residence in Santo Tomás, but by 1927 Gabriel lived with his daughter, Rosaura Arce de Piedra, and her husband Sofonías, a land owner and employer. Rosaura had brought to her marriage an illegitimate child, a circumstance which had also befallen her younger sister, María Antonia, also a dependent resident with her baby daughter, her father, and her younger brother Joaquín. In effect, this particular family had been saved from total pauperization by the advantageous marriage of a daughter, despite her having a child out of wedlock.

Two final examples are even more bleak. Both were cases of deceased persons whose parents were listed as nineteenth-century laborers (*jornaleros*) in the probate proceedings, hardly a mark of distinction. Napoleón Chavarría Arce filed for probate of his wife's, Eduvina (also known as Liduvina) Barquero González's, estate in 1932.[38] She had died at age fifty in 1930, leaving a son, José Chavarría Bolaños, as heir along with his father. The family had been listed in the 1927 census as headed by Napoleón, a laborer without property other than a mortgaged house, his wife, son José (also a laborer), and an eighteen-year-old daughter Cruz. Both males were registered voters, however, and had received some primary education, as had the daughter. In the probate proceedings five years later it was revealed that the house had been mortgaged to a resident of Santo Domingo since 1924, for 318 pesos, and that son José also owed this person 100 pesos. The house was sold for 500 pesos to pay these debts, reducing even further the pathetic resources of the surviving members of the family.

Pedro Arce Villalobos appeared in the 1927 census as a thirty-seven-year-old oxen conductor or *boyero* who worked in the public roads on his own account. He rented a house, had no property, but was literate and registered to vote. He headed a household with his wife Otilia Barrantes Fonseca (28) and their children Carmen (8), Mardoqueo (6), and María Teresa (2) Arce Barrantes. Upon his death in 1938 Pedro Arce was reportedly a resident of La Garita, Alajuela. His house in San Miguel with its twenty-seven-area lot was sold for 300 pesos to pay similar mortgage to one María Chacón Bolaños.[39] The future of children such as the Arce Barrantes was indeed bleak. Grandchildren of Santo Domingo's jornalero class, they were virtually condemned to follow in their footsteps, despite the valiant efforts of their enterprising father in the cartage trade. For the few who managed to escape such disadvantage and poverty, the coffee economy proved rewarding; for the many, it offered no relief from the constant struggle to survive without property or security in an unpredictable world of early death, low wages, and chronic underemployment.

However, if virtually none of the Zamora or other wealthy clans might be found among the downtrodden laboring classes, many of these had relatives among the propertied. Even those as unfortunate as Gabriel Arce and his children formed part of a landed household headed by his son-in-law. Their sense of dispossession must certainly have been muted by their own kin ties, as well as by the weight of "respectable" smallholder opinion in the community at large. When one of these local notable households found itself in probate proceedings and was foreclosed upon by Tournón or by Julio Sánchez, would their seasonal laborers, themselves often the children of smallholders or kin of other landowning coffee producers, be more likely to identify with their unfortunate fellow producers, or as laborers against their now bankrupt employers?[40] More to the point, how were seasonal laborers, very often kin groups headed by women with more prosperous male relatives, to develop, much less openly express, an ideology of employer-worker conflict? Paternalism, patriarchy, and familial honor, tied to an inherently ambiguous class structure, made it extremely difficult for those less favored by coffee culture to articulate an ideology of class antagonism and exploitation of their own. Rather than low wages, poor conditions, and short seasons, the workplace conversation of impoverished smallholders and laborers likely echoed the local propertied classes' trinity of concerns: weather and yields, world coffee prices, and the justice of the prices set by local processors. To discuss other topics was to identify oneself as not part of that imagined "nation" of smallholding coffee producers, as having given up any illusion of standing in village society. To make claims for labor and its interests independent of those of direct producers was to question a creed, to behave incomprehensibly, to become a man or woman marked as inferior in both current condition and future prospects. For many in Santo Domingo, family and kin both disguised local class polarization and inhibited any overt expression of it outside of the popular dichotomy of processors and money lenders versus smallholding producers.

Santo Domingo in the First Half of the Twentieth Century

If the portraits of class experiences drawn above correspond to real lives, how might one characterize the general trend of such experiences over the first half of the twentieth century? Where did most people fall along such a continuum and what were their responses to their situation? While a well-to-do landed group did consolidate and perpetuate itself over time, largely by altering its sociodemographic behavior, the majority were likely to experience increasing land pressure and downward mobility.

Land Scarcity and Downward Mobility

For those who did not emigrate to San Isidro, or later to western Alajuela, prospects were for increased difficulty of access to farming land. Five different types of indirect evidence all point in this direction. First, census records, although very imprecise, show that roughly half of households reported some capital worth in 1844, while only 17 percent of males were employers and 21 percent self-employed in 1927 (Table 5.2).[41] Likewise, the number of farm owners declined substantially (see note 15). Second, the rate of out-migration reached alarming proportions by mid-century (see note 17), as the district's residents became increasingly impoverished. Third, average land areas in probate inventories decline by the late nineteenth century, although they stabilize at around seven hectares thereafter (Table 5.3). The percentage of cases of estates under one hectare increased dramatically as holdings over ten hectares declined similarly. Fourth, the frequency of forced sales or liquidation of threadbare estates, basically houses and lots, increases dramatically in the twentieth century. Of these 153 cases (of 630 total probate inventories) nearly 80 percent are registered after 1900. Likewise, sale of rights among heirs in hopes of avoiding liquidation increases in this same time period.[42] Most important, by tracking a generation of male heirs of property holders in probate before 1927 to the census of that year one can show that 43 percent were wage laborers, only 22 percent self-employed, and 35 percent employers (Table 5.4). Even among heirs over fifty years of age in 1927, fully one-third were

TABLE 5.2
Male Occupations in Santo Domingo, 1927

Occupational status	Number	Percentage
Laborer	430	62
Self-employed	144	21
Employer	115	17
Total	689	100

Source: ANCR, Estadística y Censos, Censo de Población, 1927, Nos. 201–5.

TABLE 5.3
Size of Landholding in Probate: Santo Domingo, 1840–1939

Size of estate (hectares)	Time period (percentages)				Total	
	1840–79	1880–99	1900–19	1920–39	Cases	Percentage
Less than 1	16	38	42	46	153	35
1–4.9	34	31	35	24	135	31
5–9.9	13	12	14	15	59	14
10–19.9	21	10	5	6	48	11
20–49.9	11	6	1	3	24	6
50 and over	5	3	2	6	17	4
Total	100	100	99	100	—	101
Cases	116	115	97	108	436ᵃ	
Mean (hectares)	12.96	7.13	6.09	7.69		

Source: ANCR, Sección "Mortuales de Heredia."
ᵃThere were 194 cases in which no reliable size of estate could be calculated.

wage laborers rather than self-employed or employers. Heirs of property holders in the first half of the twentieth century in Santo Domingo could expect to fare worse than their parents. How much worse depended upon factors of chance, industriousness, and above all patience in waiting for proprietorship until relatively advanced age. Small wonder, then, that nearly half the district's residents chose to leave.

Class Differences and Life Chances

Prior to the coffee revolution of the mid nineteenth century, major demographic differences fell along the urban versus rural, or city versus village axis, with only weak differentiation along socioeconomic lines internal to villages themselves.[43] In other words, both the village rich and poor married rather young (an average age of twenty-four to twenty-six for males and twenty to twenty-two for females), formed agricultural households at

TABLE 5.4
Male Heirs and Proprietorship in Santo Domingo, 1927

Occupational status	Age in 1927 (percentages)			Cases	Percentage
	Under 30	30–49	50 and over		
Laborer	63	40	34	46	43
Self-employed	30	23	18	24	22
Employer	7	37	48	37	35
Total	100	100	100		100
Cases	27	30	50	107	

Sources: Same as Tables 5.2 and 5.3.

TABLE 5.5
Types of Households in Santo Domingo,
1927

Type of household	Number	Percentage
Simple nuclear	199	49
Simple male-headed	26	6
Simple female-headed	57	14
Complex male-headed	84	21
Complex female-headed	38	9
Total	404	99

Source: Same as Table 5.2.

marriage, showed little differentiation in fertility/mortality behavior, and lived within either single or two-parent nuclear (noncomplex) households rather small in size (four to five members). Coffee, scarce land, and class polarization would dramatically change this by the early twentieth century, in both sociodemographic and sociopolitical terms.

According to parochial records, average ages at marriage increased during the twentieth century, particularly for propertied (*agricultor*) males.[44] Using the 1927 census originals, we find the average age at marriage was 27.1 for men and 24.6 for women and, revealingly, 28.7 and 22.2 for age at leaving home. In other words, marriage was increasingly less synonymous with new household formation for men.[45] Average household size was increasing steadily, from roughly 4.5 to 5 members at mid nineteenth century, to 5.5 to 6 in rural households of Santo Domingo in 1927. More important, household complexity increased dramatically, with fully 30 percent of all households composed of complex units in 1927, two-thirds of these headed by males (Table 5.5). Where household complexity and multigenerational "stem" families had been very infrequent residential units at mid-century, some 10 of 404 households in 1927 contained a married son or daughter with their spouse (and often children) in male-headed households.

Even more indicative of the class-specific nature of these demographic changes is the frequency of sons and daughters remaining "at home" until their twenties and thirties. By 1927 proprietors/employers were far more likely to have elder sons at home, married or not, than laborers (Table 5.6). Children as old as thirty or more could regularly be found in these households, something virtually unheard of half a century before. Land scarcity and anxiety over inheritance was leading Costa Rican rural society toward greater household size and complexity as surely as was rising fertility and declining infant mortality rates.[46]

If class differences had begun to take on a demographic face, what of

TABLE 5.6
Retention of Grown Children by Occupation of Household Head,
Santo Domingo, 1927

		Male-headed, two parent households (father age 40 or older)				
		Number with	Average number of 15 or older		Median age of eldest	
Occupation	Cases	children 15 or older	Sons	Daughters	Sons	Daughters
Laborer	62	39	.73	.68	19	20
Self-employed	21	15	.95	.91	19	20
Employer	48	40	1.63	1.21	22	20

Source: Same as Table 5.2.

other areas of life chances, such as citizenship, empowerment, and standing in the community? To exercise citizenship meant fundamentally to exercise the vote, empowerment depended directly upon access to formal education, and community standing could best be seen in home ownership and access to property ownership in general. In these areas class differences were patent, but Santo Domingo's less-favored sons shared to a quite surprising degree in these elements of community membership and standing.

The broadening of the franchise in Costa Rica was a continuous process from the 1909 municipal reform, if not before. Surprisingly, nearly one-half of Santo Domingo's self-declared laborers claimed to be registered to vote (Table 5.7). Nevertheless, voter registration increased in direct relation to proprietorship, with nearly all "owner/employers" registered. Still, the figures, as with formal education and home ownership, stand in stark contrast to what one might surmise regarding the rest of Central America at this time.

Costa Rica's liberal reformers of the 1880s gave great attention to the

TABLE 5.7
Voter Registration among Santo Domingo Males by
Occupational Status, 1927 (Percentages)

	Laborer	Self-employed	Employer
Registered	49	54	80
Did not know	10	3	6
Not registered	41	43	14
Total	100	100	100
Cases	430	144	115

Source: Same as Table 5.2.

TABLE 5.8

Educational Attainment by Generation in Santo Domingo as of 1927

| | Years of formal education (percentages) | | | | | | | | | | | | | |
| | Males | | | | | | | Females | | | | | | |
Year of birth	1	2	3	4	5+	0	Cases	1	2	3	4	5+	0	Cases
1908–1917	22	24	26	9	7	12	289	17	23	27	14	9	10	278
1898–1907	6	25	28	19	10	12	189	9	24	27	14	10	16	222
1868–1877	13	29	12	2	7	36	85	10	25	3	3	1	58	93

Source: Same as Table 5.2.

educational apparatus, especially mass primary education.[47] While the ideological-control intent of these efforts was patent, and much criticized more recently, the profound impact of these reforms in the countryside is clearly revealed in the Santo Domingo data. Most residents of the district (including women!) received some formal education, usually two or three years. While only 30 or 40 percent of residents could read and write in the 1880s and 1890s, liberal reform would soon change this situation. Educational achievement increased dramatically across the board for those born in the twentieth century (Table 5.8). By this time nearly all had some access to education including women and the poor. The opening of a teachers' training school in the 1910s in neighboring Heredia offered further stimulus to the education and professional ambitions of local residents.[48]

Indeed, the emergence of reformist ideas and agitation depended upon both smallholder access to schooling and literacy sufficient to digest the increasingly frequent broadsides against the "trust" and in the name of the true "nation" of coffee producers. For radical pamphleteers and newly trained lawyers such as Santo Domingo's native son Juvenal Fonseca Villalobos, the liberal reform's educational achievements were both precondition and vehicle for the construction and communication of the smallholders' cherished past and imagined future.[49]

If most families in Santo Domingo saw their fortunes decline in the twentieth century, many still expected to own their own homes, however humble they might be. Indeed, downward mobility for the landed often meant being reduced to home and garden plot ownership rather than total dispossession. Thus proletarianization, while a real and constant threat for many, did not remove entirely for laborers the possibility of home ownership. In this, as in all other areas, proprietors set the standard, but at least 20 percent of self-declared laborer heads of household owned their dwelling (Table 5.9). Likewise, when asked to respond whether they owned "real estate" or not, wage-dependent laborers occasionally could

TABLE 5.9
Home and Property Ownership by Occupational
Status, Santo Domingo, 1927

Home ownership (heads of household)[a]	Laborer	Self-employed	Employer
Own	20%	60%	72%
Mortgage	3%	2%	0%
Rent	77%	38%	28%
Cases	208	167	96

Real estate ownership (males)[b]	Laborer	Self-employed	Employer
Own	13%	35%	77%
Do not own	87%	65%	23%
Cases	430	144	115

Source: Same as Table. 5.2.

[a]Includes women heads of household, nearly all in the self-employed category.

[b]Includes all males who declared an occupational status (basically those 14 or 15 and older). Some 186 women also responded positively to the question.

be found among the propertied. Although only 13 percent of laborers held registered real estate, this compares to only 35 percent of the so-called self-employed. While these may be the most unreliable of items in the census declaration, they suggest once again a very complex continuum from pauper to proprietor in which petty bourgeois ideals and behavior could offer credible if uncertain rewards in coffee-based society.

Land Tenure and Coffee Production at Mid-century

A century of coffee production in Santo Domingo led to the problem of *minifundio*. But unlike other Latin American contexts, the minifundio was not the counterpart of *latifundio*. Rather, the employer of the minifundista reserve army of labor was a family-farm-owning resident in the district itself. Employers such as these saw themselves as direct producers, just as their poorer neighbors, in opposition primarily to processors rather than labor. Moreover, they did their best to convince their neighbors, rich and poor, of the accuracy of this self-image. Far from repressing the organizational efforts of the poor, their more effective tactic was to preempt the leadership of the very popular movement itself, defined as the productive "nation" of coffee growers versus the oligarchy of processors and financiers.

TABLE 5.10
Size of Farms and Coffee Plantings, Santo Domingo, 1955

Farm size (manzanas)	Percentage of all farms	Coffee planting size (manzanas)	Percentage of all coffee plantings
1 or less[a]	13	1 or less[a]	27
1.1–3	32	1.1–3	38
3.1–5	13	3.1–5	14
5.1–10	22	5.1–10	14
10.1–20	11	10.1–20	4
20.1 or more	9	20.1 or more	2
Total	100	Total	99
Cases	599[b]	Cases	544[c]

Source: ANCR, microfilm from Dirección General de Estadística y Censos, rolls 83 and 85.

[a]No farms under 1 manzana were reported, but coffee plantings as small as 0.1 manzana were reported on farms of 1 manzana or more total land area.
[b]One missing value (land area illegible on microfilm).
[c]Fifty-six farms had no coffee plantings.

The two sides of this curious coin can readily be seen in the results of the 1955 agricultural census. Sub-family farms (labor surplus family units) accounted for a majority of cases, even more clearly in coffee plantings (Table 5.10). Fully 58 percent of farms were five manzanas or less and 79 percent of coffee plantings fell in this category. At the same time, however, only 11 of 600 owners had more than twenty manzanas in coffee, hardly a latifundista group. The real center of local power was in the 42 percent of owners holding five manzanas or more, and the 34 percent with coffee plantings of more than three manzanas, roughly the farm size at which nonfamily wage labor for harvest would assume critical importance.

Family-farm coffee producers depended upon wage labor virtually only for the harvest. Their minifundista neighbors willingly provided it. Labor demands peaked in November and December, with 19.5 percent of farms reporting peak demand in the former month and 53.7 percent in the latter. Outside of the harvest season very little wage labor was required. Almost 50 percent of farms had no wage labor at all in May (the off-season, when the census was taken), and another 25 percent had only one salaried employee at that time. During the harvest the median number of wage and nonwage workers was seven, with 68 percent of farms reporting ten or fewer. Only 10 percent of farms had fifteen or more harvest workers, and only 43 of 600 owners had twenty workers or more. Salaried employees were even fewer in number. Roughly one quarter of the harvest labor was

TABLE 5.11
Chemical Fertilizer Use and Coffee Planting Size,
Santo Domingo, 1955

Coffee planting size (manzanas)	Chemical fertilizer used (%)	No chemical fertilizer used (%)	Total cases
1 or less	16	84	146
1.1–3	34	66	208
3.1–5	47	53	77
5.1–10	49	51	78
10.1–20	38	62	24
20.1 or more	90	9	11
Cases	187	357	544

Source: Same as Table 5.10.

provided by unpaid family members, but only 17 percent of farms used no salaried labor at all in the harvest. Of the 83 percent that did, the average was six, and 76 percent employed ten or fewer salaried workers in the peak harvest season. A final indication of the stark dichotomy between minifundistas and family farmers can be seen in the ninety-five cases of "owners" who were working full time on another farm for wages in May, in nearly every case owners of farms of one or two manzanas.[50]

Relatively little of the post-1948 technical and political revolutions in coffee cultivation, so well analyzed by Raventós, were yet evident in the 1955 census in Santo Domingo.[51] However, what evidence there was pointed in the direction of increasing farm sizes and the falling behind of minifundista producers. While specialization in coffee was very advanced, with 66 percent of the average farm's land in coffee and 30 percent of farms, particularly the smallest, totally monocultural, improvements in cultivation were not yet widespread. Only 146 of 600 producers reported any access to credit, and 108 of these obtained it from private sources rather than the state banking system, which was to assume a dominant role thereafter. Virtually nothing but the *arábigo* coffee variety was being used, and only 128 of 544 coffee producers reported any groves replanted in the preceding three years.[52] Finally, only 187 of 544 farms reported using chemical fertilizers, the other principal source of increased yields since 1948.

The infrequent use of replanting, hybrids, and chemical fertilizers is indeed surprising. By the 1930s extensive data showed up to 50 percent increases in yields with fertilizer use. Its use and the reorganization of production using wage labor gangs for systematic replanting in the eastern district of Turrialba in the 1950s were responsible for that region's lead in yields nationwide.[53]

TABLE 5.12
Coffee Yields by Planting Size, Santo Domingo, 1955
(Percentages)

Coffee planting size (manzanas)	Yield (fanegas per manzana)				Cases
	0–4.9	5.0–9.9	10.0–14.9	15.0+	
1 or less	23	51	22	4	139
1.1–3	16	58	24	2	207
3.1–5	14	48	34	4	77
5.1–10	4	61	32	3	77
10.1–20	8	42	38	12	24
20.1 or more	9	36	36	18	11
All plantings	16	54	27	4	535
Cases	83	289	143	20	

Source: Same as Table 5.10.

The introduction of chemical fertilizers was distorted in favor of large farms (Table 5.11), as were yields in general (Table 5.12). Thus the impact of chemical fertilizers would further distance large producers' yields from those of the minifundistas. Sub-family farms were likely to be incorporated into larger units, especially the 84 percent of owners of one-manzana plots who used no chemical fertilizers. The success of the family farmers in incorporating elements of successive "green revolutions" was predicated, in large part, on their absorbing the remnants of sub-family farm units unable to finance new cultivation techniques and fertilizer use to boost yields.

In light of what is known about the spectacular impact of fertilizer use on yields over the past four decades, the Santo Domingo data show relatively little immediate impact (Table 5.13). Mean yields for those who did use fertilizer were only slightly higher than for those who did not, although there was a measurable difference in the likelihood of very low

TABLE 5.13
Coffee Yields and Chemical Fertilizer Use, Santo Domingo, 1955

Yield (fanegas per manzana)	Percentage of coffee plantings			Fertilizer		Cases
	Santo Domingo	San Isidro	Average	Used	Not used	
Less than 5	8	26	16	14	16	83
5–9.9	53	55	54	54	54	289
10 or more	39	18	30	32	29	163
Cases	322	213	535	185	350	535
Mean yield	8.74	6.49	7.8	8.0	7.74	

Source: Same as Table 5.10.

(under fanegas per manzana) or high (ten or over) yields depending on fertilizer use. Yields in Santo Domingo, at generally lower altitudes, were substantially higher than in San Isidro, and fertilizer usage was also more widespread in Santo Domingo, although it had not yet led to any spectacular results according to the 1955 census declaration.

Coffee production and land tenure in mid-twentieth-century Santo Domingo was precisely what the probate and census records would have suggested earlier: widespread minifundio and impoverishment alongside a family farmer group enjoying remarkable stability over time. No more than a half dozen properties in the district might seriously be considered very large farms and none true latifundia. Nevertheless, the well-to-do coffee producer group clearly dominated, and the secret of its apparent stability and hegemony must be sought in its changing pattern of inheritance.

Inheritance, Smallholding, and Class

Partible inheritance led to minifundio and microscopic properties in Santo Domingo and there is considerable evidence for this in the probate and census records described above. However, partible inheritance was clearly not responsible for a limitless fractioning of farm properties. Each estate had an average of four to six potential heirs over the entire century 1840–1940, and median farm sizes in probate plummeted to just over one hectare in the twentieth century, even if the mean size remained virtually constant after the 1880s at six to eight hectares (Table 5.3). While many families were losing any hope of making a living off the shrinking land base, nevertheless the middling-sized farm (5 to 9.9 hectares) maintained its share of estates (13, 12, 14, and 15 percent) over the four time periods. Likewise, farm size distribution in the 1955 agricultural census (Table 5.9) shows a still substantial group of, in effect, family farmers, with 33 percent of owners in the 5.1 to 20 manzana range, 46 percent in the 3.1 to 20 range, and fully 55 percent above 3.1 manzanas. The truly large estates declined over time, as minifundios proliferated, but the middling group appears to avoid change. How can one explain this contradiction between a geometric growth in the number of heirs and minifundios and a relative stability in the middle-sized farms?

Probate inventory proceedings purport to reveal the distribution of goods among heirs. However, the formal declarations themselves are an extremely poor guide to the effective transmission of property. Over the entire century (1840–1940) partibility was the norm, under colonial-era as well as liberal legislation after the 1880s.[54] The modalities of expressed respect for partibility changed with legislative innovations, but each generation went to great lengths to act out (or feign) a commitment to "jus-

TABLE 5.14

Distribution of Probate Inventories, Santo Domingo, 1840–1939

		Sex (%)[a]		Residence (cases)[b]				
Time period	Total cases	Males	Females	Santo Domingo	San Miguel	Santa Rosa	Santo Tomás	San Isidro
1840–79	122	53	47	103	4	5	1	6
1880–99	185	52	48	99	13	25	27	15
1900–19	173	57	43	79	23	21	21	27
1920–39	147	48	52	59	29	13	16	28
Cases	627	330	297	340	69	64	65	76
Percentage		53	47	55	11	10	11	12

Source: Same as Table 5.3.

[a]Three cases in which the sex of deceased could not be determined.

[b]Sixteen cases in which no residence could be determined.

tice" and partibility in familial transmission of property. Before we question the accuracy of these declarations we need to describe their internal patterns and changes over time.

Formal distribution of inheritance varied little over time. Roughly half of the deceased were of each sex in all time periods (Table 5.14), and partibility, in one form or another, was the expressed norm in the large majority of cases (Table 5.15; types 1, 2, 7, and to some extent, 3 and 4 are reconcilable with partibility). Nevertheless, several changes were revealed in the probate records themselves. The number of cases of residents outside of Santo Domingo itself increased dramatically (Table 5.14). The frequency of forced sales spiraled in the twentieth century (note 42;

TABLE 5.15

Inheritance Patterns in Santo Domingo: Distribution of the Estate (Percentages)

Distribution	All estates	Male deceased	Female deceased	Number of cases
1. One-half to spouse, remainder partible	32	37	25	182
2. Fully partible	17	16	18	97
3. Forced sale or total liquidation	27	24	29	153
4. Sale of rights among heirs	8	6	10	44
5. Sons favored	1	1	1	6
6. Daughters favored	0	0	0	2
7. All to spouse	7	7	7	39
8. All to parents or other relatives	9	8	10	52
Cases	574[a]	305	270	575

Source: Same as Table 5.3.

[a]Fifty-five missing values — estates not categorizable or without information.

TABLE 5.16
Inheritance Patterns in Santo Domingo: Forms of Receipt of Inheritance (Percentages)

Type of inheritance	Time period				Cases
	1840–1879	1880–1899	1900–1919	1920–1939	
1. Indivisible rights	84	62	19	16	243
2. Properties to each heir	2	2	4	5	17
3. "Material division" of properties for each heir	1	6	16	13	51
4. Cash from sale	6	15	38	34	130
5. All to one heir[a]	7	15	23	31	103
Cases	116	158	151	119	544[b]

Source: Same as Table 5.3.

[a]Nearly always the surviving spouse or parent.

[b]Eighty-six missing values or cases not categorizable or insufficient information.

Table 5.16). Heirs increasingly claimed to be eschewing "shares" or "indivisible rights" in single properties in favor of "material division" of the land in question.[55] Liberal changes in inheritance law after the 1880s were used not to favor individual heirs at the expense of others (allowable for the first time), but rather to leave all property to the surviving spouse, a holding action of sorts in expectation of future partibility (Table 5.16). In addition, families increasingly used "advances" on inheritance to children to assist them in migrating, particularly after the 1880s, to San Isidro or later to western Alajuela.

However, perhaps the single most important twentieth-century change in inheritance practices, the restriction of partibility and discrimination against daughters in land transmission, is virtually never even hinted at in the probate documents themselves. Rare indeed is the case of admitted sale of all rights to one heir, such as when the eleven brothers and sisters of Ismael Madrigal Arce, all residents of San Isidro in 1932, ceded their rights in a mixed-crop farm of approximately 3.5 hectares for small cash payments and for the nearly 1,000 pesos Ismael had spent on expenses of the deceased parents.[56]

Inheritance patterns prior to the twentieth century had been quite respectful of daughters' formal rights. In the nineteenth century one could even argue, based on perhaps impressionistic evidence, that daughters were more often than not favored with home places and house lots (a form of "protective" favoring to be sure) over brothers, who were expected to move at least a short distance and build their own homes.[57] However frequent or infrequent, women's property ownership was clearly recognized as separate from that of their husbands, both in probate and in the

TABLE 5.17

Gender and Inheritance in Santo Domingo

Siblings in 1927 census	Propertyholders in 1955 census		
	Appear as	Do not appear as	Total
Males	42	49	91
Females	9	88	97
Total	51	137	188

Cases = 33 families with at least 2 blood-related children in the household in 1927, at least 1 of whom appeared in the 1955 agricultural census.

Source: Same as Tables 5.2 and 5.10.

1955 census records. As widows they may have been virtually "socially obliged" to report male relatives as "administrators," but the property was clearly legally theirs. Finally, while there were only 2 cases in 630 of daughters being overtly favored at the expense of sons, there were family histories in which daughters later appear as land owners without their brothers being so fortunate.

The proof of a change in inheritance patterns which allowed farm sizes to remain fairly stable is not to be found in the probate records. Nor was there any single hard-and-fast pattern which developed over time. Rather, it was a strong, unofficial tendency by which sons were favored and daughters lost in the bargain. After a study of the 1955 agricultural census listing in detail, various owners could be traced back to their families of origin in the 1927 population census. In Table 5.17 the gender-specific consequences of an unofficial pattern of nonpartible inheritance are clear. Sisters virtually never held land if none of their brothers did, while the reverse was more the rule than the exception. Whereas no rigid inheritance rules had developed, a petty bourgeois, male-dominant, "farmer-like" pattern had begun to emerge, solidifying and clarifying class boundaries in agriculture. This was so despite the fact that coffee culture in Santo Domingo was not driven in this direction by any technologically imposed (i.e., mechanization such as in cereal grain production worldwide) minimum farm size.

Reformism, Smallholding, and Class

Two excellent studies have recently examined the important historical relationship between the National Liberation party's post-1948 support for the coffee producer cooperative movement and the consolidation of a "family farm" model in the coffee economy.[58] Both Raventós and Cazanga have shown that related benefits of this socially reformist model have been the creation of a cooperative processing and marketing structure to partially replace private capital, a remarkable increase in yields owing to state financing of replanting and chemical fertilizer use, and hybrid development. All of this has allowed for a surprisingly small "family farm" unit size to assimilate successive waves of green revolution technology. However, as Raventós has shown, the very success of reform in resolving the processor/producer contradiction in favor of producers and in vastly increasing yields has led to a new basic social contradiction between producers (now collectively capitalized via state support) and seasonal wage labor. Without any hope of mechanizing coffee picking, family farmer producers have required ever larger and more impoverished seasonal migratory labor contingents to harvest their burgeoning yields. Moreover, as Cazanga has demonstrated, the wealthier members of the producers' cooperatives have consistently dominated state and cooperative coffee policies, making them ever more conservative and defensive of the interests of capital and the cooperatives' special privileges.

The study of coffee producers in Santo Domingo adds to these findings by pointing up the emergence and consolidation of a petty bourgeois group of producers in the coffee economy well in advance of any major reformist triumph politically. Family farmer producers were far more the beneficiaries than the products of the post-1948 reformist programs for the coffee economy. Wealthy producers were clearly diverging from their poorer neighbors socially and demographically before 1927 and this surely accelerated thereafter. No package of reforms would have likely saved the 27 percent of growers with one manzana or less (84 percent of whom used no chemical fertilizer), nor would they affect equally the 17 percent who worked full-time on someone else's farm, compared to the producer who met or exceeded the average of fifteen to twenty fanegas harvested from two to three manzanas of coffee in 1955. Indeed, Santo Domingo's experience suggests that petty bourgeois reform such as that witnessed in 1948 and thereafter, however historically and politically "popular," was basically defensive of relative privilege in agriculture. Those who stood to benefit most from reform were no more than a minority, however visible and influential, of even the agricultural population. Their family tree may have been popular, with peasant roots, but its branches led to private property worked by seasonal wage labor. Populist discourse, in this case, was logically as well as conjuncturally antileftist and antilabor.

On a larger scale, the history of smallholding and coffee in Santo Domingo suggests a high likelihood of internal class differentiation among direct producer households, toward the consolidation of a petty bourgeois group in agriculture, regardless of crop-related features impelling higher minimum farm sizes (so lacking in our own case). Indeed, one of the most striking findings of this study was the emergence of nonpartibility and favoring of sons, without any mechanization or new technological impetus for maintaining stable farm sizes. Class formation, stability, and reproduction would seem to have been impetus enough for the well-to-do, in particular males, to recognize themselves as a class and erect defensible class boundaries, at the expense of siblings in general and sisters in particular, as well as a century-old inheritance pattern.

Small wonder, then, that the reformist zeal of petty bourgeois smallholders should dissipate so quickly upon victory in 1948. Having fought for the virtues of private property against perceived monopoly on the one side, and the threat of proletarianization on the other, their invocation of the commonwealth of direct producers/workers would cease when such a symbolic unity was no longer a partisan necessity. Administering state-bank credit, fertilizer distribution, coffee processing and marketing, and consumer goods distribution are profoundly conservatizing and routinizing activities for even the most historically militant cooperative movements.[59] In effect, the "socialism" of wages in the coffee harvest was as far as these producers had ever imagined going in the direction of leftist reform. Petty bourgeois behavior and hegemony were clearly revealed in the 1927 census. Any conservative tendencies after 1948 were not simply the creation of the reforms or reformers themselves, however much their success may have contributed to them. Key behavioral and sociopolitical changes evident in Santo Domingo came about not so much as a consequence of reformist distribution of land or resources but by pre-reform restriction of their distribution. The coffee producers' cooperative movement, one of the most visible legacies of the 1948 civil war, triumphed because of the strength of the nonprocessor but wealthy coffee producer group. If this group's consolidation and political empowerment has been more visible since 1948, its emergence and self-consciousness have deep roots in the late nineteenth and early twentieth centuries.

Notes

1. Fernando Picó, *Amargo café (Los pequeños y medianos caficultores de Utuado en la segunda mitad del siglo XIX)* (Río Piedras, 1981); idem, *Libertad y servidumbre en el Puerto Rico del siglo XIX: los jornaleros utuadeños en vísperas del auge del café* (Río Piedras, 1979); Laird W. Bergad, *Coffee and the Growth of*

Agrarian Capitalism in Nineteenth-Century Puerto Rico (Princeton, 1983); William Roseberry, *Coffee and Capitalism in the Venezuelan Andes* (Austin, 1983). Thomas Holloway, *Immigrants on the Land: Coffee and Society in São Paulo, 1886–1934* (Chapel Hill, 1980).

2. Some of the best recent studies of the historical evolution of smallholder regimes do not deal with coffee-based societies at all. See Franz J. Schryer, *The Rancheros of Pisaflores: The History of a Peasant Bourgeoisie in Twentieth-Century Mexico* (Toronto, 1979); Florencia E. Mallon, *The Defense of Community in Peru's Central Highlands: Peasant Struggle and Capitalist Transition, 1860–1940* (Princeton, 1984); Eduardo Archetti and Kristi Anne Stolen, *Explotación familiar y acumulación de capital en el campo argentino* (Buenos Aires, 1975). The work by Archetti and Stolen deals with a perhaps atypical (within Latin America) transition to mechanized farming by Italian immigrants in Santa Fé, Argentina, while Schryer's work parallels that of Roseberry and Bergad in its basis in aggregate figures for land tenure and change over time. Mallon's work provides a more detailed view of the "winners" within smallholder society, Schryer's "peasant bourgeoisie," based largely on oral history sources.

3. Picó, *Amargo café*.

4. Carolyn Hall, *El café y el desarrollo histórico-geográfico de Costa Rica* (San José, 1976); idem, *Cóncavas: formación de una hacienda cafetalera* (San José, 1978); Ciro F. S. Cardoso, "Formación de la hacienda cafetalera costarricense, siglo XIX," in Enrique Florescano, ed., *Haciendas, plantaciones, y latifundios en América Latina* (México, 1975), 635–67; Héctor Pérez Brignoli, "Economía política del café en Costa Rica, 1850–1950," *Avances de Investigación*, No. 5 (Universidad de Costa Rica, 1981); Samuel Stone, *La dinastía de los conquistadores* (San José, 1975); Gertrud Peters Solórzano, "La formación territorial de las grandes fincas de café en la Meseta Central: estudio de la firma Tournón (1877–1955)," *Revista de Historia* (Heredia, Costa Rica), Nos. 9–10 (1980): 81–167; Marco Palacios, *El café en Colombia (1870–1970): una historia económica, social, y política* (Bogotá, 1979); Absalón Machado, *El café: de la aparcería al capitalismo* (Bogotá, 1978); Charles Bergquist, *Coffee and Conflict in Colombia, 1886–1910* (Durham, 1978); idem, *Labor in Latin America* (Stanford, 1986).

5. The most influential exponent of smallholder-oriented reformism was Rodrigo Facio in his classic *Estudio sobre economía costarricense* (San José, 1942). For modern-day models based on householder production, see Pérez, "Economía política del café."

6. See Hall, *El café y el desarrollo*, and Peters, "La formación."

7. On the origins of smallholding in Costa Rica, see Elizabeth Fonseca, *Costa Rica colonial: la tierra y el hombre* (San José, 1983); and Lowell Gudmundson, *Costa Rica before Coffee* (Baton Rouge, 1986).

8. Bergquist, *Labor in Latin America*.

9. The terms are those of Facio, the intellectual leader of the pre-1948 reformist movement. For further details see Jorge Enrique Romero Pérez, *La Social Democracia en Costa Rica* (San José, 1977); Gudmundson, *Costa Rica before Coffee*, chap. 1. Bergquist's analysis (*Labor in Latin America*) of the rightward drift of

Venezuelan reformism and of the ambiguities of Columbian smallholder reformism offer suggestive parallels with the Costa Rican experience.

10. For an analysis highlighting the importance of this antilabor component of local reformism in explaining the differing response of the United States to Costa Rica in 1948 and Guatemala in 1954, see Jacobo Schifter Sikora, *Costa Rica 1948* (San José, 1982), 203–47.

11. Aggregate and anonymous data sources are particularly good in Costa Rica, with published population census returns after 1864 and a very detailed coffee producer census taken in 1935 (referred to above) and another general agricultural census in 1955. For this particular study basically four data bases were developed for Santo Domingo–San Isidro (an exercise replicable for virtually any portion of the Central Valley using the same sources). All four include identification by full name (given and, in three of the four cases, both surnames). They are: a population census schedule for 1846, a more detailed one for 1927, some 630 probate inventories between 1840 and 1940, and the originals of the published agricultural census for 1955, owner by owner, farm by farm. The 1846 count for Santo Domingo provides names for only heads of household and their spouses, with little information on kin ties within the household, while the 1927 count is extraordinarily precise on both of these as well as on demographic and economic items. Only 2,371 individuals of the 6,089 reported for Santo Domingo could be found, and none of the 2,744 inhabitants of San Isidro (subsequently, much of the San Isidro was located in the archive and is now available for consultation). The lack of complete records limits the number of family histories or linkages which can be made with other data bases but should not bias those obtainable.

The probate inventory information was codified for computer-based file keeping, as were all four data bases individually. Probate files include information on size of land holdings, land use, number and names of heirs, types of inheritance and distribution of the estate, as well as gross and net worth. The 1955 agricultural census originals exist only on microfilm at the Archivos Nacionales in San José (the location of all four of the data sources described here), an unwitting gift of the Dirección General de Estadística y Censos and not fully cataloged until after 1990. The census covers nearly the entire nation and consists of a lengthy questionnaire completed for each property owner, giving information on all aspects of farm operation, from ownership to cropping, inputs, labor recruitment, credit, and even fertilizer use. Some 600 cases are reported for Santo Domingo (345) and San Isidro (265), which roughly corresponds to the total number of owners reported in the published census figures. Given the number of cases involved, as well as the considerable gaps in the 1927 population census, record linkages were done by hand, while each individual data base was analyzed statistically using a SAS computer package. Combining these data sources allows for the tracking of numerous smallholding households and families over long periods of time. The larger research project on class formation and inheritance in the coffee economy includes a similar reconstruction of the Desamparados-Tarrazú region south of San José, characterized by much lower yields, earlier and more severe impoverishment of smallholders, and growth of the problem of minifundio. A parallel study of class and coffee in the colonization zones of western Alajuela province can be found in Mario Samper, *Generations of Settlers* (Boulder, 1991).

12. San José (and a very few growers in the city of Heredia) had begun coffee cultivation for export in the late 1830s and 1840s.

13. *Revista del Instituto de Defensa del Café* 5 (1937): 185, 301.

14. Ibid.; and for property holding in 1927 the published census of that year by Dirección General de Estadística y Censos.

15. The comparison of land ownership over time is somewhat deceptive in that no holdings under one manzana were registered in 1955, thus understating the number of "owners." However, both probate and census records show a marked concentration and restriction of operating farm ownership, as distinct from house lots, garden plots, or backyard coffee groves. The figures themselves were 811 property owners in Santo Domingo and 442 in San Isidro in 1935, versus 345 and 265 respectively in 1955.

16. At least five owners of the undoubtedly primitive beneficios of the 1880s had been residents of Santo Domingo, while outside ownership was the rule in 1935. See *Revista del Instituto de Defensa del Café* 5 (1937): 185,301; Archivos Nacionales de Costa Rica (hereafter ANCR), Fomento, No. 35 (1887); Gobernación, No. 28957 (1878).

17. Dirección General de Estadística y Censos, *Censo de Población, 1950.*

18. The area of "Quintana" was named for the second wife (Luisa de Quintana) of the Alférez and Teniente de Gobernador Sebastián de Zamora who first owned land in the area. In the early eighteenth century their son, Sargento Mayor Antonio Aurelio de Zamora, requested some nine *caballerías* of land, or 12.2 percent of present-day Santo Domingo's thirty-two square kilometers. Zamora then sold the land in lots of about one caballería to his associates, from whom one may assume arose several additional place names. See Edwin González, "Santo Domingo de Heredia: análisis demográfico y socio-económico (1853–1920)" (licenciatura thesis, Universidad Nacional, Heredia, Costa Rica, 1978), 14–17, citing Luis González Flores, *Origen y desarrollo de las poblaciones de Heredia, San José y Alajuela durante el régimen colonial* (San José, 1943), 37, note 11.

19. The collective portrait of land tenure among the wealthy is based on the following probate inventories filed between 1846 and 1878: ANCR, Mortuales Independientes de Heredia (hereafter MIH), Nos. 132, 144, 173, 174, 182, 245, 553, 560, 562, 584, 613, 629, 655, 880, 887, 974, 982, 987, 1,002, 1,364, 1,379, 1,458, 1,459, 1,563, 1,564, 1,751, 1,876, 2,324, 2,332, 2,337, 2,566, 2,573, 2,578, 3,040, 3,041, 3,400, 3,407, 3,408, 3,415, 3,425, 3,444, 3,450, 3,451, 3,455, 3,458, 3,459, 3,496, 3,499, 3,685, 3,698, and 3,700.

20. One particularly good example of this practice and its mental and linguistic contradictions can be seen in the locals' use of the term *cerco(s)*. While one might logically assume that "*un cerco de maíz*" or "*cerco de labranza*," etc., referred to a fenced crop area, in fact local usage defined the term as any sown or cleared plot. In several probate inventories the distinction is made between cercos of plantings or clearings in preparation for same, and other "*cercos con (sus) cercas (correspondientes)*." On the *cercos* versus *cercas* and *en común* questions see ANCR, MIH Nos. 132 (1846), 144 (1854), 629 (1874), 655 (1878), 1,379

(1869), 1,458 (1857), 1,563 (1846), 2,324 (1845), 2,566 (1846), 2,573 (1849), 3,408 (1867), 3,496 (1859), 3,685 (1848), and 3,698 (1857).

21. Surviving fragmentary documentation on liberal reform-era (1850s and 1860s) deeding of public lands in the Caricias/Cuascua area between Santo Domingo and San Isidro shows small-scale claims and grants in the few manzanas rather than large ones in caballerías. An excellent study of the titling process and out-migration from this area is by Margarita Torres, "Los campesinos de San Rafael de Heredia, 1830–1930: de usufructuarios comunales a propietarios privados" (Licenciatura thesis, Universidad Nacional, 1991). These records are partially preserved in the loft of Heredia's municipal building, as part of the Municipality's *Actas*. They will no doubt soon be lost, due to use of the loft as a makeshift kitchen for the municipal employees' noon meal.

22. Source material on the contradictions of a petty bourgeois ideology which was both reformist (antioligarchic) and defensive if not reactionary (vis-à-vis worker ideology) can be found along with the statistical studies of the *Revista del Instituto de Defensa del Café*. The following headings suggest the kinds of issues dealt with: "Por el trabajador rural," "El café, distribuidor de riquezas," "Un producto que pudieramos llamar socialista," "A quién debe corresponder la plusvalía del suelo?" (to the worker or direct producer, based on the teachings of Adam Smith rather than any "socialist" or "communist" ideology); 1 (1934–35): 202–4; 3 (1935–36): 560–63.

23. Long ago Richard Hofstadter contrasted North American agricultural regions and their responses to populist politics (lukewarm in the capitalized, mixed-farming old Northwest, fervent in the indebted and monocultural wheat and cotton belts) on the basis of the latter's use of the term (hired) "help" versus "laborer" or "worker" in the former. Kin-based labor recruitment, even when salaried, and its ideological manipulation helped "soften" class differences and antagonisms within a petty producer-based reform movement. For similarly perceptive analyses of kin and gender ideologies in Latin America, see Florencia Mallon, *The Defense of Community*, and "Gender and Class in the Transition to Capitalism: Household and Mode of Production in Central Peru," *Latin American Perspectives* 13 (1986): 147–74.

24. The Anglophone term *trust* was often used by Costa Rican reformist defenders of producers (identified with "the nation") against processors. See Victor Hugo Acuña Ortega, "La ideología de los pequeños y medianos productores cafetaleros costarricenses (1900–1961)," *Revista de Historia* 16 (1987): 137–59, and "Patrones del conflicto social en la economía cafetalera costarricense (1900–1948)," *Revista de Ciencias Sociales* (Universidad de Costa Rica), 31 (1986): 113–22.

25. For Tournón see Peters, "La formación," and for Sánchez see Ana Virginia Arguedas Chaverri and Marta Ramírez Arias, "Contribución al análisis de empresas: el caso de Julio Sánchez Lepiz" (Licenciatura thesis, Universidad Nacional, Heredia, 1985).

26. Since colonial times mule-based transport often led to considerable accumulation of wealth. In Costa Rica major fortunes were made in cart transport during the second half of the nineteenth century. That this particular fortune

proved long-lived can be seen in the fact that the Nobel Prize–winning former Costa Rican president, Oscar Arias Sánchez, is the grandson of Julio Sánchez.

27. See Acuña's works, cited in note 22, and Manuel Marín Quirós, "Discurso ante la asamblea de productores de café, celebrada en el Teatro Júpiter de Guadalupe, en la tarde del domingo 27 de marzo de 1932," *Revista de Historia* 16 (1987): 133–35.

28. On the post-1948 innovations and their consequences see Ciska Raventós, "El café en Costa Rica: desarrollo capitalista y diferenciación social de los productores, 1950–1980" (Postgraduate thesis, Universidad de Costa Rica, San José, 1983); and "Desarrollo económico, estructura y contradicciones sociales en la producción de café," *Revista de Historia* 14 (1986): 179–95. José D. Cazanga, *Las cooperativas de caficultores en Costa Rica* (San José, 1987) (based on a late 1970s thesis at the Universidad de Costa Rica). See also the excellent study of Anthony Winson, *Coffee and Democracy in Modern Costa Rica* (London, 1989).

29. For processor/producer conflict see, ANCR, MIH, Nos. 1,081 (1899), 3,816 (1914), 4,652 (1909); Remesa 982, No. 2 (1924), 296 (1921), 298 (1912); Remesa 1,294, No. 93 (1933). Of the 630 inventories, roughly 75 to 100 might be considered of well-to-do owners without processing plants (only four cases refer to these). Representative examples include: Nos. 467, 629, 698, 719, 729, 735, 1,425, 1,901, 2,796, 2,799, 3,153, 3,186, 3,476, 3,553, 3,580, 3,762, 3,834, 4,596, 4,766 (1874–1920); Remesa No. 1,168, Nos. 4, 86, 101, 122, 182, 244 (1919–1928); Remesa No. 1,294, Nos. 29, 67, 160, 161 (1931–1937); Santo Domingo, Alcaldía Unica, Nos. 56, 99, 147 (1898–1903).

30. Of 600 farmers surveyed in 1955, only 146 reported access to credit, 108 from private sources.

31. ANCR, MIH, Remesa No. 1,168, No. 4 (1923).

32. Ibid., No. 4,596 (1920). All subsequent reconstructions also employ the 1927 and 1955 census originals as described in note 11.

33. Ibid., Santo Domingo Alcadía Unica, No. 141 (1900).

34. Ibid., No. 3,751 (1887). For detailed analysis of the extraordinarily successful settlers from San Rafael de Heredia in Naranjo, see Margarita Torres, "Los campesinos de San Rafael de Heredia." For a case of a family heavily indebted to local processor lenders which was able to acquire forty hectares of public lands in Tilarán in highland Guanacaste Province, see ANCR, MIH, Remesa No. 1,294, No. 93 (1933).

35. Ibid., No. 2,202 (1883).

36. Ibid., Santo Domingo Alcadía Unica, No. 112 (1905).

37. Ibid., No. 70 (1907).

38. Ibid., Remesa No. 1,168, No. 125 (1932).

39. Ibid., Remesa No. 1,472, No. 3 (1939).

40. For examples of this see ANCR, MIH, No. 287 (1899–1903); 1,081 (1899); 4,652 (1909); Remesa No. 1,168, No. 184 (1929); 303 (1927).

41. The 1844 census referred to is not the one used for reconstruction (1846). The 1844 count is part of ANCR, Congreso, No. 5,424. All males over roughly fourteen declared occupations in 1927 while only heads of households did in the

mid-nineteenth-century counts. The 1927 declaration was very precise, asking "what" the occupation was, "where" it was undertaken, and "on whose account."

42. See Table 5.15. The fact that several different administrative sources (Juzgado Civil, Remesas, Alcaldía Unica, etc.) are combined in the probate section of the archive, with radically different distributions across time periods, suggests the need for caution in any generalizations regarding change over time.

43. For a fuller discussion of family and household in nineteenth-century Costa Rica, see Gudmundson, *Costa Rica before Coffee*, 88–124.

44. Ibid., 107.

45. Values for women are lower owing to the frequency of single motherhood and heading of households by such young women.

46. For similar findings on the impact of market agriculture amid growing land scarcity, see Anne Hagerman Johnson, "The Impact of Market Agriculture on Family and Household Structure in Nineteenth-Century Chile," *Hispanic American Historical Review* 58 (1978): 625–48; and Elizabeth Anne Kuznesof, "An Analysis of Household Composition and Headship as Related to Changes in Mode of Production: São Paulo, 1765 to 1836," *Comparative Studies in Society and History* 22 (1980): 78–108.

47. See, for example, Astrid Fischel Volio, *Consenso y represión: una interpretación sociopolítica de la educación costarricense* (San José, 1987).

48. Literacy figures come from González, "Santo Domingo," who quotes 1883 and 1892 census reports. A detailed study of the early-twentieth-century graduates of the Normal School in Heredia would likely shed considerable light on these questions.

49. For material on Fonseca, one of twelve children of a middling landed family with a house and three small pieces of crop land in Santo Domingo in 1893, see Acuña, "La ideología," 145, and ANCR, MIH, No. 465 (1893). Fonseca was an organizer of producer cooperatives and prolific author of opinion pieces published in the major daily of the time, *Diario de Costa Rica*.

50. These responses were included in the census forms analyzed in Tables 5.10–5.13 and described in note 11.

51. Raventós, "El café en Costa Rica" and "Desarrollo económico."

52. Of these fully 109 had one manzana or less replanted. Virtually all coffee was more than ten years old and of the mid-nineteenth-century arábigo variety characterized by much greater height and lower yields than twentieth-century hybrid varieties.

53. Studies of fertilizer use and yields are reported in the *Revista del Instituto de Defensa del Café* 1 (1935): 19. For Turrialba see, Antonio Manuel Arce, "Rational Introduction of Technology on a Costa Rican Coffee Hacienda: Sociological Implications" (Ph.D. diss., Michigan State University, 1959).

54. Under colonial-era legislation, only one-seventh of the deceased's estate could be freely disposed of in favoring any heir. After 1882 all such restrictions were theoretically lifted.

55. This was in large part a reflection of a decline in the number of *potreros* or pasture lands and less-developed properties which were almost always the ones

given in *derechos* or *acciones* without any material division. Coffee groves were supposedly divided very precisely, both monetarily and physically, although one might well doubt the truthfulness of these claims over time.

56. ANCR, MIH, Remesa No. 1,168, No. 41 (1932).

57. For similar findings see Alida Christine Metcalf, "Fathers and Sons: The Politics of Inheritance in a Colonial Brazilian Township," *Hispanic American Historical Review* 66 (1986): 455–84. For an exceptionally clear case of this involving Santo Domingo residents, see ANCR, MIH, No. 2,202 (1883).

58. Raventós, "Desarrollo económico"; Cazanga, *Las cooperativas*.

59. For similar processes of growing conservatism among militant farmer co-operatives in the United States and Canada, see Garin Burbank, "Agrarian Socialism in Saskatchewan and Oklahoma: Short-run Radicalism, Long-run Conservatism," *Agricultural History* 51 (1977): 173–80, and Steven Hahn, *The Roots of Southern Populism* (New York, 1983).

Six

In Difficult Times: Colombian and Costa Rican Coffee Growers from Prosperity to Crisis, 1920–1936

MARIO SAMPER KUTSCHBACH

T HROUGHOUT LATIN America, coffee has been — and continues to be — cultivated on very diverse types of productive units, often in close and sometimes conflictive interaction among growers. The dynamics of the relations between peasant-farmer households and owners of capital differ not only from one country to another but also — quite significantly — among coffee-producing regions of each country. They also vary, of course, over time, as external and domestic conditions which affect them change and influence each other. Thus, for example, a region where large estates predominated during earlier stages of agro-export growth may evolve toward more independent household-based production as a consequence of the specific ways in which local as well as international processes are played out in the context of specific social forces. Conversely, peasant coffee production may be weakened by the manner in which world-market and other external conditions are "internalized," and by concrete power shifts at a national or regional level.

Colombia and Costa Rica offer two especially appropriate cases for a comparative historical discussion of such changes. By the early twentieth century, both included regions where family-labor farms were especially important, and others where coffee was produced primarily on larger farms. Toward 1930, both countries faced an adverse world-market situation for their main export commodity, owing to a combination of trends in the coffee sector itself and the overall impact of the 1929 economic depresssion. However, specific outcomes, and especially the consequences for various types of productive units, differed significantly from one country to the other, but also among regions within each one.

Why was household-based coffee production alternatively strengthened or weakened as the apparent prosperity of the 1920s gave way to
the crisis of the following decade? This question can only be answered
through a historical analysis of the socioeconomic and sociopolitical processes that affected the viability of various types of production unit in each
case. Rather than assuming an inherently greater "resilience" of peasant
coffee farming or an intrinsic economic and political advantage to coffee-
producing estates, this study will address the issue of how, why, and with
what consequences one or the other outcome ensued.

The vicissitudes of peasant farmers and estate owners in the coffee
regions were, of course, part of broader societal transformations, specifically in terms of class relations, and must be discussed in relation to them.
The prospects for peasant farming and for capitalist enterprises, as prosperity gave way to crisis, were affected in many and often decisive ways
by society-wide redefinitions in terms of economic and political power
among the major social forces of the time. Simultaneously, the specific
developments in key coffee-producing regions were crucial for these predominantly rural societies where coffee was not only the major export
product but also the commodified expression of fundamental class conflicts and solidarities.

The issues raised are not merely academic, inasmuch as coffee growers
in Latin America, and especially those relying to a large extent on household labor, once again face a major, though different, critical juncture.
The recent changes stemming from socially differentiated — and differenti-
ating — technological transformations, concentration and centralization
of capital in production, processing, and marketing, and shifting power
relations are now set in the context of a regional economic crisis, a redefinition of the growth model, and fundamental changes in the world
coffee market. As in the past, specific social outcomes will result from
complex, conflictive interactions among social forces in each case, and
from the ways in which external factors are "internalized."

Coffee Producers in Costa Rica and Colombia

A prior comparative analysis of Costa Rican and Colombian coffee cultivation[1] indicates the existence of certain specific interactions between social and technological factors of coffee production and processing which
are essential to an understanding of the agricultural history of these two
countries during the 1920s and 1930s. Such interactions, as they relate to
broader societal processes, can also help explain the experience of diverse
production units and coffee-growing regions within the context of the

international economic crisis. Briefly summarized, they can be stated as follows.

In both countries numerous coffee production units were based on family labor, which interacted in various ways with larger enterprises (e.g., those with more than 60,000 trees). In the early 1930s, large enterprises directly controlled less than 25 percent of each country's coffee trees, and perhaps a somewhat higher percentage of production. Farms under 20,000 trees (which include most domestic units as well as sub-family holdings)[2] accounted for 68 percent of the total number of coffee trees in Colombia (1932), and for 60 percent in Costa Rica (1935). Yet indirectly, agroindustrial and commercial capital controlled most of the other factors associated with coffee production, such as financing, final processing, and marketing. Furthermore, there was a strong tendency toward subdivision of small coffee farms, via inheritance or other mechanisms, which by the 1930s was reflected in the fact that coffee groves with fewer than 5,000 trees accounted for almost nine-tenths of the total number of farms in either country, and, at least in Costa Rica, the majority of these small farms were actually sub-family holdings with under 1,000 trees.

Colombian coffee growers were concentrated in three main regions (Map 6.1), separated from each other and from the coasts by substantial geographical obstacles: Santander, to the east near Venezuela, which had been the first to engage in this venture since the mid nineteenth century but subsequently declined in importance; the intermediate-altitude areas of Cundinamarca and eastern Tolima, in central Colombia, starting in the latter part of that century; and the main areas of settlement and coffee production in the west, Antioquia and Viejo Caldas, from the late nineteenth century on.

Costa Rican coffee producers, instead, were located in a far smaller and geographically continuous area known as the Valle Central, actually a tectonic depression which contains a number of small valleys (Map 6.2). In the core zone of colonial settlement, known as the Meseta Central, coffee production began in the 1820s, and subsequent processes of settlement permitted the expansion of this crop, along with others, toward the west (especially after construction of the Carretera Nacional in the 1840s, an ox-cart road to the Pacific) and eastward (mainly since the building of the railroad to the Atlantic in the 1870s).

Distances to the Caribbean and Pacific ports, and internal transportation difficulties, were therefore far less significant in the Costa Rican than in the Colombian case and were more rapidly overcome. This was important not only to the early expansion of coffee production in the Central American country but also to the very different systems of processing and

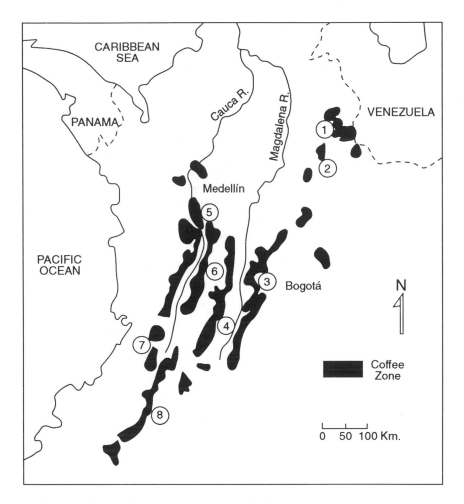

1 = Norte de Santander   5 = Antioquia
2 = Santander (Sur)   6 = Caldas
3 = Cundinamarca   7 = Valle
4 = Tolima   8 = Cauca

Map 6.1. Principal Coffee-Growing Areas of Colombia in the 1920s and 1930s. *1,* Norte De Santander; *2,* Santander (Sur); *3,* Cundinamarca; *4,* Tolima; *5,* Antioquia; *6,* Caldas; *7,* Valle; *8,* Cauca. *Sources:* J. Parsons, *La colonización antioqueña en el occidente de Colombia* (Bogotá, 1979, 3rd ed.), 177; Palacios, *El café en Colombia,* 64–74.

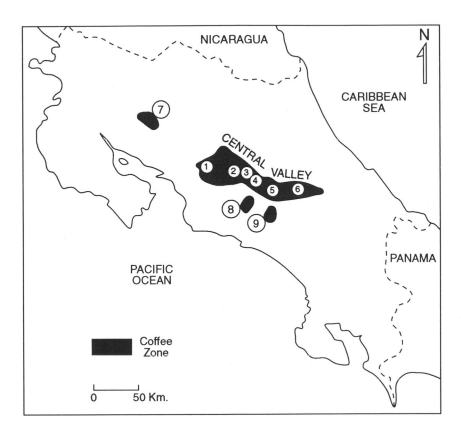

1 = San Ramón
2 = Alajuela
3 = Heredia
4 = San José

5 = Cartago
6 = Turrialba
7 = Tilarán
8 = San Ignacio
9 = Los Santos

Map 6.2. Principal Coffee-Growing Areas of Costa Rica in the 1920s and 1930s. *1*, San Ramon; *2*, Alajuela; *3*, Heredia; *4*, San Jose; *5*, Cartago; *6*, Turrialba; *7*, Tilaran; *8*, San Ignacio; *9*, Los Santos. *Sources:* G. Sandner, *La colonización agrícola de Costa Rica,* vol. 1 (San José, 1962), fig. 13; C. Hall, *El café y el desarrollo histórico-geográfico de Costa Rica* (San José, 1976), 16; Hall, *Costa Rica: una interpretación geográfica con perspectiva histórica* (San José, 1984), 158.

the conditions under which small coffee growers related to merchants and processing firms.

The relative importance of peasant farmer production versus *hacienda* (estate) production varied significantly from one region to another in each country.[3] Colombia's coffee haciendas were mostly located in the central-eastern departments, especially Cundinamarca, which had been settled earlier and where coffee production had been important for a longer period than in western Colombia. While there were some coffee-producing haciendas in western Colombia, especially near Medellín, large land grants had been subdivided in the process of southward settlement in that part of the country, and many peasants also had access to public lands, individually or collectively.

In Costa Rica most large coffee estates were situated in the eastern part of the Valle Central, an area of relatively recent settlement. Peasant farming was more important in the central and western sections of the tectonic depression. However, haciendas and peasant farms coexisted in all coffee-producing regions of both countries, in often conflictive manners which require case and comparative analysis.

With respect to the social concentration of coffee production, as reflected (partially) in the number of trees and size of holdings, there were therefore certain affinities between Cundinamarca, in Colombia, and Costa Rica's eastern Central Valley. This is not to say, however, that social relations were essentially the same or even very similar in these two very different regions. There were affinities in terms of landholding distribution and size of coffee farms, too, between the remaining areas of the Costa Rican Valle Central and most of western Colombia. Although the same caveat applies, social relations seem to have been more similar in some respects.

Interaction among members of rural domestic units and capital owners, in coffee-producing regions, could take place on several different levels, including commercial exchange, various systems of access to land, diverse labor relations, credit, and other social relations associated with coffee growing, processing, and marketing. There were, then, many interrelated forms of peasant household participation in the production process. Their effect on the direct producers and on capital accumulation varied with the different regions and the span of time, responding to the specific conditions governing the participation of peasant farmers in the various markets. These conditions were determined by direct and indirect controls exerted by capital owners on production, land, processing, credit, and marketing. These were the bases of complementarity and also of fundamental conflicts between direct producers and capital owners.

In terms of actual coffee production, both small and large production units were characterized by a low level of technological innovation, similar cultural practices and traditional varieties, and crop diversity at the individual farm level. There were no major economies of scale during this stage, and differences in yields were not the result of a predominance of specific kinds of production unit (such as haciendas or peasant households) but of differences in soils, climate, crop density, and other such factors. Differences in yield were also the result of soil depletion or aging trees. Future production was dependent on these factors as well as on the percentage of new trees that had not yet reached maturity.

A greater or lesser seasonal concentration of harvest labor requirements was in fact determined by climatic conditions for each case, although the pattern of social organization of this activity was dependent on the type of production unit. In both Colombia and Costa Rica there were pronounced seasonal labor "peaks," but in the latter the harvest was conducted once a year, during a three- to four-month period, while in the former there were usually two harvest seasons (*principal* and *mitaca*). Tasks such as picking, processing, and selecting coffee berries therefore took longer to complete in Colombia than in Costa Rica. Both haciendas and peasant households in Colombia were more self-sufficient in terms of labor than in Costa Rica, where the seasonal variations were much more acute.

However, no type of production unit was able to fully standardize its labor needs for coffee-related tasks in either country, and their members often engaged in other productive activities, whether on the same farm or elsewhere. Even middling peasant coffee growers had seasonal labor shortages and/or surpluses, and for this reason they often had to hire workers and also, at times, work for wages themselves. There was, of course, the additional option of maintaining a diversified cropping system as well as nonagricultural activities to smooth labor cycles to a certain extent.

Coffee processing during the years covered by this study was technically and socially very different in both countries. In Costa Rica coffee processing was centralized in relatively large, capital-intensive, water-based processing centers where the berry was readied for export. In Colombia, although some large farms processed the coffee they grew, peasant farmers generally pulped, washed, and dried their own harvest, which was then sold to threshing centers which would finish processing. This division into two separate stages resulted primarily from the need to reduce domestic transportation costs in this country, although other factors were involved.

The systems employed in coffee processing in Costa Rica and Colombia during this time affected the relationship between independent producers and capital owners. Both the system of credit for future crops in Costa Rica (the *adelantos*) and that of selling harvests beforehand in Colombia (the *prenda agraria*) were risky for the producer who might be unable to fully repay his creditors in case of bad harvest or low prices. In both instances commercial capital already functioned as an extension of agro-industrial capital, rather than as an independent intermediary function. Moreover, the need to sell the harvest without delay and the general status of medium and small producers in Costa Rica made them quite vulnerable to the virtual oligopoly/oligopsony of the processors/buyers. In Colombia, especially in the western region, peasant farmers who had the choice of selling their coffee pulped or in the berry were still subject to vast marketing networks controlled by the major entrepreneurs who manipulated prices. For that purpose, processing and export firms had purchasing agents in the towns, but also reached secret agreements among each other. Nevertheless, small farmers had greater leeway in choosing the timing and location of their sale of partially processed coffee beans, despite the constraints derived from their subordinate position in the coffee business.

Social relations in the coffee-producing areas of Costa Rica resembled more closely those in western Colombia than those in Cundinamarca, especially before the partial breakdown of coffee haciendas there. Of course, there were subregional variations in landholding and in the relative importance of wage versus family labor, both within Costa Rica's Central Valley and within the areas of Antioqueño settlement. Yet in both cases there was a combination of modern capitalistic enterprises and numerous small to medium farms. The variegated land tenure pattern was associated with labor systems which were at times competitive and at times complementary. In Cundinamarca, the predominance of large estates until the mid-1920s was accompanied by that of more traditional social relations where land usufruct was often exchanged for labor obligations.

In Costa Rica as in Antioquia, although there was some sharecropping especially in the latter case, free contractual wage labor tended to be the predominant social relation of production on coffee-producing haciendas. There was a resident work force year-round on such estates, often alternating between coffee, sugar cane, and other activities. Seasonal peaks in labor demand, somewhat less pronounced in the Colombian case, were supplemented by the work of wives and children of permanent laborers, as well as by hiring temporary, nonresident workers, often paid by task or on amount harvested.

Formally independent peasant cultivators, quite numerous in both Costa Rica and the Antioqueño region, had access to substantial amounts of land and controlled a major part of coffee production. They were, as previously mentioned, subject to the control of processing and export firms through mercantile/financial mechanisms. In Costa Rica, the dominance of centralized wet-processing and the lower transport costs led to more direct ties between small producers and agroindustrial capital, which in turn generated specific and explicit social tensions. In western Colombia, the separation of artisanal depulping in small tanks from the more centralized *trillado* (husking) created at least the appearance of greater independence for peasant farmers, less pressured to sell quickly or to a given firm. Yet they too faced an effective oligopsony, ably disguised by secret price-setting arrangements among the main processing and export firms, whose owners, as Palacios has shown, were more than willing to set partisan politics aside for the sake of extraordinary profit.

In Cundinamarca, until the mid-1920s, free contractual wage labor on the estates and coffee production on independent small farms were less important than in either western Colombia or Costa Rica. Instead, large haciendas involved in coffee production but with much uncultivated land came to have major areas under various types of tenancy and sharecropping arrangements. From the late 1920s to the mid-1930s, it is precisely this pattern of land usufruct and labor organization that is going to rupture, as a consequence of internal pressures and regional social conflicts as well as society-wide processes.

The technical and social organization of coffee production in Costa Rica and Colombia, with the regional variations briefly discussed above, is the necessary background for any understanding of the ways in which external conditions were "internalized" in each case. When the seeming prosperity of the 1920s was followed by crisis in the next decade, new tensions were grafted on those stemming from prior social processes, with different outcomes in each case.

World Market and Local Crises

In order to understand the impact of macroeconomic variables on the different types of coffee production units and on social relations in coffee regions, we must first compare certain tendencies and fluctuations of this economic sector in both countries. It is beyond the scope of this essay, however, to conduct any detailed analysis of economic growth and inflation in the 1920s and the recession of the following decade, or their effects on the Latin American economies, which have been well documented elsewhere. Our aim will be to discuss certain shared characteristics and some differences between the coffee-growing sectors in these countries, as they responded to changing conditions of the international economy and specifically of the market for coffee.

World coffee production during these two decades faced a twofold crisis on the international market.[4] On the one hand there developed an imbalance between a constantly growing supply and a stagnant demand in the 1920s. The apparent prosperity of the times and high prices for coffee during that decade exacerbated an already problematic situation because of the resulting increase in coffee plantations and surpluses. On the other hand the international economic crisis of the early thirties lowered coffee prices on the world market at the same time that the aforementioned new coffee growing areas were beginning production. As a result of this two-fold crisis (structural imbalance and short-term downturn)[5], world coffee prices not only began to decline earlier but dropped further and took longer to recover than those of other agricultural export products such as sugar cane and cotton. Yet coffee production, relatively inelastic in the short term, did not decline in response to low prices. It actually tended to increase for the aforementioned reasons, although new plantings probably did come to a halt temporarily. Since only Brazil could actually influence international prices significantly, as an individual exporting country, by withholding coffee from the world market, other producers tended to maintain or increase their exports whenever possible. In addition, Colombian and Costa Rican coffee enjoyed a more favorable market situation for their high-quality coffee, even in difficult times.[6]

Due to the importance of coffee growing to each national economy, the severe and prolonged drop in prices certainly affected foreign trade in both countries, reducing export revenues. However, the increased volume of production and exports partially counteracted this effect. Coffee from both Costa Rica and Colombia continued to find a market outlet, and it is debatable whether or not the impact of the crisis of 1929 on coffee was the single major factor behind economic problems facing both countries at least up until 1931.

Former Costa Rican President Alfredo González Flores conducted an economic study in 1936 in which he concluded that the crisis of 1929 in his country "did not stem from problems in the coffee industry," pointing out that although prices fell in 1930 and 1931, the appreciation of gold increased purchasing power. Coffee became a critical factor only in 1932 as a result of low yields, low prices, and a devalued British pound.[7] According to Flores, internal causes of the crisis could be traced back to 1927, when the country experienced high foreign debt coupled with inflationary practices.[8] In contrast to this, a study conducted by economist Carlos Merz during the same year argued in favor of government policy, stressing that coffee had a major impact on the country's economy as a whole and that "the problem was not with production but with prices. Selling the crop is not a problem either, because all of the coffee produced has been placed easily on the international market."[9] The problem was, therefore, fundamentally external, price-related, and closely associated with the international recession.

Subsequently, in light of the discrepancies about the nature and origins of the crisis, both of the above mentioned contemporary theses were carefully evaluated by sociologist José Luis Vega, who concluded that Flores was basically correct. In other words, low prices for coffee only worsened a situation which had its origins in prior economic processes and policies. However, he added that Flores's short-term, monetaristic perspective kept him from realizing that as the price of Costa Rican coffee declined in London (the country's principal market) "there occurred a steady, progressive, and significant devaluation of the country's labor, despite constantly increased volumes."[10] The increased volume was not a response to the economic hardships of the thirties; instead it was the simple result of the crop expansion of the previous decade.

Colombia presents a similar scenario of increased exports in the 1920s and 1930s stemming from the crop expansion in several regions during previous years.[11] The collapse of the international coffee market caused significant impact in Colombia's coffee sector as a result of declining prices during the years 1929 to 1933. The full effect of the collapse was somewhat diminished by increased volume of exports and a drop in the cost of imports. Because of this the overall impact on terms of trade, and especially the purchasing power of Colombian coffee exports, was moderate. According to researcher José Antonio Ocampo, the breakdown of international capital flow, which began in 1929, with increased service payments on the national debt resulting from credit obtained during the previous decade had a much more detrimental effect on Colombia.[12]

In short both Costa Rica and Colombia experienced the international economic crisis, in part as a rapid decline in coffee prices and a drastic reduction of capital flow, after a decade of increased borrowing abroad and possibly deteriorating terms of trade. A greater volume of production and of exports helped soften the impact, as did the favorable position of their coffee on the international markets during the 1930s. As we have seen, the increase in volume was partly due to expansion of the area planted in coffee during the 1920s, and also to a relatively favorable situation of mild coffees in the world market during the difficult 1930s. Let us compare the three indicators discussed above — volume, price lists, and total export value — for our two cases throughout the period before reaching some general conclusions about the behavior of the coffee sector of these economies during the period.

As shown in Figure 6.1, Colombian and Costa Rican coffee production continued to grow at a similar rate during the 1920s, and in the case of

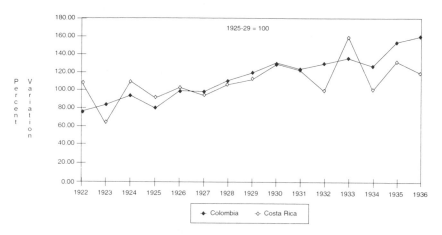

Fig. 6.1. Costa Rican and Colombian Coffee Production, 1922–1936. *Sources:* J. A. Ocampo and S. Montenegro, "La crisis mundial de los años treinta en Colombia," *Desarrollo y Sociedad* 7 (1982), 86; A. Samper, *Importancia de café en el comercio exterior de Colombia* (Bogotá, 1948), 89; C. Merz, "Coyuntura y crisis en Costa Rica de 1924 a 1936," *Revista del Instituto de Defensa del Café* IV (1936), 606; J. L. Vega, *Hacia una interpretación del desarrollo costarricense: Ensayo sociológico* (San José, 1983, 2nd ed.), 289.

Colombia it continued its sustained growth into the 1930s. In Costa Rica production was more erratic after 1931 as a result of an alternating pattern of large and smaller harvests during the following three years. The well-known biannual compensatory effect typical of such crops, due to biological recovery of the plants after heavy harvests, was less noticeable in aggregate figures for Colombia as a result of its greater regional differences, while in Costa Rica the effect was much more noticeable as a result of its reduced geographic area. Price lists for both countries declined in a similar fashion during the period in question, but the price of Costa Rican coffee decreased less in the early 1930s than that of Colombia's (see Figure 6.2). The trends in value of both countries' coffee exports during the twenties and thirties (see Figure 6.3) were similar, although the decline began earlier in Colombia.

Taken as a whole, there were no fundamental differences in terms of the effects of problems in the international market on the exports of both countries in question, which could suffice to explain differing social processes in the respective coffee regions. Yet the literature does suggest that the social impact of the international economic crisis among groups of producers varied rather substantially from one country to the other.

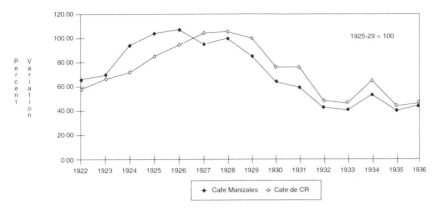

Fig. 6.2. Price of Colombian and Costa Rican Coffee, 1922–1936. *Sources:* Ocampo and Montenegro, "La crisis mundial," 46; Merz, "Coyuntura y crisis," 606; Vega, *Hacia una interpretación del desarrollo costarricense,* 289.

Economic Viability of Coffee Farms

While historical research on Colombia stresses the vulnerability of haciendas to the economic difficulties of the 1930s, studies on Costa Rica stress, rather, the vulnerability of peasant farmers. Let us follow the reasoning in each case, to assess possible explanations of these divergent analyses as well as their actual historical basis.

In Colombia several studies have emphasized the peasant farmers' ability to cope with economic hardships. Antonio García, one of the first to research this aspect (in Caldas, the prototypical smallholder area), concludes that "the small farm is best able to support a tendency of coffee prices to decline, and its selection process cannot be surpassed."[13] Marco Palacios, while considering other factors, also states that given prevailing conditions in the coffee markets and the expansion of Colombian capitalism, the small peasant farm is a much more viable productive unit than the old precapitalist hacienda, and adds:

A peasant farmer's "cost structure" is more resilient and has more options. In a nation where institutions are as weak as they were in Colombia during the first half of the twentieth century, the outcome of the crisis will be less traumatic if a single-crop export economy were based on peasant households, since it is easier to transfer the negative impact of the crisis to the peasant farmer reducing his income further. However, the credit and market crisis must still be resolved.[14]

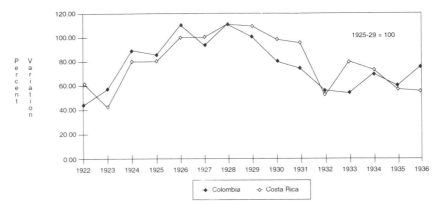

Fig. 6.3. Value of Costa Rican and Colombian Coffee Exports, 1922–1936. *Sources:* Samper, *Importancia de café,* 14; Vega, *Hacia una interpretación del desarrollo costarricense,* 308.

Domestic units are therefore, to follow this line of reasoning, more viable forms of production during short-term crises, since they exclude costs that would make larger operations unprofitable. In addition, it is easy for the sectors controlling marketing and credit to transfer the brunt of an economic crisis to these peasant households. These factors contributed to the decline of the large haciendas in Colombia's east-central regions during the thirties due to a "possible loss of profitability as a result of the international crisis," in addition to domestic "financial and management problems and the financial weakness of many *hacienda* owners" associated with heavy indebtedness and mortgage payments.[15]

In addition to continuing the strong emphasis of Colombian historians and other social scientists on the historical capacity of the peasant farmers to resist crises (an emphasis derived in part from the difficulties experienced by some haciendas during these years), Palacios also points to several other factors that explain the demise of several haciendas in the Cundinamarca and Tolima region, including: the establishment of a common front between tenant farmers and day laborers in haciendas regarding the conditions of their relationship with the haciendas and then with respect to the land itself; a legitimacy crisis of the hacienda system, which was exacerbated by an acceleration of intra-elite conflict and of political-ideological struggles; loss of leadership on the part of landholders in the central region with regard to entrepreneurs in Antioquia; the existence of a strongly populist trend in Colombian liberalism; and an economic policy which tended to strengthen peasant coffee farming as well as entrepreneurial profitability in marketing rather than solve the economic and financial troubles of the hacienda system.[16]

Recent studies such as that conducted by Bejarano and Kalmanovitz, in discussing the decline of haciendas in central Colombia,[17] suggest that the antiquated forms of labor relations practiced in the haciendas were also weakened by industrialization and urbanization processes which provided alternative sources of employment for the laborers, the low productivity of these labor relations when compared to independent or salaried workers, and the penetration of capital into rural areas and subsequent revaluation of land.

In contrast to the above, several authors in Costa Rica indicate that as of 1931 the drop in the price of coffee and land affected "the coffee growing sector and especially the small farmer, who was not able to withstand the effects in terms of production costs. Subsequently, they found themselves forced to sell their land to large producers at low prices. In some cases the banks repossessed the land so as to cancel the small farmer's debt."[18] Land sales and foreclosures during the 1930s may have helped increase the concentration of landholding in the Central Valley, as well as the supply of rural wage labor, and contributed to the expulsion of migrants toward remote frontier regions and urban centers. Nevertheless, according to Gertrud Peters, most creditors were not interested in obtaining ownership of these small, widespread lands which would prove expensive to manage. The absorption of these small land parcels by large haciendas was a geographically selective process.[19] Other measures employed by creditors to recover interest payments included the temporary management of a debtor's land for a period of two to three years.[20] Some coffee-processing centers either stopped purchasing coffee from their clients or set very low prices, which resulted in protests from small and medium producers. In addition, the lack of work available in certain coffee-producing areas substantially reduced the income of peasant-farmer families, which depended partly on salaries. In essence, available research indicates that the crisis in Costa Rica's coffee sector struck hardest at the level of domestic units that were in a disadvantageous position when dealing with processing centers and the land-poor (i.e., deficit-yielding and sub-family) units, which were heavily dependent on income from off-farm wage work. Land-poor status was due to processes of socioeconomic differentiation among peasant farmers, capital accumulation by agroindustrial firms, and subdivision of peasant holdings via inheritance.

It should be noted that even though the crisis of the thirties certainly affected coffee enterprises in Costa Rica, there was no large-scale dismantling of haciendas or widespread foreclosures of processing centers. As a matter of fact the latter, which controlled financing, processing, and marketing, survived in part because they were able to transfer the brunt of the crisis to their "clients," primarily small and medium producers. This situation, while it did not completely ruin small-scale Costa Rican coffee farmers, forced them to organize and seek state regulation of relations between processors and small farmers, which finally came about in 1936. Here it is important to add, for comparative purposes, that small and medium producers in Costa Rica did not mobilize together with salaried workers as a united front. The relative "transparency" of the conflicting interests of such coffee farmers and the processing firms, whom they viewed as a monopolistic group, may paradoxically have helped to obscure their potential affinity with other social sectors whose interests also conflicted with those of the agro-export bourgeoisie.

Moreover, in contrast to Colombia, there was no attempt to dismantle large landholdings of major coffee estates in the Central Valley, no fundamental questioning of private property there. The same was not true for uncultivated landholdings in other, more remote parts of the country which were experiencing spontaneous colonization. The absence of major internal conflict in the haciendas (with the exception of a few isolated instances of labor conflicts) is related to the scarcity of tenant farming and sharecropping in the haciendas and to the fact that most land was under production. However, other variables (discussed below) related to the roles played by the large coffee producers in Costa Rican society. Large coffee barons in Costa Rica enjoyed a stronger position within the structure of the dominant class than did their counterparts in Cundinamarca and Tolima at the time.

Coffee and Politics

The political environments wherein individuals and collective social forces from the coffee sectors of Costa Rica and Colombia interacted during these two decades were similar in some respects, yet different in other critical ones. Both countries were governed by elected governments in which the "coffee oligarchy" had significant influence over public affairs. In both countries the state intervened to ease social tensions, which had become increasingly conflictive in rural areas, and in the process to legitimize the role of the state. The countries differ, however with respect to the composition of the politically dominant class at the time: Costa Rica's single-crop economy, concentrated in a relatively small region, was controlled by a rather cohesive, homogeneous coffee elite. Colombia's diversified economy, complex social structure, and major regional variations were the foundation for a more fragmented oligarchy which also had to share political power with an emerging industrial bourgeoisie and other social sectors.

The conflict between liberal and conservative factions was played out in very different ways in Costa Rica and Colombia from the late nineteenth to the early twentieth century — far less violently in the former case, where there was no protracted civil war, than in the latter. However, mechanisms of elite rule through formally democratic means had clearly been established or reestablished in both countries by the 1920s, albeit under liberal predominance in Costa Rica and conservative prevalence in Colombia until 1936. During these decades, political institutions in both countries responded to social conflict and popular mobilization by implementing limited reforms, especially moderate in the Central American case. In Colombia, social confrontations were perhaps more severe, and while there was also more violence, the strength of popular mobilization and the course of political developments led to more substantial reforms. Despite such variations, there was clearly a gradual redefinition of the role of the state in both cases from a laissez-faire to a moderately interventionist function. As the traditional socioeconomic and sociopolitical model showed its weaknesses and social tensions were more openly expressed, the need for reforms became increasingly apparent, while popular mobilization and a changing political scenario created the conditions which made them feasible. The resulting adjustments were both a response to immediate pressures and a search for means to maintain or reestablish stability of the social order.

The goals, means, and depths of political and social reform in one or the other country were certainly diverse. In Costa Rica, for example, liberal leaders such as three-term president Ricardo Jiménez and other members of the "Olimpo" responded to increased social tensions and the rise of adversarial groups by adopting policies of mild reform that would appease the main contenders in rural and urban settings, while they expanded their own base of political and specifically electoral support. Open conflicts were thus channeled toward relatively peaceful, legal, and institutional solutions directed by the state, which did not effect fundamental transformations of the social structure and political leadership in the following years. However, popular grievances were partially addressed, and major sociopolitical upheavals were avoided.

During the 1920s the Partido Reformista, headed by the priest-turned-general Jorge Volio, campaigned on a mixed platform of populism and socialism in support of the popular cause. The party stressed two points: "la tierra al que la trabaja" (a slogan borrowed from the Mexican Revolution) as a means to address conflicts in the country's peripheral areas, and

second, the fundamental opposition of interests between the coffee oligarchy (the *argolla*) and the salaried and unsalaried popular sectors.[21] During
these years social and political pressure forced Costa Rica's liberal government to legally expropriate contested properties located outside the
Central Valley. Persons affected by these expropriations received double
indemnity in lands elsewhere. These measures, however, did not affect
coffee properties, which were mainly located within the Central Valley.[22]

In the following decade the Partido Reformista practically disappeared
and popular political mobilization was increasingly led by the newly organized Communist party, which focused its organizational work on the
rural and urban salaried workers. With the exception of minor movements in support of better wages in the coffee hacienda region of Turrialba, this party concentrated its efforts in rural areas on workers in the
banana plantations of the Atlantic.

During the early 1930s, there was also an independent movement by
small and medium coffee producers, owners of their farms but subject to
the "triple monopoly" of credit, processing, and marketing. Their objective was to challenge the "trust" formed by processing firms and generally
improve their situation vis-à-vis agro-industrial capital. This nonpartisan
but politically influential movement forced the liberal state to intervene
once again, this time to regulate relations between these sectors through
legislation and institutional development, especially by creating the Instituto de Defensa del Café.

In Colombia the relationship between the state and the interests of
large coffee growers was more complex and unstable. The Federación
Nacional de Cafeteros (created in 1927) assumed a series of economic
functions and became a strong political interest group which Kalmanovitz
accurately described as "a private State within a not-very-public State."[23]
By the 1920s ongoing debates discussed "the social function of property,"
and Law 74, passed in 1926, required that landholders, under litigation,
prove ownership of the land beyond a doubt. Peasant farmer unrest contributed to the weakening of the conservative regime and paved the way
for the rise of liberal agrarian policies. In effect, the conservative Republic
was supplanted by liberal governments, especially the one headed by
López Pumarejo (the "Revolución en Marcha"), which adopted measures
that significantly altered the structure of social-agrarian relations and
other relations of power.

Conflicts on coffee haciendas in Cundinamarca and Tolima, which initially focused on tenant contracts, working conditions, and the right to
freely market crops grown on workers' plots, evolved into refusal of
colonos and tenants with outstanding debts to pay them off, contending
that the land was theirs. Squatters also took lands belonging to coffee

haciendas. This trend was characteristic of agrarian struggles between 1930 and 1936, when existing conflicts, openly expressed since 1918 and especially in the late 1920s, became more pronounced as a result of the crisis and its social consequences. Renters, colonos, *agregados*, and day laborers in parts of central Colombia formed de facto alliances in pursuit of specifically peasant objectives. In the early thirties, workers terminated by the public sector were returning to the countryside, many of them with union experience, and joining forces with the already mobilized peasant sectors. Their collective actions effectively questioned the often dubious title of large landholdings, which frequently corresponded neither to the legally registered property nor to the actual units of production.[24]

Peasant demands received political support not only from leftist Liberal activists and members of the Communist party but also, during the crisis, from a Liberal government determined to modernize the Colombian state, modify existing forms of landholding to be in consonance with social needs, reduce the power of land barons resisting change, and serve as a catalyst to industrialization.

Land legislation and court rulings from 1927 to 1936, which declared that land not being exploited economically was subject to expropriation by the public domain, contributed to the dismantling of some haciendas and the massive expulsion of tenant farmers, sharecroppers, and colonos from others. In addition to pressuring estate owners to modernize their farms and eliminate backward labor relations, this liberal legislation intended to endow the state with "a legal argument to intervene and solve land disputes without having to resort to force, while at the same time contributing to legitimize the authority of the State."[25]

Sociopolitical processes such as those briefly mentioned above are as important as socioeconomic ones in the survival of the modern coffee plantation in the case of Costa Rica (and in certain areas of Colombia) and the general decline of the traditional coffee hacienda in major regions of Colombia, especially in Cundinamarca and Tolima. Rather than explaining the vitality of peasant-farmer or hacienda production in terms of greater or lesser abilities to withstand short-term economic adversity at the start of the thirties, this comparative analysis refers us to the internal status of the haciendas in each region, and to the sociopolitical context of agrarian struggle in these countries. In terms of the former, the following aspects were important: forms of organization and control of labor, the amount of uncultivated land, and the haciendas' financial stability or instability. Sociopolitically, the position of the coffee estate owners within the ruling class is a crucial issue; we must also consider whether or not they had to deal with organized social forces effectively challenging their power, such as the alliance between tenants and wage earners and a liberal government determined to pass legislation counter to the interests of certain sectors of the landed elite.

Hacendados and Small Farmers

The very different sociopolitical situations discussed for Costa Rica and Colombia contrast sharply with the absence of any marked difference in the coffee sectors' macroeconomic behavior in these countries. On the other hand, within Colombia itself haciendas faced much greater difficulties in some areas than others, and even in those where problems were greatest, not all were affected equally. Given the different social outcomes and contrasting explanations, we should inquire if an explanation in terms of the greater economic viability of Colombia's peasant farms and of Costa Rica's haciendas is not, to some measure, an a posteriori conclusion, arrived at as a result of the observed "collapse" of Colombia's east-central haciendas and the proven resiliency of peasant farmers there at the time, and as a result of the soundness of Costa Rica's haciendas and the difficulty experienced by its domestic units and sub-family units. No doubt historical outcomes tend to influence the interpretation of events, but one must explain why similar difficulties in the coffee sector of the economy have different effects, either strengthening or weakening peasant coffee production. Given that there were no clear macroeconomic differences in this regard, we must provide additional comments on the economic viability of certain kinds of productive units while taking a closer look at political and other factors. We must therefore comparatively evaluate the significance of specific socioeconomic and sociopolitical processes affecting the viability of coffee-producing farms and haciendas.

First, the economic status of large and small coffee production units in terms of profitability in Costa Rica and Colombia, as a specific component affecting the general problem of viability, was more complex than one might assume on the basis of the outcome, that is, the breaking down of large coffee estates.

In Costa Rica the crisis of the 1930s hit the peasant farmers hardest, but it also affected large producers. Since the 1920s overall yields in coffee production in Costa Rica showed gradual decline as a result of aging trees, low levels of soil fertility due to nutrient depletion, technological stagnation, and other related factors.[26] When these are added to the aforementioned "devaluation of labor" and the short-term crisis at the beginning of the thirties, one can see that difficult times were in store for all coffee growers, not just for small producers. For example, market problems and foreclosures affected both small and large producers, but not to the extent of radically altering the regional weight of these two types of production units.[27] Certainly producers who did not process their own crop were hardest hit, because they had to sell their harvest at very low prices in some instances and were turned down completely in others by those in control of processing and marketing. This was the result of the existing relationship between the many geographically widespread producers and a virtual monopsony which had controlled prices in the years prior to the crisis. It was not without reason that small and medium coffee producers finally organized during these two years to confront the processing "trust." And even though the Costa Rican state did not adopt any populist policies that would weaken the socioeconomic strength of the estate owners, it responded by regulating the relationships between producers and processors, so as to ease tensions between them. The state also approved moratoria on farmers' overdue debts and thereby put a curb on farm auctions.

In Colombia, a good number of haciendas in Cundinamarca had experienced economic difficulties since the 1920s, as can be seen from their debts. Cundinamarca, an area of earlier settlement, may have had a somewhat lower productive potential by the time, especially when compared with the western areas of the country where Colombia's economic axis, especially for coffee, was centered at this time. During the decline of prices and social turmoil of the 1930s the situation took a turn for the worse, and some haciendas were parceled out although others were not. The question that now comes to mind is why did the crisis have this varied effect on the large haciendas of Cundinamarca? In an attempt to address this issue, Palacios states that "there seems to be a high correlation between heavy indebtedness and the eventual parceling of an hacienda."[28] In a detailed economic study on coffee profits per region and type of productive unit conducted by Mariano Arango, we can observe two things: first, it seems that conditions for peasant farmers were not necessarily better than they were for the large hacienda owners, because whatever they gained by not having administrative costs "they lost to the local merchants and money lenders who paid them less for their coffee than they did the large landowners,"[29] and second, profit margins in Cundinamarca during the decade of the 1930s were comparatively favorable. Furthermore, in Cundinamarca when one compares areas with haciendas to other areas dominated by peasant farmers (taking into consideration both salaries and yield per hectare), one can see that the major cause of stagnation in the haciendas in the region between 1932 and 1943 is attributable mostly to social problems stemming from struggles for possession of the land, and not to economic conditions or profits.[30] Hence, the decline and parceling out of a significant number of haciendas in Cundinamarca during this time requires an explanation that takes into consideration other factors besides profitability, especially since hacienda production in southwest Antioquia was far from decadent at this time.[31] As was the case with Costa Rica, organized social forces played as significant a role as economic phenomena in shaping the outcome for the different kinds of production units.

Hence, in neither Costa Rica nor Colombia can we discover clear evidence to indicate that the difficulties experienced by domestic units and haciendas and their capacity to resist adverse economic situations can be explained solely in terms of profitability in a strict sense. We must refer, then, to other factors that will shed light on the greater or lesser viability of haciendas or small production units in Colombia and then Costa Rica. In summary, we will review some of the factors indicated earlier, emphasizing their interrelatedness in specific historical-geographic spaces.

In Colombia internal tensions and conflicts in the haciendas, mentioned earlier, led to serious confrontations in rural areas during the 1920s, as thousands of more or less organized peasant farmers struggled first for improved contractual arrangements and then for the land itself. Between 1925 and 1935, such movements acquired great momentum within and without the coffee-producing regions, to the point of seriously challenging the existing land tenure systems and rural class relations. In the context of the populist movement headed by Gaitán, of a Communist party active in the agricultural sector, and of the liberal reformism of President López, these conflicts eventually culminated in the effective distribution of lands belonging to haciendas. In central Colombia, some estates were subdivided under direct pressure by organized peasant movements and/or through government intervention, usually with ample compensation. Others were partially or completely fragmented more or less voluntarily by their owners. The end result was that a major coffee-producing region where large haciendas had been the predominant, though not the exclusive form of land tenure, was converted in the direction of a much greater peasant-farmer participation in terms of property and agro-export production. Once the objectives in terms of redistribution of land were attained, and especially after the enactment of Law 200 in 1936, the movement tended to subside.

Changes made to tenant laws did not cause as much havoc in the west as they did in the east-central coffee-producing region, because production relations were more flexible and could adjust more rapidly as a result of the greater number of household production units and the importance of modern capitalist enterprises based primarily on salaried workers.[32] In the case of tenant farmers who also worked for wages on the estates, the economic crisis meant lower prices for their products, lower salaries, and an increase in land rental relative to other costs.[33] This no doubt had an effect on their claims and organizational efforts. In contrast to the east-central region, the western area of Colombia did not experience such major struggles for subdivision of landed estates (except for some parts of the extreme south of recent settlement) during these years. And this in spite of the struggle between the "ax and the paper" during the colonization of Antioquia, when there were numerous, sometimes violent, conflicts between peasant settlers and more or less legal landowners over supposedly public land.[34] Violence did not cease there, but relatively large coffee estates survived those difficult times.

The geographic and thematic framework of the struggle for land in Colombia during the twenties and thirties surpasses the possibilities of this work. However, for our purposes we will ask why in certain zones and not in others there were alliances among colonos, tenant farmers, and day laborers who united against the estate owners of the east-central coffee-producing departments. Palacios has shown that haciendas with the smallest percentage of total land dedicated to coffee growing were hardest hit by the agrarian struggles.[35] In addition, Bejarano points out that "in Cundinamarca . . . only peripheral lands were subject to parceling where the tenants had their plots, and not the core area of the haciendas dedicated to coffee."[36] In general, agrarian conflicts on coffee haciendas during these years were focused on those landholdings with large numbers of tenant farmers, sharecroppers, or agregados, those haciendas with large amounts of untilled land, or those located in zones of recent settlement where disputes raged over ownership of large areas. In contrast, areas where landholding and unit of production tended to coincide usually did not experience acute conflicts over land ownership.

In Costa Rica, in contrast with Colombia (see Maps 6.3 and 6.4), conflicts over ownership of the land in these years occurred on peripheral, non-coffee-producing areas, such as Guanacaste, the Central Pacific, and the Atlantic. Peasant farmers outside of the Central Valley during these years struggled against the massive appropriation of land by foreign companies linked to the railroad, banana and mineral exploitation, and absentee landlords dedicated to extensive cattle grazing.[37] Conflicts within the Central Valley centered on prices paid for coffee (and also sugar cane), more specifically the relations between producers and processors.[38] One of the major factors influencing this pattern of development was the fact that the Central Valley had been colonized before the end of the nineteenth century, and, as a result, migrations were toward outlying regions of the country. It was during this time that substantial land concessions to the railroad and related companies were being made in these same areas beyond the Central Valley. The status of land and the general agrarian structure in the Central Valley was fairly stable by this time, and although there

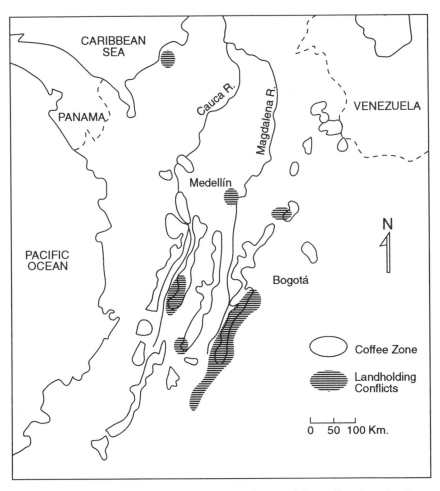

Map 6.3. Principal Areas of Landholding Conflicts and the Coffee-Growing Zone in Colombia, 1920–1936. *Source:* C. LeGrand, "Labor Acquisition and Social Conflict on the Colombian Frontier, 1850–1936," *Journal of Latin American Studies* 16 (1984), 45.

may have been some sharecropping, production units and established landholdings tended to coincide. As a result, most coffee-growing estates in the Central Valley did not experience the tensions that existed inside haciendas in Cundinamarca. However, the complete centralization of processing led to conflicts between the processors (who also controlled credit) on the one hand, and small and medium coffee producers on the other.

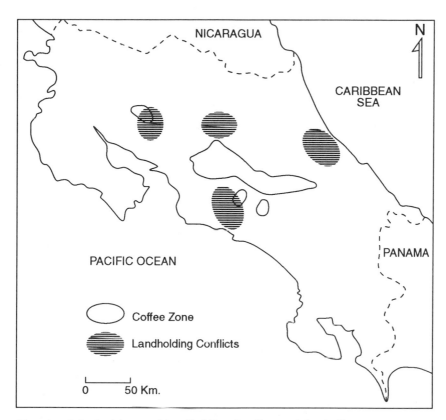

Map 6.4. Principal Areas of Landholding Conflicts and the Coffee-Growing Zone in Costa Rica, 1920–1936. *Sources:* L. Gudmundson, *Hacendados, precaristas y políticos: la ganadería y el latifundismo guanacasteco, 1800–1950* (San José, 1983); National Archives, Sección Gobernación, documents 7906, 7891, 8054; Sección Congreso, documents 12476, 12481, 14269, 14403, 14584, 15160, 15995, 16360, 17155, 17188, 17193.

Conflicts between producers and processors in the Central Valley and the struggles over land ownership in the outlying regions existed within a sociopolitical framework receptive to reform as a result of newly organized social forces and political expressions of popular demands. In both the 1920s and 1930s, as mentioned above, nominally liberal governments adopted moderately reformist policies as a means of reducing tensions. Such measures included well-remunerated expropriation of lands occupied by so called *parásitos* (the pejorative term used then for squatters) in outlying areas and legislation to regulate relations between producers and coffee processors.

Meanwhile, in Colombia claims by peasant farmers in coffee zones between the years 1920 and 1936 went from improving contract conditions inside haciendas to direct conflict for the land. As indicated above,, conflicts in Costa Rica's Central Valley focused on prices, while those in outlying regions focused on possession of the land. It is also worth noting that there was no direct connection between these two forms of social unrest in Costa Rica.

By 1930 Costa Rica and Colombia had little arable agricultural frontier left in readily accessible areas neighboring with coffee-producing regions. In both instances increased social tensions led to direct government intervention, somewhat more limited in the Central American case. In Costa Rica the parceling of large landholdings occupied by squatters on the agricultural frontier was coupled with a policy of even larger concessions in other parts of the country, thereby increasing rather than reducing the concentration of property. Similarly, large haciendas in the Central Valley were not affected by these squatters or by parceling policies. In Colombia, on the other hand, there was real distribution of arable properties in Cundinamarca's coffee-growing areas where there existed major social conflicts while other departments basically maintained their existing agrarian structures.[39]

In Costa Rica, as we have seen, units of production tended to coincide with property rights on coffee farms to a much greater extent than in Cundinamarca, before the subdivision of estates there. Smallholders' security of title to the land in this Central American case contrasted with peasant farmers' various forms of land usufruct and labor obligations in that Colombian region. Renters, sharecroppers, and rural wage laborers in the South American case came together in pursuit of the increasingly tangible dream of proprietorship, finally obtained, in many cases, through collective and individual efforts. In Costa Rica, instead, landed and landless seem to have remained separate, and the vast majority of coffee estates survived unquestioned and intact. Conflicts over land tenure in Colombia, though widespread, were especially acute in certain major coffee-producing regions. In Costa Rica they occurred primarily in the more or less peripheral areas, outside the Central Valley.

As indicated earlier, coffee growing in Costa Rica and Colombia during this period produced historical events and consequences that offer many possibilities for comparative studies in terms of technical and social organization as well as sociopolitical relations. The natural environment, soil fertility, and climatic conditions affected yields; the seasons affected harvests and labor demand; geographic obstacles influenced transportation costs and modes of processing. We have seen how coffee growing was profitable in small and large production units, which combined in various forms in the different regions and led to diverse interrelationships of labor, credit, land sales, product marketing, and sociopolitical and personal relations. Also discussed were the specific forms of subordination of direct producers to owners of capital in the coffee sector of both countries, and the significance of the forms of these relations and the conditions under which they occurred. In this manner relationships between small and medium producers and the marketing and finance sectors were different depending on specific conditions regarding the degree of centralization of processing. In the case of Costa Rica, control by large water-based processing centers was almost total, while in Colombia the process was divided into two phases controlled by direct producers and by threshers.

Individual conditions of coffee haciendas also differed according to the way production was organized within each (e.g., the number of tenant farmers, agregados, day laborers, etc.), according to existing levels of indebtedness and the general financial vulnerability of the haciendas, and according to the amount of total land used for coffee growing, as well as the percentage of tilled and untilled land within the haciendas. When economic hardships increased along with social conflicts, the specific interrelationships between direct producers and capital owners proved essential in the conservation or transformation of regional agrarian structures. The sociopolitical processes of the time played a major role in the dynamics of these interactive relationships. Fundamental social conflicts, in each case, did not result directly from the international economic crisis or the more protracted difficulties of the world coffee market, although preexisting tensions were exacerbated by them. While the main objective of peasant struggles in coffee-producing regions of Colombia came to be land tenure, in Costa Rica the key issue was the relation between small-scale producers and agro-industrial capital. In the former case, a broad-based movement incorporated other sectors of the rural population with common aspirations or, at least, the same antagonists. In the latter, the movement was fundamentally one of middling coffee farmers, forging political rather than social alliances. In both cases, these movements were relatively successful in attaining their immediate objectives; and in both, state intervention facilitated the necessary changes while at the same time co-opting the movement and maintaining or reestablishing social order.

In this study I have attempted to go beyond descriptive comparisons and contrasts in order to analyze reasons for the viability of peasant farmer and hacienda systems of coffee production during the period. I have questioned the assumption that either peasant farming or hacienda production was inherently more apt to survive economic crisis. Interrelations between endogenous and exogenous factors, or the ways in which prior history and ongoing class confrontations influenced the "internalization" of external conditions in times of crisis, have been discussed. This cannot be understood without reference to the concrete social relations through which environmental and technological factors, social organization of production, and sociopolitical and cultural aspects interact and lead to historically specific outcomes of such crises. It has been necessary to address the ways in which coffee production was organized in each country and region, the internal situation of the various types of units of production, the fundamental social conflicts and their political expressions, the formation of alliances and the goals pursued by organized social forces, the relative strength or weakness of coffee-based agro-export interests within the ruling classes, the changing role of the state in these societies, and related factors. Despite its inevitable shortcomings, this analytical exercise does allow us to place each of these cases in a broader perspective and inquire how and why such outcomes came about, rather than assuming their inevitability. In addition, I hope to have also provided some elements of interest for a wider-ranging comparative discussion on coffee production and changing class relations in Latin America during critical junctures, past and present.

Notes

I wish to thank the participants in the conference on "Coffee and Class Formation in Latin America Before 1930" for their comments and suggestions.

1. For editorial reasons, the first three sections of a longer version of this essay are not included here. They dealt, respectively, with the Latin American context of the time; the general characteristics and social organization of coffee growing in Costa Rica and Colombia, based on the coffee censuses; and relevant technological aspects of coffee cultivation, as well as its processing and transportation in the two cases. The original text and tables were published in Spanish by *Estudios Rurales Latinoamericanos* 12 (1989). An expanded English version of the socioeconomic analysis of coffee production in the two countries is forthcoming.

2. For a conceptual and empirical discussion of these categories, in general and as they apply to coffee production, see Mario Samper, *Generations of Settlers: Rural Households and Markets on the Costa Rican Frontier* (Boulder, 1990). Unless otherwise indicated, the data for Colombia in 1932 are derived from the coffee census carried out that year by the Federación Nacional de Cafeteros, and those for Costa Rica in 1935 are from the census survey by the Instituto de Defensa del Café de Costa Rica (IDDCCR) and published in the *Revista del IDDCCR* between 1935 and 1937.

3. The term *hacienda*, as used here, is akin to the "supra-family unit of production" discussed in Samper, *Generations of Settlers*.

4. A detailed analysis of this twofold crisis can be found in Mario Samper, "Caficultura, producción familiar, y haciendas, 1920–1936: análisis comparado a

partir del caso costarricense y colombiano," *Estudios Rurales Latinoamericanos* 12 (1989).

5. For an extensive discussion of this dual crisis, see Celso Furtado, *The Economic Growth of Brazil* (Berkeley, 1965), 193–224.

6. A complete discussion of the coffee market and Brazil's "valorization schemes" is well beyond the possibilities of this study. Suffice it to say, following Carlos Manuel Peláez, "An Economic Analysis of the Brazilian Coffee Support Program: Theory, Policy, and Measurement," in Carlos Manuel Peláez, ed., *Essays on Coffee and Economic Development* (Rio de Janeiro, 1973), 181–248, that prior valorizations had actually increased production within and without Brazil, and during the 1930s other countries were unwilling to participate in the price support schemes.

7. Alfredo González Flores, *La crisis económica de Costa Rica. Su origen, proceso, y factores que la han agravado. Medidas recomendables para procurar el reajuste económico* (San José, 1936), 78–79.

8. Ibid., 15–32.

9. Carlos Merz, "Coyuntura y crisis en Costa Rica de 1924 a 1936," *Revista del Instituto de Defensa del Café* 4 (1936): 620.

10. José Luis Vega, *Hacia una interpretación del desarrollo costarricense: ensayo sociológico* (San José, 1980), 170.

11. Jesús A. Ocampo and Santiago Montenegro, "La crisis mundial de los años treinta en Colombia," *Desarrollo y Sociedad* 7 (1982): 44.

12. Jesús A. Ocampo, comp., *Historia económica de Colombia* (Bogotá, 1987), 209–14.

13. Antonio García, *Geografía económica de Caldas* (Bogotá, 1978), 557.

14. Marco Palacios, *El café en Colombia*, 2d ed. (México, 1983), 381–82 and 462.

15. Ibid., 363–66.

16. Ibid., 356–63.

17. Jesús A. Bejarano, *Economía y poder. La SAC y el desarrollo agropecuario colombiano, 1871–1984* (Bogotá, 1985); Salamón Kalmanovitz, *Economía y nación: una breve historia de Colombia* (Bogotá, 1988).

18. Gonzalo Cortés, "La crisis económica de 1930" (History thesis, Universidad de Costa Rica, 1983), 63. Vega, *Hacia una interpretación*, 187, deals with the rural exodus and the concentration of property during the thirties.

19. Gertrud Peters, "La formación territorial de las fincas grandes de café de la Meseta Central: estudio de la firma Tournón (1887–1955)," *Revista de Historia* (Costa Rica, 1980): 138–39.

20. This was the system that was implemented according to Julio Sánchez Lépiz in 1932 (Ana Virginia Arguedas and Marta Ramírez, "Contribución al análisis de empresas: el caso de Julio Sánchez Lépiz [1862–1934]" [History thesis, Universidad Nacional, Costa Rica, 1985], 323).

21. Mario Samper, "Fuerzas sociopolíticas y procesos electorales en Costa Rica, 1921–1936," *Revista de Historia*, special edition in honor of Dr. Paulino González (1988).

22. Regarding the role of the Partido Reformista, see Marina Volio, *Jorge*

Volio y el Partido Reformista (San José, 1973); on the political expression of agrarian issues at the time, see Samper, "Fuerzas sociopolíticas."

23. Kalmanovitz, *Economía y nación*, 348.

24. For a more complete discussion of this social movement, see Charles Bergquist, *Labor in Latin America: Comparative Essays on Chile, Argentina, Venezuela, and Colombia* (Stanford, 1986), especially pp. 310–59, who also refers to the abundant Colombian literature on the subject.

25. Bejarano, *Economía y poder*, 197.

26. Héctor Pérez, "Economía política del café en Costa Rica, 1850–1950," *Avances de Investigación* (Centro de Investigaciones Históricas, Universidad de Costa Rica) 5 (1981).

27. Carolyn Hall, *El café y el desarrollo histórico-geográfico de Costa Rica* (San José, 1976), 102, affirms that "the great depression had a greater effect on the Turrialba region [mostly haciendas] than on the Central Plateau or the Alajuela–San Ramón region." Nevertheless, the haciendas in Turrialba were not dismembered as they were in Cundinamarca.

28. Palacios, *El café*, 366.

29. Mariano Arango, *El café en Colombia, 1930–1958* (Bogotá, 1982), 35.

30. Ibid., 37.

31. Ibid., 94.

32. Absalón Machado, *El café: de la aparcería al capitalismo* (Bogotá, 1977), 330–31.

33. Palacios, *El café*, 358.

34. Jorge Villegas, "Pleitos de tierras entre colonos y propietarios en la colonización antioqueña," *Revista de Extensión Cultural* (Universidad Nacional de Colombia, Medellín) 5–6 (1978), describes these conflicts well, which were characterized as such by Alejandro López.

35. Palacios, *El café*, 380.

36. Jesús A. Bejarano, *Ensayos de historia agraria colombiana* (Bogotá, 1987), 52.

37. Lowell Gudmundson, *Hacendados precaristas y políticos: la ganadería y el latifundismo guanacasteco, 1800–1950* (San José, 1983).

38. Victor Hugo Acuña, "Patrones del conflicto social en la economía cafetalera costarricense (1900–1948)" (paper presented at 45th conference of Americanists, Bogotá, 1985).

39. Bejarano, *Ensayos de historia agraria*, 57.

Seven

Labor System and Collective Action in a Coffee Export Sector: São Paulo

MAURICIO A. FONT

NEW PATTERNS of class relations have often appeared in Latin America in the context of emergent forms of economic organization linked to production for export markets.[1] The phenomenal growth of world trade between 1850 and 1930 stimulated the expansion of agricultural export sectors responsible for the fateful deepening of behaviors and institutions associated with capitalism — the market, systematic profit-making, free labor migration, and the wage system.[2] Born of the global expansion of capitalism, the question — a big one indeed — is under what general conditions the resulting class structure consists mainly of proletarians, serfs, petty-commodity producers, or some other category.

Noting the clear subsumption of export agriculture to global capitalist development since 1850, some authors have characterized Latin American direct producers or cultivators as proletarians, subject to processes of capitalist immiseration and polarization — and potential or actual militant participants of horizontal, often politicized, collective action.[3] Others have called attention to the "peasantlike" or even "unfree" characteristics and behaviors of export cultivators,[4] often focusing on clientelism for accounts of political participation. While this possibility has been neglected in the past, there is growing awareness that export sector expansion may lead to the emergence of independent small and medium holders.[5]

The debate is not only over the extent and character of various types of class formation in given areas and periods, but also over their general causes, including the role of exports-led frontier expansion. For instance, in opposition to Bergad's view of nineteenth-century Puerto Rican coffee cultivators as proletarians, Brass recently portrayed them, as well as those of Colombia and Brazil, as "unfree." One of the latter's theoretical arguments — seemingly conceded in Bergad's reply to Brass — restates the well-known Nieboer-Domar thesis to the effect that labor scarcity in the context of exports-propelled frontier expansion led and leads to repressive measures and "unfree" labor systems.[6] Chirot attempted to derive from the same hypothesis and the analysis of the "second feudalism" of Eastern Europe a more ambitious enserfment hypothesis applicable to all export-oriented peripheral societies.[7] In contrast, Winson touches on a diametrically different principle with regard to the agro-export economies of Argentina and southern Brazil after 1850: "Where a potential labor did not exist locally . . . relatively high money wages embodying more or less free contractual relations were essential institutional prerequisites to attract an immigrant labor force."[8] In turn, Bauer has challenged the generalized view of Latin American peonage.[9]

Proletarian, peon, or farmer? Free or unfree? Militant firebrand or acquiescent follower? What factors condition class formation in Latin America's agricultural export economies and export cultivators' political participation and collective action? This article explores these questions in terms of the labor systems and patterns of social relations and social conflict generated in the coffee economy of São Paulo between 1889 and 1930, particularly during the 1920s. At the time São Paulo was the largest coffee export sector of all times and one of the largest export sectors of Latin America. The direct producers or cultivators of coffee in São Paulo have also been characterized in varying terms. This essay reconsiders the *colono* system in light of structural complexity and presents evidence from colono strikes and other forms of participation and conflict in the coffee zone.[10] More generally, it suggests that the extent to which landlords succeed in proletarianizing or enserfing direct cultivators may depend on their having access to ample supplies of labor and their ability to monopolize land and related economic opportunities, something which ultimately hinges on state power.

Background and Analytical Elaboration

New forms of production did indeed accompany the growth and consolidation of the coffee economy in the western plateau of the state of São Paulo after the 1870s. This eventually included the emergence of an alternative agrarian economy based on small and medium holders.[11] One of the most important questions about this case is how the latter differentiation may have been related to the prevailing labor system in the large estates.

Most of the labor force required for the expansion of the Paulista coffee economy was formed by immigrants — mostly Italian, but also Spanish, Portuguese, other Europeans, and later, Japanese — who traveled to São Paulo often under a government-sponsored program. These immigrant laborers were known as colonos. The colono labor system inaugurated a new chapter in the development of São Paulo and Brazil. Before its full adoption in the 1880s, the predominant enterprise system in the much smaller coffee economy was the large estate (*fazenda*) based on slavery and experimental forms of tenancy.[12] The new agricultural system of the western plateau of the state represented a considerably freer labor force.[13]

Unlike traditional *hacienda* or slave plantation systems, the new Paulista fazenda of the 1880s made wider use of wage labor and profit-making based on the appropriation of surplus value. Generalizing, some authors apply to the entire Paulista labor force of this period a theory of class formation and collective action which indicates or implies widespread proletarianization, pauperization, and a working class seemingly prone to violence or, given proper conditions, strikes and other forms of contention.[14] As Stolcke and Hall would have it,

the transition . . . to the colonato was a process of increasingly systematic exploitation of labor . . . Once a capitalist labor market had been created, planting rights restricted to the basic minimum, and increasingly severe labor discipline instituted, conditions effectively disappeared for individual struggle at the level of work . . . By the turn of the century immigrants constituted a homogeneous mass, subject to more or less uniformly harsh conditions . . . For those who remained in agriculture, low wages or any additional exactions by planters, such as non-payment of wages, the prohibition of food growing, or a reduction in wages, could trigger off collective action in the form of strikes. Contradictorily, by increasing labor discipline, planters created the very conditions for collective — and thus much more damaging — actions by the immigrants.[15]

As to the level of rancor in the relations between estate owners and colonos, the same authors present what they call "a famous though by no means atypical" example. This occurred "when Francisco Augusto Almeida Prado, a planter belonging to the prominent Prado family, was so careless as to stroll through his coffee fields one day without the protection of his bodyguards. Several of his laborers took advantage of the situation and murdered him, riddling his body with knife wounds, and chopping it into pieces with their hatchets and hoes."[16]

The aforementioned portrayals of the colono as "unfree" and politically acquiescent under the weight of the clientelistic system known as *coronelismo*[17] or, conversely, as potentially able to save and become independent producers[18] contrast rather sharply with the above view. This is also the case with a third view, which presents fazendas in semiarcadian terms. As Harvard professor Robert Ward put it in 1911, after a trip to fazenda Santa Veridiana (owned by the Silva Prado family, the quintessential traditional coffee family in the state): "All these Brazilian fazendas have a peculiar charm — an appearance of solidarity, of comfort, of peace, and of prosperity — as they lie there, surrounded by the wealth of their coffee trees, with cattle grazing on the neighboring fields and with the ever-busy, picturesque Italian laborers caring for the precious crop, whose market prices are quoted daily in all the important papers throughout the civilized world."[19]

Arguments that attribute a uniform proletarian or servile fate to colonos between the 1880s and 1930 overgeneralize and make an empirical error. Worse, they misconceive the system and the dynamic forces responsible for important structural changes. The expansion and consolidation of the coffee economy of São Paulo during this period was far from a simple process of reproduction of a secure and predominant large estate. Actually, a great deal of differentiation was taking place, including the expansion of petty-commodity production among colonos and the emergence of small and medium holders, which challenged the predominance of the fazenda and imbued the system with structural properties it lacked otherwise.[20] Pure proletarianization and enserfment models exaggerate the role of the large fazenda, neglect that of immigrant colonos, and give an inadequate, static account of processes of class formation, political contention, and change.

An alternative approach to collective action and political participation in São Paulo and comparable export economies would differ from the proletarianization-cum-pauperization and the traditional enserfment and clientelistic approaches by centering on the causes, components, and consequences of differentiation — particularly of interactions between competing forms of production. Building on a line of analysis found in Hirschman and Paige,[21] the alternative approach could be seen as centering on "micro modes of production" often associated with various staples. Such a micro dialectical approach would study vertical coalitions in dynamic terms with an eye to integrate them with the analysis of class action and conflict. With respect to São Paulo, the elaboration of such an approach would entail drawing a balance sheet between characterizations of the colono as a close approximation to a proletarian or a first step toward independent agriculture. It also calls for a systematic reassessment of whether the colonato expressed the ironclad predominance of modern capital under the capitalist large-estate system known as the fazenda and whether the colono's typical political behavior or propensity was either to succumb to planters under the weight of traditional clientelistic relations or to engage in militant behavior or other forms of participation.

Labor System, Differentiation, and Conflict in São Paulo

Most authors have emphasized one aspect of the standard colono contract to characterize the system as precapitalist (even "feudal"), proletarian, or farmer-in-the-making. The contract provided for a mixed system of payments as well as usufruct of land plots.[22]

Spindel, Hall, and Martínez Alier, and Stolcke and Hall emphasize the proletarian and exploited nature of the colonato and its overall functionality to the capitalist mode of production represented by the fazenda. The latter refer to "homogeneous and proletarian working conditions" in the coffee estates. Spindel emphasizes the "superexploitation" inherent in the colono contract—extraction of value not only via surplus value (through wage) but also by making the working family responsible for its own reproduction through subsistence agriculture in inter-row cropping or family plots. This line of reasoning treats the subsistence element of the colonato as part and parcel of a process of primitive accumulation functional to the hegemony of planter capital. These authors often quote Dean, who argued that food production made the colono responsible for his own reproduction; in this light, the sale of surpluses was necessary to complement wages so low that workers otherwise had great difficulties in making ends meet. While maintaining basically the same position, Stolcke and Hall emphasize the cost of the reproduction of labor and its functionality in terms of occupying the labor force all year around. While recognizing the "subsistence" dimensions of the colonato, they view it as capitalist wage labor.[23]

In contrast, Gorender views the Paulista labor system as "a latifundiary plantation mode of production aided by dependent peasant forms," a perspective derided in Stolcke and Hall and supported in Foerster, one of the first academic sketches of the Paulista coffee economy. Foerster referred to the "somewhat feudal organization . . . [reminiscent] of slave days" and to a "patriarchal organization [of production] suitable for slave societies," but which "ill comports with the ideal of free labor." A still different perspective is that of Holloway, who, approaching the colonato from the perspective of an emergent smallholding system, maintains that a large number of colono families were able to save and achieve independent status as small producers.[24]

Regardless of what may have been the logic and precise relative weight of the three forms of payment—amount of money per thousand trees cared for or cultivated, amount of money per volume of harvest, or daily wage for other tasks — there is no question that the relationship between worker and planter entailed a cash bond. (One, it should be stressed, negotiated on a year-to-year basis and involving the use of an official notebook or log of all transactions.) However, to generalize that the colono was uniformly a full-fledged proletarian — immiserated or not — may be acceptable in a static and subregional sense, but appears too simplistic in dynamic and broader regional terms.[25]

While the paucity of decisive evidence hampers a definitive adjudication among alternative accounts, there are enough grounds to advance a more complex sketch of the colonato which incorporates the kernel of truth in the above views but does not reduce to any one of them. As a starting point, it should be noted that, by themselves, wages as such in the large estates were generally low at least until approximately 1914, and would have barely permitted the colono family to make ends meet and provide for its reproduction. A subsidized immigration program replenished the labor force each year, creating a permanent reserve army and making chronic low wages possible. If a continuous flow of fresh immigrants had not been enough, local "peasants" known as caipiras constituted a second pool of cheap labor in what was effectively a segmented labor market.[26] While there were significant temporal and spatial variations, wages as such would not have permitted the savings required to buy and maintain a significant amount of land.[27]

Thus the question of upward mobility hinges on the significance of the colono's own crops and animal husbandry, that is, on the importance of land usufruct. The views of the colono as either proletarian or peón agree in emphasizing the subsistence nature of the family plots and inter-row cropping. Many of the arguments minimizing the importance of land usufruct rely on data reported by Dean for a fazenda in an aging region suggesting that it may not have been very large.[28] Dean found that colonos consumed 70 percent of what they produced and that the remaining 30 percent did not amount to much real saving. But there are several problems in extrapolating these figures to other periods and subregions. Dean derived the value of cash crops by multiplying the quantity recorded in the fazenda books times staple prices for the late 1880s. However, prices then were lower than those prevailing in subsequent years (e.g., 15 milreis per cart of corn, in Dean's data, versus 20, 25, 30, and even 40 milreis in 1901–3, according to Spindel and Holloway).[29] Dean's figures are averages for families in a large estate past its prime. However, those families with particularly favorable endowments of labor and fresh land (as in the frontier) must have produced higher quantities and commercialized considerably more than 30 percent of their total output.[30] Also, since planters

TABLE 7.1

Budgets of Colono Families in Brazil, 1897–1922 (in Current Milreis)

Setting	Family makeup	Income Wages	Income Crops	Income Animal	Expenses	Net
1. Taquaritinga 1897	2 workers	905	260	?	583	582
2. Taquaritinga 1901	2 workers	560	180	150	547	342
3. Ribeirão Preto, 1903	2 workers	480	130	140	550	200
4. Mogiana region, 1903	4 workers	1,400	920	?	2,320	1,407 (U.S.$338)
5. Noroeste region, 1922	3 workers (Japanese)[a]	2,875	1,240	?	2,996	1,119 ($135)
6. circa 1922	6 workers	3,480	1,740 (est.)		2,350 (est.)	2,870 (est.)
7. circa 1922	2 workers	1,750	875 (est.)		1,130 (est.)	1,495 (est.)
8. circa 1922	1 worker	640	320 (est.)		780 (est.)	180 (est.)

Sources: Cases 1–4, Holloway (1974), 101–4; Case 5, Tsuchida (1978), 179–80; Cases 6–8, Maistrello, quoted in Stolcke and Hall (1983), 198.

[a] 2d year in Brazil.

sometimes pressured colonos to sell part of their crops to them at low prices, it would be natural to suspect underreporting by the latter. Lastly, Dean's figures do not include income from the sale of animals as well as animal and other household products.

In general, a significant number of the colono families exercised de facto operational control of land, both in the cultivation of coffee as well as in the management of assigned plots. Available analyses of "typical" family budgets vary in their assessment of the contribution of land usufruct to total colono income, but they could be quite high. Table 7.1 summarizes actual and partially estimated family budgets.

Judging by these examples, the sale of cash crops and animal products constituted a very substantial source of income. Data for the first five cases suggest that sale of cash crops and animal products may have generally amounted to at least 50 percent of wages. If we use this very conservative figure to estimate net income for three partial budgets reported in 1922 (cases 6–8 in Table 7.1), the resulting figures show levels of potential savings significant enough in the best of cases to make possible the accumulation in a few years of the capital needed to purchase a private family plot. The budget for a Japanese family reported as typical in Tsuchida[31] (case 4 in Table 7.1) corroborates this conclusion (this family had been in the country only two years; its income should have increased in subsequent years).

The recognition of the structural complexity and protean character of the colono role under the dynamic conditions of export sector expansion and frontier settlement is a major step in building a more adequate sketch. As discussed by Foerster, the colono contract was elastic across estates, times, and regions. Whatever the intended functionality of land usufruct to capital accumulation at the level of the large coffee estate, colono production of cash crops and animal products came to constitute a form of embryonic petty production.[32] If, on the one hand, the lot of the incoming immigrant who remained (a majority seem to have repatriated[33]) became low-level wage earning, it is also the case that for a significant minority the colono experience provided enough saving to make the transition to smallholding agriculture.[34]

A more elaborate account of the above process has been discussed elsewhere and need only be summarized here.[35] Several factors interacted with the colonato and allowed a significant number of immigrants, most of whom entered the state as substitutes for slaves, to become independent producers. A fluid (and fragmented) labor market and opportunity structure prevented the institutionalization of the colonato as a labor system based on a permanent labor force. Immigrant laborers were thus able to search for better opportunities within or outside the fazenda system, while planters remained dependent on continuous flows of fresh immigrant labor. Unwilling or unable to rely on money wages for all or most of his labor costs, the planter used land—acquired at little or no cost from the vast reserves of unexploited public lands—in the incentive packages offered to colonos. The latter thus functioned as producers of food staples as well as proletarians.[36] The intended purpose of land usufruct was to make the colono responsible for his own subsistence and reproduction. However, the dramatic increase in demand for food crops allowed families with sufficient labor power to achieve substantial savings by orienting the usufruct of plots to the production of cash crops.

Born out of the fazenda export sector, the alternative agrarian economy based on small and medium holders and mobile colonos developed a dynamic of its own which underpinned the emergence of alternative land tenure and utilization arrangements. Alternative producers thriving on the cultivation of diverse agricultural products, including coffee, became an important element of social organization. These processes undermined the monopoly of land, labor, and markets traditionally claimed by the traditional large planters. By 1920, the alternative economy produced more than a third of the state's coffee, most food staples (in particular corn, beans, and rice), and a significant share of its cotton. As Paulo Prado, an unsuspect source, put it in 1924, "all non-export crops are in the hands of old colonos."[37] The social differentiation inherent in these processes entailed the appearance of alternative elites with economic and political interests in land markets, regional development, and the commercialization of cash crops. In fact, without coalitions with these power holders it is doubtful that immigrants could have exercised effective ownership of the land.

In conclusion, the crucial proximate conditions affecting the levels of economic and political participation by colonos in São Paulo centered on the interaction between a changing context driven by a frontier and the structural character of the colonato. Available coalition partners and channels of participation were pivotal.

Rural masses in São Paulo were often the victims of overwhelming exploitative forces, to be sure. They may have also been more susceptible to manipulation than urban groups. But it is also apparent that a significant number of upwardly mobile colonos and petty producers were able to follow rational strategies oriented to the pursuit of an independent livelihood. That the alterations in the opportunity structure attendant to frontier expansion, changing socioeconomic structure, urbanization, and industrialization provided meaningful bases for economic choice in the major economic decisions of *cultivators* was only half the picture. As important was the likelihood that their claims to independent production would be honored in a polity traditionally controlled by landlords.

Patterns of Mobilization and Participation

To what degree did the colonos and other rural strata in the state of São Paulo form revolutionary unions, peasant leagues, or other forms of militant political action? Did political dynamics in the state permit the enfranchisement of immigrants? To what extent did the state government uniformly act as a direct instrument of planters in responding to the claims of immigrant colonos?

COLLECTIVE ACTION AND CLIENTELISTIC COALITIONS. While some authors have emphasized actual or potential radicalism by the immigrant colonos and rural masses of São Paulo, the sources studied for evidence of collective action in the coffee zones of the state between 1918 and 1930 show no reliable record of major rebellions, political or major strike activity, revolutionary unions, social movement, or any major form of widespread horizontal political behavior.[38] The proletarianization-cum-pauperization hypothesis indicates that colonos had a high propensity to strike and engage in collective action, and did not do so more often largely because of outright planter repression or little bargaining power due to abundant labor.[39] While it is true that the latter factors were present and must have inhibited collective action, this does not imply that they were necessarily the most important explanations for the low levels of actual collective action.[40]

The view that subsidized immigration was responsible for creating a saturated labor market and was thus the major inhibiting factor implies that there were no major labor shortages during this period and that periods of relative imbalances in immigration flows must have been responsible for higher levels of strike activity and militancy. Coupled with the assumption of homogenization, this view also implies that strike activity should be uniformly distributed in the coffee economy and that their claims had a "clearly proletarian content."[41] But there are reasons to doubt all these arguments.[42]

Evidence about the relative paucity of "horizontal" forms of political collective action by immigrants, while incomplete, are telling in this regard. With respect to strike activity, the record shows a significant number of them, but they tended to be restricted in geographical scope and in demands. This is the case with all of the seventy-six strikes reported between 1920 and 1925 in the annual report of the Patronato Agrícola.[43] Eleven of the twenty-three strikes in 1923 were against delays in the last phase of the coffee harvest apparently caused by heavy rains. Colonos were reported to have signed new contracts in faraway zones and were eager to go west to plant maize, beans, and rice. Another frequent reason for striking was delay in payments of wages. In 1918, thirteen of the twenty recorded strikes were so prompted.[44]

These strikes were often limited to one fazenda and did not involve large numbers of individuals. The eighteen strikes of 1925, for example, had 353 participants in total. Two of the largest strikes involved 35 Japanese families demanding the firing of an abusive foreman and 156 families striking over wages.

The largest wave of colono strikes before 1930 had taken place between 1911 and 1913 and were concentrated in the older areas of the Mogiana and Paulista regions, particularly Ribeirão Preto and Bragança.[45] In contrast with the accounts of these events provided by Stolcke and Hall, these were not years of decreased immigration. While the average level of foreign immigration to the state between 1899 and 1910 was 36.2 thousand, the corresponding figures for the period 1911–13 were 61.5, 98.6, and 116.6 thousand.[46] As noted by these authors themselves,[47] there was indeed an increase in immigration flows in 1911–13 — a rather sharp one,

TABLE 7.2

Colono Claims at *Patronato Agrícola*, by Nationality and Year, 1922–1928

Nationality	1922	1923	1924	1925	1926	1927	1928	Total
Italians	202	540	276	269	281	258	329	2155
	(35%)	(44%)	(32%)	(26%)	(23%)	(26%)	(30%)	(31%)
Spaniards	122	244	148	157	218	177	189	1255
	(21%)	(20%)	(17%)	(15%)	(18%)	(18%)	(17%)	(18%)
Portuguese	74	162	140	136	137	143	158	950
	(13%)	(13%)	(16%)	(13%)	(11%)	(15%)	(14%)	(14%)
Brazilians	95	176	195	225	213	208	253	1365
	(16%)	(14%)	(22%)	(21%)	(18%)	(21%)	(23%)	(19.5%)
Others	86	96	115	262	351	191	175	1276
	(15%)	(8%)	(13%)	(25%)	(29%)	(20%)	(16%)	(18%)
Total: Known	579	1218	874	1049	1200	977	1104	7001
nationality	(100%)	(100%)	(100%)	(100%)	(100%)	(100%)	(100%)	(100%)
Total: Unknown	179	46	131	186	139	107	86	874
nationality								
Grand total	758	1264	1005	1235	1339	1084	1190	7875

Source: São Paulo, Secretaria da Agricultura, *Relatório*, 1922–1928.

indeed.[48] Since the restitution of the right to plant food crops within the coffee groves was a main claim in the 1913 strike in Ribeirão Preto,[49] it would seem that the question of the right to produce food was as critical a claim as any other — something which is more compatible with the alternative hypothesis about the importance of land usufruct.[50]

There is no record of colonos, tenants, smallholders, or other rural ranks forming militant peasant leagues or similar agrarian movements, such as those being formed in many parts of Latin America at roughly the same time. Strikingly, approximately at the same time as rural conflict was beginning in Colombia, and in Mexico the Revolution had as battle cry the death of *caudillos*, São Paulo exhibited a high degree of relative peace. By and large, and in contrast with the rest of Brazil, the Paulista countryside was quiet in terms of other forms of social movement. While the northeast of Brazil had a high incidence of messianic movements during the 1920s, only a small one was reported for São Paulo, a comparatively minor movement in the area of Jau. Of more concern to the police were the bands of thoroughly disliked gypsies roaming the countryside.

Colonos and small landholders did articulate plenty of grievances and claims during the same period via the Patronato Agrícola and other mechanisms of mediated participation. Table 7.2 shows a total of almost 8,000 personal claims articulated through the Patronato between 1922 and 1928 — an average of more than 1,000 per year. Most of these claims demanded compliance with work contracts, rerecruitment (after dismis-

TABLE 7.3
Colono Claims in São Paulo, by Type and Year, 1922–1928

Claim type	1922	1923	1924	1925	1926	1927	1928	Total	%
Payment delays	31	20	13	41	54	62	69	290	7.4
Settling accounts, travel expenses	3	19	17			90	139	268	6.9
Fazenda sale before paying colonos				14	6	4	3	27	.7
Wages, harvesting prices, and units		54	5	9	5			73	1.9
Fines and unfair deductions	55	40	30	38	74	64	75	376	9.6
Better housing	8	3	3	8		2	2	26	.7
Inadequate means of subsistence	20	11	4	14	19	11	2	81	2.1
Prohibition of sale of surplus crops		12	12	14	8			46	1.2
Breach of contract	156	87	64	89	133	121	129	779	19.9
Demands written contract	18	9	8	15	6	3	2	61	1.6
Irregularities in "caderneta" (work card)				15	39			54	1.4
Contract rescinded		33	35	49	9	3	3	132	3.4
Use of force to retain colono	4	4		38				46	1.2
Confiscation of colono property	12	18	23	40	12	8	7	120	3.1
Confiscation of property to prevent departure	21	15	18	11	18	8	7	98	2.5
Illegal retention of caderneta	11		8	4	4	3	5	35	.9
"Bad treatment" and similar grievances	29	32	14	46	37	27	16	203	5.2
Lay-offs	42	89	86	105	127	120	72	641	16.4
Other	47	55	31	67	125	176	48	549	14.1
Total	457	502	311	618	676	702	579	3905	100%

Source: São Paulo, Secretaria da Agricultura, Relatório, (1922–28).

sals), cancellation of (unfair) fines, prompt payment of wages, and the like (see Table 7.3).

The network of foreign consuls throughout São Paulo constituted a source of important allies for immigrants in the Paulista countryside. They monitored working conditions and played a major advocacy role before the Patronato and other levels of the Paulista and Brazilian government. Their arguments were recorded and normally heard, since not doing so could affect the likelihood of further immigration. Besides permanent consuls — with at least one in every major town or city, and a network of subagents often related to newspaper operators and journalists — there were also frequent visits by ambassadors of foreign governments. The Italian consular system was the most active. Of the 488 consular claims processed at the Patronato between 1920 and 1928, the Italian consuls accounted for an annual average of 57 percent — ranging from 41 percent in 1923 to 76 percent in 1927.[51]

THE ITALIANS: PARTICIPATION, CLIENTELISM, AND INCORPORA-
TION. Italians accounted for more than half the immigrant flow and were thus by far the most numerous immigrant "colony" in São Paulo. Consular estimates reported 800,000 Italians in São Paulo by 1906–8, most from northern Italy, at a time when the state population was 2.5 to 3 million.[52] Half a million of those who arrived after 1889 did so with travel subsidies from the state of São Paulo, which by 1918 had spent $14 million for this purpose. According to several estimates, Italians accounted for seven- to eight-tenths of the coffee labor force in the 1900s. (In 1910, 35 percent of the population of 400,000 of the city of São Paulo was Italian born, mostly from the north.)[53]

The Italians pioneered in the proliferation of mutual aid societies and clubs. It seems that such associations were at least as oriented to the promotion of incorporation and welfare as to any other major goal. Dean reports lack of solidarity from workers in towns and cities with those in the fazendas. The associational life of Italo-Paulistas was frequently differentiated by regional origin.[54] These people were closely monitored by the government. Most associations evolved into hospitals, insurance programs, social and cultural clubs, and less frequently, trade unions. Another very significant form of participation of immigrants was in newspapers, which played an important role in promoting participation among the Italians and in defending their interests.[55] Interestingly, Baily states that for Italian immigrants politics in São Paulo were "more open and participation more meaningful than in Argentina."[56] Immigrants often articulated progovernment and statist support through their associations. For example, at a time when the local planters were in a power struggle against the ruling party, the Sociedade Operaria Humanitaria Italiana of Araras endorsed its candidate for the state presidency in 1924.[57] The immigrant elite also cultivated political goodwill through commercial associations such as the Italian Chamber of Commerce.

There are indications that, while immigrants played leading roles in the organization of the (urban) labor movement,[58] many Italians may have avoided direct political contention. In 1904 an "Italian Colonial Congress" in São Paulo voted against direct political contention.[59] This undid the efforts that had been made at the turn of the century by a Comitato

Permanente degli Elettori de Origine Italiano, which is said to have received little support in any case. When there was an effort later to form a politically oriented Federazione della Societa Italiana dello stato di San Paolo, only fifteen out of more than one hundred associations joined and it eventually failed.[60] According to Baily, the Italians of São Paulo were also less militant than their counterparts in Argentina. Many immigrants during this period seem to have followed a deliberate strategy to leave politics to Brazilian-born politicians — "to concentrate on economic activities," as it was expressed to me by an octogenarian informant, who came as part of a colono family shortly after 1900 and became a prosperous coffee broker.[61] Since immigrants cultivated ties to the fatherland and tended to be perceived by themselves and others as "foreign subjects," the odds of successful direct political participation were low and probably made this a sensible strategy. Moreover, the political system remained elitist, distant, and well-structured. Also, to attempt to articulate direct contacts could incur the displeasure of local powerholders and their private guards.

In this way the mass of colonos and smallholders may have given the politicians a fair amount of "slack" and ample room for political maneuvering. This was an arrangement not unlike that emerging at roughly the same time in American cities under political bossism. Both entailed "machines" which aggregated votes and claims in exchange for selective incentives, often using extralegal or fraudulent means. At the same time, a new type of politician — closer to a political boss than to a landed patriarch — was emerging in São Paulo. But in important ways the political and economic interests of socially mobile immigrants were antagonistic to the fazenda and its claims to monopolize land, labor, and local supremacy. The total sum of selective exchanges linking emergent political brokers and these "clients" generated a quantum of demands on the political system which challenged the coffee fazenda system and planter hegemony. The impetus from these antagonistic and previously unincorporated interests reinforced a process of bureaucratic autonomy.

The professional politicians had reasons to cultivate and expect support from immigrants. Italian mainstream participation often served to promote the political centralization and autonomy of the governmental apparatus. Even elite figures such as Matarazzo cultivated a mediational approach to participation. They concentrated on economic activities and retained a sense of being Italian (which was also a social response to the aristocratic airs and snubs of the traditional Paulista elites, who mercilessly reminded them of their "nouveau riche" status). Formal politics as such was left to professionals who, as was the case with Washington Luís (São Paulo's leading political figure in the 1920s and Brazil's last president in the Old Republic), were willing to protect basic interests of the immigrants. Carlos de Campos's 1924 presidential platform reiterated the theme of Washington Luís's earlier platform and messages that the key aspect of immigration into the state was "colonization" and nation building rather than merely providing manpower to the coffee fazendas. Since early in his career Washington Luís had played a significant role in promoting the enfranchisement of immigrants.[62] The national platform of PRP's Julio Prestes in 1929 also declared that immigration was to be faced "from the standpoint of the formation of nationality, rather than the question of manpower for the coffee fazendas."[63]

Discussion

The above overview of social structure, contention, and political participation by or with respect to immigrants in the São Paulo of the 1920s emphasizes a view of the Paulista coffee export sector and its labor system in terms of differentiation and changes related to the expanding frontier.[64] While other factors were no doubt present, differentiation was certainly one of the most important factors affecting the forms and levels of collective action and participation by colonos.

That horizontal forms of action were relatively sporadic, isolated, and oriented to economic rather than broad political issues gives an inkling of a critical related factor. The evolving political system in São Paulo had ceased to be identified wholly with the planter; the colono and smallholder saw in the state politicians potential coalition partners in their struggle for citizenship status. The political system was gradually gaining in complexity and dynamism. Through the labor relations board known as Patronato Agrícola, through openness to the pressures from consuls and other agents, and through permeability to immigrant enfranchisement via political bosses, the political system can be said to have been gradually integrating the immigrant. This movement was neither automatic nor primarily due to elite generosity; it was propelled by relentless pressure from "below."[65]

The entrepreneurially minded in São Paulo, whether native or immigrant, did not have a feudal landlord class to dislodge via a "bourgeois revolution." While perhaps not as progressive vis-à-vis capitalist development as often portrayed, Paulista planters had presided over the expansion of an economy based on free labor and offering more opportunities than the rest of Brazil or much of Latin America. The labor force was "free" in an obvious but not trivial sense: Italians and others who came to São Paulo had done so of their own choice and were generally free to leave the fazendas or even the state — as many did indeed do, not rarely disillusioned with their fate. Those who stayed played a major role in the modern development of the state.

Conclusion

If the arguments presented above qualify simple applications of the proletarianization model, they do the same for the hypothesis that when the amount of land in relation to labor is large, landlords will succeed in using political force and judicial means to limit the mobility of labor. The latter, of course, is negated by the experience of areas of recent settlement.[66] If the analysis reported here is correct, Brass's characterization of the entire Paulista economy in terms of the enserfment hypothesis is on the wrong track, at least for the period between the 1880s and 1930s. The arguments presented here provide grounds for maintaining that cultivators in certain export economies may experience much more differentiation than allowed for by the enserfment hypothesis.

It should be noted that the Paulista case also exhibits from the very beginning of the process of export-led frontier expansion one of the main conditions posited by Chirot and Domar as leading to enserfment, the prior historical experience of an established landlord class. In São Paulo, a previously existing landlord class could not prevent a significant number of cultivators from pursuing independent livelihoods and were increasingly compelled to adopt a relatively free labor system.[67] If São Paulo's experience prior to 1930 does not fit the generalization of either the enserfment or proletarianization hypotheses to all forms of export-oriented capitalism, it is largely because of conditions not unlike those which also prevented uniform enserfment or proletarianization in areas of recent settlement. Specifically, the findings support the position that more consideration should be given to the various forms and roles of petty and family production.[68] Under conditions such as those prevalent in São Paulo prior to the 1930s, modes of cultivation characterized by the partial noncommodification of labor appear to confer upon certain labor family units a strength and protean quality with the potential of leading to the formation of family-sized and medium-sized forms of production. This situation entails contrasting labor processes and political behaviors.

A major condition affecting the eventual fate and behaviors of would-be independent producers is what happens at the level of the elites and the state. Aspiring petty producers need coalitions with emergent elites, even if they entail elite-controlled forms of mobilization and participation, to gain reliable access to land and markets. To the extent that such alternative elites are available, direct cultivators' political organization and participation will tend to take forms rather different from those expected from more uniform agrarian systems. Moreover, differentiated interests embedded in the reality or perception of success in this regard mitigate against the likelihood of revolt, as do the vertical or multiclass political bonds.[69]

This line of analysis may also be useful in understanding many instances of conflict where cultivators support elite-led political movements in rancorous opposition to other rural popular strata. At the same time as rural strata in São Paulo appear to have been contributing to the rise of new forms of political intermediation, including a new breed of politician, those of Mexico and parts of Colombia were asking for the heads of *caciques* and other political bosses. A key difference seems to be that through those new political brokers and processes a critical mass of aspiring immigrants in São Paulo could hope to make valid important claims.

Finally, the likelihood that in São Paulo elite differentiation may have created conditions inhibiting agrarian revolt contrasts with analytical arguments and findings about the relationship between these factors in Walton and Wolf.[70] The Paulista experience suggests that whether elite differentiation may be conducive to revolt depends on another factor identified by Walton, the existence of a political system with sufficient resources and autonomy to mediate the relationships between emergent classes and traditional elites. There is evidence that, particularly after World War I, the state government and ruling party in São Paulo were emerging as a force of their own, claiming operational and substantive autonomy with respect to the narrow interests of particular economic groups.[71] Rather than a mere instrument of planter dominance as often argued, the Paulista polity also seems to have been undergoing a process of realignment in favor of new elites and groups, many of them immigrants or of immigrant descent, linked to processes of development oriented to the internal market.

That is, if at least through 1930 the Paulista immigrant labor force could not be wholly characterized as either serflike or proletarian labor, this was due in no small part to elite differentiation and state formation. While other factors played important roles, an increasingly complex polity emerged as the critical arena deciding the question of the emergence of forms of agriculture alternative to the large estate.[72] We can conclude that, under such general conditions as found in São Paulo, landlords will succeed in fully proletarianizing or enserfing their labor when they can monopolize land and dispose of considerable state power.

Notes

The research reported here is part of a broader study of the collective action of the coffee elites of the state of São Paulo, Brazil. I am thankful for support from the City University of New York and Rutgers University's Research Council.

198 MAURICIO A. FONT

1. Fernando Henrique Cardoso and Enzo Faletto, *Dependencia y desarrollo en América Latina* (México, 1976); Jeffrey M. Paige, *Agrarian Revolution: Social Movements and Export Agriculture in the Underdeveloped World* (New York, 1975); Eric R. Wolf, *Europe and the People without History* (Berkeley, 1982), 382–83.

2. Kenneth Duncan and Ian Rutledge, eds., *Land and Labour in Latin America* (Cambridge, 1977); Arnold J. Bauer, "Rural Spanish America, 1870–1930," in Leslie Bethell, ed., *Cambridge History of Latin America, 1870 to 1930*, vol. 5 (Cambridge, 1986); Anthony Winson, "The Formation of Capitalist Agriculture in Latin America and Its Relationship to Political Power and the State," *Comparative Studies in Society and History* 25 (1983): 83–104; William Glade, "Latin America and the International Economy, 1870–1914," in Bethell, *Cambridge History of Latin America*, vol. 5.

3. Laird Bergad, *Coffee and the Growth of Agrarian Capitalism in Nineteenth-Century Puerto Rico* (Princeton, 1983); Michael Hall and Verena Martínez Alier, "Greves de colonos na Primeira República" (Paper in the II Seminário de Relações de Trabalho e Movimentos Sociais).

4. Tom Brass, "Coffee and Rural Proletarianization: A Comment on Bergad," *Journal of Latin American Studies* 16 (1984): 143–52; William Roseberry, *Coffee and Capitalism in the Venezuelan Andes* (Austin, 1983); Catherine LeGrand, "Labor Acquisition and Social Conflict on the Colombian Frontier, 1850–1936," *Journal of Latin American Studies* 16 (1984): 27–49.

5. Thomas H. Holloway, *Immigrants on the Land: Coffee and Society in São Paulo, 1886–1934* (Chapel Hill, 1980); Bauer, "Rural Spanish America," 156–57. For a broader argument see Harriet Friedmann, "World Market, State, and Family Farm: Social Bases of Household Production in the Era of Wage Labor," *Comparative Studies in Society and History* 20 (1978): 545–86; idem, "Household Production and the National Economy: Concepts for the Analysis of Agrarian Formations," *Journal of Peasant Studies* 7 (1980): 158–84. An important reference point for debates about Latin American labor systems is the broader debate about modes of production and transitions to capitalism in Latin America. Pointing to evidence of unfree labor and extraeconomic coercion, Ernesto Laclau, "Feudalism and Capitalism in Latin America," *New Left Review* 67 (May-June, 1971): 19–38, rejected the argument in Andre Gunder Frank, *Capitalism and Underdevelopment in Latin America: Historical Studies of Chile and Brazil* (New York, 1967), that Latin America has been capitalist since the sixteenth century (see also Immanuel Wallerstein, "The Rise and Future Demise of the World Capitalist System: Concepts for Comparative Analysis," *Comparative Studies in Society and History* 16 (1974): 387–415. Laclau's position calls for a view of Latin American agriculture in terms of the transition to capitalism from precapitalist modes of production. This line of reasoning dovetails with analyses positing distinct, regionally based processes of agrarian capitalist development. Duncan and Rutledge, *Land and Labour*, chap. 1, for example, identify three such different processes, based on proletarianization, increased coercion, and hybrid peasant/wage labor. An even richer conceptual matrix for the general questions raised here is the corpus of debates among European historians and other social scientists about the transition from feudalism to capitalism.

6. Bergad, *Coffee and Agrarian Capitalism*; Brass, "Coffee and Rural Proletarianization"; idem, "Free and Unfree Labour in Puerto Rico during the Nineteenth Century," *Journal of Latin American Studies* 18 (1986): 186–94; Bergad, "On Comparative History: A Reply to Tom Brass," *Journal of Latin American Studies* 16 (1984): 153–56; Evsey D. Domar, "The Causes of Slavery and Serfdom: A Hypothesis," *Journal of Economic History* 30 (1970): 18–32.

7. Daniel Chirot, "The Growth of the Market and Service Labor Systems in Agriculture," *Journal of Social History* 8 (1975): 67–80; see also Charles Tilly, "Flows of Capital and Forms of Industry in Europe, 1500–1900," *Theory and Society* 12 (1983): 123–43. Philip Corrigan, "Feudal Relics or Capitalist Monuments? Notes of the Sociology of Unfree Labor," *Sociology* 2 (1977): 435–63, makes the even more ambitious argument that labor constraint and coercion generally increase with the expansion of capitalism.

8. Winson, "The Formation of Capitalist Agriculture," 94. In areas of "recent settlement," export agriculture has been consistently linked to smallholding or family-based tenancy (Friedmann, "World Market, State, and Family Farm"; Mauricio A. Font, "Export Agriculture and Development: A Bigger Role for Smaller Holders?" *Sociological Forum* 1 [1986]: 733–39; idem, "Coffee Planters, Politics, and Development in Brazil," *Latin American Research Review* 22 [1987]: 69–90) and what Paige has called commodity price reform movements. Grosso modo, the comparison of prototypical East and West European experiences shows different forms of labor and political behavior embedded in differentiated systems of commercial agriculture (see also Tilly, "Flows of Capital").

9. Bauer, "Rural Workers in Spanish America: Problems of Peonage and Oppression," *Hispanic American Historical Review* 59 (1979): 34–63; idem, "Rural Spanish America." For a critique, see Brian Loveman, "Critique of Arnold J. Bauer's 'Rural Workers in Spanish America: Problems of Peonage and Oppression,'" *Hispanic American Historical Review* 59 (1979): 478–85.

10. The main intention of this essay is not to adjudicate among the various general theoretical perspectives or to argue for any of various possible characterizations of the Paulista labor system. It merely seeks to raise questions about existing approaches to both and to argue for a sharper theoretical focus on the latter in terms of a broader comparative framework.

11. Holloway, *Immigrants on the Land*. This period also marks the beginning of the complex and increasingly dynamic capitalist economy which in a few decades made São Paulo perhaps the most important center of industrialization and economic development in Latin America.

12. Robert Franz Foerster, *The Italian Emigration of Our Times* (Cambridge, Mass., 1919).

13. The literature on the colono system includes Warren Dean, *Rio Claro: A Brazilian Plantation System, 1820–1920* (Stanford, 1976); José de Souza Martins, *O cativeiro da terra* (São Paulo, 1979); Cheywa Spindel, *Homens e máquinas na transição de uma economia cafeeira* (São Paulo, 1980); Holloway, *Immigrants on the Land*; Brasílio Sallum, Jr., *Capitalismo e cafeicultura: oeste paulista, 1888–1930* (São Paulo, 1982); and Verena Stolcke and Michael Hall, "The Introduction of Free Labor on São Paulo Coffee Plantations," *Journal of Peasant Studies* 10 (1983): 170–200.

14. Hall and Martíñez Alier, "Greves de colonos"; Stolcke and Hall, "The Introduction of Free Labor"; Michael Hall, "The Origins of Mass Immigration in Brazil, 1871–1914" (Ph.D. diss., Columbia University, 1969).

15. Stolcke and Hall, "The Introduction of Free Labor," 181.

16. Ibid., 185.

17. Maria Isaura Pereira de Queiroz, O mandonismo local na vida política brasileira e outros ensaios (São Paulo, 1976).

18. Holloway, Immigrants on the Land.

19. "A Visit to the Brazilian Coffee Country," National Geographic Magazine 22 (1911): 908–31.

20. As noted by Charles Tilly, my arguments about São Paulo parallel those made by Jan de Vries for seventeenth-century Netherlands: increasing petty production at the base of processes of transformations to more dynamic and productive capitalist systems.

21. Albert Hirschman, "A generalized Linkage Approach to Development, with Special Reference to Staples," Economic Development and Cultural Change 25 (Supplement, 1977): 67–98; Paige, Agrarian Revolution.

22. For descriptions of the colono contract, see Foerster, The Italian Emigration, 292–93; Spindel, Homens e máquina, chap. 2; Holloway, "Migration and Mobility: Immigrants as Laborers and Landowners in the Coffee Zone of São Paulo, 1886–1934" (Ph.D. diss., University of Wisconsin, 1974), chap. 3; Maria Silvia C. Beozzo Bassanezi, "Absorçao e mobilidade da forca de trabalho numaã propriedade rural paulista (1895–1930)," in Edgar Carone, ed., O café: anals do II Congresso de História de São Paulo (São Paulo, 1975); Sallum, Capitalismo e cafeicultura.

23. Spindel, Homens e máquina; Hall and Martínez Alier, "Greves de colonos"; Stolcke and Hall, "The Introduction of Free Labor"; Dean, Rio Claro.

24. Stolcke and Hall, "The Introduction of Free Labor," 199; Foerster, The Italian Emigration, 290–99; Holloway, Immigrants on the Land.

25. For discussions of other aspects of Paulista dynamics and social structure, see Font, Coffee, Contention, and Change (London, 1990); idem, "Export Agriculture and Development Path," Journal of Historical Sociology 3 (1990): 329–61; idem, "City and Countryside in the Onset of Brazilian Industrialization," Studies in Comparative International Development 27 (1992): 26–56; idem, "Coffee Planters, Politics, and Development." It should be stressed that the arguments made here pertain to the period 1880–1930, particularly after World War I. Prior to the 1880s the colono system as such was not fully developed and appears to have had more elements of "unfree" labor. Since the 1930s, it seems to have become progressively simplified, coming closer to a form of rural wage labor, often temporary, offering much lower opportunities for mobility (V. Caldeira Brandt, "Do colono ao bóia fria: transformações na agricultura e constituição do mercado de trabalho na Alta Sorocabana de Assis," Estudos CEBRAP 19 [1977]). That is, if the doors of opportunity may have swung open to a significant degree between 1880 and the 1930s, they seem to have opened less and less since then. The closing of the frontier was no doubt a main factor in this regard.

26. See Chiara Vangelista, Le Braccia per la fazenda: immigrati e caipiras nella

formazione del mercato del lavoro paulista (1850–1930) (Milan, 1982), who concluded that the above forces of fragmentation precluded the consolidation of coffee cultivators as a homogeneous large rural labor force.

27. Variations were tied to the expansion of the frontier. More than half of the state was claimed and settled after 1910. The "westwardly march of coffee" fanned out from the central region following the construction or extension of several different railroads, the main ones being the Paulista, Mogiana, Soroca-bana, and Noroeste. The emergent subregions took the name of the railroads, qualified by how far west they were. These subregions differed in many ways: fertility of the soil, amount of land available for colonos and for crop expansion, wage structure, land tenure and class structure, and the like. At the time, sub-regions were described as old, intermediate, or frontier proper. Authors who have analyzed the expansion of coffee in terms of spatial and temporal variations result-ing from the moving frontier include Sergio Milliet, *Roteiro do café e outros ensaios* (São Paulo, 1941); José Francisco de Camargo, *Crescimento da população no estado de São Paulo e seus aspectos economicos*, 3 vols. (São Paulo, 1952); Pierre Monbeig, *Pionniers et planteurs de São Paulo* (Paris, 1952); Roberto Simon-sen, "Aspectos da história econômica do café," *Revista do Arquivo Municipal de São Paulo 65* (Separate issue, 1940): 149–226; Caio Prado, Jr., "Distribuição da propriedade fundiária rural no estado de São Paulo," *Revista Geografia* 1 (1935): 231–39; Holloway, *Immigrants on the Land*; Martin T. Katzman, "The Brazilian Frontier in Comparative Perspective," *Comparative Studies in Society and History* 17 (1975): 266–85; Souza Martins, *O cativeiro da terra.*

28. Dean, *Rio Claro*, 175.

29. Spindel, *Homens e máquinas*, 118; Holloway, "Migration and Mobility," 101.

30. Dean, *Rio Claro*, 118.

31. Nobuya Tsuchida, "The Japanese in Brazil, 1908–1941" (Ph.D. diss., Uni-versity of California, Los Angeles, 1978).

32. See also Vangelista, *Le braccia per la fazenda.*

33. See Wilson Cano, *Raízes da concentração industrial em São Paulo* (Rio de Janeiro, 1977).

34. Holloway, *Immigrants on the Land.* As early as 1915, an Italian vice-consul critical of the fazendas stated that colonos who had been in São Paulo for many years generally "had been able to save and become smallholders." Paulo Sergio Pinheiro and Michael Hall, *A classe operária no Brasil, 1889–1930* (São Paulo, 1981), 102.

35. In Font (1990a, 1992, 1987). My arguments build on Holloway (1974).

36. Sallum, *Capitalismo e cafeicultura.*

37. *Revista do Brasil* (July 1924): 4.

38. Much of the material discussed in this section comes from reports (Re-latório) of the secretary of agriculture of the state of São Paulo and systematic day-by-day readings of the three main newspapers in the state, *Correio Paulistano, O Estado de São Paulo*, and *Diario Nacional.*

39. Stolcke and Hall, "The Introduction of Free Labor."

40. An interesting contrast: among the nitrate workers of Chile at roughly the

same time, large availability of labor and notoriously higher levels of repression in the export sector did not prevent workers from launching an impressive workers' movement and frequent collective action, including a general strike in 1907, which contributed decisively to the rise of the Chilean left (Charles Bergquist, "Exports, Labor, and the Left: An Essay on Twentieth-Century Chilean History" [The Wilson Center, Latin American Program, Working Paper, 1981]). Another contrast: much of the rest of Brazil witnessed a great deal of rural as well as urban agitation during the 1920s. There is no record of major rural labor conflict in São Paulo even when there was a collapse of authority in the state during the rebellion of 1924.

41. Hall and Martínez Alier, "Greves de colonos," 3.

42. Regarding the issue of labor supply, Stolcke and Hall do not adequately explain why, if workers were always abundant, planters were often complaining about shortages. They dismiss planter cries as mere "laments" or "debating points" to assure abundant labor and counter European measures against migration to São Paulo ("The Introduction of Free Labor," 183). This does not explain why planters would continue to cry out after European resistance to subsidized migration subsided. Considering the high labor turnover rate in the fazendas, it seems likely that these cries reflected true shortages in at least some subregions. Interestingly, Vangelista's quantitative analyses show that wages did not generally change with either sudden rises in demand for labor or surges of immigration.

43. The Patronato Agrícola (translated as Agricultural Protective Bureau by Foerster in 1919) was a rural labor relations board created by law in 1911 in part to show that São Paulo protected its foreign-born labor force and was thus deserving of more immigration (O Estado de São Paulo [December 9, 1910], 6). Because many planters did not pay colonos in bad years, claiming more pressing mortgage obligations, in 1907 a federal law gave the colonos a first lien on the coffee crop. The Patronato was to enforce this and other state laws on behalf of the colonos. It did not start effective operations until several years after 1911. While at first some of its rulings appear to have benefited planters, it became progressively more evenhanded. By the 1920s planters often complained of a pro-colono bias. Its yearly reports appeared in the Relatório of the Secretaria da Agricultura. Data for 1920–25 come from Relatório of the Secretaria da Agricultura (1923, p. 156; 1924, p. 99; 1925, p. 126). These figures should probably be used as low estimates of overall activity. Since strike activity in the fazendas was generally underplayed by the traditional Paulista elites and authorities, it is possible that strikes were more frequent than reported by the Patronato. On the other hand, checks using other newspapers and sources failed to identify significantly higher levels of strike activity during this period.

44. São Paulo Secretaria da Agricultura, Relatório (1928).

45. See also Dean, Rio Claro, 179–80.

46. See Holloway, "Migration and Mobility," 168.

47. Stolcke and Hall, "The Introduction of Free Labor," 183.

48. On the same page these authors also refer to "a moderate rise (in money wages between 1902 and 1910) due to the relatively small number of immigrants entering São Paulo and the large number of departures." Immigration levels were very low, to be sure. But time-series data for the two fazendas studied by Bassanezi

and Holloway fail to show any increase in money wages during this period (see graphs in Mauricio A. Font, "Planters and the State: The Pursuit of Hegemony in São Paulo, Brazil, 1889–1930" [Ph.D. diss., University of Michigan, 1983], 698–700). Also, while Stolcke and Hall seem to argue that the strikes were primarily motivated by the need to maintain the value of real wages in the face of inflation, it is far from clear that there was a great deal of the latter at that particular point.

49. José Arthur Rios, "Aspectos políticos da assimilação do italiano no Brasil," *Sociologia* 20 (1958): 336.

50. Incidentally, in this case the planters organized themselves in the form of a "League" and sought support from the Patronato Agrícola, which ruled in their favor — showing that in its early years the Patronato could be pressured to work as an instrument of planter control.

51. *Relatório*, Secretaria da Agricultura, São Paulo, 1922–28.

52. Foerster, *The Italian Emigration of Our Times*, 288–91.

53. Samuel L. Baily, "The Role of Two Newspapers in the Assimilation of Italians in Buenos Aires and São Paulo, 1893–1918," *International Migration Review* 12 (1978): 321–40.

54. Dean, *Rio Claro*; Rios, "Aspectos políticos."

55. Baily, "The Role of Two Newspapers."

56. Ibid., 337.

57. *Correio Paulistano* (February 25, 1924: 3,7,M).

58. Baily, "The Italians and the Development of Organized Labor in Argentina, Brazil, and the United States, 1880–1914," *Journal of Social History* 3 (1969): 123–34.

59. Rios, "Aspectos políticos," 22.

60. Ibid.

61. See also ibid. and Eugenio Banardelli, *Lo Stato di S. Paulo d el Brasile e l'Emigrazione Italiana* (Turin, 1916).

62. The Constitution of 1891 gave foreigners who were in Brazil prior to November of 1889 six months to express their desire to preserve their nationality of origin (Rios, "Aspectos políticos," 311). As secretary of justice in the late 1900s, Washington Luís interpreted federal immigration law to read that practically by default all immigrants married to Brazilians, parents of Brazilian children, or owners of property were to be considered Brazilian — unless they declared otherwise. This reading of the law was reaffirmed by President Arthur Bernardes when there was a challenge to the law in 1923. *O Estado de São Paulo* caustically pointed out that immigrants in São Paulo had more rights than in their countries of origin (*O Estado de São Paulo* [August 2, 1929: 3,3T]). In 1928 the Supreme Court decided that naturalization did not depend on the immigrants' public statement of their status, but on the holding of an elector's card (begging the question, it declared that this was so because possession of an elector's card could not have taken place without the prior show of documents proving citizenship).

63. *O Estado de São Paulo* (December 18, 1929: 6,1,T).

64. Cultivators and other groups linked to the emergence of an alternative economy in the state were part of an emergent alliance significant enough to elicit major defensive responses from the traditional coffee elites. In fact, the politics of

traditional planter elites in the 1920s can be seen as a response to restore their full
hegemony in the state (see also Font, *Coffee, Contention, and Change* and "Coffee
Planters, Politics, and Development."

65. Again, the above analysis does not deny that outright proletarianization or
immiseration — or even enserfment, for that matter — may have taken place in São
Paulo. (Incidentally, during the period in question proletarianization increasingly
took place within family-operated units employing complementary labor power.)
The point is that in São Paulo there was sufficient mobility and differentiation to
contribute to the emergence of an alternative economy not exclusively centered on
the large fazenda and to justify aspirations of personal advancement which undermined collective action.

66. The contrast with the famous Turner thesis is sharp: according to the latter
the frontier plays a key role in the emergence of independent producers and a
democratic society, or at least did so in the United States.

67. This case may not necessarily negate the hypothesis: the key concept is
labor scarcity (Chirot, "The Growth of the Market"), but there is debate about the
extent of effective labor scarcity between the 1890s and 1910 as well as through
the 1910s and 1920s. A new structural situation emerged with the "closing of the
frontier" and the progressively heavier reliance on internal migration starting in
the late 1920s.

68. Friedmann, "World Market, State, and Family Farm"; idem, "Household
Production and the National Economy."

69. It is also likely that in São Paulo lack of community solidarity undermined
"peasant" capacity to revolt. Massive rural revolts have been associated with
strong cultivators' communities in Russia, France, China, Mexico, and other cases
(Barrington Moore, *Social Origins of Dictatorship and Democracy: Lord and
Peasant in the Making of the Modern World* [Boston, 1966]; Eric R. Wolf, *Peasant
Wars of the Twentieth Century* [New York, 1969]; Theda Skocpol, *States and
Social Revolutions* [Cambridge, 1979]). Settlements in São Paulo's expanding
frontier often lacked institutionalized solidarity and corporativeness. Colonos, of
course, lived in the large estates (see, e.g., Ward, "A Visit to the Brazilian Coffee
Country," 914) and exercised a great deal of geographic mobility. No tradition or
well-established normative order was there to be broken in São Paulo. Since the
fact that immigrants actually pioneered in the emergence of mutual aid and comparable societies suggests that they did have the capacity to act collectively, it
seems more likely that the main determinants of their behaviors had to do with the
structure of interests and related mobilizational factors.

70. John Walton, *Reluctant Rebels: Comparative Studies of Revolution and
Underdevelopment* (New York, 1984); Wolf, *Peasant Wars*. The latter linked the
likelihood of revolt to power crises derived from the appearance of new elites —
entrepreneurs, merchants, political brokers — and the threat they posed to established landlords.

71. Font, *Coffee, Contention, and Change.*

72. The state has been recognized as a major actor in the emergence and
consolidation of settler and smallholding systems in Canada, Australia, and other
areas of recent settlement, including the United States (e.g., Friedmann, "World

Market, State, and Family Farm"; Phillip McMichael, *Settlers and the Agrarian Question: Foundations of Capitalism in Colonial Australia* [Cambridge, 1984]; Carl Solberg, "Land Tenure and Land Settlement: Policy and Patterns in the Canadian Prairies and the Argentine Pampas," in D. C. M. Platt and Guido di Tella, eds., *Argentina, Australia, and Canada: Studies in Comparative Development* [New York, 1985]).

Eight

Wage Labor, Free Labor, and Vagrancy Laws: The Transition to Capitalism in Guatemala, 1920–1945

DAVID MCCREERY

> Property in money, means of subsistence, machines, and other means of production does not yet stamp a man as a capitalist if the essential complement to these things is missing: the wage-laborer, the other man, who is compelled to sell himself of his own free will.
>
> Marx, *Capital*

DURING THE early 1920s, a debate broke out in the Guatemala City newspapers over the need for labor reform in the coffee export sector. This is of interest not only because in those years material of substance rarely appeared in the press, but because labor was, and had been for half a century, the coffee elite's most vexing concern. Whereas the country possessed abundant land for coffee and had since the 1870s received a substantial inflow of foreign capital, *brazos* ("arms," or workers), planters complained unceasingly, were in constant short supply. Whether such shortages were real or imagined, and whether, if real, they resulted from population declines, because workers fled the abusive practices of the *fincas* (coffee estates) and the state, or because of an innate reluctance of the Indian to abandon a life of sloth and vice was much discussed after 1920, as was what should or could be done about it. The debate waned in 1924 when coffee prices revived, only to appear again in 1928–29 with the first indications of the Great Depression. This unprecedented airing of the labor question set the framework for a major overhaul of the laws governing rural workers in the 1930s. The operation of these laws, in turn, helped expose conditions which prompted an end to legal extra-economic coercion and the transition to capitalist free labor in 1944–45. Why, in a period of little more than twenty years, did Guatemala's landed elites abandon a four-hundred-year-old system of labor mobilization and control that seemed to have served them well?

From the Conquest the cash and export sector of Guatemala's agricultural economy relied on coerced labor.[1] Though black slavery was of little consequence and abolished soon after independence, a system of forced labor drafts called *repartimientos* before independence and *mandamientos* after 1821 together with debt peonage persisted into the twentieth century. When agricultural elites shifted from cochineal to coffee in the 1860s and 1870s, export production expanded to an unexampled degree, engrossing large areas of the country until then little touched by export agriculture. A new generation of liberals rode the coffee boom to power in 1871, organizing a relatively efficient, centralized state that rested on a professionalized army and a *ladino*[2] militia and was able to project an unprecedented presence into the countryside.[3] To mobilize workers for coffee, the state expanded the use of mandamientos and peonage and pushed the search for labor deep into the western highlands and the Alta Verapaz, where most of the majority indigenous population lived. The two labor forms of forced drafts and debt peonage made an interlocking system: under the 1894 general labor law[4] only a debt of at least fifteen pesos for work on an export finca exempted the Indian, in law if not always in fact, from the hated mandamientos. This was a powerful incentive. A few Indians for personal reasons abandoned their communities and took up residence permanently on the plantations as *colonos* (resident workers), but most continued to live as subsistence farmers and handicraft manufacturers or traders in the highlands and to go reluctantly to the fincas two or three months a year to clean the groves and make the harvest.

Coercion worked, and it helped to guarantee substantial profits for Guatemala's planters, but the uncertainties attendant on World War I and the price instabilities that followed it made planters increasingly uneasy about the condition of the coffee economy. Exports had peaked in 1906 and stagnated thereafter (Table 8.1), while world prices for coffee tended to swing in wild and unpredictable arcs (Table 8.2). A decline in the value of the country's paper money against gold, from six pesos to the United States dollar in 1900 to fifty-four pesos in 1922,[5] generally benefited the planters, who sold abroad for hard currency and paid their production expenses at home in increasingly worthless pesos.[6] But by the late teens the peso's gyrations had become so violent and so unpredictable that growers and merchants alike found it increasingly difficult to plan or to calculate costs and profits.[7] These problems, together with the government's dismal

TABLE 8.1
Coffee Exports in Guatemala (Five-Year
Averages in Quintales)

Years	Exports
1900–1904	681,368qq
1905–1909	807,914qq
1910–1914	773,765qq
1915–1919	845,282qq
1920–1924	930,983qq
1925–1929	992,516qq
1930–1934	963,979qq
1935–1939	990,249qq

Sources: C. L. Jones, Guatemala, Past and Present
(Minneapolis, 1940), 210; Grieb, Guatemalan Caudillo, 147.
1 quintal = 100 pounds.

performance in the wake of a disastrous 1917 earthquake and the 1918 flu
pandemic, prompted the mass of the population, segments of the elite, and
foreign diplomats to come together in 1920 to bring down long-time
dictator Manuel Estrada Cabrera.

The fall of Estrada Cabrera touched off a decade of uncertainty and
change.[8] Among the first things to be ended were the mandamientos. If
some writers argued that corvée labor was an embarrassment to a modern
nation and a symbol of the hated past regime,[9] for most planters the real
problem lay elsewhere. Above all, they lamented the caciquismo (bossism)
which allowed state officials to manipulate the drafts to their own profit
and allowed the more wealthy, and especially foreign, growers a monopoly on labor.[10] Most planters seem to have been happy to see mandamientos go. And, of course, debt peonage remained. By the 1920s most
highland Indians owed money for labor to coffee plantations, but whatever their debt none would leave the community for the coast each year
until they received an additional advance from the finca's representative.
The effect, together with finca and recruiter fraud, was that Indians rarely
worked off what they were said to owe. Typically, their debt rose to far
more than the nominal fifteen pesos the law demanded, as Table 8.3
indicates.

While some interpreted such large debts as evidence of hopeless "slavery"[11] to the fincas, the laborers and many finqueros (finca owners) understood the situation more clearly. The workers hated peonage and sought
at every turn to escape its demands, but to be without a debt to an export
plantation was to be liable for mandamientos (until 1920), military re-

TABLE 8.2
Guatemalan Coffee Prices (U.S. Dollars per
Quintal)

Year	Price
1915	13.63
1916	13.47
1917	11.83
1918	14.23
1919	26.26
1920	20.36
1921	14.58
1922	16.52
1923	17.83
1924	24.74
1925	27.89
1926	26.95
1927	25.10
1928	25.33
1929	22.54
1930	16.55
1931	15.20
1932	11.82
1933	10.31
1934	12.11
1935	9.31
1936	9.73
1937	11.10
1938	9.38
1939	9.45

Source: International Institute of Agriculture, *The World's Coffee* (Rome, 1947), 432.

cruiting, forced road work, and other extortions of the state and state agents, demands from which only a *patrón* (employer) offered some protection. Too, the recruiter was usually the Indians' only source of ready or emergency cash. This gave little reason to seek to escape debt. The imperative, in fact, was quite the opposite. It was to the worker's advantage to extort as much money from the finquero as possible, to, in effect, build up the employer's investment in him. A bigger debt, rather than being a burden, gave the *mozo* leverage. If pressed too hard by a finca, he could almost always find another employer ready to buy his debt, or he might simply run away, change his name, and seek work in another area. In their scramble for workers, planters routinely, and rather shortsightedly, hid runaways and provided them false papers to evade past obligations. Indians also crossed over into Mexico or Belize to escape finca and state

210

DAVID McCREERY

TABLE 8.3
Debts for Workers on South Coast Fincas,
Guatemala, 1929

Finca	Average Debt (Guatemalan pesos)
Mocaya	$928
Santa Abundancia	$1,246
El Regalo	$2,252
Olas de Moca	$4,027
La Patria	$972
Milan	$1,823

Source: AGCA, Jefe Político, Sololá, 1929.

pressures and to earn higher wages. Because the power a specific finca owner had over any given individual member of his work force — as opposed to class power — was extremely limited, he was forced into constant negotiations. One obvious result was the Indians' ability to push their debts to unexpected levels.

The collapse of prices after 1919 turned the attention of coffee growers to the need to improve production efficiency, and this attention focused on labor. A few planters dared to suggest that local custom squandered labor: "Such is the system of making our *mozos* work, without getting the profit from them that we should, that we are, on the one hand, wasting thousands and thousands of days' work on each *finca*, and, on the other, failing to take advantage of thousands and thousands of days' work that we could get from the workers we manage to obtain."[12] Most, though, felt that their problem was quite the opposite and lay in a shortage of available workers.[13] There had been no published census since 1893,[14] so no one had a clear idea how many Indians in fact existed in Guatemala. Some expressed the opinion that the absolute number had declined in recent decades, the result of alcoholism, disease, and emigration. Others argued that the problem was not population size but the mobilization and control of workers.[15] How, then, might more and cheaper labor be obtained?

The process of the primitive accumulation of capital[16] in late-nineteenth-century Guatemala had stopped short of converting all production factors into full market commodities. The liberals ended restrictions on interest rates, encouraged the formation of banks and the growth of commercial lending, and welcomed foreign capital. The new regime also eased access to land for commercial production by selling off public and church lands and by regularizing land measurement, titling, and transfer.[17] Even so, precapitalist restrictions continued to weigh on land. Not only did

Indian community *ejidos* (communal lands) in many areas survive largely intact, but the state allowed or assisted the villages to expand these.[18] Those few villages unfortunate enough to be in the direct path of coffee's advance were overwhelmed and their population converted into colonos and day laborers,[19] but most Indians lived not in the piedmont where coffee flourished but in the adjacent highlands. Their cold, dry ejidos were of little immediate use to coffee growers,[20] and the state usually confirmed and titled these to the villages, as well as granting or selling them additional lands from the public domain, in the highlands and in those areas of the hot country not needed for coffee.[21] Villagers held this land in a variety of hybrid forms of possession, often with a general municipal title legally registered and recognized by the state, under which individuals enjoyed private property or life tenure or shifting cultivation depending on local custom.[22]

The Indian peasantry of the western highlands and the Alta Verapaz inhabited a socioeconomic formation structured by the articulation of subsistence and petty commodity production with a superordinate and exploitative export economy. Precapitalist relations of production/exploitation predominated in the export sector, although cash wages tended to disguise these. It is important to be clear on this. There is some tendency to confuse capitalism with the accumulation of money, the mechanization of production and, especially, the presence of cash wages. But capitalism rests not on a pool of money or the existence of modern productive equipment but on a specific social relationship of production/exploitation. Guatemala had been caught in the toils of international capitalism—first in the guise of merchant capital and then as industrial and finance capital—since the sixteenth century, but this integration or articulation[23] took place initially only at the level of circulation. With the second generation of liberals that came to power in the 1870s, capitalism came to dominate the ideological superstructure characteristic of the state and elites, but it failed to penetrate to any serious degree, much less revolutionize, productive relations. Whereas cochineal growers (1830–70) had flirted with capitalist free labor, the spread of coffee after 1871 prompted the reimposition, tightening, and generalization to areas previously little affected of extraeconomic, or direct, coercion. Dominance of the local economy by a capitalism external to Guatemala, whether in the form of the cacao boom of the sixteenth and seventeenth centuries or that of coffee in the nineteenth, had the effect of strengthening rather than weakening precapitalist work relations in the countryside.

By the early 1920s solutions to the problem of brazos put forward in editorials and letters to the newspapers increasingly focused on *trabajo libre* (free labor). This was not capitalist free labor. Such was impossible, the argument went, because the Indian lacked the "civilized needs" that would drive him into the wage labor market.[24] Most of the rural inhabitants of early twentieth-century Guatemala were not free in the capitalist sense not only because of direct coercion but also because most still had access to land or similar resources. The Indian communities controlled the means of their own reproduction and retained the ability, impeded to be sure by the effects of coerced labor, to set these means in motion. They used cash and in some instances actively sought wage labor, but most were not yet dependent on either for subsistence. Indeed, no theme was more persistent among the elites than that of the drunken, lazy Indian who would not work because he had no need to.[25] As long, it appeared, as he was satisfied with "a rude shack, almost without clothing, crammed together with the family in a space of two or three meters, in nauseating promiscuity, victim of a thousand superstitions, getting drunk at every opportunity"[26] coercion would be required.

Pejoratives aside, this was essentially a correct analysis of the Indians' situation, at least before the 1920s. So long as the indigenous population could supply its subsistence (including ritual) requirements from its own resources, it had little reason to labor in someone else's coffee fields. If an individual voluntarily looked for cash wages, this typically was for a specific purpose, for example, to pay for a ceremony or buy food to tide him and his family over until the next harvest. Higher wages meant he would work less. What resulted was the well-known "backward bending labor supply curve,"[27] the despair of nineteenth-century colonial administrators and export producers the world over. The highland Indian understood and responded to the opportunity to make higher wages[28] but not to that of simply making more money. As a result, some elites argued the Indian was hopeless and must either be eliminated as had been done by the North Americans or swamped by the immigration of "healthy elements."[29] Others, a minority, believed him to be the victim of past treatment, treatment that had brutalized him and taken away his incentives, and thought that he might yet be educated to economic rationality.[30]

Why did the Guatemalan state not confiscate village ejidos, smash the communities, and free up land and labor for capitalist production as the coffee elites of neighboring El Salvador apparently did?[31] One explanation sometimes offered for the survival of precapitalist socioeconomic formations articulated with capitalism is that capitalism essentially functionalizes such communities, allowing and even assisting them to survive in order to produce and reproduce cheap labor power for the export economy.[32] The villages also supply cheap food and handicraft manufactures, and they offer a potential market only partially tied to the wages of the export sector. Thus the survival of precapitalist communities may help to

offset capitalism's tendency toward a falling rate of profit. The more astute planters in Guatemala recognized the value to them of the highland
villages as food producers and labor reserves, and the land policies of the
liberal state reflected this. Given the availability of direct coercion for
worker mobilization and the different types of land involved, the preser-
vation of the ejidos cheapened labor and pacified the countryside.

But to reify "capitalism" into a historical actor obscures more than it
illuminates. Individual planters, the elite/planter class, and their state,
operating within a framework set by the changing conditions of the national economy and international capitalism, plainly sought to create and
maintain relations of exploitation which would return them the greatest
profits. However, the cross currents and contradictions at work in this
environment were enormously complex and not easily reduced to schematic representation.[33] As a result, whatever theory might have dictated
to be in their best interest, some finqueros, and particularly those with
excess land available on which to colonize workers, did hope to break up
the communities and shake out the inhabitants.

What stopped them was Indian resistance. The villagers were ingenious, tenacious, and on occasion violent in defense of community resources and in opposing egregious exploitation on and by the fincas.
Overt opposition to state policies by the indigenous population had fallen
off dramatically after the 1870s, a logical response to the growing power
of the liberal state,[34] but burst into the open again in the 1920s during a
decade of political instability. Reports of "uprisings," resistance to state
and finquero authority, and the ominous news that the Indians in the
countryside were organizing against their long-time oppressors filled the
newspapers.[35] *El Imparcial* reported strikes and unrest in the coffee areas
of Colomba, Coatepeque, Xolhuitz, and Chocolá, as well as attacks on
ladinos and land battles in Ilón, San Lucas Sacatepéquez, and other communities.[36] Peasants and urban workers came together to press joint demands.[37] The change in atmosphere from the apparent tranquility of the
Estrada Cabrera years may have been in part one of perception, for the
newspapers now reported occurrences which in the past they might have
ignored or concealed,[38] but it reflected also both the temporary weakness
of the central state, which allowed accumulated grievances to bubble to
the surface, as well as the influences of contemporary events in Mexico
and Nicaragua.

Resurgence of open Indian resistance underlines the point that the persistence or the destruction of a precapitalist socioeconomic formation
articulated with capitalism cannot be theoretically predetermined. Each
encounter is historically contingent, dependent on the stage of capitalist
development, the form of contact between the bearers of international

capitalism and the precapitalist formation, and the internal structure and current "health" of that formation.

But if the turmoil reminded elites of the limits of their power, coercion would continue at least until an adequate number of Indians offered themselves spontaneously for wage labor. In the context of 1920s Guatemala the much-discussed trabajo libre meant that work might be of free selection but it would be obligatory. The mozo "may choose between obligatory labor on public works, military service, or *trabajo libre*, which for an Indian could not be other than work on the *fincas*."[39] Enforcement would require a strong vagrancy law. An 1870s law remained on the books,[40] but it defined vagrants as "those who do not have a profession, trade, income, salary, occupation or means of support by which to live." This was a measure for urban crime control, not the mobilization of agricultural labor. If the threat of punishment as a vagrant was to serve effectively to coerce rural workers, a new law aimed specifically at the population in the countryside was needed, together with effective instruments for its implementation. To police the countryside the state relied on *ladino comandantes locales* (local military commanders) and small and poorly trained, but well-armed, militia detachments, recruited from ladino villages and among the ladino officials, shopkeepers, and labor recruiters in Indian communities. To back these up, most planters agreed that a full-time rural police force similar to El Salvador's national guard was required.[41] There was also the problem of how to keep track of individual workers. Highland Indians caught up in forced labor often adopted "ladino names" for use with government officials and labor recruiters. They changed these when convenient and lent each other documents to evade the authorities. Most of the indigenous population, too, lived not in the central part of the villages but in outlying hamlets,[42] where the *comandante* found it difficult to keep track of them. The solution most commonly proposed was that all Indian males be made to carry, in addition to the debt record, or *libreta*, that the existing law demanded, a registered *cédula de vecindad* (identity card).[43]

A transition to trabajo libre also presented the problem of what to do about existing debts. Should these be abolished at once or worked off, and if worked off, over how long a time period? Might the mozos be allowed to pay in money what they owed for labor? Should new *habilitaciones* be made? Though planters complained in other circumstances of the cost of carrying mozo debts,[44] when opposing the abolition of these they rarely brought up the losses they must inevitably suffer. This tended to confirm the suspicion that much "debt" was little more than fiction, the result of creative bookkeeping by the fincas rather than any genuine outlay of capital. The finqueros protested instead that abolishing debts would reward mozos who had failed or refused to work off what they owed.[45] Employer resistance to ending debt peonage was above all, it appeared, a moral question! While comments in the newspapers suggested that most planters opposed the immediate end to labor debts and rejected also the idea that Indians be allowed to pay back debts owed for work with money,[46] they had much more trouble agreeing upon a scheme for genuine reform.

A number of proposals for a new labor law surfaced in the years 1920–24. Because most varied only in detail, it is sufficient to look briefly at just two, one put forward in 1921, and subsequently slightly modified, by the newly created Ministry of Agriculture, and a second advanced by the planters' Asociación de Agricultores Guatemaltecos (A.G.A). "All labor will be free," proposed the Ministry of Agriculture, with the restrictions that no contracts could be made for work outside the country[47] and no mozo might be taken on by an employer without exhibiting a *boleto de solvencia* (written proof of having cleared all debts with previous employers). Debts contracted for work might be paid off in money. Public officials were not to work as labor recruiters, but they could grant a worker a boleto de solvencia if such was due and an employer refused it. Any man claiming to be looking for work would be punished as a vagrant if he did not find employment within a specified time.[48] The ministry withdrew the draft in response to planter protests and returned it a year later with several changes.[49] The new version made it more difficult to repay with money advances made for labor, specified and tightened the conditions under which a worker might leave a finca when his contract expired, and shifted responsibility for patron-worker disputes from the courts to the local officials of the finca's municipality.

Complaining, nevertheless, that the government was meddling in affairs of which it was ignorant, planters through the A.G.A. presented their own project. Existing debts would be worked off over no more than two years and future advances limited to the equivalent of sixty days' labor. Banned too were contracts for work outside the country, the activities of *tratistas* (freelance labor recruiters), who drove up labor costs and labor recruiting by public authorities. No worker in debt to one employer was to be contracted by or to receive an advance from another. Only in the case of severe illness would a mozo be allowed to repay labor debts with money. Every worker was to carry a *boleto de trabajo* (a work ticket) with his name, the amount of work done each month, and the finca to which he was in debt; failure to produce this would be taken as proof of vagrancy.[50] With its provisions for ending long-term debts and for limiting advances, the A.G.A.'s proposal would have moved more aggressively than that of the Ministry of Agriculture to cheapen the costs of labor recruiting and in the direction of trabajo libre, but there were no major or substantive conflicts between the two proposals nor any of the others seriously entertained in these years.

When coffee prices rebounded in 1924, the elite's uncharacteristic self-examination faded from the press. No new labor law emerged. Custom asserted itself, with the results one writer described:

We Guatemalans continue to be the most disorganized in the world as regards wages and working conditions. Our *caja* ["box" = the measure used in harvest labor] of coffee varies [among fincas] from 70 to 185 pounds and hardly two fincas are the same. Wages run 10 to 60 pesos a task.[51] On some fincas they do not provide food while on others they provide without cost meat, milk, chile, beans, corn, lye, and salt. The majority of fincas cajole workers with dances, clothes, alcohol, and many presents, in addition to our disastrous system of unlimited advances.[52]

Only in 1928 did doubts resurface. Although prices continued to be good in that year, dealers sold much coffee in anticipation of the harvest, and futures prices anticipated the Depression.[53] Instead of rationalizing production in the recent bonanza years, planters' efforts to expand output to take advantage of market opportunities had thrown them into frantic competition for workers, driving up costs. Efforts to attract labor depended less on increasing money wages than on offering workers the much more powerful incentive of free or below-market-price corn. Levels of corn production remained fairly constant in these years (Table 8.4), but corn prices and, more significantly, corn imports soared (Tables 8.4 and 8.5). Coffee planters brought in large quantities of grain to secure "their" mozos and for use in enticing workers away from other employers. For a short time the Indians must have enjoyed a paradise of corn! Even with these increases and additional expenses, however, Guatemalan wage costs remained lower than those of competitors in other nearby countries, or so writers claimed in the late 1920s. Even so, lower levels of productivity, the result of outdated machinery, inadequate and monopolized communications, and a reluctant, coerced labor force, kept Guatemalan planters' real production costs relatively high.[54]

Worried by this competition and offended by their workers' evident affluence, Guatemala's finqueros again rehashed in the newspapers many of the problems and proposals for labor mobilization and control raised in the early years of the decade.[55] State officials and tratistas continued to prey on them, they complained; the end of mandamientos had not stopped *caciquismo*. Competition from the big fincas, and particularly those controlled by the resurgent German companies,[56] drove up wages and monopolized labor. Lazy, ignorant Indians defrauded their employers and the

TABLE 8.4
Corn Harvests and Imports, Guatemala,
1921–1940

Year	Harvest (quintales)	Imports (kilograms)
1921	3,132,412	
1922	2,989,298	
1923	2,488,972	975,072
1924	2,492,973	491,086
1925	2,403,440	240,727
1926	1,967,310	8,109,606
1927	2,386,190	427,015
1928	1,966,594	22,346,588
1929	2,803,618	18,458,424
1930	3,436,621	1,083,493
1931	2,921,379	2,057
1932	3,163,184	40
1933	2,954,679	579,436
1934	2,848,061	20,119
1935	3,074,760	834
1936	3,280,096	597
1937	6,182,224	4,755,636[a]
1938	6,220,918	1,634,356
1939	7,020,628	641
1940	10,019,980	659

Source: Ministerio de Agricultura, *Memorias, 1922–1940* (Guatemala, 1922–1940).

[a]For an explanation of this sudden "jump" in production, see McCreery, *Rural Guatemala*, chap. 10.

state — the irony here seems to have escaped the planters — by continuing to run up multiple debts with various fincas and then evading work. Proposed solutions repeated the familiar ones of free but obligatory labor, a vagrancy law requiring a minimum number of days' work a year, an end to wage advances, and the imposition of improved instruments of social control.

A new element evident in the debates of the late 1920s was an awareness among the coffee planters of the growth in the nation's population. The census taken in 1921, but not published until the end of 1924,[57] revealed that, far from declining as many had claimed to fear, the size of the indigenous population had increased markedly in the decades since 1893 (see Table 8.6). As the Depression took hold, the possibility began to work its way into elite consciousness that in many communities the inhabitants might no longer have access to enough land or other resources to

TABLE 8.5
Corn Price Indexes in Guatemala, 1920–
1935

Year	Index
1920	67
1921	84
1922	87
1923	100
1924	103
1925	100
1926	127
1927	101
1928	160
1929	145
1930	95
1931	60
1932	55
1933	67
1934	68
1935	46

Source: Ministerio de Fomento, *Memorias, 1922–
1936* (Guatemala, 1922–1936).
Index, 1923 = 100.

support themselves without recourse to the wage sector. Increasingly, Indians voluntarily sought work on the fincas, work which, at least in the early years of the Depression, was often not to be had.[58] Ecological degradation, population growth, and new tastes acquired on the plantations or with plantation-earned cash in fact had begun to create new needs among the inhabitants of the highland villages. The problem of brazos to the employers' minds was coming more and more to focus on control rather than simply on numbers.

In general, the coffee growers of Guatemala weathered the Depression remarkably well.[59] There was a burst of panic selling of fincas in 1930, but the market soon stabilized.[60] After a brief hesitation,[61] planters responded aggressively to the fall in coffee prices by increasing production and attempting to reduce labor costs. Employers cut wages or, rather than pay wages at all, only credited a worker's debt account, and they also tried to limit advances or, with less success, stop them altogether.[62] The government lowered interest rates, made small amounts of cheap credit available to hard-pressed finqueros, and issued a stop law to prevent creditors from foreclosing on plantations.[63] Most of the business houses and banks did not wish to take over debtors' property in any event but instead rolled

TABLE 8.6

Guatemalan Population Statistics, 1893 and 1921

Sample Indian departments	1893	1921	Percentage of increase[a]
Sololá	70,039	104,283	48
Sacatepéquez	42,713	46,453	9
Quiché	92,753	138,076	49
Huehuetenango	117,127	137,166	18
San Marcos	89,322	176,402	49
Total Indian Population	883,228	1,299,927	47
Total Population	1,356,678	2,004,900	48

Source: Dirección General de Estadística, *Censo general de la República de Guatemala Levantado el 26 de febrero de 1893* (Guatemala 1894); *Censo de la República de Guatemala* (Guatemala 1924).

[a] Some of the growth in individual departments (e.g., Sololá and San Marcos) represented migration from other departments, and in other cases it may in part reflect a more accurate count.

over existing financing to keep debtors in business and making payments on their debts.[64]

With the seizure of power by General Jorge Ubico in 1931, serious debate again disappeared from the newspapers.[65] It is thus impossible to outline the specific sequence of events or decisions which led up to a general overhaul of rural labor laws in May 1934, but the reforms followed directly from the arguments of the preceding ten years. Decree 1995, enacted on May 2, 1934, ended long-term debt servitude, and Decree 1996, issued six days later, put in its place a new vagrancy law specifically intended to mobilize cheap labor for the rural fincas.[66] The state abolished debts because of "the constant conflicts between employers and workers resulting from disagreements over debts provoked by the activities of recruiters and because advances restrict the freedom of work and convert the laborer into an object of undue exploitation by those who contract his services."[67] Decree 1995 outlawed the activities of the infamous tratistas, prohibited future wage advances, and allowed planters and mozos two years in which to work off existing debts. In effect, planters gained two years of free or nearly free labor in the worst years of the Depression at the cost of the partial loss of debts of often dubious provenance. They soon discovered, however, that, regardless of the law, the inhabitants of the highland communities would not work without advances, and that prohibition came to nought. But by having the courts refuse to uphold contracts to the contrary, the state did succeed in limiting advances to what could be worked off in a single season or year.

The struggle for control of labor power continued transmuted but un-

abated. Few of the Indians had the cash or the desire to pay off what they
owed, and they sought instead to work as little as possible or to evade the
recruiters' grasp entirely until the two years elapsed. Some of the recruiters, for their part, sought to convert debts originally contracted for labor
into common debts of money at interest, for which the Indian would still
be liable after the Decree 1995 deadline passed.[68] Finca agents in other
cases tried to foreclose on any real property, particularly land, that the
worker possessed. Such tactics did not always proceed smoothly. In the
town of Nebaj, for example, a recruiter conspired with a local notary to
rewrite labor contracts into debt notes and deceived illiterate Indians into
signing these. When a delegation of the elders of the town led a large
crowd to the local comandante to complain, he panicked and threatened
them. In the scuffle that followed an Indian hit him with a broom. The
crowd quickly disarmed the small garrison without injury, but knowing
what was sure to follow, most of the Indians fled to the hills. The government rushed troops to Nebaj, arrested seven of the supposed leaders, and
threatened to try 138 of the local population for sedition.[69] More typically, and for obvious reasons, the Indians adopted a less confrontational
approach, seeking simply to stay out of sight and hand until time ran out.

In addition to the traditional definitions, the new vagrancy law, Decree
1996, labeled as a vagrant anyone without sufficient property to provide
an "adequate" income, anyone contracted for work on a finca but who
had failed to comply with their agreement, and anyone without a contract
for agricultural labor who did not cultivate at least three *manzanas*[70] of
coffee, sugar, or tobacco, four manzanas of corn, wheat, potatoes, vegetables, or other food products, or three manzanas of corn in the hot country
giving two harvests a year. Few Indians had access to such relatively large
amounts of land.[71] Subsequent clarification[72] provided that those who
cultivated ten or more *cuerdas*[73] of land, but less than the amount that
gave a labor exemption, were to work 100 days a year for wages. Those
with less than ten cuerdas owed at least 150 days. The law also required
that all agricultural laborers now carry a new form of *libreta*, to be renewed each calendar year, in which employers were to record the number
of days worked for wages. Those convicted as vagrants would be jailed or
fined.

At the same time that the state reformed the labor laws, Ubico further
tightened control over the countryside. He replaced elected local officials
with appointed intendants, usually an individual from outside the community, put into effect the much-discussed identity cards, and stepped up
the activities of the Treasury Police (the *Montada*).[74] Those arrested as
vagrants commonly fell into the hands of the authorities at check points as
they entered or left town or during sweeps of the outlying hamlets by the

Montada or local police and village authorities. The courts took as proof of vagrancy the failure to produce an up-to-date libreta or certificate of exemption. Those accused sometimes attempted to defend themselves by claiming that they never had worked on a finca and were not required to have a book—a holdover defense from the old peonage system, which did not address the demands of the new vagrancy law—or by claiming that they had a profession that gave them a living or access to enough land in their home community or elsewhere to exempt them from compulsory labor. Certainly the most ingenious, if unsuccessful, defense was that of the individual who affirmed that, "in his heart he did not consider himself a vagrant"![75] Others said they were *tinterillos* (scribes/fixers), between employments, or that they worked as local or traveling merchants. The courts went to considerable lengths to attempt to verify the prisoners' claims, usually telegraphing the authorities in the home community or giving them the opportunity to retrieve documents, and they regularly exonerated those found not liable under the law.

The most frequent complaint of that part of the rural population that had a profession or access to land was that local authorities obstructed their efforts to obtain the necessary certification.[76] Intendants sought to generate the maximum number of workers possible from their communities to satisfy their superiors and to curry the favor of powerful finqueros. As a result, officials ignored villagers' work or trade or purposefully undermeasured their plantings. Although there was no legal basis for such, some intendants refused to accept land cultivated in the village common as meeting the requirements of the law. Chamelco, for example, began for the first time to charge rent for the use of ejido land, apparently to establish a firmer basis of individual possession to satisfy the vagrancy law.[77]

But even efforts such as Chamelco's were no guarantee against abuses if intendants continued to respond primarily to bribes from planters and recruiters. The inhabitants of Comitancillo, for example, complained that instead of being allowed to work on the fincas they chose, they were forced by the intendant to go to the estates he favored and by which, presumably, he was bribed. When they resisted, he jailed and beat them.[78] The Indians of Aguacatán repeatedly pointed to similar abuses by their intendant, apparently without much relief.[79] By the late 1930s and early 1940s the recruiters' usual tactic was to denounce as vagrants men contracted to work on their employer's finca but who had, or so it was claimed, failed to appear or to complete the agreed-upon tasks. The courts refused to convict a person of vagrancy if he could show that he had worked the number of days for wages required by law, even if not on the finca that had entered the case against him. Nonetheless, they also ordered him to fulfill any outstanding contracts. The judges handling vagrancy cases ruled repeatedly that no one could be forced to commute their sentence, but some intendants pressured convicted Indians to accept work offered by preferred recruiters or planters, who were only too happy to pay the Indians' fines. In effect, some intendants sold mozos to the highest bidder or briber.

The villages resisted the vagrancy law as they always had fought state pressure, with appeals to *tata* ("grandfather") *presidente*, evasion, fraud, and, occasionally, violence.[80] But resistance was muted not only by the effective coercive power of the Ubico regime but also by a sense among the indigenous population that the law was much fairer than had been those of the Estrada Cabrera years.[81] Decree 1996, they recognized, extended the requirements of trabajo libre to the non-Indians as well as Indians among the rural poor, and the police swept up ladino and Indian "vagrants" alike. This was a welcome change from the petty tyrannies of the past half century. It did not mean, of course, that they submitted to labor demands willingly.[82] Those who could afford it paid off the intendant to obtain genuine or fraudulent certifications of cultivation or merchants' exemptions. Tinterillos did a lively business in forgery. Indian and ladino employers struck deals with mozos to work for less than the required number of days for nothing or only for food, in exchange for a notation of the required 100 or 150 days as needed.

One group of ladinos immediately and adversely affected by the new laws were the recruiters and the shop and tavern keepers who dominated the cash economy of all but the most isolated of highland Indian towns. Most had arrived late in the nineteenth century specifically to profit from the opportunities created by labor recruiting and the cash generated by the coffee boom.[83] They survived, and a few prospered, by dispensing large quantities of alcohol during the recruitment season, trafficking in mozos, and selling cheap consumer goods. These sources of profit now were both reduced and made more precarious. The end to indefinite labor debts generally weakened the network of credit by which the ladinos kept and exploited their clientele, and the Depression brought lower wages and smaller advances for their customers to spend. The abolition of debts probably had little real economic impact on the fincas, but it wiped out many shopkeepers and tratistas.[84] The Indians, they lamented, were "only wait[ing] for the month of May to arrive without working, because that is the date Decree 1995 goes into effect."[85] One effect of these changes was that in the 1930s the flow of ladinos into the highland villages began to reverse itself. Trade and commerce were re-Indianized in some communities.[86] Finqueros tended to see the tratistas and other village ladinos as parasites that complicated recruitment and raised labor costs and did not regret their passing. In addition, Ubico's ambitious road building program meant that the state could increasingly rely on full-time state agents for internal repression and had less need of the old ladino local militia units.

The laws that ended long-term debts and imposed a new definition of vagrancy hastened a process of socioeconomic differentiation within the indigenous population already accelerated by forced participation in the coffee economy. Rich by local standards, Indians could now more easily avoid finca labor by owning or cultivating enough land, by obtaining a merchant's exemption, or by bribing the intendant.[87] The eagerness of poor Indians to avoid having to leave the community meant that anyone with land available could easily obtain cheap labor. The exit of ladinos opened new commercial opportunities. Indians moved into the formerly ladino-dominated areas of shopkeeping and mule and truck transport, and former *caporales* (Indian foremen) took over labor recruiting directly. These opportunities, if less attractive than they had been to the ladinos, were valuable to Indians both for the profits they promised and the exemptions they offered. Finally, and perhaps unexpectedly, the new laws may actually have increased Indian access to land. To stabilize their labor force, the fincas registered plots of land of the requisite size for their workers, whether on the lowland plantation itself or on highland labor reserves known as *fincas de mozos*.[88]

When anthropologists in the 1930s undertook the first generation of intensive field studies in highland Guatemala, they found land shortages to be widespread. Raymond Stadelman,[89] for example, in his investigation of corn production in the department of Huehuetenango, calculated that villages needed one and a half acres of arable land per inhabitant for subsistence agriculture to be viable. On this basis, only three or four of the twenty-three towns he surveyed had enough.[90] At the same time, an evident emerging balance of supply and demand, and even oversupply, of labor for the export sector could be read in government libreta figures (see Table 8.7). Sales of these required work cards indicated the yearly availability of 180,000 to 200,000 agricultural laborers. By contrast, the number of workers needed to make the crop in the 1930s was not more than 140,000 to 150,000 a year, based on only 100 days' labor per mozo.[91] Clearly, state-enforced extraeconomic coercion of labor was less and less necessary, and less and less economical. But the planters resisted giving up their guarantees, and the vagrancy law continued in force into the 1940s.

Ironically, it was in the death throes of the repressive Ubico regime that direct coercion of agricultural labor also breathed its last. Under rising pressure from students and the urban middle and working classes, Ubico abandoned office in 1944, turning government over to a junta headed by one of his followers, General Frederico Ponce. It was Ponce, an unlikely

TABLE 8.7
Libreta Sales, 1937–1942

Year	Indian departments	Ladino departments	Totals
1937	100,597	49,828	150,425
1938	182,875	59,948	242,823
1939	165,084	69,142	234,226
1940	89,270	31,671	120,941
1941	123,308	48,550	171,858
1942	142,029	48,932	190,961

Source: Ministerio de Agricultura, Memorias, 1938–
1944 (Guatemala, 1938–1944).

Note: These figures do not include the department of
Guatemala; the selection of "ladino" versus "Indian"
departments is necessarily somewhat arbitrary.

reformer if ever one could be imagined, who "in a desire to pander to [i.e.,
gain the support of] the rural population" arbitrarily suppressed the libreta [vagrancy] system.[92] But this by no means ended the matter. Ponce,
in turn, fell to the October 1944 revolution that for the first time brought
genuine popular reform to Guatemala and life back to the newspapers.
Again the question turned to labor, and the old complaints of the "lazy"
Indian and warnings that an end to coercion would mean labor shortages
reappeared. But the indigenous population now found many more public
defenders: "Capitalism thinks of the Indian as forever the trash collector,
but many times it is the traveler [in the highlands] who feels small when
confronted by the noble spirit, the high morality, and the grace of these
men of the mountains, so poorly understood."[93] Finally, in May of 1945
the Congress, intent on converting Guatemala's agriculture to a capitalist
basis, passed yet another rural labor law.[94] This ended the use of libretas
and did not require a specific number of days of labor per year. Now
vagrants were simply those without work or a profession or without an
income or property adequate to sustain them. The new regime wrote this
into the 1945 constitution. Free labor had come to Guatemala.

Precapitalist labor forms persisted in Guatemala from the first days of
the colony to the 1920s because they served the interests of the planters
in the cash and export sectors and because the indigenous peasant communities resisted the commodification of their work and material resources. The post-Estrada Cabrera governments ended mandamientos not
so much to relieve the burden on the villages as, and ultimately with
marginal success, to limit the extortions of the fincas by departmental and
local officials. Debt peonage continued but was the subject of intense

debate whenever the economy stumbled. The turning point came in the late 1920s and early 1930s with, on the one hand, the awareness among the elites of the population growth that the belated publication of the 1921 census made clear, and, on the other, when the initial declines in production during the first years of the Depression revealed to the finqueros and the villagers alike the existence of more Indians seeking work than there was work immediately available. Centuries of exploitation had created a situation of "reproduction-destruction[95] in the countryside": the communities persisted but suffered a growing population and a downward ecological spiral and increasingly needed the finca wages for survival. But a ruling class as conservative as Guatemala's was not yet ready to abandon coercion. Instead, in 1934 the dictator adopted the halfway measure of free but obligatory labor enforced by a new definition of vagrancy. The sale of libretas under this law gave the first reliable count of available brazos, many of whom were without sufficient land or handicraft manufacturing or trade to support themselves. It revealed an emergent sufficiency of free labor. In 1944 and 1945 the state and the planters finally abandoned legal extraeconomic coercion. Short-term debts persisted, as did the use of real or threatened coercion and violence to discipline and cheapen labor, but in the 1940s the basis for extorting the surplus from the direct producers shifted from direct coercion to economic necessity.

Notes

I wish to thank William Roseberry, Charles Bergquist, Chris Lutz, and Steve Webre for their comments. Research for the essay was carried out under a Fulbright Senior Research grant.

1. Material on agricultural labor before 1920 is drawn from two articles by David McCreery, "Debt Peonage in Rural Guatemala," *Hispanic American Historical Review* 63 (November 1983): 735–59, and "An Odious Feudalism: Mandamientos and Commercial Agriculture in Guatemala, 1853–1920," *Latin American Perspectives* 13 (winter, 1986): 99–117, as well as McCreery, *Rural Guatemala, 1760–1940* (Stanford University Press, 1994), chaps. 3, 7, and 8. Except in rare instances where women were drafted as cooks, forced labor and vagrancy laws applied only to men; women could and did enter into debt peonage, either directly or as a result of relations with a male relative, but men predominated in this category too.

2. In Guatemala a *ladino* is an individual of "national" or "Spanish" culture, though the differences are often expressed in racial and even "caste" terms. Ladinos hold themselves to be superior to Indians and use this supposed superiority to belittle and exploit the indigenous population. On ladinos see Benjamin N. Colby

and Pierre L. van den Berghe, *Ixil Country: A Plural Society in Highland Guatemala* (Berkeley, 1969), and Kay Warren, *The Symbolism of Subordination: Indian Identity in a Guatemalan Town* (Austin, 1978).

3. David McCreery, "Hegemony and Resistance in Rural Guatemala," *Peasant Studies* 17 (1990): 157–77.

4. Rosendo Mendez, comp., *Leyes vigentes de agricultura* (Guatemala, 1937), 203–8.

5. James P. Young, *Central American Currency and Finance* (Princeton, 1925), 39.

6. Real wages for agricultural workers fell sharply in these years: McCreery, "Debt Servitude," 749; on the advantages to the planters of a depreciating exchange rate, see Ministerio de Fomento (Guatemala), *Memorias — 1902* (Guatemala, 1902), 136.

7. Victor Bulmer-Thomas, *The Political Economy of Central America since 1920* (Cambridge, 1987), 12.

8. On the politics of the 1920s see Joseph Pitti, "Jorge Ubico and Guatemalan Politics in the 1920's" (Ph.D. diss., University of New Mexico, 1975), and U.S. State Department, "Documents Relating to the Internal Affairs of Guatemala," 1910–1929, microfilm rolls #3–9.

9. For example, *El Imparcial* (Guatemala City, June 26, 1920).

10. *Diario de Centro América* (Guatemala City, February 1, 4, and 12, May 3, and September 20, 1919); Guillermo Rodríguez, *Guatemala en 1919* (Guatemala, 1919), 104.

11. The government in 1923 set the daily minimum wage on public works at eight pesos a day: *El Imparcial* (July 19, 1923). Wages for agricultural work in the mid to late 1920s were generally in the range of 10 to 15 pesos, though some individuals working off old contracts received considerably less. On the "slavery" of finca labor, see *Diario de Centro América* (April 30, 1921); planters, for their part, argued that the Indian was enslaved only by his vices: *El Imparcial* (September 26, 1922).

12. *El Imparcial* (November 30, 1922).

13. *Diario de Centro América* (September 20, 1919); *El Imparcial* (July 6 and November 30, 1922, and June 9, 1923).

14. In 1916 the U.S. embassy in Guatemala reported that President Estrada Cabrera considered census material a military secret and did not allow it to be published: U.S. State Department, "Internal Affairs of Guatemala," microfilm roll #20.

15. Compare, for example, *El Imparcial* (November 25 with November 30, 1922).

16. The best introduction to the much-talked-about but little studied process of primitive or original accumulation remains Marx, *Capital*, vol. 1, pt. 8.

17. McCreery, *Rural Guatemala*, chap. 6.

18. On land in the period 1820–1930 see David McCreery, "State Power, Indigenous Communities, and Land in Nineteenth-Century Guatemala, 1820–1920," in Carol Smith, ed., *Indian Communities and the State: Guatemala, 1540–1988* (Austin, 1989).

19. See, for example, the example of Pochuta: Instituto Indigenista de Guatemala, "Pochuta, monografía #264" (Guatemala City, n.d.).

20. McCreery, "State Power." The exception was the Alta Verapaz, where coffee and community lands more directly overlapped and where Indian communities aggressively resisted the expansion of the fincas: for example, see San Cristobal Verapaz, Archivo General de Centro América (AGCA)-Sección de Tierras (ST), Paquete 7, expediente 3.

21. The area of Pamaxán and Panan on the south coast seems to have been less sought after for coffee than the Costa Cuca to the west or Escuintla to the southeast (see Felix McBryde, *Cultural and Historical Geography of Southwest Guatemala* [Washington, D.C., 1947]: map following page 14) and, therefore, more readily available to highland towns seeking to title hot country land: AGCA, Ministerio de Gobernación (MG), legajo 28658, expedientes 108 and 190, and titles in the AGCA-ST for, among many other communities, Santiago Atitlán, San Pedro La Laguna, San Martín Sacatepéquez, Concepción Chiquirichapa, Totonicapán, Santa Catarina Ixtahuacán, Santa Lucía Utatlán, and Momostenango.

22. Ruth Bunzel, *Chichicastenango* (Seattle, 1959), 16, gives a good summary of what was probably the typical pattern for land holding in the villages by the 1920s and 1930s; for a slightly different situation, or at least interpretation, see McBryde, *Cultural and Historical Geography*, 95. An excellent study of historical patterns of land tenure is Shelton Davis, "Land of Our Ancestors" (Ph.D. diss., Harvard University, 1970).

23. On "articulation" see Aidan Foster-Carter, "Can We Articulate Articulation," in John Clammer, ed., *The New Economic Anthropology* (New York, 1978), 210–49; and Harold Wolpe, ed., *The Articulation of Modes of Production* (London, 1980), intro.

24. *Diario de Centro América* (June 17, 1920); *El Imparcial* (June 26, 1920, May 18, 1921, and July 6, 1922).

25. For example, *Diario de Centro América* (June 26, 1920, and May 18, 1921) and *El Imparcial* (July 6, 1922).

26. *El Imparcial* (July 6, 1922).

27. G. Arrighi, "Labour Supplies in Historical Perspective: A Study of the Proletarianization of the African Peasantry in Rhodesia," *Journal of Development Studies* 6 (1970): 185–224.

28. For an eighteenth-century example of Indians shifting from lower to higher wage areas, see AGCA, A3, legajo 224, expediente 4033.

29. On this, see a series of articles by Carlos Wyld Ospina in *El Imparcial* (January 31, February 6 and 10, 1928; November 22, 23, and 28, 1929).

30. *El Imparcial* (April 7, 1923). An earlier, more systematic exposition of this point of view is to be found in Antonio Batres Jáuregui, *Los indios: su historia y civilización* (Guatemala, 1893), pt. 3.

31. David Browning, *El Salvador: Landscape and Society* (Oxford, 1971), 208; Rafael Menjívar, *Acumulación originaria y desarrollo del capitalismo en El Salvador* (San Salvador, 1980); Héctor Lindo-Fuentes, *Weak Foundations: The Economy of El Salvador in the Nineteenth Century, 1821–1898* (Berkeley, 1990).

32. This explanation is developed most thoroughly, with an extensive bibli-

ography, in chapter one of Alain de Janvry's *The Agrarian Question and Reform-ism in Latin America* (Baltimore, 1981).

33. For a treatment of recent state autonomy and intra-elite conflict, see Susan Berger, *Political and Agrarian Development in Guatemala* (Boulder, 1992).

34. McCreery, "State Power" and "Land, Labor, and Violence in Highland Guatemala: San Juan Ixcoy, 1893–1945," *The Americas* 45 (October 1988): 237–49.

35. *Diario de Centro América* (October 11, 1921); *El Demócrata* (Guatemala City, July 17, 1922); *El Imparcial* (November 29, 1922, October 24, 1923, and February 14, 1928).

36. AGCA, Jefe Político (JP), Sololá, 1920: finqueros to JP, June 12 and Sep-tember 2, 1920, and July 10, 1923, and many similar from this and other depart-ments; *El Imparcial* (November 1 and 29, 1922, and October 24 and July 1, 1924).

37. AGCA, JP Sololá, 1929, Federación Obrera de Guatemala to Ministerio de Gobernación, April 24, 1929; *El Imparcial* (February 14, 1928; April 25 and 27 and May 2, 1929).

38. The bloodiest attack on ladinos in the half century before 1930, the up-rising at San Juan Ixcoy in 1898, rated barely a mention in the national press (McCreery, "Land, Labor, and Violence"). A major catalyst to good reporting in the 1920s was the founding in 1921 of Guatemala's first modern newspaper, *El Imparcial*.

39. *El Imparcial* (March 18, 1926).

40. Decree 222, September 14, 1878, *Recopilación de Las Leyes de Guate-mala*, vol. 2 (Guatemala, 1881), 201–4.

41. *El Imparcial* (October 7, 1922).

42. On the spacial structure of highland Indian municipalities, see Sol Tax, "The Municipios of the Midwestern Highlands of Guatemala," *American Anthro-pologist* 39 (1937): 423–44.

43. For example, *Diario de Centro América* (April 21 and 29, May 10 and 19, 1921); *El Imparcial* (March 17, 1923).

44. Juan Antonio Alvarado, *Tratado de cafecultura práctica*, vol. 2 (Guate-mala, 1936), 470.

45. *El Imparcial* (April 7, 1923).

46. *Diario de Centro América* (May 30, 1921).

47. Planters, especially those in San Marcos on the Mexican border, were obsessed with the drain of labor across the frontier: AGCA, Fomento letters vol-ume #14928, Jefe Político San Marcos to Ministro de Fomento, November 12, 1921. On why the workers fled to Mexico, see *El Imparcial* (October 14, 1922).

48. *Diario de Centro América* (June 1, 1921).

49. *Diario de Centro América* (May 30, 1921, and April 24, 1922).

50. *Diario de Centro América* (March 17, 1923).

51. Guatemalan coffee plantations traditionally assigned and paid for work either by the day or the *tarea* (task). In theory the two involved approximately the same amount of labor but in fact wide variations occurred, usually to the worker's disadvantage (McCreery, "Debt Servitude").

52. Alvarado, *Tratado*, 2: 456.

53. Victor Bulmer-Thomas, "Central America in the Inter-war Period," in Rosemary Thorp, ed., *Latin America in the 1930s* (London, 1984), 284. This was in large part a result of the enormous Brazilian harvest of 1927–28.

54. By the 1930s International Railroads of Central America, a subdivision of the United Fruit Company, controlled all but a few miles of Guatemala's rail system and owned the chief Atlantic port. It used this control to favor its banana exports at the expense of other shippers. For a brief treatment of transport problems in these years, see Kenneth Grieb, *Guatemalan Caudillo* (Athens, Ohio, 1979), chap. 9. On the costs of coerced labor, see *El Imparcial* (April 27, 1929, and August 26, 1943); Alvarado, *Tratado*, 2: 459.

55. For example, *El Imparcial* (June 12, 1928, October 25, 1929, and January 2, 1930).

56. On the formation of the best known of these, Central American Plantations Company [CAPCO], see Regina Wagner, "Actividades empresariales de los alemanes en Guatemala, 1850–1920," *Mesoamérica* 13 (1987): 120.

57. Dirección General de Estadística, *Censo de la República de Guatemala, 1921* (Guatemala, 1924).

58. Ministry of Agriculture, *Memoria — 1933* (Guatemala, 1933); *El Imparcial* (January 7, February 12, and October 1, 1930).

59. Bulmer-Thomas, *Political Economy of Central America*, chaps. 3 and 4.

60. This is evident in the yearly mortgage/sales records published in the *Memorias* of the Ministerio de Gobernación and in the histories of individual fincas evident in the Registros de Propiedad Inmueble, Guatemala City and Quetzaltenango.

61. Bunzel reports, for example, that many planters "did not bother to pick the 1932 harvest" (Bunzel, *Chichicastenango*, 11).

62. For example, *El Imparcial* (October 29, 1930); Ministerio de Agricultura, *Memoria — 1932* (Guatemala, 1932), 509; AGCA, B119.21.0.0, legajo 47790, expediente 86; Bulmer-Thomas, *Political Economy of Central America*, 49.

63. Grieb, *Guatemalan Caudillo*, 58–59.

64. Interviews with retired finqueros; mortgage records of individual fincas in Registro de Propiedad Inmueble.

65. On Ubico, see Grieb, *Guatemalan Caudillo*, and Pitti, "Jorge Ubico," chap. 8.

66. Méndez, *Leyes*, 214–15 and 244–47.

67. Ibid., 244.

68. For example, AGCA, B119.21.0.0, legajo 47800, expediente 471.

69. Jackson Lincoln, "An Ethnographic Study of the Ixil Indians of the Guatemalan Highlands" [1945], Manuscripts in the Microfilm Collection of Middle American Cultural Anthropology, University of Chicago, #1); Colby and van den Berghe say the seven were shot (Colby and van den Berghe, *Ixil Country*, 155); for a dramatic account of these events, see David Stoll, "Evangelicals, Guerrillas, and the Army: The Ixil Triangle under Rios Mont," in R. Carmack, ed., *Harvest of Violence: The Maya Indians and the Guatemalan Crisis* (Norman, Okla., 1988), 101.

70. A manzana equals approximately 1.7 acres.

71. For the benefits that the new vagrancy law brought the better-off Indians, see Warren, *Symbolism of Subordination*, 150.

72. Raymond Stadelman, "Maize Cultivation in Northwestern Guatemala," *Contributions to American Anthropology and History* 6 (1940): 94.

73. In rural Guatemala the cuerda varies according to local custom between twenty-five and fifty square *varas* (yards).

74. Except as specifically cited, the following paragraphs are based on a large amount of material in the records of the courts which heard appeals of vagrancy cases: for example, AGCA, Archivo General de Los Tribunales (AGT), Huehuetenango, Juez de Paz, 1932–38 and 1942–44, Quiché, 1937–40 and 1943–44, Sololá, 1938–1944, and Chiquimula, 1940.

75. AGT, Juez de Paz, Quiché, criminal, 1937–38, leg. 15, #673.

76. B119.21.0.0, leg. 47800, exp. 53 and 75, and leg. 47804, exp. 19.

77. Antonio Goubaud, "San Juan Chamelco," manuscripts in the Microfilm Collection of Middle American Cultural Anthropology, University of Chicago, #23.

78. AGCA, JP San Marcos [administrativo #17], 1936; Municipality of Comitancillo to President, August 21, 1936.

79. AGCA, B119.21.0.0, leg. 47801, exp. 1 and leg. 47802, exp. 64.

80. AGCA, JP Sololá, September 9, 1936; JP San Marcos, August 21, and November 25, 1936 [administrativo #17]; *El Imparcial* (August 13, 1943).

81. Warren, *Symbolism*, 150–51.

82. On ways to "beat the system," see *El Norte* (Cobán, June 5, 1937) and *El Imparcial* (August 13, 1943).

83. Colby and van den Berg, *Ixil Country*, chap. 2.

84. Tani Adams, "San Martín Jilotepeque: Aspects of the Political and Socioeconomic Structure of a Guatemalan Peasant Community" (unpublished 1979 manuscript in the files of the author), 32.

85. AGCA, JP Sololá, April 13, 1936.

86. See, for example, the history of changes in San Pedro Sacatepéquez (San Marcos) outlined in Waldemar Smith, *The Fiesta System and Economic Change* (New York, 1977), and the life of the protagonist of James D. Sexton, ed., *Son of Tecun Uman* (Tucson, 1981), and *Campesino* (Tucson, 1985).

87. Douglas Brintnall, *Revolt against the Dead* (New York, 1979), 112; Warren, *Symbolism*, 150.

88. See, for example, *matrículas de mozos* (registries of workers) for San Juan Ostuncalco (municipal archives) and Sumpango (AGCA).

89. Stadelman, "Maize Cultivation," 105 and 134. See also Charles Wagley, "Economics of a Guatemalan Village" (American Anthropological Association Memoir #58, 1941): 31, and McBryde, *Cultural and Historical Geography*, 74. This contrasts with the picture Ruth Bunzel paints for Chichicastenango in these years in *Chichicastenango*, 43.

90. Of course, some communities had other resources (e.g., salt springs), engaged in handicraft manufactures and trade, and rented land in more fortunate municipalities, but overall a growing shortage of local opportunities was clear.

91. This is based on an assumption of fifteen days' labor per quintal (100 lbs.) of coffee.

92. *El Imparcial* (January 22, 1945).

93. *El Imparcial* (May 22, 1945).

94. Decree 102, May 22, 1945, in Augusto Zelaya Gil y Manuel Antonio Lucerno, eds., *Resúmen de leyes de la República, clasificados y anotados por secretarías* (Guatemala, 1955), 255.

95. On this, see Foster-Carter, "Can We Articulate Articulation?"

Nine

Indians, Communists, and Peasants: The 1932 Rebellion in El Salvador

HÉCTOR PÉREZ BRIGNOLI

O N FEBRUARY 5, 1932, a Mr. McCafferty, head of the American Legation in San Salvador, made the following report to his government:

The Legation has reported from time to time during the past year various communist outbreaks, or allegedly communist outbreaks, in San Salvador as well as the activities of Augustín Martí [*sic*], the communist leader. Opinions have been expressed that real communism could not flourish in this country owing to the mild climate and plentifulness of food and the lack of necessity for many clothes and much shelter. During recent weeks, however, it has become more and more apparent that communist leaders, many of them foreigners, with the aid of communist propaganda chiefly printed in the United States, have taken advantage of the growing discontent among the workers on the coffee plantations.

The conditions that have permitted this rather sudden rise in so-called communism are well known. Farm workers have been often miserably underpaid and have been working under conditions on some fincas which have been certainly intolerable. On the fincas of many of the richest landowners in Salvador, conditions have been the worst. Medical attention has not been available, [and] workers have been compelled to purchase their few necessities at advanced prices from stores maintained by the finca proprietors. Frequently, it has been asserted that a farm animal is of far more value to the proprietor than the worker for there is generally a plentiful supply of the latter.

Taking advantage of the supposed weakness in the de facto Government about January 20, and directed by communist leaders, the workers led successful and horrible revolts. For the most part, the finca owners had perceived the rising danger and had come to the capital where, as it turned out, they were entirely safe. Their farm managers, administrators, sub-administrators, as well as the police, telegraph operators and local officials in the small country villages were the ones to feel the brunt of these attacks. The movement was confined almost entirely to the region between San Salvador and Ahuachapán y Sonsonate. In this area severe fighting occurred between the Government forces and the communists after the latter had successfully taken several towns and villages. The sanguinary intentions of the communists, which strangely enough did not seem as in the usual case to require the stimulus of alcohol, was shown in numerous gory and lustful attacks. Women were raped and butchered, others had their breasts cut off, and men were so hacked by machetes that it was impossible to identify their corpses. Houses were ransacked and others completely destroyed. Shops were looted of all their stocks. As far as is known, only one foreigner, an Italian named Redaelli, the local manager in Juayúa for a large Italian firm, was killed, but the movement did not take any anti-foreign character.

The Government took strong repressive measures and, fortunately, owing to payment of some of the arrears in salaries and the utmost precautions, found its troops loyal. The official estimate of dead communists has now surpassed 4,800 but this is believed to be somewhat exaggerated. A remarkable feature of the armed attacks on the communists was the coolness and courage with which the poor Indians who could not possibly have given any coherent idea of what communism really is, met their death. Photographs which have arrived in the capital show them before firing squads with quisical [sic], almost amused expressions on their faces. In innumerable cases, people were executed not because there was any evidence of their communism but rather because they told the Government forces that they were communists.[1]

Such a lengthy quotation was chosen because of the quality of this document. It is the best summary I have come across of the peasant uprising of 1932. The observer has a clear picture of the political, economic, and social situation in El Salvador, expresses neither sympathy for the rebels nor trust in official versions of events, and reports on the developments almost as they were happening, for the sole purpose of providing *concise and confidential* information. What we have here, in other words, is an experienced and knowledgeable observer who understands the event and the circumstances surrounding it, but who has been able to "distance" himself from it, and who has no personal or institutional reasons to hide, omit, or exaggerate anything. McCafferty also puts the events in a certain causal sequence: (1) communist agitation and growing discontent among coffee workers; (2) a bloody rebellion in a clearly defined geographical area; and (3) violent repression imposed upon the entire Indian population.

Many of the problems of interpretation faced by scholars of the 1932 rebellion are cleared up in other diplomatic and confidential documents from the time. On December 22, 1931, the military attache of the U.S.

legation, Major A. R. Harris, whose permanent residence was in Costa Rica at the time,[2] informed his government that the social and economic situation in El Salvador was explosive, since "90 per cent of the wealth of the Nation is held by about half of 1 per cent of the population" and "thirty or forty families own nearly everything in the country." Harris thought "the situation in El Salvador today is much like France was before its revolution, Russia was before its revolution, and like Mexico was before its revolution" and added that "the situation is ripe for communism and the communists seem to have found that out." The "inevitability" of the rebellion was obvious to many observers in the months preceding the uprising, as was the dyad of factors: agrarian unrest and communist agitation. U.S. naval officers stationed in Acajutla, after consultations with their British counterparts, arrived at the conclusion that even though agrarian unrest created discontent and helped to make conditions ripe for revolt, it was definitely part of an "organized effort to foster communism," given the existence of propaganda and declared sympathizers and the organization of simultaneous attacks. The officers thought (naively, of course) that "most of the agrarian element is without any education whatever and any organized movement planned or carried out by them is most unlikely." Their attitude coincided with the prevailing feeling in San Salvador that the movement had been essentially communist in nature.[3]

Participants in the 1932 rebellion were peons from coffee plantations, Indian peasants, and communist leaders, united perhaps by shared ideals. In any case, the one thing that brought them all together was the repression that led to the revolt. Was this a bitter by-product of coffee? Or was it the result of political circumstances understandable only within the context of El Salvador in 1932? Was it the stifled prelude to a "modernizing" revolution, or perhaps the last gasp of some "primitive" revolutionaries doomed to failure? The aim of this essay is to provide some answers to these questions, which are as complex as they are thought provoking.

Sources

The sources available can be divided into three types. The first consists of detailed descriptions of the events themselves and the context in which they occurred, produced at the time of the events. Included in this group are the journalistic records of Joaquín Méndez, published shortly after the insurrection.[4] The testimony this journal provides is invaluable even though the author makes no attempt to hide his sympathies for the government and the army. Containing much more information on the political context of the rebellion are the reports sent by the U.S. Legation in San

Salvador in 1931 and 1932.[5] These documents make it possible to trace step by step the increase in sociopolitical tensions, through the eyes of observers not directly involved in the social conflict. These files also contain samples of the political propaganda used at the time, as well as several government documents. Further invaluable testimony is found in two reports issued by Commander Victor G. Brodeur,[6] in charge of the Canadian destroyers sent to Acajutla by the British navy at the request of the British consul, D. J. Rogers. Brodeur visited Sonsonate and San Salvador during the insurrection, met with the military leaders and Hernández Martínez, and evaluated the situation in terms of the eventual need for intervention.

The book by Jorge Schlesinger and the testimony of Miguel Mármol, though written many years after the uprising, contain very valuable information.[7] Schlesinger wrote to warn the Guatemalans of the danger of a similar insurrection. To do so, he used numerous original documents supplied by the government of Hernández Martínez. Much of the documentation appears in the appendix of the book. The testimony provided by Mármol, one of the leaders of the Communist Party of El Salvador, was collected by Roque Dalton in 1966, that is, thirty-four years after the fact. The fact that so much time had transpired affected not only Mármol's recollection of the events but also his interpretation of them. Thus the book is invaluable in reconstructing the life of this militant politician, his modus operandi, and his view of the world, but it is much more limited in revealing the motives and strategy behind the rebellion.

Certain statistics contribute to understanding the socioeconomic situation in El Salvador in 1932. The 1930 census and the *Anuarios Estadísticos* contain information that deserves further study.[8] The coffee census carried out between November 1938 and March 1939 is the first modern study of this type.[9] Even though it was conducted quite a while after the events of the rebellion, it provides ample detail on the structure of coffee production, assuming that it had not changed much since 1930. Also available, especially in the diplomatic documents mentioned earlier, are fairly detailed descriptions of working conditions on the farms and the living conditions of the peasants.

There is abundant bibliography available on the rebellion, even though most of its authors emphasize political aspects. The work by Thomas Anderson is still the most complete and detailed study of this event, and is intended to provide a descriptive reconstruction of the different incidents in the uprising.[10] Segundo Montes analyzes the rebellion in an anthropological study of the institution of *compadrazgo* in the Indian region.[11] Alejandro Marroquín studies the phenomenon in the context of the crisis and Depression of the 1930s, while Everett Wilson analyzes the social unrest that preceded the rebellion.[12] The political context has been examined by several authors from different points of view. David Luna focuses on the dictatorship of Hernández Martínez, while Rodolfo Cerdas studies the strategies of the Third International.[13] North American policy toward El Salvador was analyzed by Kenneth Grieb.[14] Rafael Guidos Vejar considers that the rebellion was part of a process of political struggle and readjustments of the "power bloc" between 1871 and 1935.[15]

Passing, but important, references appear in the works of Abel Cuenca, Ricardo Gallardo, Alastair White, and Leon Zamosc.[16] Few authors have compared the 1932 uprising with other peasant rebellions. Douglas Kincaid did so recently in connection with the revolt of the Nonualco Indians in 1833 in El Salvador and the mobilization of peasants that affected several regions of the country in the 1970s.[17] He tries to show how, in all three cases, community solidarity combined with other elements: Indian ethnicity in 1833 and 1932 and the Catholic religion in the 1970s. Alignment in terms of class, though it played a role in all three cases, seems to have been much less important.

Interpretations

The rebellion and its causes have been the subject of numerous interpretations. This can be attributed to two different phenomena. First, the complexity of the events themselves, and the context in which they took place, is such that different interpretations are possible. Second, the rebellion, or at least a mythical version of it, conditioned political life in El Salvador between 1932 and 1980, affecting the perception and strategies of all classes and political forces involved. Below I offer a classification of the different interpretations.

Some interpretations underscore political insurrection and the communist attempt at seizing power; others focus on the origin and nature of the social conflict, relegating politics to a secondary position. The interpretations that focus on the political aspects can be classified into at least three types, depending on the emphasis given to conspiracy, provocation, or mistaken strategy. The theory of *conspiracy* was invented by the government and soon became the "official" interpretation of the insurrection. At first it was disseminated through the press, then taken up again in the books by Méndez and Schlesinger. As the theory goes, the Communist Party of El Salvador had organized an elaborate conspiracy, infiltrating the masses of Indians and peasants, even trying to persuade some sectors of the army. The economic and social crisis and the ineptitude of the government of Arturo Araujo had set the stage for this. The repression and strong-arm tactics of General Hernández Martínez had saved the country from falling into the hands of communism.[18]

The left, especially the leaders of the Communist Party of El Salvador, offered a different interpretation, which was, however, very similar to the first in that emphasis was placed on the *provocation* of the government. Hernández Martínez needed to consolidate his power. It was in his interest both to exaggerate the scope of the insurrection and to provoke the masses to justify violent and bloody repression, as a lesson to all. Abel Cuenca, who was a leader during the insurrection, does not hesitate to write: "The insurrection, cleverly provoked by the government, which refused to recognize the victory of the workers in certain municipal elections, broke out in several departments on January 22, 1932. The mass of people involved in the insurrection was under the direction of no one, carrying out widespread and chaotic semi-armed actions that were quickly and bloodily wiped out and put down by government forces."[19] Alejandro Dagoberto Marroquín, a communist leader during the 1940s, lists the "provocations" of the government, and thinks that Hernández Martínez had a perfectly calculated plan for all of it.[20]

Other leaders and analysts have underscored the importance of what we could call a *mistaken political strategy*, for which the Communist Party of El Salvador was directly responsible. Mármol's recounting, in 1966, of the events he lived through follows along these lines, as do the comments added by Roque Dalton. Mármol says that "the lack of coordination, the disappearance of the National Committee at the most critical moment, inattention to security measures, and the lack of organization at the national level for the purely military aspects of the insurrection were, in my opinion, the principal causes of the military failure, and, hence, the total failure."[21] Mármol mentions in passing the influence of the political guidelines of the Third International, a subject studied in detail by Rodolfo Cerdas Cruz. He comes to the conclusion that the leaders of the International were not serious or thorough enough in their theoretical and empirical analyses, and that they had no respect for the national sections. Thus they were able, in the case of El Salvador, first to foment an insurrectional strategy that led to a tragedy and then to condemn the defeated leaders as "macheteros," sectarians, and extreme leftists.[22]

Let us now move on to the consideration of the interpretations that emphasize the social conflict and the basically peasant nature of the insurrection. In 1961 Abelardo Torres explained the connection between the expropriation of lands that took place during the liberal reform (1881–82), which brought an end to common and community lands, and the agrarian discontent caused by the violent usurpation of lands and the 1932 insurrection. To quote him:

In the first year mentioned [1932], during the campaign for President of the Republic, one of the parties constantly spoke of dividing up the lands, thus sowing the seeds of a future uprising. When Arturo Araujo, in whose name the campaign promises had been made, won, the peasants demanded that he begin to divide up the lands of the wealthy. The government smashed several local uprisings aimed at demanding land. At that time, the worldwide crisis was being felt fully in El Salvador. Coffee could not be sold at any price, farmers could not begin their seasonal agricultural work, and the peasants were unemployed. This combination of circumstances, together with the agitation of some leaders from the far Left who took advantage of the situation to organize and indoctrinate the masses in preparation for a class struggle, led to the largest peasant uprising in the history of Central America.[23]

Here, the peasant problem is of primary importance, while communist agitation is relegated to a secondary position. David Browning, in his well-known work on the agricultural landscape in El Salvador, develops and expands upon Torres's thesis.[24] He studies both the expropriations of the liberal period and the projects for agrarian settlements developed by the government immediately following the insurrection. Even though such projects were a totally inadequate response, in view of the magnitude of the agrarian problems in the country, at least they indicate that the government had become aware of the social unrest.

Everett Wilson's dissertation detailed the social disruption that accompanied the steep increase in coffee exports in the first decades of the twentieth century, and underscored the role played by ethnic divisions between Indians and mestizos.[25] The rebellion occurred, after all, in an area in which the population consisted primarily of Indians. In fact, several Indian chiefs took part. Ricardo Gallardo recognized how important the agrarian conflict and the social unrest were, but also felt that "the racial factor played an important part in many of the abuses, acts of violence and murders carried out during those black days."[26]

Leon Zamosc tries to clear up the "social roots" of the insurrection, but his methods are purely deductive, lacking sources on the rebellion itself. His line of reasoning is as follows: (1) the Salvadoran economy was characterized by a capitalist "pole" represented by the coffee sector; (2) the economy was not autonomous or a self-centered system, which means that it was highly dependent upon the larger "world system"; (3) the proletarian or semi-proletarian workers on the coffee plantations were key groups in terms of the potential for a class struggle in El Salvador, especially in light of the extreme conditions of exploitation and misery that prevailed in the 1920s; (4) the government of Romero Bosque (1927–31) tried to open up the political system as part of a new strategy of domination; (5) this did not work, however, since the pressure and mobilization of the masses was as uncontrollable as it was radical; and (6) all of this led to a crisis during the tenure of Araujo (1931), and, "alarmed, the dominant classes decided that there were no conditions to go on with democratic strategies of domination." The military coup followed. According to Zamosc, the base of the insurrection lay with the temporary and permanent workers on the plantations, the vanguard of a broad alliance of "plebeian classes" who joined the class struggle with a socialist and proletarian strategy, but never as "primitive rebels."[27]

In other recent interpretations, the rebellion is presented as a typically peasant uprising, with ethnic overtones and political agitation led by the Communist party, in which other sectors (for example, the Labor party of president Araujo), had their own purposes. This is the type of analysis offered by Alastair White and Segundo Montes.[28] Even though no one has yet said so, all of this suggests the possibility that there were really two insurrections, similar in some ways and different in others: one an Indian and peasant insurrection, and the other a communist conspiracy. The first took place between January 22 and 25, 1932. The second was aborted by the government when Farabundo Martí and other leaders of the Communist Party of El Salvador were arrested in San Salvador on January 18 and an attempted military uprising at the headquarters of the Sixth Regiment failed on the evening of January 16.

A more thorough study of the insurrectional movement itself and the development of a comparative perspective, both indispensable, are the goals of this essay. However, our methodological strategy must, because of the lack of, or incomplete nature of, the sources, accept two things: first, that it is impossible to discover exactly how far-reaching the mobilization of unions and the communist political agitation were, though we do know that it took place in the 1920s and that it had a great influence throughout the movement. Second, we lack direct testimony from Indians or peasants. This means that the discontent that existed in the agrarian sector can be reconstructed only indirectly by resorting to observations by people who, though interested, are relatively far removed from the peasants, and by referring to structural, statistical indicators.

The next section looks at the macroeconomic and macrosocial context of the insurrection, from the basic characteristics of the expansion of coffee growing in El Salvador to some statistics on the rebel regions, and describes the "agrarian unrest" as accurately as possible. I then consider the Indian problem from two different angles: (1) the role of the *cofradías*[29] and their place in national politics; and (2) the "mysterious" denial of the Indian component of the Salvadoran population. Next I reconsider the movement itself, in an attempt to identify the patterns of social confrontation and the possible causes of the uprising. Finally I offer some comparisons and interpretations.

Expansion of Coffee Growing and Agrarian Unrest:
The Regions in Rebellion

In El Salvador the expansion of coffee production came late but was fast-paced. In the decade of the 1880s, coffee overtook indigo, accounting for more than 70 percent of total exports.[30] In the decades of the 1920s and 1930s, it reached 90 percent of total exports. No other country in Central America has ever depended so heavily on one export commodity as El Salvador did on coffee.

Exact data on the total area planted in coffee did not become available until the first coffee census, conducted in 1938 (Map 9.1). However, looking at the export trends (Figure 9.1), there is no doubt that there was substantial expansion in the latter years of the nineteenth century and the early years of the twentieth. Around 1910, production in El Salvador was considerably beyond that in Costa Rica — the pioneer in coffee growing in Central America — and economic progress was everywhere. Dana G. Munro, an astute observer, stated that El Salvador was one of the most prosperous countries of the isthmus, with a government and army that conducted their affairs in an orderly and efficient fashion. Because of the work ethic of its people, the fertility of its soil, and the progressive outlook of its upper classes, the country seemed to have a bright future, including improvements in political and social conditions.[31] What was the social cost of this successful and rapid expansion? This question can be divided into several aspects.

In the first place, there was an important change in the agricultural landscape, which has been admirably described by David Browning.[32] El Salvador became a showplace of well-kept coffee plantations, and the village Indians and mestizos lost their lands (owing to laws from 1881 and 1882 abolishing community-owned lands) to private ownership. As Browning said, "This new appraisal of the land was shared by only a few of those who lived on it."[33] Thus the lines were drawn for a social and ideological conflict of huge proportions, between a growing mass of dispossessed peasants imbued with the tradition of common access to the land, and an elite class of entrepreneurs who, together with the government, were bent on an almost unlimited expansion of agricultural exports. The connection between the privatization of the soil and the concentration of land tenure becomes more apparent if viewed in macrosocial terms and over the long term, specifically, if we compare agriculture in El Salvador just prior to the end of common lands, based on the "land survey" of 1879,[34] with the situation depicted in the coffee census of 1938 and the first national agricultural census in 1950. Rafael Menjívar has offered a persuasive interpretation of this process in terms of the Marxist notion

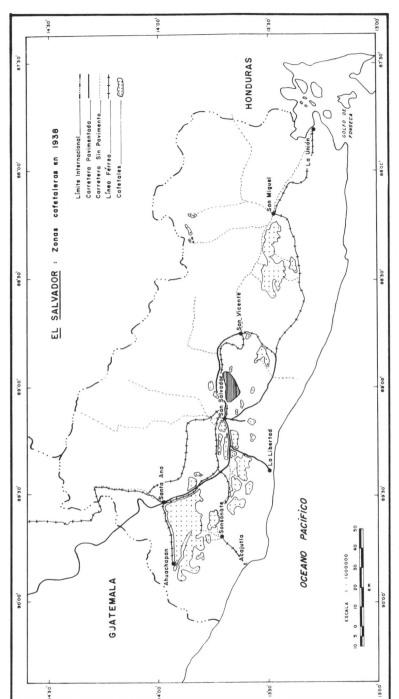

EL SALVADOR : Zonas cafetaleras en 1938

Límite Internacional
Carretera Pavimentada
Carretera Sin Pavimento
Línea Férrea
Cafetales

HONDURAS

GOLFO DE FONSECA

La Unión

San Miguel

San Vicente

San Salvador

Santa Ana

Ahuachapan

Sonsonate

Acajutla

La Libertad

OCEANO PACIFICO

GUATEMALA

ESCALA 1 : 1000000

10 5 0   10   20   30   40   50
Km

Map 9.1. Coffee Zones of El Salvador in 1938

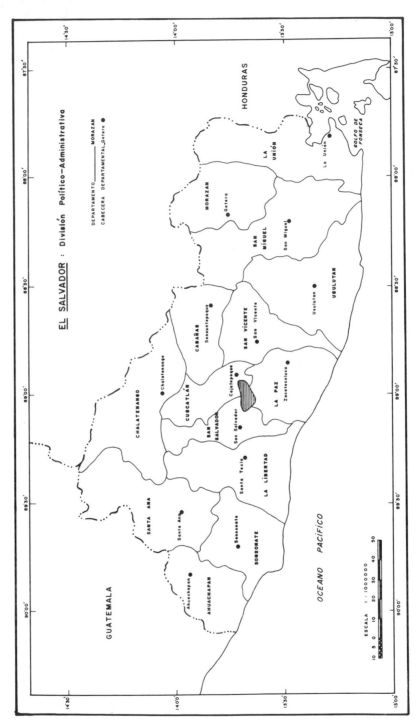

Map 9.2. Political-Administrative Divisions of El Salvador

242

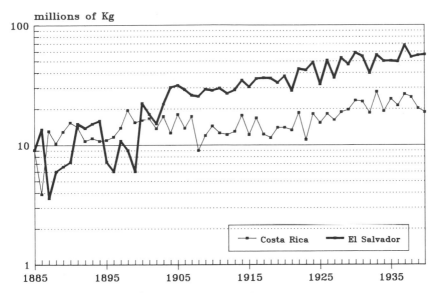

Fig. 9.1. Coffee Exports from El Salvador and Costa Rica, 1885–1940. *Sources:* Official data from *Anuarios Estadísticos;* FAO, *The World's Coffee* (Rome, 1947), 98–99.

of "primitive" accumulation of capital. After analyzing the information compiled in the "land survey" of 1879, he estimates that the area of the common lands equaled 22 percent of the agricultural land in the country, and states that the lands of the Indian communities were not included in this survey. He concludes his calculations by estimating that 40 percent of the agricultural lands, in 1879, were owned jointly.[35]

On the basis of the available documents, at least for now, no definitive conclusion can be reached. This, nonetheless, is very important if we wish to move from the macrosocial plane, from the slow evolution of the agricultural landscape, to one that is much more precise chronologically and related to the mobilization of peasants and to specific events. That is, if the objective is to link changes in the ownership of agricultural land with increased social conflict and the growth of the peasant rebellion, as was stated by David Browning: "In the case of Juayúa, the 1881 abolition of *tierras comunales* merely legalized a process of alienation of their lands that was already well advanced. The ultimate reaction of the villages to this situation was demonstrated when, in 1932, Juayúa became the headquarters of the largest peasant uprising Central America has experienced."[36] We cannot state that Browning is mistaken if we look at his argument from the perspective of long-term factors. His reasoning is, however, rather incomplete as an explanation of the 1932 uprising. Even if we accept that the "structural" causality is correct (the relationship between expropriation and rebellion), it is obvious that an equally crucial set of "intermediate variables" must be identified.

Let us return now to the social cost of expanding coffee cultivation. The concentration of land ownership and of processing and marketing of coffee advanced at their own pace and in their own way.[37] In 1938, when the first coffee census was conducted, 455 producers (4 percent of the total) owned almost 63,000 *manzanas* (53 percent of total land area) on farms of more than fifty manzanas. In addition, there were some 207 *beneficios* (processing facilities) and a similar number of exporters. Juan Pablo Duque, an engineer commissioned by the National Federation of Coffee Growers of Colombia, traveled throughout Central America between December 1936 and March 1937. In his technical report, he did not hesitate to characterize the situation in El Salvador in the following words: "This country is faced with a grave social problem because its coffee-producing lands are not sufficiently divided up; living and working conditions of the workers are substandard; their ration of food is neither enough nor nutritional; sanitation problems have not been solved, and, on top of all this, the problem of the Communists in the country is very serious."[38]

How far back does this particularly unfair and concentrated structure of coffee-related wealth go in El Salvador? Many have expressed the opinion that in the 1920s there was a dual process. On the one hand, there was a rapid expansion of the area planted in coffee, with the subsequent increase in volume exported. On the other, many peasants and small farmers were losing their lands to the large estates. Complaints and expressions of bitterness about this process appeared regularly in the newspaper *Patria*, published by Alberto Masferrer in the late 1920s.[39] In a survey conducted in 1928, it was estimated that 350 coffee growers had farms larger than seventy-five manzanas,[40] a situation close to that recorded in the census ten years later. In 1920, the U.S. consul reported 337 important coffee growers.[41] It appears that the coffee elite was already well established in the 1920s. Another consular report, this one from 1929, reported that all the land that could be used for growing coffee had already been planted, that the network of roads was the best in Central America, and that long-term financing was the major problem faced by the growers. It also read:

Until recent years the plantations were practically all limited in size and yields were consequently small. Land was cheap and planters would often mortgage their holdings in order to raise sufficient funds to develop them or purchase new pieces. Much of the profit from crops has been used to improve the land. Large plantations have been formed by a few individuals and companies by buying small tracts from time to time and these employ large-scale production methods, modern transportation, improved housing for labor, efficient organization and accounting systems.[42]

In summary, this is a description of a typical process of capitalist concentration. The greater productivity of the Salvadoran farms was reflected not only in increased exports: yields per surface unit were particularly high, and the aforementioned engineer, Duque, was able to confirm the superiority of same as compared to those of the rest of Central America.[43]

Now let us examine the situation with regard to labor. Diplomatic records supply ample references to the deplorable situation of rural workers. In his final report on the landing of Canadian marines at Acajutla on January 23, 1932, Commander V. Brodeur wrote the following:

Present conditions are best illustrated by a concrete example, which came under the personal observation of the Commanding Officer. On a certain coffee plantation, during normal times about 150 men are employed; but during the picking season, from January to May, about 500 extra workers, including children of 15 years old and upwards and many women, are taken on. These common laborers work as much as ten hours a day in some cases, for which they are paid 25c a day local money, equal to about 12c U.S. currency, or gold as it is usually termed. (The average exchange in 1931 was 9.88 Colons to the £). In addition they are given their food consisting of a handful of beans and a few tortillas (small, flat and exceedingly indigestible cakes made of maize) and coffee to drink; the cost of feeding each worker per day is at the most 1c. The season's yield of coffee from this plantation is valued in the neighborhood of £100,000; and a small calculation will show that labor for the whole season costs at the most £2,000. Even taking into account that it takes several years to bring the plantation to such a state of annual yield, and also expenses connected with outlay on acreage and plant, upkeep and taxes, etc., all of which means a considerable financial drain, even so the profits are large enough to justify the payment of a decent living wage to the plantation-workers.[44]

Shortly thereafter, Brodeur accurately described the working conditions: "low wages, incredible filth, utter lack of consideration on the part of the employers, conditions in fact not far removed from slavery."

Our overview of the context has taken us from the expansion of coffee growing to the agrarian conflict. This is not enough, however, to explain completely the 1932 insurrection. The rebellion took place in a clearly defined geographical area, which can be seen in Map 9.3. What characterizes that rebel zone? Are there features, in comparison with the rest of the country, that explain, at least partially, the rebellious nature of this zone?

246

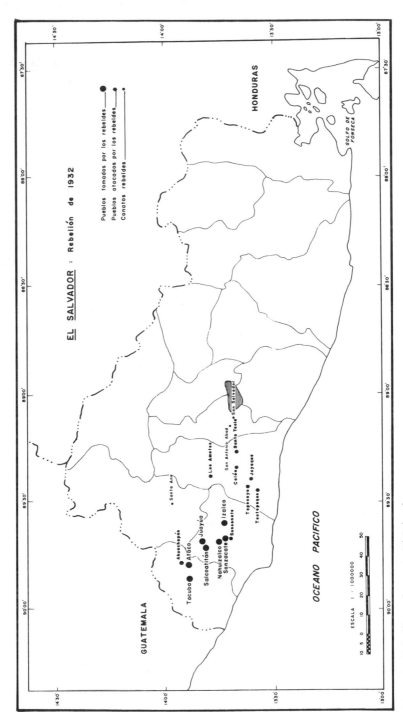

Map 9.3. Rebellion of 1932 in El Salvador

Table 9.1 can help in answering this question. This table includes some significant indicators taken from the censuses of 1930 and 1938, and from the *Anuarios Estadísticos* of the time, and presented by department. Unfortunately, the information cannot be broken down by municipalities. The indicators selected are the result of a very careful process of selection and control. The quality of the information selected was considered along with its relevance to the purposes of this study. All data considered uncertain or unreliable was discarded.

Between 55 percent and 63 percent of the rural population lived in the zones where the insurrection took place (Ahuachapán, Sonsonate, and, in part, La Libertad), a percentage similar to that of other zones in the central and eastern parts of the country. San Salvador, as was to be expected, had a much lower percentage, whereas Chalatenango, Cuscatlán, Morazán, and Cabañas were more rural, typical of zones that are more backward and isolated (See Map 9.1, showing the coffee-producing zones and the major means of communication). The rebel zone had the highest percentage of Indian population, and made major contributions to coffee production. The percentage of day laborers did not vary much from department to department, but was higher in San Salvador, where there were more artisans. The percentage of owners of real estate (houses and farms) was similar in all the coffee-growing departments, with a greater percentage of owners in the zone surrounding the areas under cultivation (Chalatenango, Cuscatlán, Morazán, etc.).

The increase in population between 1918 and 1930 contains a number of significant regional variations, but does not seem to be connected with any other characteristic of the rebel zone. The records of those prosecuted in 1931 would seem to dismiss the idea that the rebel zone was showing signs of "social decomposition" evidenced by high crime rates. Other indicators refer to the distribution of coffee-producing lands and were taken from the 1938 census. The Gini coefficient measures roughly the concentration of ownership of land. The rates are similar throughout the coffee-growing zone, with the national average being 66 percent. Only in zones that were backward and on the periphery, such as Chalatenango and Cabañas, is the rate lower than in the country as a whole. More precise than the Gini coefficient, and to a certain extent a control variable, is the situation of growers who had between one and ten manzanas, who could be considered small property owners. The general trends are the same as those indicated for the Gini coefficient, but it should be mentioned that this sector of producers seems to have been more important in Sonsonate than in other coffee-growing zones.

The sixth column of Table 9.1 includes the percentage of common lands with respect to the agricultural lands of each department in 1879,

TABLE 9.1
Statistical Indicators for El Salvador

	Santa Ana	Ahua-chapán	Sonsonate	La Libertad	San Salvador	Chala-tenango	Cuscatlán	La Paz	San Vicente	Cabañas	San Miguel	Usulután	Morazán	La Unión
Percentage of rural population in 1930	64.17	63.33	54.84	60.45	35.02	71.34	71.47	55.33	65.14	83.34	66.07	64.11	77.35	72.86
Percentage of Indian population in 1930	2.62	26.03	34.69	7.39	5.93	0.02	0.03	0.00	0.00	0.02	0.01	0.00	0.01	0.05
Percentage of owners of real estate in 1930	5.81	6.39	6.05	6.17	7.13	14.59	11.01	9.64	9.10	9.34	2.90	6.40	9.47	9.49
Gini Coefficient, coffee farms, 1938	62	57	67	71	66	24	45	58	57	33	59	63	58	63
Percentage of artisans in 1930	3.66	2.47	3.28	2.97	9.53	1.07	2.67	2.81	2.79	1.18	1.85	2.21	1.08	1.19
Percentage of common lands in 1878	4.3	20.0	34.0	27.0	20.0	8.7	12.0	n.d.	8.0	10.0	n.d.	19.0	45.3	14.5
Percentage of day laborers in 1930	21.70	20.44	20.82	23.10	14.86	24.89	23.31	22.18	20.87	24.33	23.31	23.06	24.68	21.68
Percentage of coffee production in 1930–31, with respect to the national harvest	40.59	12.21	5.53	16.52	2.37	0.14	1.08	2.87	1.00	0.57	5.02	11.14	0.57	0.34
Prosecuted judicially in 1931 (per 1,000 inhabitants)	2.27	2.21	2.63	2.73	5.84	2.49	3.91	3.22	2.60	4.42	4.59	3.27	4.31	3.70
Percentage of land owners with 1 to 10 manzanas (coffee, 1938)	42	50	41	43	35	17	32	50	41	47	46	51	30	50
Percentage of the land on farms of 1 to 10 manzanas (coffee, 1938)	15	24	17	10	22	41	51	29	25	60	15	13	27	11
Population increase, by departments, in percentages (1918–1930)	22	11	27	37	46	16	14	9	22	33	33	34	18	36

just prior to the expropriations of the liberal reform. Even though the estimates are fairly broad and cannot be considered highly exact, their significance is undeniable: Ahuachapán, Sonsonate, La Libertad, and San Salvador were affected by the expropriations more than other places. Two other things need to be mentioned. The department of Morazán, which also had a high percentage of common land, was relatively peripheral and did not play a major role in the expansion of coffee growing. The calculation presented refers only to common lands and does not include the lands of the Indian communities, which, as we know, were also expropriated. In summary, what seems to distinguish the region of the insurrection from the rest of the country is the proportion of Indian population in coffee-growing departments[45] and the formidable process of expropriation during the liberal reform.

Indians, Cofradías, and Politics

The 1930 census revealed that 5.6 percent of the population of El Salvador was Indian. An expert on the issue, Barón Castro, estimated that the figure was more like 20 percent.[46] Even though it is impossible to arrive at an exact figure, there is no doubt that the 1930 census underestimated the Indian population.

Toward the end of the nineteenth century, Rafael Reyes, the Director of Statistics, estimated that the Indian population was 55 percent of the total,[47] whereas the results of the 1888 census (which only included certain departments) indicated that the Indian population equaled 45 percent in Ahuachapán, 37 percent in Sonsonate, 7.5 percent in San Vicente, and 22 percent in Cabañas.[48] In the series *Monografías Departamentales*, published between 1909 and 1914, another expert on this issue, Santiago I. Barberena, stated that in Ahuachapán, Sonsonate, and La Paz, approximately 50 percent of the population was Indian, while in Cuscatlán the proportion was even greater. In addition, there were minority groups of Indians in La Unión and Morazán. Of course, all of these figures are fragmentary, and often not completely accurate, but they all point in the same direction. No matter how intense the process of acculturation, it does not seem feasible that over a period of fifteen to twenty years the Indian population could have declined so drastically, especially if we remember that it was concentrated in specific zones. What seems to have happened is that statistical criteria for classification changed during the 1920s. This is the only explanation for the figures recorded in the 1930 census. It should also be pointed out that all of this was taking place at a time when the ruling class and the intelligentsia of the country believed that in El Salvador the so-called Indian problem did not exist.[49]

Religious cofradías had been, for centuries, a fundamental link of solidarity among Indians.[50] From the point of view of power relations, their
importance increased once the communities and the common lands were
abolished, and national politics fell under the typical model of an "oligarchic republic." The first occurred, as we know, in 1881 and 1882; the
second became a reality in the elections of 1914, when the Meléndez-
Quiñónez family took power. From that point, and up to 1932, the Indian
cofradías became a fundamental piece in the clientelism that fed each
presidential election. This is why Jorge Schlesinger, in referring to the chief
of Izalco, did not hesitate to say, "The leadership of that cofradía gave the
Indian Ama power over all similar associations under his command, making him a true chief in the midst of a regime that appeared to be republican. Through the cofradías, Ama controlled more than 30,000 indians,
which is why politicians wanted him on their side."[51]

Following the classic clientelist model, the cofradías always lined up
behind the official candidate, who was sure to win as long as the elections
were not truly open. Therefore, it was no surprise when, in 1931, the
cofradías of Izalco supported Dr. Gómez Zarate, apparent heir of president Romero Bosque. According to Schlesinger, once in power, the Labor
party of Araujo tried to co-opt Ama, but without much success. Ama
preferred to join the communist ranks, and "a few months of propaganda
was all it took to turn this honest and hard-working man . . . into a true
believer of the red creed."[52] There is no way to prove the veracity of
Schlesinger's comments. However, his text can also be taken a different
way: the cofradías seemed to act with relative independence, and the
political haggling of Ama was really aimed at promoting the interests of
autonomous groups, in other words, his own.

In any case, there seems to be no question that the political activity of
the Indian religious cofradías, before and during the insurrection, was
fundamental.[53] These institutions of ethnic and cultural solidarity, reinforced by their semiclosed nature, provided the organizational framework
for Indian mobilization and doubtless served to underscore the Indian
component of the rebellion.

The Movement

We have already said that the lack of sources makes it impossible to re-
create the motives and ideas of the participants. We can, however, analyze
facts related to the insurrection. This means reassessing the accounts by
Joaquín Méndez, written almost as the events were happening.[54] The
validity of the accounts, for the purposes of this essay, is even greater if we

consider that the author was a journalist in the service of Hernández Martínez. If there is one thing we cannot accuse Méndez of, it is of showing favoritism to the rebels, and we can accept the notion that he did all he could to describe subversive activities.

According to Méndez, the participants in the rebellion were Indians who marched on the towns to attack them and eventually take them over (see Map 9.1). They appeared as a poorly organized mob (more or less 2,000 in Sonzacate, and some 500 in Nahuizalco), armed with nothing more than rocks, sticks, and machetes. They announced their arrival with such shouting and screaming that the whites and mestizos were filled with fear. They caused the deaths of some twenty mestizos, most of whom were guards and police.[55] The attacks consisted of ransacking certain houses, businesses, and public offices, and the setting of an occasional fire. At no time was there any indication of a plan for political organization. The inevitable drunkenness and continuous yelling were the common denominator in the towns taken by the rebels. In Nahuizalco, they forced the women to make tortillas for them, and in Juayúa they commandeered several automobiles and made the drivers chauffeur them through the city. In Juayúa, they also made the town's band play, without giving "the musicians a moment's rest."[56] If we remove the word *Communist* from Méndez's story, as well as two or three references to "modern conveniences" of the time (telegraph, automobiles, etc.), what is left is not surprising: it is the story of a violent act, similar in every detail to the riots and rebellions of Indians during colonial times, which Severo Martínez Peláez studied in such detail.[57] Let us review the "instruments" of Indian violence during the colonial period: stones pulled up from the streets, clubs, machetes, and hatchets; ransacking prior to the setting of fires; and a "lot of screaming, especially from the women in the mob."[58] Those killed were always henchmen or officials particularly hated because of their abuses and excesses. The mob was not acting on a plan, and its only intention was "to punish and stop excesses." The rebellions, on the other hand — Severo Martínez reserves this category for the Zendal Indians (Chiapas, 1712) — even though the causes were the same as in the riots, were well planned and were seeking the overthrow of the Spanish.[59]

Inasmuch as we do not know what motivated the Indian rebels in 1932, and since, in contrast with the colonial uprisings, what followed was not a judicial prosecution of those involved but rather such violent repression that it annihilated them physically, it is impossible to decide if the movement should be called a riot or a rebellion. That it was planned is evident, if we accept the idea of a Communist conspiracy and admit that it broke out simultaneously in different places. But something important is missing if we observe the behavior of the rebels and the fact that the general call to revolt was answered in only a few nearby towns where the population was predominantly Indian. In any case, the similarities with colonial violence are striking. Officials from the American Legation in San Salvador apparently agreed, refusing to come right out and classify the movement as Communist. Just as in colonial times, Indian solidarity, as manifested in the cofradías, helped in planning the rebellion, leaving the Indian chiefs to answer to the authorities and die as ignominiously as their predecessors had centuries before.

Of course, what still has to be determined is what set the movement off. There is sufficient evidence to support the argument related to agrarian unrest in the zone of the insurrection. Another factor is the important role the solidarity and cultural identification of the Indians played in fostering the spirit of insurrection. But what was the spark that set off the uprising? It is here where the communist conspiracy played a major role, but exactly how things developed is not clear. Schlesinger reprints a general call to insurrection, attributed to the Communist party, which is really a call to slaughter.[60] Mármol denies the authenticity of the document, and insists that it was a fabrication of the Hernández Martínez government, designed to confuse and incite. He does accept, however, the existence of the conspiracy and notes that there were changes in the date set for the uprising. According to Mármol, the arrest of Farabundo Martí only hastened the tragedy, since there was no way to retract the order. The discontent of the masses could not be contained, and the insurrection ensued.[61]

In all of this, there is the supposition that the only political element that led to mobilization was the agitation of the Communist party. We know that this was not the case. Throughout 1931 there was considerable political effervescence, and during the election campaign that put Araujo in power the subject of agrarian reform had been spoken about openly.[62] In addition, Araujo's movement had the support of relatively influential intellectuals and professionals, including Alberto Masferrer. To discuss whether or not such an order was given, where it came from, and whether or not it was heeded, is to a certain extent futile, since it will probably never be possible to answer the question completely. There are three points, however, about which there is no doubt: (1) the insurrection took place on the evening of January 22; (2) it was preceded by a relatively long period of political agitation, which included a presidential campaign, a coup d'état on December 2, 1931, and municipal elections in early January 1932 ; and (3) the insurrection took the form of a classic Indian rebellion.

Let us return to the spark that finally provoked the uprising. Severo Martínez explains that the outbreak of colonial Indian violence occurred when the cord broke that linked the omnipresent *anger* caused by exploitation with the equally present *fear* resulting from repression and, in general, the system of domination.[63] With this context and the labyrinth of possible causes in mind, we can now address, albeit with conjecture, the role of Communist agitation among the Indians in 1932. What this message did was unblock the fear and offer the possibility of finding allies within the broader national context. The social effervescence experienced in El Salvador in the years prior to the rebellion and the change in socioeconomic relations due to the rapid and violent increase in coffee production at the end of the nineteenth century and beginning of the twentieth are the reasons why the origin of this "unblocking" element was so modern and urban. Thus it was that communism in the twentieth century played the same role as the visions of the Virgin in the Zendal rebellion (Cancuc, 1712), the "Speaking Cross" in the Caste War of the Yucatán (1847–1902), or the visions of the "speaking stones" in the case of the Chamula Indians (Chiapas, 1868).[64]

Repression and Racism

The brutal manner in which the uprising was repressed is only too well known: "A few short days of indescribable terror produced tragic results for the people of El Salvador: twenty-five thousand people—laborers, peasants, capitalists, professionals, religious ministers, women, the elderly and children—lost their lives in the cities and villages. Execution squads carried out their bloody work night and day, as birds of prey devoured those who fell during the fratricidal struggle."[65] Without entering into unnecessary detail as to the exact number of victims,[66] it is important to reflect on two crucial aspects: who was in charge of the repression, and against whom was it directed?

The army and different police corps, acting on orders and equipped with modern weapons,[67] played a very important role in controlling the towns in rebellion (see Map 9.4). Also, from the moment of the outbreak of the insurrection, the government organized a civilian guard force, made up of volunteers under the command of military officers, which was put in charge of patrolling and repression. Farabundo Martí, Mario Zapata, and Alfonso Luna, the leaders of the Communist Party of El Salvador, under arrest since January 18, were tried and executed on January 31. For the next several months, persecution and death awaited all who had participated in or sympathized with the uprising.

Who was really persecuted? In the first place, obviously, are the Communist leaders and militants, whose identification was made easier by the fact that the party had participated in municipal elections in early January,

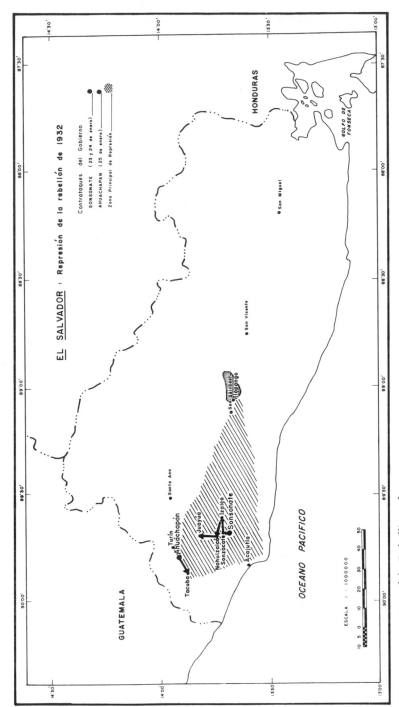

Map 9.4. Repression of the Rebellion of 1932

at a time when voting was public. Next, by association, were union leaders, and, then, real and suspected sympathizers. Under martial law and the curfew imposed, many abuses occurred and personal vendettas were carried out. This was confirmed years later by Castro Canizales, one of the military officers that overthrew Araujo. In his words, the capital had become "a cemetery."[68]

The brunt of the massacre was borne, however, by the Indian rebel zones. To truly understand the motives behind the repression, it is necessary to clarify who was seen as the enemy and why. A plantation owner in Juayúa published a very interesting account in *El Diario de Santa Ana* of his experiences during the insurrection. It was February 1, 1932. His description of the rebels is detailed: he calls them a "horde of wild savages" in which "all the Indians were affiliated with communism." He identified many of those involved in the uprising: "In the mob, in this huge uncontrolled mob, were all of them: almost two hundred of my workers, and those of my neighbors and my brothers." He held nothing back in his descriptions:

They, who are crafty by nature, and who come from a race inferior to ours, a conquered race, need little to ignite their deep-felt passions against the mestizos, because they hate us and always will. Our most serious mistake was to grant them civil rights. This was bad for the country. They were told that they were free, that the nation was also theirs, and that they were entitled to elect their own leaders and act as they saw fit. Of course, they took this to mean that they could steal, destroy property and kill their employers.

The author also offered a simple solution to the problem:

It is our wish that this race be exterminated. If it is not, it will come back even stronger, more experienced and less stupid, and ready, in future attempts, to do away with all of us. We need a strong reaction from the government, without asking for anybody's opinion, because there are those who counsel forgiveness; those whose lives have yet to be threatened. They did the right thing in the United States, getting rid of them, with bullets, rather than letting them stop progress. They killed the Indians first because they were never going to change. Here, we have treated them as if they were part of our family, shown them every consideration, but you should see them in action! Their instincts are savage.[69]

For this plantation owner, to say Indian is to say Communist, and the solution he offers is extermination. After reading his arguments, it is easy to see how anticommunism and racism[70] combined to offer a justification for the repression, behind which the oligarchy and the middle class rallied.

Conclusions

Agrarian unrest in the coffee-growing zones and social agitation, with
plenty of opportunity for the actions of the Communists, were both factors in El Salvador in 1932. The peasant rebellion, nonetheless, took place
almost exclusively in heavily Indian zones. The bloody repression that
ensued was felt most in the same region, leading to the virtual extinction
of those visibly Indian, on the pretext of the existence of a Communist
threat.

The patterns of social confrontation are intertwined and, therefore,
difficult to interpret. At the base, there is a serious conflict between land
owners, peons, and peasants, made even worse by the economic crisis and
the rapid changes in the distribution of land that took place in the decades
prior to and because of the expansion of coffee cultivation. This conflict,
however, despite the fact that it was exploited politically by the party of
President Araujo, the unions, and the Communist party, was not enough
to cause the insurrection. This took place in areas heavily populated with
Indians and was an expression of another basic conflict: the clash between
Indians and mestizos. The Communist conspiracy died with the failure of
the insurrection in the army and the arrest of the principal leaders days
before the date set for its initiation.

The dynamics and intensity of the repression are also the result of a
complex intermingling of solidarities. Mestizos, landowners, and the middle class lined up behind the forces of repression, and made anticommunism and racism their cause. The "conspiracy" theory was the justification
for closing down the political system and brutally doing what the liberals
at the end of the nineteenth century had long dreamed of doing: to teach
the peons and peasants to work harder. In this context, it is not surprising
that those who opposed this viewpoint should see it as a giant "provocation" orchestrated with very clear political motives in mind.

In the midst of all this, those involved were really just the most recent
actors in a play begun a long time ago. When Feliciano Ama was hung in
the town of Izalco, his executioners thought they were saving the country
from communism. What actually happened was that a long and unequal
struggle, begun by the Conquistadors in the sixteenth century, finally
came to an end. The Communist leaders paid dearly for following a political line that was as utopian as it was naive, and it took them many years to
admit that not everything was a conspiracy by Hernández Martínez and
the coffee oligarchy. The middle classes, terrified as they were of both
Indians and communism, thought they were defending the rule of law and
civility. Actually, what they were doing by contributing to these sad and

tragic events was mortgaging the democratic future of their country for decades to come.

Notes

I thank Héctor Lindo-Fuentes, Aldo Lauria, Fabrice Edouard Lehoucq, and Arturo Taracena Arriola for their comments and suggestions. I assume full responsibility for the content of this essay.

1. American Legation, San Salvador, *Correspondence, 1932*, vol. 3, File 800, General Conditions Report, Dispatch 57, pp. 11–13, National Archives, Washington, D.C.

2. Ibid., vol. 4, 1932. Files 800.B to 800.2, Salvador Economy, no. 4000b, Degree of Economic Development, copy of report sent by Major Harris from San José, Costa Rica.

3. Ibid., vol. 4, U.S. Naval Dispatch, January 29, 1932, from COMSPERON to OPNAV.

4. Joaquín Méndez, *Los sucesos comunistas en El Salvador* (San Salvador, 1932).

5. American Legation, San Salvador, *Correspondence, 1931*, vol. 5, file 800; vol. 6, file 800 to 810; *Correspondence, 1932*, vol. 2, file 330; vol. 3, files 574 to 800; vol. 4, files 800.B to 800.2; vol. 5, files 801 to 814.4; vol. 6, files 815.4 to 891, National Archives, Washington, D.C.

6. Complete versions of these reports appear in Leon Zamosc, "The Landing That Never Was: Canadian Marines and the Salvadorean Insurrection of 1932," *North-South: Canadian Journal of Latin American and Caribbean Studies* 11 (1986): 131–47.

7. Jorge Schlesinger, *Revolución Comunista* (Guatemala, 1946); Roque Dalton, *Miguel Mármol: los sucesos de 1932 en El Salvador* (San José, 1972).

8. *Población de la República de El Salvador: censo del primero de mayo de 1930* (San Salvador, 1942); the *Anuarios Estadísticos* has been published annually by the Dirección General de Estadística y Censos since 1911.

9. *Primer Censo Nacional del Café* (San Salvador, 1940).

10. Thomas R. Anderson, *Matanza: El Salvador's Communist Revolt of 1932* (Lincoln, Neb., 1971).

11. Segundo Montes, *El Compadrazgo: una estructura de poder en El Salvador* (San Salvador, 1979), 177–200.

12. Alejandro Dagoberto Marroquín, "Estudio sobre la crisis de los años treinta en El Salvador," *Anuario de Estudios Centroamericanos* 3 (1977): 115–60; Everett Wilson, "The Crisis of National Integration in El Salvador, 1919–1935" (Ph.D. diss., Stanford University, 1969). A Spanish translation of chapters 2, 4, and 6 of Wilson appears in Rafael Menjívar and Rafael Guidos Vejar, eds., *El Salvador de 1840 a 1935, estudiado y analizado por extranjeros* (San Salvador, 1978), 151–239.

13. David Luna, *Análisis de una dictadura fascista latinoamericana: Maximiliano Hernández Martínez, 1931–1944* (San Salvador, 1961); Rodolfo Cerdas Cruz, *La hoz y el machete: la Internacional Comunista, América Latina, y la Revolución en Centroamérica* (San José, 1986).

14. Kenneth J. Grieb, "Los Estados Unidos y el ascenso del general Maximiliano Hernández Martínez," in Menjívar and Guidos Vejar, *El Salvador de 1840 a 1935*, 243–69.

15. Rafael Guidos Vejar, *El ascenso del militarismo en El Salvador* (San Salvador, 1980).

16. Abel Cuenca, *El Salvador, una democracia cafetalera* (Mexico, 1962), 104–9; Ricardo Gallardo, *Las Constituciones de El Salvador*, vol. 1 (Madrid, 1961), 737–48; Alastair White, *El Salvador* (San Salvador, 1983), 107–13; Leon Zamosc, "Class Conflict in an Export Economy: The Social Roots of the Salvadoran Insurrection of 1932," in Jan L. Flora and Edelberto Torres-Rivas, eds., *Sociology of "Developing Societies": Central America* (London, 1989), 56–75.

17. Douglas Kincaid, "Peasants into Rebels: Community and Class in Rural El Salvador," *Comparative Studies in Society and History* 29(1987): 466–94.

18. Anderson, *Matanza*, seems to share some of the spirit, if not the letter, of this interpretation.

19. Cuenca, *El Salvador*, 105–6.

20. Marroquín, "Estudio sobre la crisis," 152–56.

21. Dalton, *Miguel Mármol*, 362.

22. Cerdas, *La hoz y el machete*, 298–305. Tirso Ricardo Melgar Bao writes that "the red insurrection in El Salvador was conducted against the positions of Farabundo Martí and the Caribbean Bureau of the Communist International," but he does not show very much evidence in support of this statement. See his "El marxismo en América Latina, 1920–1934: introducción a la historia regional de la Internacional Comunista" (Master's thesis, Universidad Nacional Autónoma de México, 1983), 219–20.

23. Abelardo Torres, *Tierras y colonización* (San Salvador, 1961), 37–38.

24. David Browning, *El Salvador: la tierra y el hombre* (San Salvador, 1975). Originial English version, *El Salvador: Landscape and Society* (Oxford, 1971), 408 ff.

25. Wilson, "The Crisis of National Integration."

26. Gallardo, *Las Constituciones de El Salvador*, 73. Jorge Lardé y Larín, *El Salvador: Historia de sus pueblos, villas, y ciudades* (San Salvador, 1957), also emphasizes the participation of Indians in his references to Izalco and other rebel towns.

27. Zamosc, "Class conflict," 70–71

28. White, *El Salvador*, 112–13; Montes, *El Compadrazgo*, 177–94.

29. Religious brotherhoods organized during the colonial period to honor the image of a saint; they held properties, bonds, and values to finance festivities and other social activities.

30. The best analysis of the competition between indigo and coffee, and of the economic and political factors involved, appears in the work by Héctor Lindo-

Fuentes, *Weak Foundations: The Economy of El Salvador in the Nineteenth Century, 1821–1898* (Berkeley and Los Angeles, 1990).

31. Dana G. Munro, *The Five Republics of Central America* (New York, 1918), chap. 5.

32. Browning, *El Salvador*, chap. 5.

33. Ibid.

34. A summary of these documents (answers by authorities to a government survey on common lands, conducted in July 1879) appears in Browning, *El Salvador*, appendix 3. An apparently complete publication appears in Rafael Menjívar, *Acumulación originaria y desarrollo del capitalismo en El Salvador* (San José, 1980), 158–69.

35. Menjívar, *Acumulación originaria y desarrollo del capitalismo*, 99. According to Lindo-Fuentes, this figure is a very high estimate (*Weak Foundations*, 129–30).

36. Browning, *El Salvador*, 207.

37. The best discussion, in economic terms, of the nature of the process of privatization of land appears in Lindo-Fuentes, *Weak Foundations*.

38. Juan Pablo Duque, "Costa Rica, Nicaragua, El Salvador, y Guatemala: informe del Jefe del Departamento Técnico sobre su viaje de estudio a algunos países cafetaleros de la América Central," *Revista Cafetera de Colombia* 7 (August 1938): 2,426.

39. Cf. Wilson, "The Crisis," chap. 4.

40. Ibid., 40.

41. Lynn W. Franklin to Sec. State, "List of coffee growers in El Salvador," Dispatch 29, March 25, 1920, Foreign Agricultural Relations Report, Record 166, Entry Box 168, File: coffee, 1912/1938, National Archives, Washington, D.C.

42. Ibid., "Salvadoran Coffee," from S. L. Wilkinson, April 25, 1929, p. 11.

43. Duque, "Costa Rica." Around 1935, yields in El Salvador were, on average, almost thirteen quintals per hectare (p. 2424), whereas in Guatemala they were barely ten (p. 2447) and in Costa Rica less than seven. See also Food and Agriculture Organization, *The World's Coffee* (Rome, 1947), 139, 180.

44. Public Record Office, London, FO-371-15814-A-4077-9-8, reproduced in Zamosc, "The Landing That Never Was," 135–6.

45. It should be mentioned that even though Sonsonate contributed only 5.53 percent of the national harvest, because of its geographical location, it is in the heart of a coffee-growing zone. It is likely that a good part of its peasant population participated in the coffee harvest on neighboring farms.

46. Rodolfo Barón Castro, *La población de El Salvador*, 2d ed. (San Salvador, 1978), 556–59. Barón Castro published the first version of this work in 1942 without having access to the data processed in the 1930 census, which were not published until 1942. This explains why he makes no reference to these figures.

47. Rafael Reyes, *Apuntamientos estadísticos sobre la República de El Salvador* (San Salvador, 1888), 13.

48. Dirección General de Estadística, *Censo general levantado en el año 1888*

(San Salvador, 1890). The census includes only the four departments cited. It is interesting to compare these figures with those from the 1930 census.

49. It is symptomatic, for example, that Alberto Masferrer, in his essay on the "vital minimum," written between 1928 and 1929, and which is supposed to be both a diagnosis of and a solution to the social problems of El Salvador, makes no reference to the Indian population and its culture (Alberto Masferrer, *El minimum vital y otras obras de carácter sociológico* [Guatemala, 1950]). Another "oversight" no less symptomatic appears in Jorge Arias Gómez, *Farabundo Martí: esbozo biográfico* (San José, 1972). The author, a militant Communist like Martí, describes the 1932 insurrection without mentioning the Indians (chap. 14).

50. Santiago Montes Mozo, *Etnohistoria de El Salvador: el guachival centroamericano*, 2 vols. (San Salvador, 1977).

51. Schlesinger, *Revolución comunista*, 25.

52. Ibid., 26.

53. Ibid. Everett Wilson and Thomas Anderson, in the works cited above, agree almost to the letter with Schlesinger's statements. The role of the cofradías is not mentioned in U.S. diplomatic documents, or in the reports by Communist leaders, for example, Miguel Mármol.

54. Méndez, *Los sucesos*.

55. Montes, *El Compadrazgo*, 184–88, compares the list of casualties provided by Méndez with those he collected during interviews in the rebel villages in 1976. He found that they coincided to a great extent, and confirmed that almost all were mestizos.

56. Méndez, *Los sucesos*, 88.

57. Severo Martínez Peláez, *Motines de Indios: la violencia colonial en Centroamérica y Chiapas* (Puebla, México, 1986).

58. Ibid., 53, 55–57.

59. Ibid., 126.

60. Schlesinger, *Revolución comunista*, 173–76. Curiously enough, this order was published in the *Diario Latino* of San Salvador on January 23, 1932 (No. 12,429) and was reprinted in Alfredo Schlesinger, *La verdad sobre el comunismo*, 2d ed. (Guatemala, 1932).

61. Dalton, *Miguel Mármol*, 334–38.

62. Anderson, *Matanza*, chap. 3.

63. Martínez Peláez, *Motines de Indios*, 48–51.

64. On the subject of religion in the Caste War and the Chamula rebellion, see Friedrich Katz, "Rural Rebellions after 1810," in Friedrich Katz, ed., *Riot, Rebellion, and Revolution: Rural Social Conflict in Mexico* (Princeton, 1988), 525–29; Victoria Reifler Bricker, *The Indian Christ, The Indian King: The Historical Substrata of Maya Myth and Ritual* (Austin, 1981).

65. Schlesinger, *Revolución comunista*, 4.

66. For an assessment of the total number of possible victims (estimates range from six to forty thousand), see Anderson, *Matanza*, 133–37. He feels that a figure of eight to ten thousand deaths is likely.

67. The telegraph, machine guns, and transportation by rail and truck were

key factors in the speed with which the uprising could be squelched (Schlesinger, *Revolución comunista,* 194–97).

68. The testimony of Castro Canizales, Julio C. Calderón, and Maceo Bustamante are reprinted and analyzed in Anderson, *Matanza,* 130–37.

69. Reprinted in Méndez, *Los sucesos comunistas,* 100–106.

70. The government of Araujo persecuted, also with clear racial overtones, the limited number of Chinese immigrants (217 in all). A discriminatory tax was imposed on their retail businesses, which led to their marrying Salvadorans, giving up their original names, and transferring their businesses. This incident, which took place in 1931, was widely reported in the press, and is another reflection on the strong racist feelings that prevailed among the middle class. On this subject, see American Legation, San Salvador, *Correspondence, 1931,* vol. 4, file 704, National Archives, Washington, D.C.

Ten

At the Banquet of Civilization:
The Limits of Planter Hegemony
in Early-Twentieth-Century Colombia

MICHAEL F. JIMÉNEZ

In the words of the Liberator: "We have tried plowing the sea. Here there is no choice but to emigrate . . . But even that might be too costly."

Gabriel Ortiz Williamson

O N MAY 1, 1914, Jesús del Corral admonished his audience at the Sociedad de Agricultores de Colombia (SAC) "to gird for combat and prepare to attend the magnificent banquet of civilization."[1] This warrant for progress reflected the optimism of export elites seemingly destined to lead their northern Andean nation into the modern world. Large coffee growers with enterprises in the fifty-thousand-square-kilometer upper Magdalena River Valley encompassing the modern departments of Huila, Tolima, and Western Cundinamarca constituted an integral part of the Colombian oligarchy.[2] Together with other elite groups, they had drawn the country back from disaster at the close of the War of a Thousand Days (1899–1903). For several decades these elites pursued a project of bipartisan rule, administrative reform, and infrastructural development. The owners of large plantations survived the vagaries of the First World War to profit from expanded coffee exports during the 1920s. All the while this planter faction of the Colombian upper class envisioned itself as a modernizing vanguard, hopeful, in the words of its principal publicist, Gabriel Ortiz Williamson, that a "new vigor, energy, purposiveness, and discipline . . . [will] contribute to the formation of the merchant, the farmer, the professor, and the man of state."[3]

The heyday of a coffee republic created by rising exports, railroads, and pragmatic gentlemen-farmers became the centerpiece of the nation's early-twentieth-century historiography. The period has been seen essentially as an extension of the Conservative, statist regime known as the *Regeneración* (1886–1902), which shepherded Colombia through the initial stages of modernization.[4] Dependency interpretations reaffirmed this view, with Tulio Halperín Donghi enrolling Colombia as "an oligarchic republic in its purest form . . . dominated by the alliances of Bogotá landowners and provincial grandee clans."[5] Similarly, Fernando Henrique Cardoso and Enzo Falleto designated this northern Andean nation as a representative case of "an oligarchic pact . . . [where] in spite of the violence of political struggle, a flourishing agro-exporting bourgeoisie managed throughout to impose temporary compromises among factions."[6] According to Charles Bergquist, in the wake of the turn-of-the-century conflict, "bipartisan export-import interests" successfully engendered "a new political and economic order which was to guide Colombia through more than three decades of political stability and the expansion of the export sector."[7] Though departing somewhat from these structuralist approaches, recent studies still emphasize the era's social and political stability. Marco Palacios has identified an atmosphere of "great corruption, peculation, and graft,"[8] while Herbert Braun deftly chronicled the construction of a political culture "spearheaded by the traditional power of the landowners."[9]

But if Colombia became a republic of coffee in the first third of the twentieth century, it was hardly a planters' republic. Elite rule in this period was riven with internal disputes and challenged from below. In particular, the coffee estate owners of central Colombia's upper Magdalena Valley, constituting the core of the nation's large-scale export agriculturalists, could not assert control over the nation's destiny. On the contrary, they succeeded neither in establishing themselves as the principal force within the Colombian oligarchy nor in creating a coherent and enduring political instrument of upper-class rule independent of the traditional political parties. Moreover, their hold over the plantation districts was often circumscribed. Finally, the coffee planters proved unable to articulate, much less enact, a hegemonic vision capable of uniting various elite factions and encompassing the vast majority of their fellow citizens. Like Southern cotton planters after the U.S. Civil War, the large coffee *hacendados* of the upper Magdalena did not emerge as the landowner core of a "classic conservative coalition" intent on launching Colombia on a modernization program.[10]

Region, Economy, and Elite Formation in the Republic of Coffee

A decade and a half after Jesús del Corral's invitation for the coffee growers to take their places at the banquet of civilization, the plantation districts in the upper Magdalena were swept by intense social and political conflict.[11] Dock workers, artisans, and laborers in construction and factories, as well as native communalists, engaged in strikes, land invasions, demonstrations, and armed uprisings throughout the region. Leftist militants joined in the late 1920s with provincial middle-class radicals and Liberal party military chieftans in a failed insurrection against the Conservative regime. These movements coincided with protests by squatters, tenants, and peons on the great estates west of the nation's capital. While responding harshly to the unrest, the authorities also attempted to settle conflicts in these wealthy, strategically located coffee districts through collective bargaining and government arbitration. In January 1929, J. R. Hoyos Becerra, Chief of the General Labor Office, recommended that hacendados sell their holdings and invest instead in bean processing and merchandising, and in industrial enterprises.[12]

That a government official in Latin America before the Great Depression should have counseled planters to yield economic power signals the fragile position of the coffee hacendados in the ruling bloc of Colombian oligarchs during the three decades after 1903.[13] Moreover, such a challenge to a major segment of the export elites suggests the playing out in this period of long-term constraints on their power and authority. During the final decades of the nineteenth century, the coffee hacendados of the upper Magdalena, despite the extraordinary growth of their enterprises, enjoyed minimal social and political leverage within the Regeneración governments. And after 1903, notwithstanding their great fortunes, their influence within the major parties and the state, and their apparent cultural hegemony, these coffee hacendados remained decidedly vulnerable. In effect, this segment of Colombia's export elite could not, during the three decades before the Great Depression, overcome their historic economic and political frailty and their limited cultural authority.[14]

At first glance, the planters' weakness is puzzling. After all, their economic fortunes had advanced rapidly after the War of a Thousand Days. Even in the face of erratic coffee prices, high transport costs, and persistent difficulties in gaining access to capital and labor, the large *haciendas* in the upper Magdalena mostly prospered in the three decades before the Great Depression.[15] Plantation varieties (known as *bogotas, girardots,* and *tolimas*) earned reputations for excellence in the North Atlantic, and many estates directly exported their beans with special markings.[16] The success of most enterprises in this period stemmed partly from the greater availability of credit and a growing, more settled population in the plantation districts. Entrepreneurial strategies based on crop diversification and tenancy arrangements also provided a cushion against international market shocks and ensured cheap and disciplined workers. The coffee haciendas served as a major pillar for an agro-mercantile elite with invest-ments in commerce, finance, real estate, and industries. At the time, these elites also went some distance toward institutionalizing their economic power. A major force behind the creation of the national agricultural lobby (SAC) in 1904, they successfully promoted the creation of a minis-try of agriculture a decade later.[17] In 1927, the planters helped establish the National Federation of Coffee Growers, a semiautonomous corpora-tion which would quickly become the principal guardian of the country's main export interest.[18] Finally, well-traveled and increasingly educated abroad, these members of the Jockey and Gun clubs, heads of philan-thropic societies, and founders of elite schools stood at the center of high society in the highland capital of Bogotá.

Why was it, then, that despite their wealth, political influence, and high social status, the planters did not dominate the Colombian oligarchy in this period? First, their economic position in the nation's ruling bloc was highly compromised. Most important, merchants, financiers, and even large growers in western Colombia acquired great influence in these years, effectively overshadowing the planters.[19] During the 1880s and 1890s, transportation improvements, a gold-mining revival, and rapid coloniza-tion of the central *cordillera* spurred a dramatic economic transformation in the mountain corridor extending from Antioquia to the upper Cauca Valley. After the turn of the century, the western Colombian business community built on these foundations, provisioning coffee smallholders with credit, closely monitoring bean quality, and undertaking merchan-dising campaigns abroad. Responding adeptly to international demand, Antioquian merchant-financiers collaborated with foreign exporters and British, German, and North American banking concerns to rationalize and expand the coffee trade out of western Colombia; by the end of the period, that region had "reportedly gone the farthest towards standard-ization."[20] This strategy paid off handsomely. Whereas prior to 1914 up-per Magdalena plantation varieties had fetched slightly higher prices than western beans in U.S. markets, the edge had been reversed a decade later.[21] Between 1913 and the late 1920s, the latter's share of national production grew from 30 to 70 percent.[22]

Western Colombia overshadowed the upper Magdalena planters in other ways. First, the Antioquian corridor garnered the lion's share of resources for infrastructural improvements as a flurry of projects in the 1920s lowered transport costs out of the central and western cordilleras to ports on the Pacific and the Caribbean. By contrast, links to the outside world remained expensive and inadequate for Cundinamarca and Tolima growers.[23] The 250-kilometer stretch of river between Girardot and La Dorada was impassable for months on end; when central Colombian varieties might have fetched high prices in foreign markets clear of western corridor coffee, mountains of beans lay stuck on upper Magdalena docks.[24] Second, the western Colombians became the principal voice in the nation's coffee lobby. Several attempts by the upper Magdalena planters to promote a coffee defense plan similar to the São Paulo valorization were frustrated by inadequate financial resources and lack of support from the increasingly influential western Colombian coffee processors and exporters.[25]

The National Federation of Coffee Growers, founded in 1927, became much the creature of the westerners, particularly the representatives from the fast-growing region of Caldas. Finally, the latter challenged the planters on their own terrain. Western Colombian settlers, businessmen, and their foreign partners moved rapidly into the region after the turn of the century. By 1930, northern Tolima, with its ensemble of plantations, smallholds, processing plants, and marketing networks had been drawn into the orbit of the western Colombian coffee interest.[26]

The coffee planters faced another major challenge from the grain and cattle hacendados of the eastern highlands and the Cauca Valley to the west who had been major pillars of the Regeneración.[27] Despite their often undercapitalized and technologically backward enterprises (with the exception of several large sugar complexes), these domestic agricultural producers benefited from Colombia's rapid population growth and urbanization in the first three decades of the century. Moreover, with their close ties to the Conservative party, they exercised formidable political clout. From SAC's formation in 1904, grain and sugar producers and cattle ranchers made common cause with coffee planters in pursuit of infrastructural improvements, credit for agricultural enterprise, and new technologies for the Colombian countryside. Large-scale producers for domestic and foreign markets also shared concerns about protecting private property and assuring discipline among the rural poor.

Yet on occasion this alliance served the coffee planters poorly. Staple producers insisted on nearly unchecked protection throughout most of the period. Between 1904 and 1927, high tariffs blocked the entry of rice, sugar, and wheat from abroad; levies on these products ranged between 60 to 100 percent above market value, higher than any others in the Americas during those years.[28] Representatives of the coffee hacendados faulted such policies for violating free-trade principles and raising labor costs. They were also frustrated in their efforts to obtain a cheap work force, unable to marshal political support for immigration schemes and facing resistance by *altiplano* elites to their recruitment efforts among the eastern highland peasantry.[29] In effect, the coffee estate owners remained in a subordinate position within the diverse agrarian segments of Colombia's ruling bloc through the 1920s.

After the First World War, a major economic transformation further diminished the position of the large coffee hacendados in this tenuous elite combination. During the so-called dance of the millions, North American and European capital penetrated various regions and sectors of the economy. Lowland coastal areas on the Pacific and Caribbean became major zones for sugar and banana plantation development by foreign and Colombian businessmen, and petroleum companies sunk wells in jungle wastes in the mid-Magdalena Valley and elsewhere.[30] While North Atlantic financiers expanded their presence and a $25 million Panama indemnity payment from the United States flowed into the country, Princeton economist Edwin Kemmerer helped reorganize the nation's fiscal and monetary structures.[31] At the same time, after the abrupt commercial downturn of 1920–21, control over the coffee trade passed from the traditional commission houses to international conglomerates such as W. R. Grace, Hard and Rand, and the American Coffee Corporation (a subsidiary of A&P founded in 1919), which established purchasing and processing centers in the upper Magdalena.[32] In turn, the tightened connections to the world economy spurred urbanization and expansion of manufacturing in Bogotá, Medellín, and other cities.[33]

These dramatic changes affected the planter elites in various ways. Their enterprises came under increasing pressure during this period. Foreign purchasing agents insisted on standardized, quality beans from the haciendas. Credit was also in short supply for agricultural enterprises, notwithstanding the Panama indemnity payments, the presence of foreign banks, and fiscal and monetary reforms. With the decline of the older commission house structure, lending terms became less advantageous to large growers, causing many to fall into debt.[34] Some did gain access to the newly founded national agricultural mortgage bank after 1925, but that institution concentrated its loans in urban real estate and housing ventures. The quickened pace of economic change, including greater employment opportunities in manufacturing, construction, and public works, led to labor shortages throughout the upper Magdalena. In 1928, the nation's central bank raised the alarm, noting that the "coffee crop is abundant, but there is fear of insufficient financing for the harvest."[35] While most haciendas managed to survive, and some even to prosper under such adverse circumstances, their owners were clearly on the defensive.[36]

The growers were also increasingly subordinated within the elite realignment of the postwar era. Large coffee producers, fearful of inflation, rising labor costs, and social protest, joined Conservative bureaucrats, financiers, importers, and other urban elite groups in calling for the cancellation of protective tariffs on foodstuffs.[37] During fierce debates at the 1929 Manizalez coffee congress, planter spokesman Ortiz Williamson, in concert with Finance Minister Jaramillo from Caldas, western Colombia's fastest-growing department, dealt a harsh rebuff to the domestic staples' producers, rejecting the plea of Pomponio Guzmán, a prominent altiplano landowner, "for love of the republic [to] eliminate this law so injurious to our great national interests."[38] But the planters did not necessarily benefit from this move against their traditional *latifundista* allies, as their erstwhile partners among the western Colombian merchant-financiers proved to be less than attentive to the concerns of large coffee growers on the eastern cordillera. The latter also found themselves at a disadvantage in the scramble for capital as urban developers, industrialists, and large merchant houses garnered ever more influence. Finally, regional elites other than the western coffee interest with links to the global economy began to exercise much more influence in the Colombian economy.

In the end, the large coffee growers may themselves have undermined the creation of a discrete planter interest within the Colombian oligarchy. As Frank Safford has shown, during the export initiatives in central Colombia's semitropical and tropical zones after independence, landowners often doubled as merchants and financiers or were closely aligned with mercantile clans.[39] Such business strategies endured well into the twentieth century. An original investor in the prestigious Banco López was Daniel Sáenz, co-owner of the two largest, most technologically sophisticated coffee plantations in the mid-Tequendama Valley southwest of the capital. Yet this descendant of José María Sáenz, the premier tobacco baron of the mid-nineteenth century, also held stocks in a cement plant, a shoe factory, real estate, and the aerial tramway to Monserrate overlooking the highland capital. He was described in the banking founding document on January 1919 neither as a *hacendado* nor as an *agricultor,* but rather as a *comerciante.*[40] Thus the uneasy perch of the coffee plantation owners near the apex of the oligarchy might have reflected their historic ambivalence about risking their capital and devoting their energies to large-scale export agriculture and perhaps also the degree to which they had already begun to follow Hoyos Becerra's prescription to make themselves over into another kind of elite.

Planters under Political Siege

In politics as well, the planters' power was similarly qualified. Having helped negotiate an end to the War of a Thousand Days, they exercised considerable influence in both parties and held important government positions during the three decades before the Great Depression. Large coffee growers joined other oligarchs in an intra-elite consensus to restrain both partisan violence and claims from below. In the longest period of political peace in the nation's history, the upper classes aimed, in Herbert Braun's words, "to *convivir*, to live together in a realm of power they felt ideally suited to inhabit."[41] This project achieved its most concrete political expression in the Republican Union, a bipartisan alliance of export interests which ousted the authoritarian regime of Rafael Reyes in 1909 and brought Carlos E. Restrepo to the presidency. The four-year administration of this Antioquian moderate Conservative sought to stabilize the nation's finances and steer the country toward a closer embrace with world markets.[42] By pursuing a modernization program above party conflict, the republican unionists hoped to replace the "roar of the canon" and the "flag-waving theorizing" of the previous century with the "whistle of the locomotive."[43]

In the three decades before the Great Depression, apart from the hiatus of the Republican Union administration between 1910 and 1914, the Colombian state proved to be often uncongenial and sometimes openly hostile to the upper Magdalena planters. In 1929, Tolima planter Julio J. Dupuy complained that his efforts to bring the concerns of coffee growers before government officials were frustrated by the "force of inertia, known by all, of the waiting rooms of public offices . . . One after another, from all the Ministers of Agriculture and Commerce to even the Presidents of various administrations, I importuned them fiercely with my constant obsession, and nothing, absolutely nothing, was I able to accomplish for the coffee interest."[44] Hyperbole aside, until the Liberal return to power in 1930, Colombia's public life was dominated by cliques of landowners, merchants, churchmen, military officers, bureaucrats, and political bosses extending from the most isolated villages to the presidential palace. Even the Restrepo administration, despite its efforts to dampen partisan competition and enact administrative reform, found itself in thrall to the Conservative networks inherited from the Regeneración. Also, given the immense influence of the Catholic Church, the Colombian state seemed very nearly a theocracy.[45] And yet in a nation consecrated to the Sacred Heart of Jesus, powerful impulses toward economic modernization, institutional change, and even social improvement existed among a bureaucratic cadre with strong nationalist, renovative pretensions.[46] Despite their formidable social status and economic influence, planters came at times to be regarded by the Conservative authorities as sources of revenue, inconvenient claimants on the public purse, and obstacles to the regime's development programs.

Taxes were a persistent source of friction between this oligarchical faction and the Conservative state. Disputes centered on export levies at the national level. In the aftermath of the War of a Thousand Days, planters had been disappointed by Reyes's lack of sympathy in this regard, and pressured successfully for removal of such charges. Joining in the ouster of Reyes in 1909, they found in the Restrepo administration a shield from state tributary exactions. On their return to power in 1914, the Conservatives reimposed export taxes and raised them once again in 1921 after the recovery from the postwar downturn. The planters battled, not always successfully, in Congress and the press to halt this extraction of funds from the coffee till.[47] These conflicts raged until 1927 when the newly formed National Federation of Coffee Growers began to manage revenues from taxes on coffee exports. This was, nonetheless, a pyrrhic victory for the planters because the western Colombians would be largely in command of this new vehicle to defend the rapidly changing coffee trade.

The planters also faced a fairly aggressive tributary state at the local level. They wrangled continually with departmental officials over cadastral evaluations, such conflicts becoming especially acute from the mid-1920s as large-scale producers faced mounting economic difficulties. In 1927, Sergio Céspedes, administrator of the Hacienda Costa Rica in Viotá, reported to the Tamayo family owners that "the cadastral commission came yesterday charged with raising the valuations. Naturally I gave them the lowest figures possible, calling their attention to the difficulties which the coffee haciendas are currently having due to the lack of hands and high wages."[48] They regarded the corvee as especially onerous and socially disruptive. Labor obligations for road building and municipal police duties not only siphoned off workers from enterprises already suffering labor scarcity, but caused, in the words of one observer, "the specter of rebellion . . . among those dark laborers, simple spirits . . . [who] just break the chains and abandon the *estancia*."[49] Similarly, planters complained bitterly about overzealous excisemen whose sorties against peasant liquor and tobacco contrabandists very nearly provoked open warfare between the state and the rural poor and undermined the tranquillity of the hacienda districts.[50]

The bureaucracy intruded as well on the landowners' traditional access to public sources of wealth through concessionaire arrangements. Seeking to deprivatize various sectors of the economy after the turn of the century, the Conservative state clashed with the planters. For example, Cundinamarca officials dislodged the Sáenz family from two profitable concessions. The first was the Portillo toll bridge on the Bogotá River, likely the most profitable such station in the Tequendama Valley, operated since 1891 by José María Sáenz and Evaristo de la Torre, another major planter.

In 1915, departmental authorities expropriated the bridge, which the Sáenz clan only regained by exerting influence at the highest levels to override a gubernatorial decree and district court judgment against them. However, treasury officials persisted in their efforts to gain control over this highly remunerative toll, finally forcing Guillermo Sáenz in 1922 to hand the bridge over to the department.[51] Three years later Sáenz business interests suffered another setback. Their monopoly over liquor production and excise collection in Cundinamarca, held from the beginning of the century, was challenged by the Conservatives on their return to power in 1914. Facing the departmental expropriation of the stake in the processing and sale of distilled spirits, the Sáenzes, co-owners of the region's largest aguardiente plant at the Ingenio San Antonio in Anapoima, failed to deter the takeover by Cundinamarca authorities.[52]

Upper Magdalena landowners in the 1920s found themselves constrained as well by official responses to disputes over land titles and rural protests. In the former case, legislation favored squatters in huge, untitled areas of central Colombia; the issue became more pressing in the middle of the decade when judicial rulings threatened landlord claims over often uncharted zones of the Sumapaz district southwest of the nation's capital and other areas.[53] In addition to conflicts over land, severe labor problems emerged in the plantation districts during these years. Large-scale export agriculture in Colombia had never been able to rely either on government-sponsored immigration or state-enforced coercive labor, in the manner of the Brazilians or Central Americans. Thus, in 1924, eager for official support to improve labor contracting, the planters had applauded the establishment of the General Labor Office within the Ministry of Industries. By decade's end, however, under attack by squatters, peons, and tenants, the great estate owners were dismayed not to receive the full support of the Conservative bureaucrats. To counter the "bolshevik" threat, Labor Office representatives recommended clearly defined contracts, the elimination of service tenancies or their conversion into sharecropping arrangements, and even, as Hoyos Becerra suggested, the sale and distribution of the haciendas to the rural poor. The planters balked at what they regarded as radical solutions to rural unrest emanating from unsympathetic, even hostile sectors of a government.

The absence of a strong regional base set further limits on the planters as well. The administrative division of the upper Magdalena into the departments of Tolima, Huila, and the western section of Cundinamarca disallowed the creation of a unified, autonomous political entity similar to that constituted by the São Paulo planters in Brazil in the same period.[54] The region's proximity to the nation's capital made it untenable for the hacendados or their business and political allies to build a separate governmental base of power. Neither any of the rustic towns on the eastern or central cordilleras nor the torrid river port cities of Honda or Girardot were serviceable as a regional capital. On the contrary, Bogotá's banks and merchant houses, schools and clubs, and governmental offices drew the hacendados inexorably to the cool, tableland capital to the east.

Post-Regeneración politics proved equally nettlesome for the planters. The partisan design of Colombia's intra-elite competition had been forged in the mid-nineteenth-century confluence of family loyalties, programmatic disagreements, competing ideologies, and regional affinities and had congealed during the Conservative retrenchment after the mid-1880s.[55] During the Regeneración, the upper Magdalena growers who had earlier supported the Liberal program of free trade, decentralization, secularization, and appropriation of ecclesial properties found themselves largely excluded from bureaucratic offices and legislative representation. They also endured taxes on exports, expropriations of property and capital, and political persecution by the Conservatives. As the country rushed headlong into its deadliest, most destructive civil war, in the late 1890s, the still largely Liberal planters, huddled in their party's peace faction, could neither achieve harmony among the competing oligarchs nor contain liberalism's more insurrectionary elements.[56]

In the wake of the War of a Thousand Days, upper Magdalena growers and other oligarchs resolved to avoid the divisive partisanship seen as injurious to their particular interests and the country as a whole. A plan early on for the establishment of an Agrarian party independent of Conservatives and Liberals fizzled. Nonetheless, the idea of an alternative to the previous century's warring bands survived among many upper Magdalena entrepreneurs and others.[57] The coalition of export interests and moderates from both parties which brought Reyes down in 1909 went some distance with the Republican Union in creating such an option. In this respect, withal its limitations and the persistence of Conservative militants in the state apparatus, the Restrepo administration came the closest to making Colombia a planter's republic during the first third of the century. Yet after 1914 and until its disbandment in the early 1920s following almost a decade of lackluster electoral performances, the Republican Union did not become a unified, coherent instrument of class rule under the aegis of the large landowning export elites.

Throughout the 1920s, the planters fought a rearguard action against other oligarchical factions within the two major parties. Though they shared common ground on social questions and economic policy with both the Antioquian entrepreneurs and domestic-oriented latifundistas in the ruling coalition, partisan resentments and differences with state bureaucrats over various issues kept them apart from the Conservatives.

Most important, they never fully captured control of the Liberal party, where they had to accede to elite factions linked to the commercial and financial sectors of the export economy as well as manufacturing and urban development.

At the same time, from early in the century, emergent middle-class claimants used the remarkably enduring system of sectarian politics to challenge the power and authority of the coffee oligarchy.[58] Economic opportunities, expansion of the bureaucracy, and increased access to education spawned ever greater numbers of lawyers, physicians, journalists, and public employees active in both parties. In Bogotá and other major cities, this group was often closely linked to the large growers by patronage, marriage, and party loyalty. Nonetheless, some politically active members of the middle class did not fully share the planters' vision of an oligarchical republic which excluded greater participation and maintained a laissez-faire approach to the economy, particularly with regard to foreign trade and investment.

Such skepticism toward the large growers found expression in Rafael Uribe Uribe's efforts to revive the Liberal party in the decade after the War of a Thousand Days. Until his assassination on the steps of the Capitol in 1914, this former chieftan of the Liberal insurgents campaigned with ferocious partisanship against Conservatives and Republic Unionists alike; his program of "state socialism" proposed governmental intervention to promote economic development and social welfare.[59] The *uribistas* scorned the gentleman-farmers, regarding them as legatees of a seigneurial past, obstacles in the way of progress, enthusiasts of free trade and other economic policies who placed their private interests above the public good, and vendors of the nation's patrimony to foreign interests in the wake of the Panamanian debacle. Uribe Uribe's newspaper opined that since, under the dominion of these elites, the Colombian people had "only obligations to fulfill and no rights to enjoy, burdens to endure and no guarantees of which to be assured . . . the government should ensure an equilibrium between the different social classes and political parties, and the oligarchy should surrender its privileges."[60] These themes would later be taken up in the 1920s by a new generation of social critics and politicians, such as Alejandro López.[61]

The hacendados fared badly in local politics as well. The upper Magdalena, described by José María Samper in 1861 as the "house of republicans," had a long tradition of resistance to the Conservatives, and to the strong central state and the oligarchy more generally.[62] Born in the midcentury era of oligarchical reform and strengthened during the Regeneración, this popular variant of liberalism emphasized individual liberties, social equality, and anticlericalism; it also demonstrated a marked tendency toward an exclusionary politics and military vanguardism, particularly in the face of the Conservative reaction.[63] After the War of a Thousand Days, popular liberalism continued to flourish in the upper Magdalena, scene of the conflict's fiercest fighting and harsh repression of the Liberal military chieftans and their followers as the conflict drew to a close. This homegrown opposition found expression in the constant round of local, regional, and national elections, where planter politicians and their delegates faced increasingly raucous and demanding plebeian voters. These lower-class Liberal loyalists distrusted the efforts by elites to dampen partisan rivalries and achieve a rapprochement with the Catholic Church, the archenemy of the popular liberals. Prior to the First World War, Uribe Uribe's followers in the region checkmated the reconstitution of planter-dominated political networks in the region. Even after his death in 1914, the uribista legacy stood in the way of the hacendados' efforts to completely reassert control over provincial liberalism. As a result, during much of the three decades before the Great Depression, the planters proved unable to take full advantage of a substantial voting bloc in the upper Magdalena countryside. Given their weak leverage over the Conservative-dominated state, they could provide neither the protection nor the patronage for effective clientelism. In the rural as well as the urban areas, the planters' efforts to remake Colombian politics in the image of their much admired English parliamentarism failed miserably.

The eruption of popular liberalism outside the traditional parties further complicated politics for the upper Magdalena elites. Early on, a Partido Obrero (Workers' party) with links to Uribe Uribe gained adherents in a major zone of guerrilla operations during the War of a Thousand Days, winning the 1911 assembly elections in Viotá only to have the results overturned by the authorities. A decade later, the newly founded Socialists gained control of a handful of municipalities through the ballot, including the port city of Girardot, which they governed into the early 1920s, sending out organizers into nearby rural areas. Toward the end of the decade, in the midst of economic crisis and official repression, a loose coalition of provincial middle-class radicals, university students, artisans, dissident Liberal politicians, and former insurgents formed the Partido Socialista Revolucionario (PSR). The example of the Soviet Union and worsening social conditions throughout the country presaged a successful, broad-based revolutionary movement. María Cano, an Antioquian labor activist, and other PSR militants sought to link their nationwide organizing efforts to local artisanal, proletarian, and peasant movements in the upper Magdalena. Strikes, land invasions, and armed conspiracies throughout the region culminated in an abortive national uprising in July

1929 as veterans of the War of a Thousand Days joined lower-class insurgents in the hopes of toppling the Conservative regime.[64]

Police and army actions in the region during the late 1920s responded forcefully to these upheavals. Strongly supportive of the repression against the PSR activists and the lower-class protestors, the landowners came into a close embrace with the most reactionary elements of the Conservative regime and stood at odds with the arbitration teams from the Labor Office.[65] Their hard line also alienated some local notables and segments of the provincial petty bourgeoisie who hoped for a peaceful resolution of these conflicts and who were not, in any event, fully incorporated into the region's unstable political elite networks. In the end, the planters' recourse to violence underscored their failure to maintain an effective local clientelism or otherwise domesticate public life in this zone. In the capital or traveling abroad, the increasingly absent landowners could only see a region plagued by pettifoggers, *macheteros,* bandits, drunken peasants, and now "bolsheviks" threatening the despised Conservatives and law and order more generally.

Contested Haciendas: Everyday Resistance and Rebellion

The obstacles posed by this radical opposition to the planters signaled the incompleteness of the great estate's dominion in the upper Magdalena. The hacienda certainly remained a towering presence, its owners managing local elections, controlling municipal courts, and supervising public works. In what Jesús del Corral referred to as a "veritable feudal regime," the coffee lords seemed to exercise near absolute mastery over peons and tenants alike.[66] Nonetheless, behind this facade of apparently unqualified power, the hacendados were caught in a web of relations with their own workers and with other segments of the population over which they did not always have the firmest grip. In effect, their hegemony was quite fractured at the very place where it might predictably have been the most secure.

Near the end of the War of a Thousand Days, Liberal Celso Román pleaded "that the tempest cease in order that people and things return to occupy the position and level to which, given their background and conduct, they are suited."[67] Almost two decades later, a Cundinamarca official complained that in the villages near the Socialist-dominated port of Girardot, the "ancient and proverbial respect for the *patrones* is fast disappearing."[68] That there had ever been such total deference to the lords by the peoples of the upper Magdalena seems unlikely, however. Since the

Spanish conquest of the northern Andes during the mid sixteenth century, the power and authority of large landowners had been significantly circumscribed at the local level. They seem not to have been able to assert complete control over their work forces almost from the outset. Neither the state nor the church proved to be very effective partners to the landed elites in guaranteeing tranquillity and social conformity. And, finally, Bogotá patricians with holdings in the region never established solid links between themselves and local notables, artisans, and petty merchants in this backwater.

Until the mid nineteenth century, the sparsely settled frontier sent tropical products and livestock to the heavily populated eastern highlands and served as a transit zone to the Caribbean Sea and to the southwest. A handful of large cattle ranches and sugar plantations, some held by the Catholic Church and Bogotá rentiers, were surrounded by a multitude of tenants, squatters, and independent proprietors. The region was populated by descendants of mostly decimated indigenous peoples, African slaves, and a thin stream of migrants from the surrounding highland zones, particularly from the altiplano to the east. "Living apart from society," in the words of one colonial official, this population generated an extensive underground economy in the upper Magdalena wilderness, defying landlords and the state alike.[69] In addition to poaching and flight from labor obligations, small-scale sugar producers undercut the large plantations in regional markets with their cheap molasses and alcoholic beverages; moreover, the authorities were hard pressed to stop widespread evasion of the excise by contrabandists.[70] Neither did the Catholic Church sink deep roots in those desolate settlements where the population "rarely attended mass, thereby endangering their immortal souls and easily exposed to the excesses caused by their proximity to nature, without fear of being caught."[71] In 1781, when the *comuneros* in the eastern highlands rose against Spanish tax policy, a bloody social and caste war broke out in the upper Magdalena. A fleeing imperial official reported from the Tequendama Valley that "justice is given affront and depreciated; and Your Majesty's sacred name blasphemed."[72] Well after independence, the region remained in the elite imagination as inaccessible and barbaric. "It is not possible," wrote Emiro Kastos dispiritedly in 1852, "however optimistic one might be, to envision for these interior places any future prosperity."[73]

From its beginnings in the 1840s, large-scale export agriculture faced a similar configuration of independent household producers and a fragile governmental apparatus. Initiatives were undertaken in tobacco, indigo, cacao, quinine, and coffee on a frontier zone with few and scattered towns and villages and a state with little presence and less authority. As the planters moved into newly settled areas or the remnants of colonial lati-fundia, their experiments with diverse labor arrangements had only lim-ited success. The great tobacco enterprises in the Ambalema district on the Magdalena's western shore during the 1860s and 1870s purportedly de-clined because of the sharecroppers' inattention to quality. In 1871, Min-ister of Finance Salvador Camacho Roldán, in a letter to British investors, allowed that labor was in short supply because wage workers simply abandoned the fields and processing tanks to establish their own plots in the adjacent wilderness.[74] A character in the classic *costumbrista* novel *La Manuela* declared that "some tenants have a stand of plantains, up to six beasts of burden, and live in open warfare with the landlords."[75]

By the late 1870s, the owners of the recently established coffee planta-tions turned to workers from the eastern highlands "where the population is large, where there is great poverty and salaries low."[76] Compared to the lowlanders, so much like the French "given to rowdy diversions," geolo-gist Alfred Hettner found the people of the altiplano akin to his fellow Germans, "serious and tranquil."[77] Before 1900, however, the flow of migrants never reached the proportions hoped for by the agrarian entre-preneurs, who discovered in any event that these countryfolk were hardly so malleable. Malcolm Deas cites the desperation of a western Cundina-marca hacienda administrator: "I'll never understand these people: they really are *indios*. Now they get a good day's wage in the harvest, one still has to force them and mule-drive them just as if one was asking them to work for nothing."[78] In addition, squatters competed with cattlemen and coffee planters for control over much of upper Magdalena's unclaimed vastness. Independent smallholders and tenants also participated in a net-work of local markets and continued to do battle with excise officials. This confraternity of peasants and provincial petty bourgeoisie proved to be enthusiasts of popular liberalism, after 1850 and at the height of the Regeneración. Many participated as chieftains and soldiery in the Liberal guerrilla bands during the several armed outbreaks between 1885 and the War of a Thousand Days, the latter finally turning the region into Colom-bia's bloodiest ground since the Wars of Independence.[79]

A war-weary upper Magdalena grew quieter after 1902 as elites in both parties sought to cool political passions. Greater stability of labor came to the great estates with the increase in migrants down from the altiplano and the crystallization of a labor system combining seasonal wage earners and permanent workers drawn from sharecroppers and service tenants.[80] The exchange of work obligations for usufruct rights on small plots gave advantages to the rural poor and growers alike. For the *arrendatarios* (service tenants), such arrangements provided both relative economic se-curity and opportunities to engage in commercial activity of considerable scope and reach. Contemporary notarial records reveal substantial tenant investment in foodstuffs, sugar, and even occasionally coffee cultivation, as well as cattle, mules, and other livestock. Particularly enterprising tenants engaged in sugar processing and liquor production. Trading in usufruct rights also appears to have been commonplace. Squatters, independent proprietors, and tenants plied local markets which could draw, according to one observer, "two to three thousand people, making transactions for considerable sums."[81] Such locations often evolved into larger, more permanent settlements with taverns, shops, and slaughterhouses connected to wider commercial networks by traveling salesmen and agents of store owners from nearby towns.

Planters gained by this system as well. The incentives of the tenancy plots — and fear of eviction — appeared to ensure a cheap and apparently docile labor force. Paternalist affection, reciprocity, and coercion cemented this economic relation.[82] Smallholder production within the great estate benefitted the hacendados in other ways. Required tenant provision of housing and meals for day laborers helped reduce capital outlays by the estates. Operating costs were also lowered by subcontracting of various tasks to the *arrendatarios,* such as the mule teams carrying coffee to railheads and river ports. In addition, the tenant household became a source of small chunks of capital for the often hard-pressed estates with managers levying tolls on their dependents for the movement of goods, licensing fees, and fines for infraction of regulations.

But this symbiosis of peasant and lord did not guarantee unblemished social concord in the upper Magdalena prior to the Great Depression. Squatters and elites clashed furiously on that vast, sparsely settled frontier march. And conflicts became endemic on the great estates themselves, especially toward the end of the period. Slowdowns, tool breakage and loss, and similar sorts of everyday, workplace resistance were commonplace in the coffee groves, processing centers, and sorting sheds. Wealthier tenants sent others in their stead to fulfill labor obligations, further loosening their ties to the hacienda. The *estancieros* struggled to defend and even expand usufruct rights. Poaching and pilferage of estate resources, such as cattle, sugar, and even coffee occurred with some frequency and tenants evaded hacienda extractions of tribute and other constraints on their participation in local markets. After the First World War, an ever more commercially active peasantry demanded freedom to cultivate coffee on their allotments. By the late 1920s, as individual bargaining with the estate managers turned more collective with unions and leagues, the issue of independent coffee cultivation assumed greater salience. In some areas, such as northern Tolima, sharecropping muted the protests to some degree. But in the eastern part of the department and in Cundinamarca, the planters' unrelenting refusal to accede to such demands and heightened pressure on workers in a declining economy escalated the conflicts dramatically, so that in the eyes of many observers Central Colombia seemed poised at the brink of a major rural jacquerie.[83]

Tense and often violent encounters between smallholders and the state further imperiled the haciendas' authority in the region. The preying by Conservative bureaucrats and local tyrants on the rural poor through labor tribute and taxation was a constant incitement to conflict in the plantation districts. Hacienda workers and tenants also had to endure the collusion of local political bosses and clerics, the latter of whom demanded onerous fees for baptisms, marriages, and burials, sometimes causing the rural poor to take flight.[84] The struggles over the excise took a particularly heavy toll on order and tranquillity in the countryside. The centuries-long effort by colonial and later republican authorities to levy duties on the lively trade in tobacco and sugar-based local brews, *guarapo* and *aguardiente,* entered a new phase in these years, as departmental bureaucracies expanded the power and reach of their excise offices, even inviting foreign police missions to modernize their tax police units. A Cundinamarca official in 1918 described peasant contrabandists as "constantly on the alert and prepared for combat, well-armed, and fully resolved to protect their industry."[85] The detention of violators of the excise and constant uproars over government intrusions into these smallholder economies kept large segments of the upper Magdalena in a constant state of alarm.

On the other hand, the rural poor regularly used the government, and the courts in particular, against the planters. Catherine LeGrand has amply documented the legal initiatives taken by squatters in the upper Magdalena and elsewhere in Colombia to gain access to contested public lands.[86] Tenants pursued their demands to grow coffee through the judicial system as well. They also registered contracts amongst themselves at notarial offices, hopeful of legitimating their household economies. As their claimsmaking turned more collective in the 1920s, tenants flooded local, departmental, and national authorities with petitions denouncing the growers and demanding formal labor and tenancy contracts. They thus channeled their protests more often than not through legal institutions, despite enduring constant fraud and corruption at the hands of local officials. Obviously, by this litigation the rural poor could not bend state power entirely away from its entanglement with the planters. Nonetheless, the latter did find themselves tied down by a peasantry which was learning with ever greater efficacy to use the legal instruments of the republican state against the powerful and wealthy.

Local tradesmen, merchants, and small-town professionals often lent their support to the independent proprietors and tenants against the hacendados and the state. Many among the local middle classes did, of course, cooperate with the large growers and their agents, collecting debts, managing estates for often absent landowners, and enforcing law and order on the latter's behalf. Yet they also remained economically dependent on the smallholders, whose produce they purchased and to whom they sold manufactured goods and rendered a host of services. Thus authorities criticized the petty bourgeoisie in the region for shielding contrabandists and for treating tax collectors "not as officials, but as private citizens and preventing them from going about their business of necessary searches and investigations."[87] Moreover, local lawyers were often the source of the interminable litigation in the upper Magdalena countryside; modestly trained *rabulas* and *tinterillos,* as they were known, became the instruments by which countryfolk used the judicial system for their own benefit. Unsurprisingly, these plebian legal practices came to be regarded by the elites as threatening private property, victimizing the peasantry, and undermining respect for authority.[88]

This connection to the peasant economy allowed the petty bourgeoisie to constitute bases of wealth and power which were often independent of the planters and did not yield easily to the demands of the state. The authorities complained repeatedly about the chicanery and autonomy of the political machines in this part of Colombia after the turn of the century.[89] "There are interests which are difficult to combat," raged a Cundinamarca official in 1919 reporting to the governor on the lack of cooperation by the petty bourgeoisie in the municipalities west of the capital.[90] Almost a decade later, a Bogotá daily declaimed the political clans in the districts of the upper Magdalena "whose deceit is everyday more disconcerting and whose violations of legal and constitutional order represent a growing danger, one if not faced up to by the Minister of Government, will sorely try the patience of the people."[91]

This complex economic symbiosis of the petty bourgeoisie and segments of the rural poor, notably smallholders and tenants, in the upper Magdalena also undermined the broader political and cultural authority of the mostly Liberal planters and representatives of the Conservative state in the region. The clearest evidence of this challenge was, of course, the broad support that popular liberalism, within the Liberal party and outside its ranks, received from the population of these districts over the entire period, at the polls, in demonstrations, the popular press, and armed uprisings. There were other manifestations as well of a powerful oppositional culture which was shared by the provincial middle classes and the more privileged segments of the peasantry, one which disavowed relations of dependence and deference, insisted on equality before the law, and demanded freedom of commerce. For example, the region was the site of constant disputes with the Catholic Church on a range of issues, from the appointment of schoolteachers to clerical interference in elections; Jesuit "missionaries" sent to the province of Tequendama in western Cundinamarca were sharply criticized for preaching openly on behalf of Conservative candidates on the eve of the balloting.[92] After the turn of the century, when Protestant missionaries journeyed into the region, they often drew large crowds despite Church interdicts.[93] In towns and villages throughout the region, followers of freemasonry and theosophical thought denounced institutional marriage and expressed disdain for traditional values and institutions. This oppositional culture was nurtured through local printing presses, social clubs, secret societies, and real and imagined armed conspiracies, as Gonzalo Sánchez has vividly shown.[94]

Such a multifaceted resistance to the hegemonic pretensions of both planters and the Conservative state as well as their priest collaborators had major consequences for elite rule in the upper Magdalena. Certainly the traditions of popular liberalism there were given renewed vitality in the confluence of political and social conflicts after the War of a Thousand Days, helping significantly to erode the power and authority of the coffee hacendados in the region. This process laid the groundwork for the rising of peons and tenants in the late 1920s and 1930s, leading ultimately to a full-blown revolutionary agrarianism in the region at mid-century.

Retreat from Hegemony

The upper Magdalena planters faced major structural, political, and cultural impediments to their dominance over Colombian society in the three decades before the Great Depression. But they were also constrained by their own inability and unwillingness to imagine a place for most of their fellow Colombians at the "banquet of civilization." Effective and enduring rulership depends on the capacity, as Rousseau suggested, to "transform force into right, and obedience into duty."[95] While the achievement of hegemony has historically involved the consolidation of economic and institutional resources, including the capacity for coercion, more is required to rule effectively. Dominant groups have usually sought to articulate a social vision encompassing and purportedly representing the values and practices of the vast majority of people in their societies, fellow elites and subalterns alike. Throughout history, the incompleteness or frailty of such a vision has contributed to ongoing contentiousness within societies, occasionally open rebellion, and, more rarely, fundamental revolutionary transformations.

The merchant-landowners who undertook major economic, political, and cultural reforms and sought to tighten the country's links to the world economy during the middle decades of the nineteenth century had articulated such a broad ideal for Colombian society.[96] Their optimism was founded on three major themes. First, the nation, defined in terms of the participation of free and equal citizens in an ensemble of republican institutions, could provide the political framework within which to achieve modernity. Second, the sociability required for citizenship in such a parliamentary regime would be generated by the free, unhindered operation of the market. Salvador Camacho Roldán, in his 1872 finance minister's report, accentuated the crucial importance of the spirit of "association . . . that spontaneous, natural, and free undertaking of the people [which] is the result of the natural functioning of the basic laws of human organization."[97] Finally, in turn, such eternal jostling of individual interests and desires would unleash society's productive resources. Secure and ample returns on capital investment could thus be assured, land would be put to productive use, and most importantly, the labor of all social classes would become the principal guarantor of the nation's future.

During the first third of the twentieth century, however, the planter interest retained little of the optimism and broad inclusiveness of its liberal forebears. There had been, of course, elite dissenters during the reform era of the 1850s through the 1870s, Liberals as well as Conservatives, who doubted that free markets and an inclusive polity could promote modernity. They proffered instead a far more paternalist, authoritarian, and statist vision which ultimately found expression in the Regeneración.[98] Through the 1880s and 1890s, even those hacendados who remained in the Liberal party found reason enough to retreat from their earlier optimism as economic crises, social unrest, and unrelenting partisan conflicts tore the nation apart. And despite the three decades of relative peace and prosperity after the War of a Thousand Days, such uneasiness did not abate. In their business offices, salons, clubs, lobby meetings, and the management of plantations, and on their frequent trips abroad, the planters turned the liberal idiom cautionary, fearful, cramped, and exclusive, thereby themselves limiting its capacity to constitute a hegemonic ideal for their society.[99]

Unsurprisingly, the continuing usage of the language and symbols of nationhood and citizenship by this upper-class group rang ever less true. On the one hand, as Eric Hobsbawm has suggested, the growing cosmopolitanization of tropical elites in this period undermined their earlier commitment to the nation-state as the principal sphere within which progress could be achieved.[100] With the distinctions between the "advanced" and "backward" worlds gaining ground among members of a planter class educated and traveled abroad, they came to regard the Colombian people as an ever less apt vehicle by which to achieve modernity. In this context, the inroads of scientific racism into Colombian intellectual life undermined the optimism of the mid-nineteenth-century republican patriciate's liberal wing. Their earlier ideal of the lower classes as solid citizens gave way to a more somber view of a commonfolk "given to degrading vices and filled with silly superstitions."[101] How could a liberal democracy be possible among those "possessed of a lesser spiritual development because they are unable to appreciate the advantages of civilization and are incapable of determining what is best for them"? Accordingly, such a people needed to be "guided by persons who are more active and ambitious than they."[102]

Nor could the middle class necessarily be relied upon to support the planters' vision of a "popular and democratic government," as the Republican Union called itself.[103] The sectarian addictions of so much of the petty bourgeoisie in town and country were regarded as obstacles to a stable constitutional regime. The planters feared the insurrectionist sensibility among provincial activists whose popular liberal tendencies they excoriated as "jacobinist."[104] But concerns about renewed civil war barely masked a deeper anxiety over Uribe Uribe's attempts at mass mobilization before his assassination in 1914. The elites heaped opprobrium on their principal adversary in those years, sardonically referring to him as "the pope of liberalism."[105] Finally state employees and politicians, many of them from the mushrooming middle class, were seen as having corrupted public life. Planter spokesman Ortiz Williamson lamented in 1924 that the "vigorous energies of our youth should be asphyxiated in the tropical underbrush of our sovereign bureaucracy."[106]

Likewise, the planters retreated from their previous expectation that the market might school the vast majority of Colombians in the ways of responsible political participation. Miguel Samper's enthusiasms in 1861 that expanded exports from the upper Magdalena would turn Colombians into "citizens of the world" now had little resonance among the large growers.[107] On the contrary, after the War of a Thousand Days, the image of the lower classes among the upper Magdalena elites congealed in the figure of the *machetero*, a violent, drunken veteran of civil war, without reason or discipline, and, in the words of Jesús del Corral, all too susceptible to "leveling rebellion."[108] Under these circumstances, the market came to be seen not as an engine of sociability which would pull all social classes along for the common good, but rather as a battleground. Thus, "association" came to be transformed from the binding of society through the balm of commercial exchange into an imperative for upper class unity in the face of the dangerous lower orders. In response, the elites

284 MICHAEL F. JIMÉNEZ

needed to set aside their partisan differences and close ranks in the Republican Union, SAC, and similar groupings. A military posture was required in everyday life, as suggested by Jesús del Corral's call to the planters to "gird for combat." This new elitist sensibility appeared also in the new methods of schooling for upper-class youth, which emphasized strength, endurance, and mental discipline.[109] In short, this Hobbesian view of the market denied that benign self-interest pursued by all citizens could guarantee order and progress.

Finally, the planters no longer regarded work as a common ground for Colombians. The hacendados celebrated their founding of the great estates during the second half of the nineteenth century in the upper Magdalena Valley. Having allegedly risked their fortunes, health, loved ones, and even their own lives in a titanic struggle to overcome nature in the tropics, these exemplar "workers of the hot country" congratulated themselves for having set the nation on a new course.[110] But most other Colombians could hardly measure up, in their view. Again, the planters regarded the ever more numerous middle-class bureaucrats and politicians as parasites feeding on the principal producers of wealth, namely themselves. Unlike the haciendas, where men of action were forged, "the sedentary life of offices" promoted dyspepsia, obesity, and neurasthenia rather than the vigor, energy, and discipline necessary to achieve economic prosperity in the modern world.[111] Neither did they spare other elite segments, as they castigated their own relatives and erstwhile allies among the traditional highland aristocracy for perpetuating that "ancient Spanish feudalism, highly prejudicial and crushing for the inferior classes."[112] But the "inferior classes" could hardly provide the foundations for a productive society anyway. The planters simply found it impossible to imagine the unmarried, ill, violent, drunken peons and tenants of their plantations in the ranks of the republic of "peasants" and "workers," as the estate owners of the upper Magdalena referred to themselves.

While the oligarchical rescripting of liberalism certainly proved inadequate to the tasks of hegemony, no viable alternative was at hand for Central Colombia's large-scale export entrepreneurs after the turn of the century. In the western part of the country, merchant-landowner, financier, and industrial elites did elaborate a potentially more inclusive social myth based on the allegedly virtuous and autonomous coffee smallholder.[113] But this mixture of agrarian nostalgia, social Catholicism, and modern management methods appears to have had little appeal for the besieged planters. Moreover, during the 1920s, those factions seeking to "modernize" liberalism through greater attention to social problems and state intervention in the economy provoked uneasiness and resentment among the large growers.[114] Finally, the upper Magdalena elites could not countenance a full-blown reactionary ideology in a Catonist mold.[115] Their unabashed cosmopolitanism and distaste for mass political action stood in the way of a virulent, nationalist agrarianism led by themselves and supported by a substantial middle- and lower-class following, particularly in the countryside.

During the Great Depression and its aftermath, the consequences of these historic limits on the planters' power and authority earlier in the century would become tragically apparent. As modernizing factions of the Colombian upper class led by Alfonso López Pumarejo undertook, however tentatively, a major economic, social, and political restructuring in the mid 1930s, the large growers resisted.[116] In alliance with other elite groups against any shift in power toward labor or the middle classes, their strategy bears many similarities to what David Rock has called an "oligarchic restoration" in reference to the Argentine *concordancia* during those same years.[117] The successful containment of reform from the mid 1930s through the 1940s emboldened the rightist reaction which partly drove the horrific social and political upheaval at mid-century known as "*la violencia.*"[118] In the end, the fractured hegemony of the upper Magdalena coffee hacendados had as its legacy neither a bourgeois pluralist democracy, a populist regime, nor a stable oligarchical order buttressed or not by the armed forces. Rather, the economic, political, and ideological weakness of the planters in this northern Andean coffee republic before 1930 helped usher in the successive, violent contestations for power, elite accommodations, and intense social conflicts of Colombia's recent past.

Notes

I deeply appreciate the critical remarks and suggestions of those who participated in the conference on "Coffee and Class Formation in Latin America before 1930," especially Charles Bergquist, Catherine LeGrand, Joseph Love, Marco Palacios, and William Roseberry. I also wish to thank colleagues and friends at Princeton and elsewhere for their helpful comments and support, including Marc Chernick, Barbara Corbett, Peter Mandler, Michael Merrill, Mary Peniston, Mary Roldán, and Eduardo Sáenz.

1. "Por los siervos de la gleba," *Revista Nacional de Agricultura* 9, Special Edition (June 1914): 7.

2. For a geographical description of the upper Magdalena basin, see Rafael Gómez Picón, *Magdalena Río de Colombia,* 7th ed. (Bogotá, 1983), pt. 1. The 1932 Coffee Census revealed that the large growers in this region produced 76 percent of the coffee in those departments, 53 percent of coffee produced by large growers nationally, and one-fifth of Colombia's total. *Boletín de Estadística* 1 (February 1933): 119–21. Another statistical compilation from the period, Diego

Monsalve's classic *Colombia cafetera* (Barcelona, 1927), also illustrates the concentration of large producers in this region.

3. "Educación física," *Revista Nacional de Agricultura* (November–December 1911): 219.

4. Robert Dix, *Colombia: The Political Dimensions of Change* (New Haven, 1967), suggests the continuities of political development in the late nineteenth and early twentieth centuries. Salamón Kalmanowitz, *Economía y nación: una breve historia de Colombia* (Bogotá, 1986), echoes this point of view from a Marxian perspective.

5. Tulio Halperín Donghi, *Historia contemporánea de América* (México, 1970), 351–52.

6. Fernando Henrique Cardoso and Enzo Falleto, *Dependency and Development in Latin America,* trans. Marjory Mattingly Urquidi (Berkeley, 1979), 97–98.

7. Charles Bergquist, *Coffee and Conflict in Colombia, 1886–1910* (Durham, N.C., 1988), 224.

8. Marco Palacios, *El café en Colombia, 1850–1970: una historia económica, social, y política* (México, 1983), 280.

9. Herbert Braun, *The Assassination of Gaitán: Public Life and Urban Violence in Colombia* (Madison, Wis., 1985), 21.

10. Steven Hahn, "Class and State in Postemancipation Societies: Southern Planters in Comparative Perspective," *American Historical Review* 95 (1990): 75–98.

11. For a review of the unrest in the late 1920s and 1930s, see Pierre Gilholdes, "Agrarian Struggles in Colombia," in Rodolfo Stavenhagen, ed., *Agrarian Struggles and Peasant Movements in Latin America* (Garden City, N.Y., 1970), 411–21; Miguel Urrutia, *The Development of the Colombian Labor Movement* (New Haven, 1969); and Ricardo Melgar Bao, *El movimiento obrero latinoamericano* (Madrid, 1988), 271–82.

12. "El problema del trabajo entre los cafeteros. Circular No. 6002-B, Enero 4, 1929," *Boletín de la Oficina General del Trabajo* (August 1919): 7–8.

13. The position of the Colombian planters contrasts sharply with export elites in central and southern South America in the nineteenth and twentieth centuries as analyzed by Anthony Winson in "The Formation of Capitalist Agriculture in Latin America and Its Relationship to Political Power and the State," *Comparative Studies in Society and History* 25 (1983): 83–104.

14. This follows Francisco Leal Buitrago's argument regarding the regional and partisan sources of elite differentiation in late-nineteenth-century Colombia, but focuses on the sectoral aspects of upper-class conflicts in that period and its aftermath. "Formación nacional y proyectos políticos de la clase dominante en el siglo XIX," in Leal Buitrago, *Estado y política en Colombia,* 2d ed. (Bogotá, 1984), 107–50.

15. In Viotá, the region's premier coffee municipality, plantings increased by over 230 percent between 1907 and 1927; almost half the bushes in that southwestern Cundinamarca district were grown on ten estates larger than 500 *fanegadas* (1 *fanegeda* = 1.6 acres). Michael F. Jiménez, "Travelling Far in Grand-

father's Car: The Life-Cycle of Central Colombian Coffee Estates. The Case of Viotá, Cundinamarca (1900–1930)," *Hispanic American Historical Review* 69 (1989): 205–6. For a contemporary portrait of the district, see the 1910 report by Swiss botanists E. Fuhrmann and E. Mayor, *Voyage d'exploration scientifique en Colombie*, vol. 5 of *Memories de la Societé neuchâteloise des sciences naturalles* (Neuchâtel, 1914), chap. 9.

16. In 1914, a North American observer recommended that the highest grade blends include 25 percent washed *bogotas*. *Spice Mill* (January 1914): 36. The penetration of North American markets by Colombian beans is described by Charles A. McQueen, "Colombian Public Finance," *Colombian Review* (June 1928): 360–67.

17. Jesús Antonio Bejarano, *Economía y poder: la SAC y el desarrollo agropecuario colombiano, 1871–1984* (Bogotá, 1985), chap. 3.

18. Bennett E. Koffman, "The National Federation of Coffee Growers of Colombia" (Ph.D. diss., University of Virginia, 1969), chap. 4.

19. Roger Brew, *El desarrollo económico de Antioquia desde la independencia hasta 1920* (Bogotá, 1977), and Fernando Botero Herrera, *La industrialización en Antioquia: génesis y consolidación, 1900–1930* (Medellín, 1984).

20. U.S. Department of Commerce, Bureau of Foreign and Domestic Commerce, *The Coffee Industry in Colombia* (Washington, D.C., 1931), 8.

21. *Revista Nacional de Agricultura* (November–December 1914): 222–25, and *Revista Nacional de Agricultura* (May–June 1924): 285–86.

22. Palacios, *El café en Colombia*, 71.

23. See J. Fred Rippy, "Dawn of the Railway Age in Colombia," *Hispanic American Historical Review* 33 (1953): 650–63, and Alfredo Ortega, *Ferrocarriles colombianos, 1920–1940* (Bogotá, 1932).

24. P. L. Bell, *Colombia: A Commercial and Industrial Handbook* (Washington, D.C., 1921), 245.

25. "Las labores del congreso cafetero," *Revista Nacional de Agricultura* (September 1920): 65–70.

26. On the Antioquian penetration into the upper Magdalena, see María C. Errazuriz, *Cafeteros y cafetales del Libano* (Bogotá, 1986).

27. Francine Cronwshaw, "Landowners and Politics in Colombia, 1923–1948" (Ph.D. diss., University of New Mexico, 1986).

28. Bejarano, *Economía y poder*, 138.

29. *El Tiempo* (April 26, 1924); and Cronshaw, "Landowners and Politics in Colombia," 54–62.

30. A portrait of expanding U.S. business interests during this period is provided by Stephen J. Randall, *The Diplomacy of Modernization: Colombian-American Relations, 1920–1940* (Toronto, 1977).

31. Paul W. Drake, *The Money Doctor in the Andes: The Kemmerer Missions, 1923–1933* (Durham, N.C., 1989), chap. 2.

32. Fabio Zambrano, "El comercio de café en Cundinamarca," *Cuadernos colombianos* 11 (1978): 391–436.

33. Jesús Antonio Bejarano, "El despegue cafetero, 1900–1928," in José Antonio Ocampo, ed., *Historia económica de Colombia* (Bogotá, 1987), 173–208.

34. In the late 1920s, Enrique de Narváez (hijo) reported that transaction fees had risen dramatically and that repayment schedules for coffee producers had shrunk from six to three months or less. *Revista del Banco de la República* (June 1928): 217–19.

35. *Revista del Banco de la República* (July 1928): 251.

36. Jiménez, "Going Far in Grandfather's Car," discusses the responses of large estate owners in Viotá to the pressures of the 1920s, revealing that although some enterprises had contracted heavy debt burdens, others passed through the years of crisis unscathed, even substantially expanding production in several cases.

37. Hugo López, *Estudio de la inflación en Colombia: el período de los años 20* (Medellín, 1977), 137. See also Finance Minister Esteban Jaramillo on this matter in his *La carestia de la vida* (Bogotá, 1927).

38. *El Tiempo* (February 18, 1929).

39. Frank Safford, "Commerce and Enterprise in Central Colombia, 1821–1870" (Ph.D. diss., Columbia University, 1965).

40. Eduardo López, *Almanaque de hechos colombianos* (Bogotá, 1919), 236–37. For further material on the Sáenz investments, see *Gaceta de Cundinamarca* (April 12, 1918): 8439; "La industria cafetera de Cundinamarca," *Revista Nacional de Agricultura* (September–October 1923): 40–42; "Disolución conyugal de Guillermo Sáenz y Ana Fety de Sáenz," Registraduría de Tierras, *Libro de registro. La Mesa*, vol. 2, folio 202, April 11, 1934. Interview with Nicolás Sáenz Dávila, Bogotá, May 6, 1980.

41. Braun, *The Assassination of Gaitán*, 20.

42. Luis Baudillo Bello, "El papel del partido republicano en la lucha por el poder entre 1909 y 1914" (Degree thesis, Universidad Nacional de Colombia, 1981).

43. "El progreso de la armonía," *Revista Nacional de Agricultura* (November 1906): 332.

44. Julio J. Dupuy, *Estudio sobre organización y defensa de la industria cafetera en Colombia* (Bogotá, 1929), 9–10.

45. Fabio López de la Roche, "Cultura política de las clases dirigentes en Colombia: permanencias y rupturas," in López de la Roche, ed., *Ensayos sobre cultura política colombiana* (Bogotá, 1978), 99–204; Humberto Bronx, *Historia moderna de la iglesia colombiana* (Medellín, n.d.), 303–42; and Ana María Bidegaín de Urán, *Iglesia, pueblo, y política: un estudio de conflictos de intereses. Colombia, 1930–1955* (Bogotá, 1985), chaps. 2 and 3.

46. Bernardo Tovar Zambrano, *La intervención económica del estado en Colombia, 1914–1936* (Bogotá, 1984), presents a compelling portrait of the modernizing, nationalistic program of the Conservative governments in this period.

47. For a summary of the debates on the export tax question from the perspective of the planters, see Gabriel Ortiz Williamson, *La libertad de exportación en Colombia* (Bogotá, 1925).

48. Weekly Correspondence, *Archivo Costa Rica* (September 21, 1927).

49. *Revista Nacional de Agricultura* (April 1, 1908).

50. Palacios, *El café en Colombia*, 237.

51. Cundinamarca, *Informe del secretario de hacienda, 1915*, 51; Cundina-

marca, *Informe del secretario de hacienda, 1916,* 103–5; and Cundinamarca, *Informe del secretario de gobierno al señor gobernador del departamento, 1922,* 101.

52. Cundinamarca, *Informe del secretario de hacienda, 1915,* 93, and *Annexo al informe secretario de hacienda, 1926,* xxvi.

53. Darío Fajardo, *Haciendas, campesinos, y políticas agrarias en Colombia, 1920–1960* (Bogotá, 1983), 29–34.

54. On Brazil and São Paulo in particular, see Joseph L. Love, *São Paulo in the Brazilian Federation, 1889–1937* (Stanford, 1980); Steven Topik, *The Political Economy of the Brazilian State, 1889–1930* (Austin, Tex., 1987); and Mauricio Font, *Coffee, Contention, and Change in the Making of Modern Brazil* (Cambridge, Mass., 1990). Also, the classic essay by Warren Dean, "The Planter as Entrepreneur: The Case of São Paulo," *Hispanic American Historical Review* 46 (1966): 138–52.

55. Frank Safford, "Social Aspects of Politics in Nineteenth-Century Spanish America: New Granada, 1825–1850," *Journal of Social History* 5 (1972): 344–70, and Malcolm Deas, "Venezuela, Colombia, and Ecuador: The First Half Century of Independence," in Leslie Bethell, ed., *The Cambridge History of Latin America,* vol. 3, *From Independence to c. 1870* (Cambridge, 1985), 507–38.

56. Helen Delpar, *Red against Blue: The Liberal Party in Colombian Politics, 1863–1899* (University, Ala., 1981), and Bergquist, *Coffee and Conflict in Colombia,* pt. 1.

57. See "El Dr. Roberto Ancizar y el Partido Agrario," *Revista Nacional de Agricultura* (April 1913): 743–46. A discussion of subsequent efforts to found an independent party of rural elites before 1930 and afterward is in Olinto Marcucci, *La revolución agraria en Colombia* (Bogotá, 1934).

58. Marco Palacios, "La clase más ruidosa," in *Estado y clases sociales en Colombia* (Bogotá, 1986), 9–86.

59. Fernando Galvis Salazar, *Uribe Uribe* (Medellín, 1962), and Eduardo Santa, *Rafael Uribe: un hombre y una epoca,* 3d ed. (Bogotá, 1972), present sketches of a life not yet the subject of a thorough biography. *Obras selectas,* Jorge Eastman, comp., 2 volumes (Bogotá, 1979), is a compilation of his writings and speeches, including his call for governmental intervention, "Socialismo del estado. Conferencia dictada en el Teatro Municipal de Bogotá, en octubre de 1904," 1:29–47.

60. *El Liberal* (March 20, 1913).

61. The leading critic of the large landowners after the First World War, the Antioquian engineer and economist López considered the latifundistas, in which category he placed the coffee planters, as major obstacles to economic development and social progress. Of his vast work, see in particular *Problemas colombianos* (Paris, 1927).

62. José María Samper, *Ensayo sobre las revoluciones políticas y la condición social de la repúblicas colombinas (Hispano-américanas), con un apéndice sobre la orografía y población de la confederación granadina* [1861] (Bogotá, n.d.), 310.

63. A seminal study of this provincial radicalism is Malcolm Deas, "Poverty, Civil War, and Politics: Ricardo Obeso Gaitán and His Magdalena River Campaign in Colombia, 1885," *Nova Americana* 2 (1979): 263–304.

64. On the PSR, see Ignacio Torres Giraldo, *Los inconformes,* vols. 3–4 (Bogotá, 1974–78); Medófilo Medina, *Historia del partido comunista de Colombia* (Bogotá, 1980), 99–156; Julio Cuadros Caldas, *Comunismo criollo y liberalismo auctóctono* (Bogotá, 1938); and José María Rojas Guerra, "La estrategia insurreccional socialista y la estrategia de contención del conservatismo doctrinario: la década de los veinte" (unpublished manuscript, Cali, 1989).

65. See, for example, a memorandum sent to the minister of industries in March 1928 by large coffee growers in southwestern Cundinamarca whose estates were under siege by peasant activists. Olaya Herrera Archive, Section 2, Folder 45, Doc 123.

66. Corral, "Por los siervos de la gleba," 11.

67. Cited in Bergquist, *Coffee and Conflict in Colombia,* 192.

68. Cundinamarca, *Informe del secretario de gobierno al señor gobernador del departamento, 1921,* 5–8.

69. Francisco Antonio Moreno y Escandón, *Indios y mestizos de la Nueva Granada a finales del siglo XVIII,* introduction and indexes by Jorge Orlando Melo, transcription by Germán Colmenares y Alonso Valencia (Bogotá, 1975), 73.

70. Gilma Lucía Mora de Tovar, *Aguardiente y conflictos sociales en la Nueva Granada durante el siglo XVIII* (Bogotá, 1988).

71. Moreno y Escandón, *Indios y mestizos de la Nueva Granada,* 73.

72. José Fulgencio Gutiérrez, *Galán y los comuneros: estudio histórico-crítico* (Bucaramanga, 1939), 258.

73. Juan de Dios Restrepo (Emiro Kastos) et al., *Museo de cuadros de costumbre* (Bogotá, 1886), 1:45.

74. Salvador Camacho Roldán, *Escritos varios* (Bogotá, 1892), 2:453.

75. Eugenio Díaz, *La Manuela* [1857] (Medellín, 1947), 79.

76. Letter of Carlos Abondano, November 12, 1878, in Juan de Dios Carrasquilla, *Segundo informe que presenta al comisario de la agricultura nacional al poder ejecutivo para el conocimiento del congreso, año del 1880* (Bogotá, 1880), 42.

77. *La cordillera de Bogotá: resultado de viajes y estudios,* trans. Ernsto Guhl [1888] (Bogotá, 1964), 312–13.

78. "A Colombian Coffee Estate: Santa Barbara, 1870–1912," in Kenneth Duncan and Ian Rutledge, eds., *Land and Labor in Latin America: Essays in the Development of Agrarian Capitalism in the Nineteenth and Twentieth Centuries* (Cambridge, 1977), 269–98.

79. There is a vast literature on the nineteenth-century civil conflicts and the War of a Thousand Days in particular, well summarized and amplified in Carlos Eduardo Jaramillo Castillo, *Los guerrilleros del novecientos* (Bogotá, 1991).

80. For discussion of these arrangements, see Palacios, *El café en Colombia,* chap. 4; Mariano Arango, *Café e industria, 1850–1930* (Medellín, 1977); Absalón Machado, *El café: de la aparcería al capitalismo* (Bogotá, 1977); and the various works of Jesús Antonio Bejarano, especially "El fin de la economía exportadora," in Darío Jaramillo Agudelo, comp., *La nueva historia de Colombia* (Bogotá, 1976), 675–739. In Viotá, one-fifth of the municipality came to be occupied by service tenants by the late 1920s, and those estates most reliant on such arrange-

ments—as opposed to exclusively wage labor—had the highest, most consistent rate of grove expansion. Jiménez, "Going Far in Grandfather's Car," 204–14.

81. "Cordillera de Subía," *Revista Nacional de Agricultura* (November 1906): 270.

82. For a discussion of relations of dependence and deference in the plantation districts, see Michael F. Jiménez, "Class, Gender, and the Origins of Peasant Rebellion in Central Colombia, 1900–1930," in Forrest Colburn, ed., *Everyday Forms of Peasant Resistance* (Armonk, N.Y., 1989), 122–50.

83. The vast array of writings on the rural unrest in the late 1920s and early 1930s includes Hermes Tovar Pinzón, *El movimiento campesino en Colombia* (Bogotá, 1975), and Gonzalo Sánchez, *Las ligas campesinas en Colombia* (Bogotá, 1977). Jesús Antonio Bejarano, "Campesinado, luchas agrarias, e historia social: notas para un balance historiográfico," *Anuario colombiano de historia social y de la cultura* 11 (1983): 251–304, presents a thorough review of the literature on this topic.

84. Jesús del Corral, "Por los siervos de la gleba," 6.

85. Cundinamarca, *Informe del secretario de hacienda al gobernador, 1918,* 44.

86. *Frontier Expansion and Peasant protest in Colombia, 1850–1936* (Albuquerque, N.M., 1986), chaps. 5 and 6.

87. Cundinamarca, *Informe del secretario de hacienda al señor gobernador, 1918,* 44.

88. *Revista Nacional de Agricultura* (October–November 1918): 1711.

89. For a provocative view of local politics in the nineteenth and early twentieth centuries, see Malcolm Deas, "La presencia de la política nacional en la vida provinciana, pueblerina, y rural de Colombia en el primer siglo de la república," in Marco Palacios, ed., *La unidad nacional en América Latina: de regionalismo a la nacionalidad* (México, 198?), 149–73.

90. Cundinamarca, *Informe del secretario de hacienda al señor gobernador, 1919,* 226.

91. *El Diario Nacional* (April 15, 1928).

92. *El Liberal* (December 16, 1912).

93. See the *Annual Reports of the Board of Foreign Missions of the Presbyterian Church in the United States of America* (New York, 1903–13).

94. Gonzalo Sánchez, *Los "bolcheviques" del Líbano (Tolima)* (Bogotá, 1976).

95. Jean Jacques Rousseau, *The Social Contract,* trans. Maurice Cranston (London, 1960), 52.

96. On this liberal vision, see Gerardo Molina, *Las ideas liberales en Colombia, 1849–1914* (Bogotá, 1973). For a provocative analysis of the limits and possibilities of that mid-century episode, see Marco Palacios, "La fragmentación regional de las clases dominantes en Colombia: una perspectiva histórica," *Revista Mexicana de Sociología* 42 (1980): 1663–91.

97. "Estudios sobre la hacienda pública. Fragmentos de la Memoria de hacienda presentada al congreso de 1872," in Salvador Camacho Roldán, *Escritos varios* (Bogotá, 1885), 3:234.

292   MICHAEL F. JIMÉNEZ

98. Jaime Jaramillo Uribe, *El pensamiento colombiano en el siglo XIX* (Bogotá, 1964), pt. 2.

99. Uday S. Mehta, "Liberal Strategies of Exclusion," *Politics and Society* 18 (1990): 427–54, discusses "the specific cultural and psychological conditions" which are the bases for the endorsement of universal capacities" within liberal thought and practice, using nineteenth-century Indian history as an example. The limits on the inclusionary, liberative, and democratic prospects of liberal thought can be seen in the Brazilian case as elegantly discussed by Emilia Viotti da Costa, *The Brazilian Empire: Myths and Realities* (Chicago, 1985), chap. 3.

100. Eric Hobsbawm, *The Age of Empire, 1875–1914* (New York, 1987), chap. 1.

101. Jesús del Corral, "Por los siervos de la gleba," 11. The prominent Bogotá physician Miguel Jiménez López, the premier exponent of this racialist ideology in this period, wrote extensively on this question, including *Nuestras razas decáen* (Bogotá, 1919) and *La inmigración amarilla* (Bogotá, 1923). See also Gustavo Adolfo Solano, *Delincuencia en Colombia* (Bogotá, 1923), and Andres Marín, *Sociología criminal* (Bogotá, 1923).

102. *Revista Nacional de Agricultura* (March 1924): 285.

103. For a clear statement on the planter political reform program, see "Manifiesto de la Unión Republicana, Mayo 12, 1912," in Baudillo Bello, "El papel del partido republicano," Annexo 4.

104. For example, *El Tiempo* editors called for "an open, civilized politics . . . Anything to the contrary is suicide for the Republic . . . Seeking to return to the old methods and aphorisms is not merely *démodé,* but something more grave: it is unpatriotic" (September 2, 1916). Eduardo Rodríguez Piñeres, the secretary of the Republican Union at its founding, would later write a history of the political crisis of the 1890s and the War of a Thousand Days in which he attacked Uribe and the War Liberals as "jacobins" whose rebellion he characterized as "the most risky and absurd adventure ever undertaken in Colombia." *Diez años de política liberal, 1892–1902* (Bogotá, 1945), 128.

105. *El Tiempo* (January 26, 1912).

106. *Revista Nacional de Agricultura* (March 1924): 285.

107. *La miseria en Bogotá* [1867] (Bogotá, 1969), 126.

108. "Los siervos de la gleba," 6. The excitement and anxiety regarding the alleged lower-class proclivity toward violence was evident in the trial of a guerrilla veteran of the War of the Thousand Days, Nicolás Jiménez, where over a thousand spectators came to observe the proceedings against the so-called *hombre-fiera* (man-beast) accused of several homicides. *El Tiempo* (April 16–June 22, 1918).

109. "Educación física," 219. An impressive example of the institutionalization of these values was the Gimnasio Moderno, an elite school founded in 1914 whose curriculum melded older patrician values of social responsibility and paternalism with a new sensibility emphasizing physical and intellectual discipline. Two introductory essays to the writings of the school's longtime director, Tomás Rueda Vargas, vividly illustrate the school's ethos. Alfonso López Michelsen, "Prólogo a la obra de Tomás Rueda Vargas," and Eduardo Carranza, "Obra de Don Tomás Rueda Vargas," in *La sabana y otros escritos de si mismo* (Bogotá, 1977), xiii–lxii.

110. Medardo Rivas, *Los trabajadores de la tierra caliente* [1899] (Bogotá, 1983), a collage of anecdotes of nineteenth-century Colombian politics, civil wars, poetry, and detailed descriptions of the tobacco, indigo, and coffee booms, became the touchstone for this planter historical narrative.

111. "Educación física," 219.

112. "Por los siervos de la gleba," 6.

113. Alberto Mayor Mora, *Ética, trabajo, y productividad en Antioquia*, 2d ed. (Bogotá, 1985); Charles Bergquist, *Labor in Latin America* (Stanford, 1986), 277–79; and Mary Jean Roldán, "Genesis and Evolution of La Violencia in Antioquia, Colombia (1900–1953)," (Ph.D. diss., Harvard University, 1992), pt. 2.

114. José Fernando Ocampo, *Colombia siglo XX: estudio histórico y antología política* (Bogotá, 1980), pt. 2, analyzes the modernizing elements in the Liberal party before 1930.

115. Barrington Moore, Jr., *Social Origins of Dictatorship and Democracy: Lord and Peasant in the Making of the Modern World* (Boston, 1966), defined Catonism as an "upper-class mythology about peasants . . . the criticism of mass democracy, the notions of legitimate authority and the importance of custom, opposition to the power of wealth and to mere technical expertise," 495. For a provocative contrast with an agrarian elite in Central Europe which did evolve a Catonist response to pressures similar to those experienced by the Colombian coffee planters, see Shelley Baranowski, "Continuity and Contingency: Agrarian Elites, Conservative Institutions, and East Elbia in Modern German History," *Social History* 12 (1987): 285–308; and Hans Rosenberg, "The Pseudo-democratization of the Junker Class," in Georg Iggers, ed., *The Social History of Politics: Critical Perspectives in West German Historical Writing since 1945* (Dover, N.H., 1985), 81–112.

116. Daniel Pecaut, *Orden y violencia: Colombia, 1930–1945* vol. 1 (Bogotá, 1987), chap. 2; Alvaro Tirado Mejía, *La revolución en marcha: aspectos políticos del primer gobierno de Alfonso López Pumarejo, 1934–1938*, 2 vols. (Medellín, 1986); and Michael F. Jiménez, "Social Crisis and Agrarian Politics in Colombia, 1930–1946" (Master's thesis, Stanford University, 1971), chap. 5.

117. David Rock, *Argentina 1516–1982: From Spanish Colonization to the Falklands War* (Berkeley, 1985), chap. 6.

118. Gonzalo Sánchez, "The Violence: An Interpretative Synthesis," in Charles Bergquist, Ricardo Peñaranda, and Gonzalo Sánchez, eds., *Violence in Colombia: The Contemporary Crisis in Historical Perspective* (Wilmington, Del., 1992), provides an excellent overview of this phenomenon. A recent study by Eduardo Sáenz Rovner, *La ofensiva empresarial: industriales, políticos, y violencia en los años 40 en Colombia* (Bogotá, 1992), presents a compelling portrait of the business community and its role in the mid-century economic restructuring amid widespread political violence and labor repression.

Contributors

Mauricio A. Font is Associate Professor of Sociology at Queens College and the Graduate School, City University of New York. His recent publications on Brazil include *Coffee, Contention, and Change* (1990), "City and Countryside in the Onset of Brazilian Industrialization" (*Studies in Comparative International Development,* 1992), and "Failed Redemocratization: Region, Class, and Political Change in Brazil, 1930–37" (in F. Devoto and T. Di Tella, eds., *Political Culture, Social Movements, and Democratic Transitions in Latin America* (forthcoming). He is working on a book on the politics of development in Latin America.

Lowell Gudmundson is Professor and Chair of Latin American Studies, Mount Holyoke College. He is the author of *Costa Rica Before Coffee: Society and Economy on the Eve of the Export Boom* and co-author of *Central America, 1821–1871: Liberalism before Liberal Reform* as well as other books and articles in Spanish and English.

Michael F. Jiménez teaches history at the University of Pittsburgh and is the author of a forthcoming study, *Red Viota: Power, Authority, and Rebellion in the Colombian Andes.*

David McCreery is Professor of History at Georgia State University and is the author of *Rural Guatemala 1760–1940* (1994).

Héctor Pérez Brignoli is Professor of History at the University of Costa Rica. A specialist in historical demography and the economic and social history of Central America, he is the author of several books and articles, including *A Brief History of Central America* (1989, first published in Spain). He is working on *A Historical Atlas of Central America.*

Fernando Picó is Professor of History at the Universidad de Puerto Rico. Among his books are *Libertad y servidumbre en el Puerto Rico del siglo 19, Amargo café, Historia general de Puerto Rico,* and *Al filo del poder.*

6 CONTRIBUTORS

William Roseberry is Professor and Chair of Anthropology at the New School for Social Research. He is the author of *Coffee and Capitalism in the Venezuelan Andes* (1983) and *Anthropologies and Histories: Essays in Culture, History, and Political Economy* (1989) and is working on a book on households.

Mario Samper Kutschbach is Professor of History at the University of Costa Rica and the National University of Costa Rica. He is the author of *Generations of Settlers: Rural Households and Markets on the Costa Rican Frontier, 1850–1935* (1990).

Verena Stolcke is Professor of Social Anthropology at the Universidad Autónoma de Barcelona and has worked extensively in Latin America. She is the author of *Marriage, Class, and Colour in Nineteenth-Century Cuba* (1974) and *Coffee Planters, Workers, and Wives: Class Conflict and Gender Relations on São Paulo Plantations, 1850–1980* (1988).

Related Titles in the Series

Index

Library of Congress Cataloging-in-Publication Data

Coffee, society, and power in Latin America / edited by William Roseberry,
Lowell Gudmundson, Mario Samper Kutschbach.
    p.   cm. — (Johns Hopkins studies in Atlantic history and culture)
    Includes index.
    ISBN 0-8018-4884-9 (alk. paper). — ISBN 0-8018-4887-3
(pbk. : alk. paper)
    1. Coffee industry — Latin America — History.   2. Latin America —
Economic conditions.   3. Latin America — Social conditions.
4. Latin America — History — 1830–   I. Roseberry, William, 1950–
II. Gudmundson, Lowell.   III. Samper K., Mario.   IV. Series.
HD9199.L382C64   1995
338.1′7373′098 — dc20   94-14193